I0454092

Wildlife Photographer of the Year

Portfolio 35

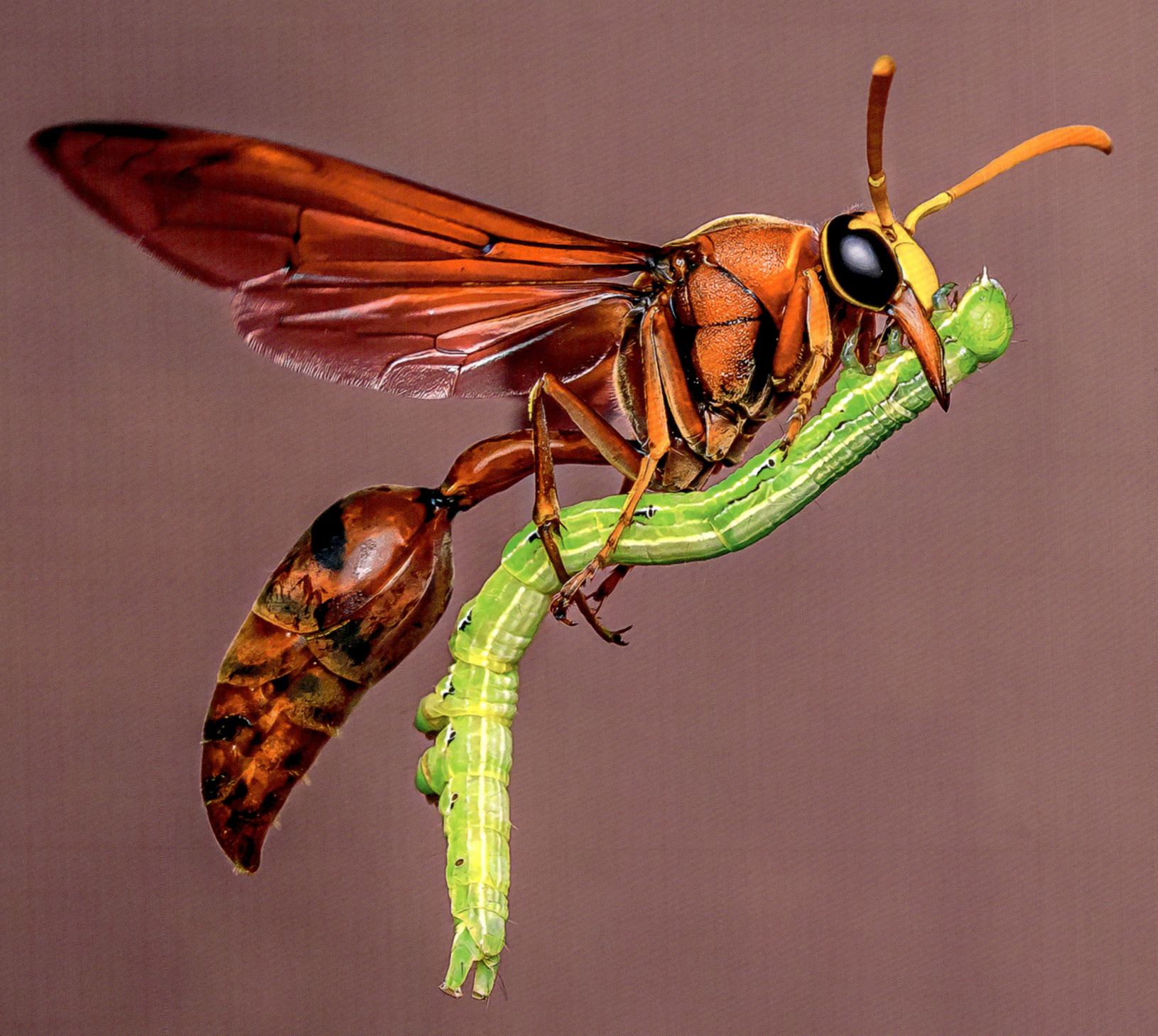

Wildlife Photographer of the Year

Portfolio 35

Published by the Natural History Museum, London

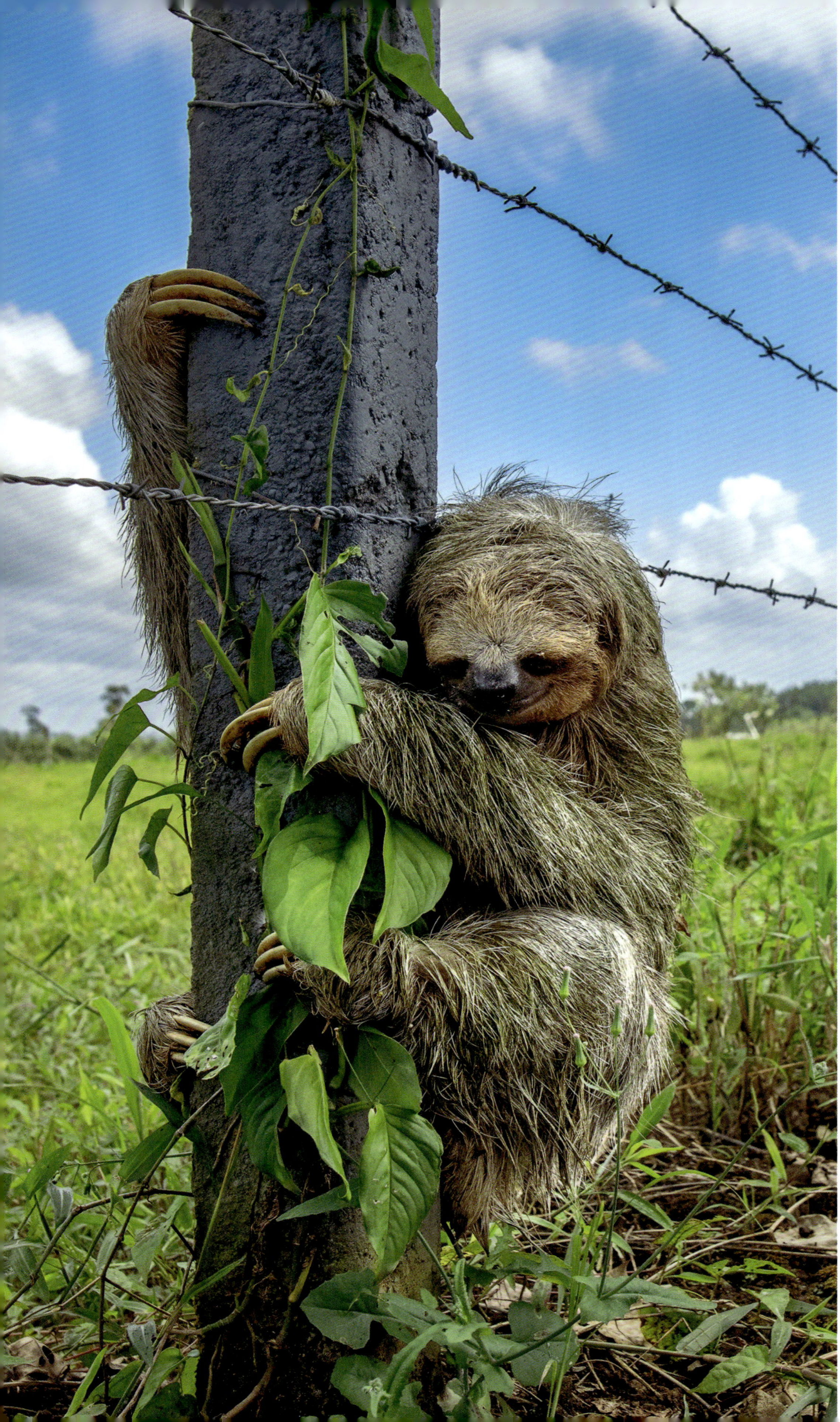

First published by the Natural History Museum,
Cromwell Road, London SW7 5BD
© The Trustees of the Natural History Museum,
London, 2025
Photography © the individual photographers 2025

ISBN 978 0 565 095727

A catalogue record for this book is available from
the British Library.

Editor Keith Wilson
Designer Bobby Birchall, Bobby&Co Design
Writers Stuart Blackman, James Fair
and Jane Wisbey
Image Grading Stephen Johnson
www.copyrightimage.com
Colour proofing Saxon Digital Services UK
Printing L.E.G.O. S.p.A, Italy

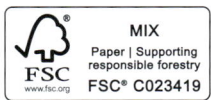

MIX
Paper | Supporting
responsible forestry
FSC® C023419
FSC
www.fsc.org

Left No place like home by Emmanuel Tardy
Previous page Special delivery by Bidyut Kalita
Foreword page Fractal forest by Ross Gudgeon
Competition page Wake-up call by Gabriella Comi

Contents

Foreword 6

Wildlife Photographer of the Year 8

The Wildlife Photographer of the Year 2025 Award 10

Behaviour: Mammals 12

Behaviour: Birds 20

Behaviour: Amphibians and Reptiles 28

Behaviour: Invertebrates 32

Urban Wildlife 40

Under Water 48

Portraits 56

Natural Artistry 64

Oceans: The Bigger Picture 74

Animals in Their Environment 80

Wetlands: The Bigger Picture 90

Plants and Fungi 98

Photojournalism 102

Photojournalist Story Award 110

Rising Star Portfolio Award 116

Portfolio Award 122

The Young Wildlife Photographer of the Year 2025 Award 130

Young Wildlife Photographers

    15–17 years 130

    11–14 years 140

    10 years and under 148

Index of Photographers 156

Foreword

As I slosh through what I hope will be the final April shower of this cold and wilful Maine spring, it occurred to me that the Wildlife Photographer of the Year competition has a rhythm that cycles through the seasons. Just when I think the dark of winter solstice will break me, the hard drive arrives, the first phase of judging begins and I lose all track of time and light. A couple of months later, the final round commences and I leave behind a frozen river and knee-deep snow for the kiss of a London spring – crocuses, daffodils and the anticipation of selecting the winning images. Now, with summer's first glow, the exhibition work takes place, all with the excitement of being among the lucky few who have seen the winning images. When fall descends, with the first fleck of frost and longer nights, we come together once more at the awards ceremony to celebrate the photographs that highlight the wild places and wildlife that depend upon healthy, intact seasons. Just like that, Wildlife Photographer of the Year has taken me on another trip around the sun.

But back to spring in Maine. When the last fear of frost has eased, I will start phase two of a project that was inspired by Jim Brandenburg, a long-time member of the Wildlife Photographer of the Year family. Known for his iconic and winning photograph of the gemsbok on a Namibian dune, his groundbreaking work with Arctic wolves and his celebration of the Boundary Waters region of Minnesota, Jim was actually a man of the grasslands. Prairies were his love. At *National Geographic*, I had the opportunity to work with him only once, ironically, on a story looking at the subtle beauty of spring. For that story Jim wrote, '...learning to make photographs on the prairie may have been a blessing for me: I was weaned on looking carefully... Each image I make feels like a prayer flag I've hung out to the universe – a celebration of nature's wonder.' Or as he once told me, 'Photographs are little miracles.'

In early April 2025 we lost Jim, this man who learned to look carefully and to revel in all seasons. Through the power of his aesthetic and his commitment to conservation, Jim inspired countless photographers to tune into their vision and their hearts. As photographer Mike Forsberg put it, 'More than any other photographer, what I learned from Jim was that it was okay to reveal one's soul while making photographs, and that to be in nature and connect with it on a visceral level was holy communion.'

What Jim also recognized was that nature is as fragile as it is strong and that we are challenging that resilience to breaking point. While I can still witness variations in the seasons, countless species are experiencing changes to the cycles that they depend upon for their survival. Without ice, harp seals can't pup. Chinook salmon can't spawn due to increased water temperatures. European pied flycatchers are out of sync with the caterpillars they need to feed their chicks, and snowshoe hares are experiencing a mismatch in their colouration – while their fur still changes from brown to white for the winter they often lack the snow that once provided camouflage. Nature cannot keep pace with such accelerated, human-made change.

What can we do? Well, inspired by Jim, I started removing grass from my yard, replacing it with a wildflower meadow. Phase one was a glorious bee- and butterfly-infused mess. Echinaceas, black-eyed Susan, oxeye daisies, butterfly weed, sunflowers and lots of milkweed mixed in with poppies and cosmos provided respite and nourishment for numerous species. Seeing monarch caterpillars was a triumph. Phase two starts in a few weeks when we double the meadow; seed packets are piled up waiting for a week of sustained soft days. My goal is a mid-coast replica of Jim's Touch the Sky prairie near his boyhood home. In the meantime, I take inspiration from Jim's photography, his commitment to community and his belief that we can all make a change, that even little steps matter. Wildlife Photographer of the Year shares these values. And the winning photographers and their photographs are the perennial proof that we can make a difference.

KATHY MORAN
Chair of the Jury

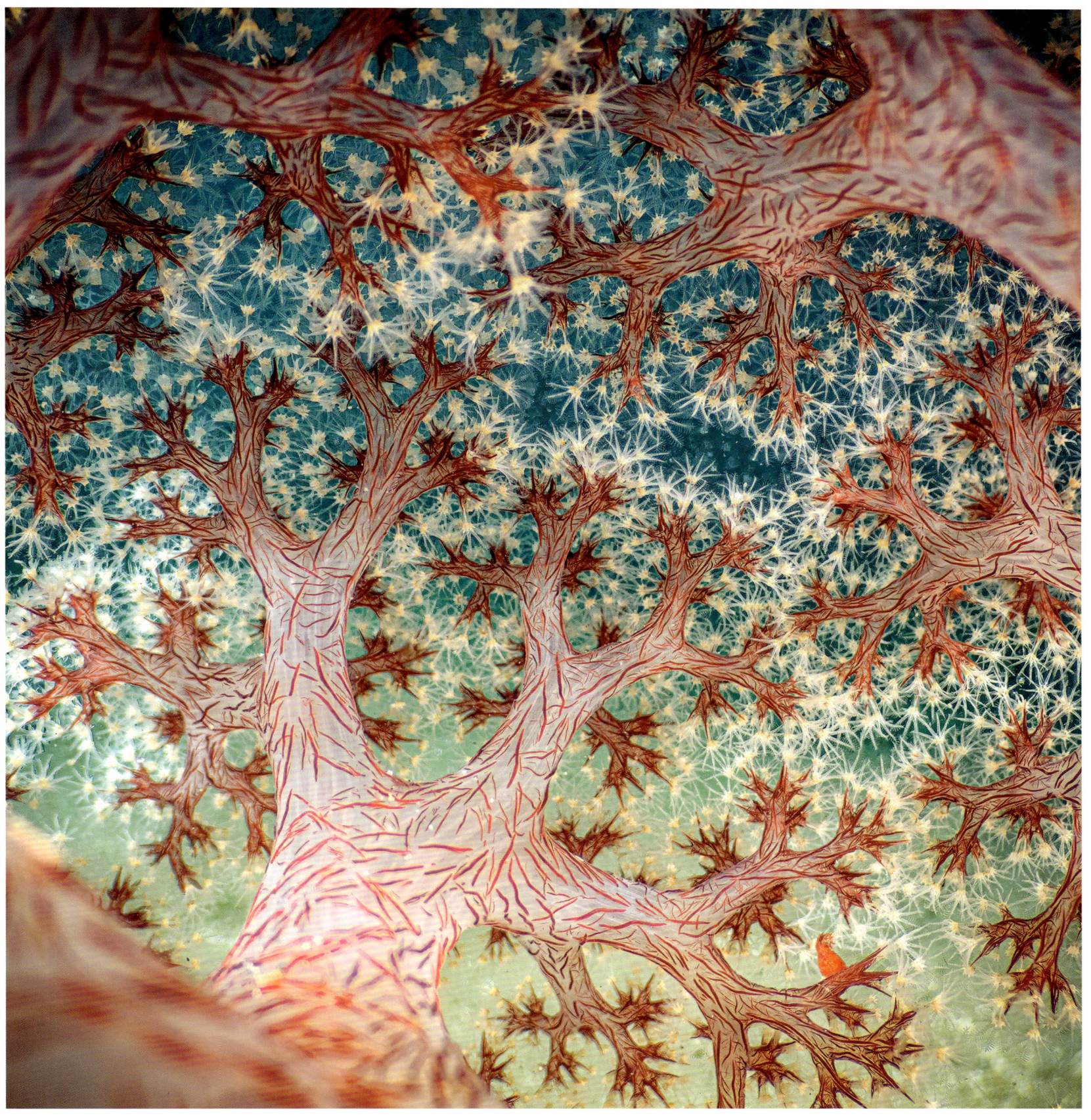

Wildlife Photographer of the Year

In another record-breaking year in the illustrious history of Wildlife Photographer of the Year, the world's greatest competition devoted to nature photography received more than 60,000 entries. The images came from far and wide – 113 countries and territories, including first-time entries from Azerbaijan and Ghana. The competition is open to professionals and non-professionals alike, with 16 different categories to choose from – plus three for young wildlife photographers. This portfolio features the final 100 images awarded in this year's competition, and serves as a companion to the world-famous exhibition touring over 35 venues globally in the months following its opening at the Natural History Museum, London.

Since its launch in 1965 with just 361 entries, and the Natural History Museum's involvement from 1984, Wildlife Photographer of the Year has continued to grow in popularity and reach. The organizers have always sought to attract as many entrants as possible – indeed, the competition is open to all, regardless of age or ability, from anywhere in the world. Furthermore, entry is free for anyone aged 26 and under, or from the more than 100 countries where the organizers deem that the entry fee might prove prohibitive. With such a large potential catchment for fresh perspectives of our natural world, the challenge for the seven-strong jury is to agree on 100 photographs that showcase the greatest variety of wildlife imagery, as well as the very best.

As you might expect, narrowing down the 60,363 submitted photographs to 100 takes time and some very serious discussion. The first round of judging is carried out remotely in January, and shortlists for each category are made based on artistic and technical merit, authenticity and storytelling insight. The jury meets for a week in February at the Natural History Museum in London, and spends long days sharing and challenging their views and perceptions about each image until agreement is reached. Exhaustive scientific and technical checks are made to verify the accuracy of any described species behaviours, and address possible infringement of the competition rules through image manipulation, including by AI. In an age of increasing disinformation, the competition organizers believe it is more important than ever for the public to trust what they see.

Increasingly, Wildlife Photographer of the Year is providing insight into humankind's harsh impact on our environment, and issues of conservation are becoming a larger part of the visual narrative for many entrants. Last year, the competition introduced the Impact Award to highlight positive conservation photo stories, as selected by the jury. This year's winner, Fernando Faciole, captures the endearing moment of an orphaned giant anteater pup following the heels of its carer at a rehabilitation centre in Brazil.

Images such as this show that Wildlife Photographer of the Year is more than a competition. With an ever-growing global reach, thanks to the touring exhibition, multimedia coverage, this portfolio book and social media feeds, it has also become a much-needed voice for nature photography, and for nature itself. Many photographers already know that their voice is best heard through a photograph. By taking part in Wildlife Photographer of the Year, they have a chance to be heard – and seen – by millions.

The 62nd Wildlife Photographer of the Year competition opens 20 October 2025, and closes 4 December 2025, at 11.30am GMT. See www.wildlifephotographeroftheyear.com

---

Judges

Gavin Broad (UK), entomologist and Principal Curator of Hymenoptera, Natural History Museum, London

Jaime Culebras (Spain/Ecuador), biologist, herpetologist and nature photographer

Jennifer Hayes (USA), marine biologist and underwater photographer

Hans Cosmas Ngoteya (Tanzania), wildlife and conservation storyteller

Andy Parkinson (UK), wildlife photographer

Akanksha Sood Singh (India), natural history filmmaker

Chair: Kathy Moran (USA), editor

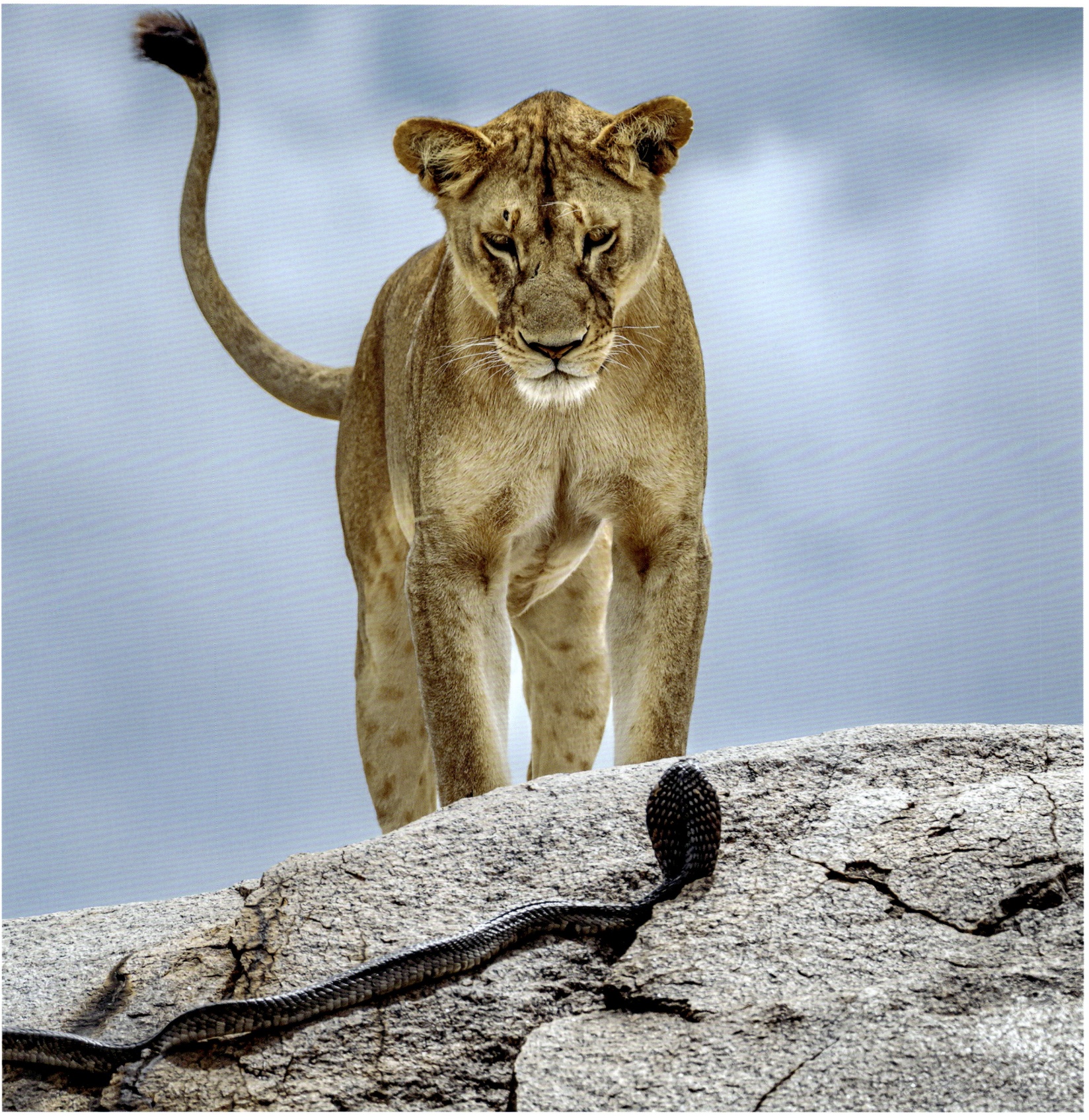

The Wildlife Photographer of the Year 2025 Award

The winner of the grand-title award goes to Wim van den Heever, whose picture was judged to be the most striking and memorable of all the category winners.

Wim van den Heever

SOUTH AFRICA

A renowned wildlife and landscape photographer, Wim van den Heever was born and raised in South Africa, where he developed his passion for photography and the natural world. He is the founder and owner of Tusk Photo, a safari tour operator based in Pretoria since 2007, and has led numerous photo safaris across Africa, as well as to the Arctic and Patagonia. Wim's photography has been widely published and recognized in many international competitions, including Wildlife Photographer of the Year. He sees his photography as a lifestyle rather than a hobby.

Ghost town visitor

An elusive and endangered brown hyena pauses as it makes a night crossing through the empty streets of Kolmanskop, an abandoned diamond mining town on the edge of the Namib Desert. Once the richest settlement in Africa, Kolmanskop attracts thousands of visitors each year. One of them was Wim, who has made regular trips here for nearly 10 years with the sole purpose of photographing a nocturnal brown hyena prowling amongst the ruins. Although the rarest of all hyena species, these largely solitary canids were known by security guards to pass through Kolmanskop on their way to scavenge carrion on Namibia's Skeleton Coast. On each visit, Wim set up camera traps in the hope of getting his picture, but the night-roaming hyenas always evaded capture. When he photographed a jackal and found a set of hyena footprints in the same area, he knew this spot, with a large empty building in the background, offered the best chance for his camera trap. On the memorable night, a sea fog rolled in, adding to the ghostly setting. 'My camera triggered three times that evening, each capturing one image at a time,' Wim recalls. 'Only one had the brown hyena.'

Nikon D810 + 17–35mm f2.8 lens at 17mm; 15 sec at f2.8; ISO 3200; 2x Nikon SB-800 Speedlight flashes; Camtraptions motion sensor.

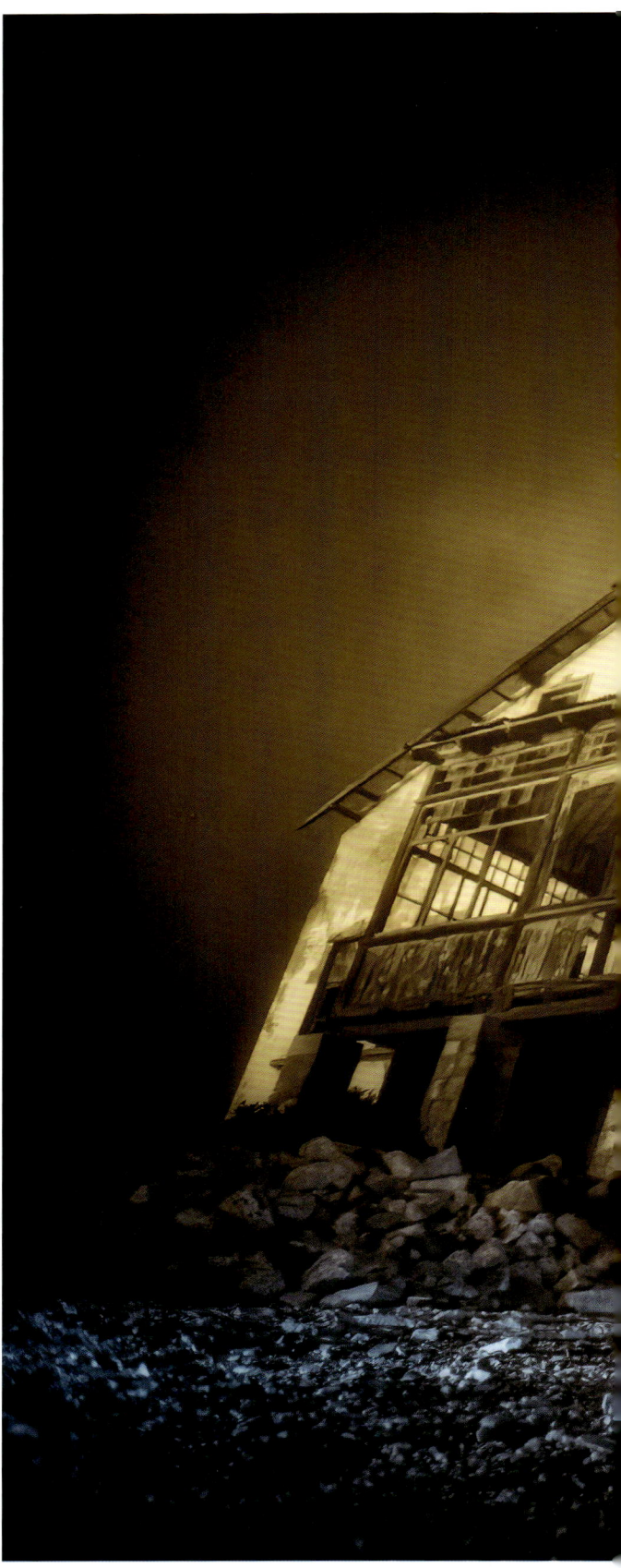

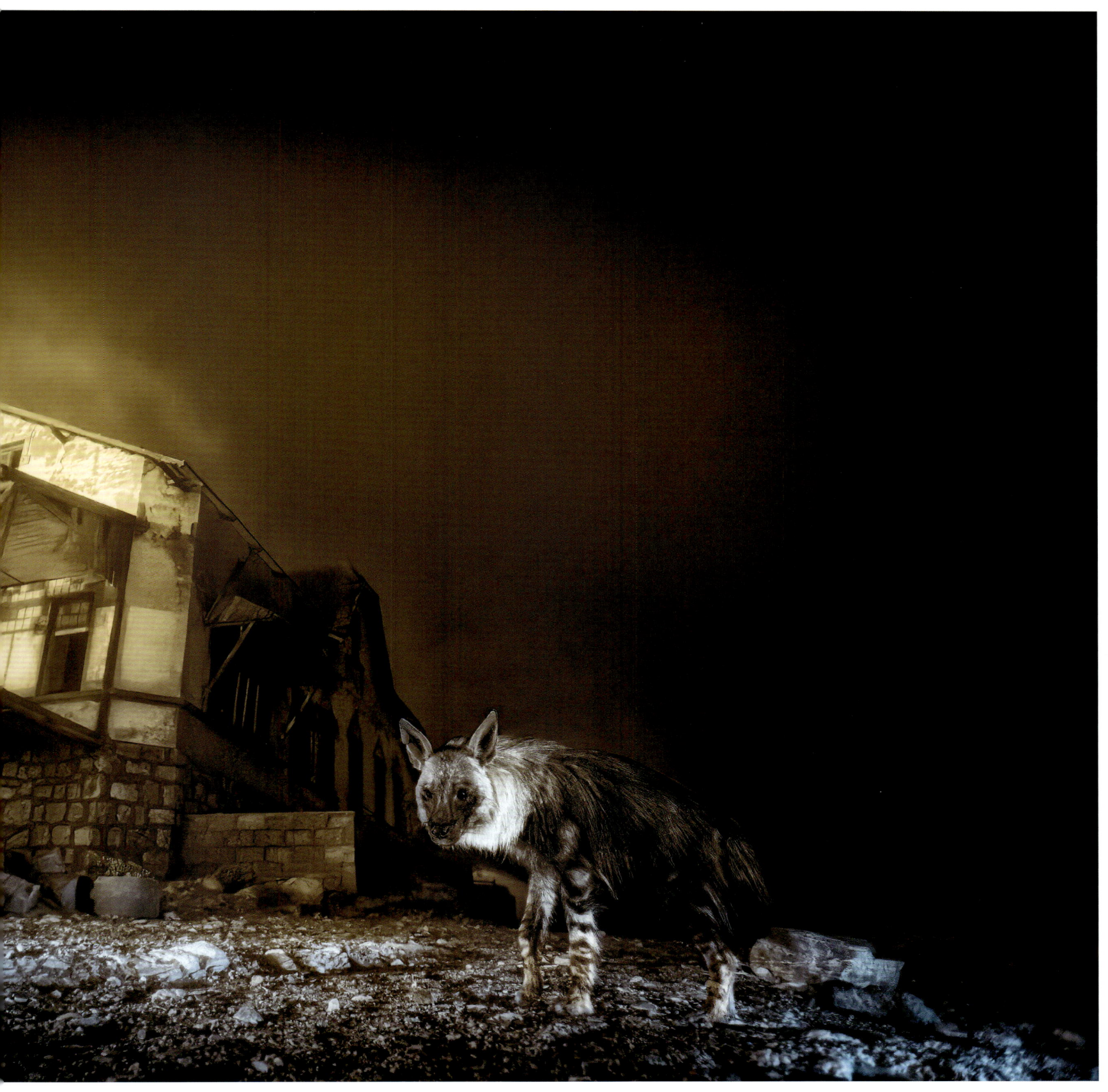

Behaviour: Mammals

Cat amongst the flamingos

Dennis Stogsdill

USA

Dennis had been keeping an eye out for servals in Tanzania's Serengeti National Park for a few days, when a call came over the radio that one of these sleek and delicately spotted cats had been seen at Ndutu Lake. What he and his friends encountered on arrival was certainly sleek and feline, but it was no serval. Its sandy fur lacked spots, and its ears were tipped with distinctive, black, pointed tufts: this cat was a caracal. And it was on the prowl. Caracals enjoy a varied diet that ranges from insects to antelope, and are renowned for the acrobatic leaps they make to pluck birds from the air, but there are few, if any, records of their hunting of flamingos. A flock of about 20 birds wading on Ndutu Lake was unaware of the caracal's presence until it sprung from the bank and hauled an unfortunate bird from the water by its wing. Caracals are widespread across Africa, the Middle East and South Asia, but very difficult to see, especially during the day in the long grass. While lesser flamingos are more visible, there are just three major breeding colonies remaining in Africa, so witnessing an interaction between these two species might become even rarer in future.

Canon EOS 1DX Mark II + 600mm f4 lens; 1/1600 at f5.6; ISO 2500.

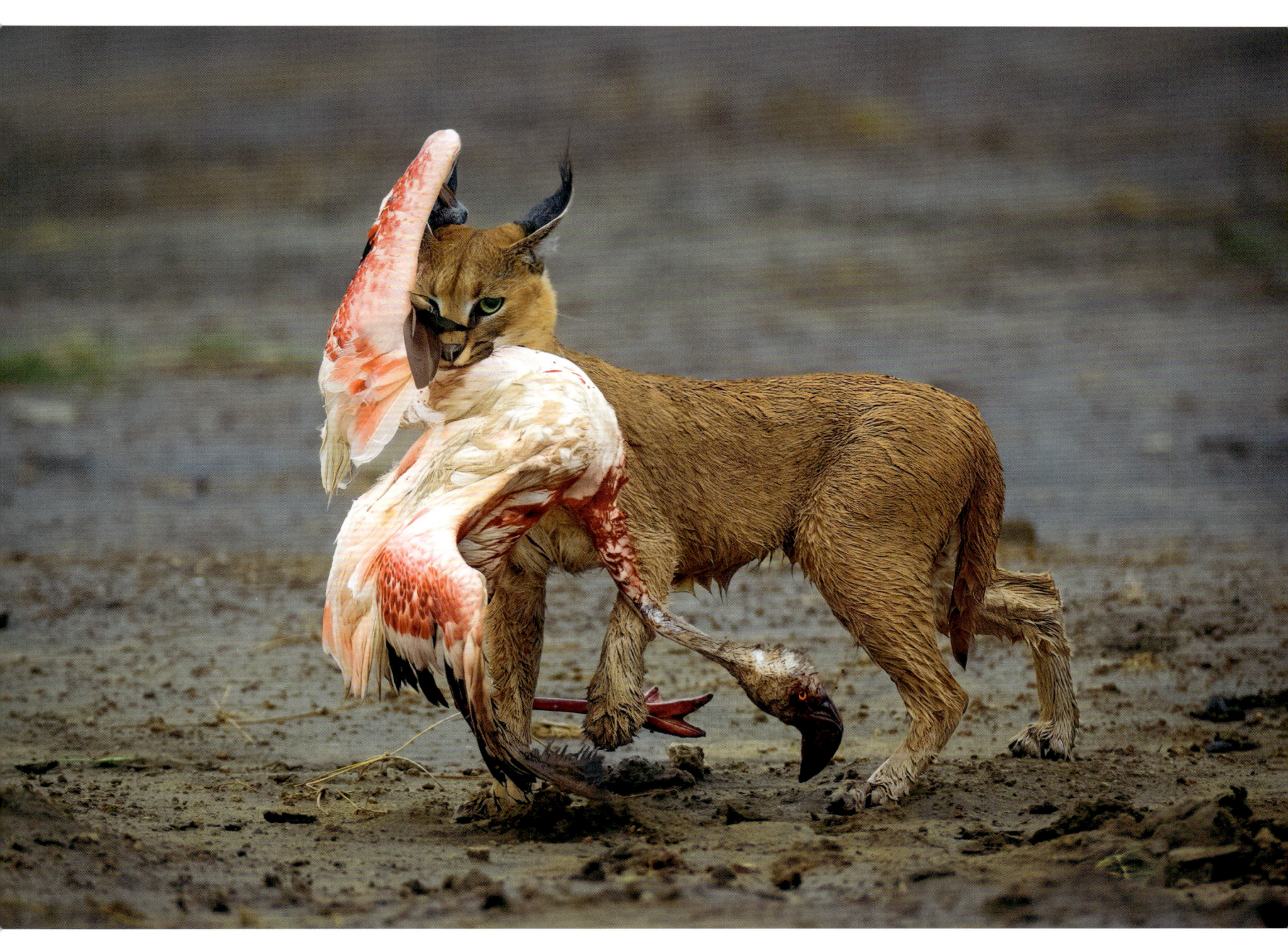

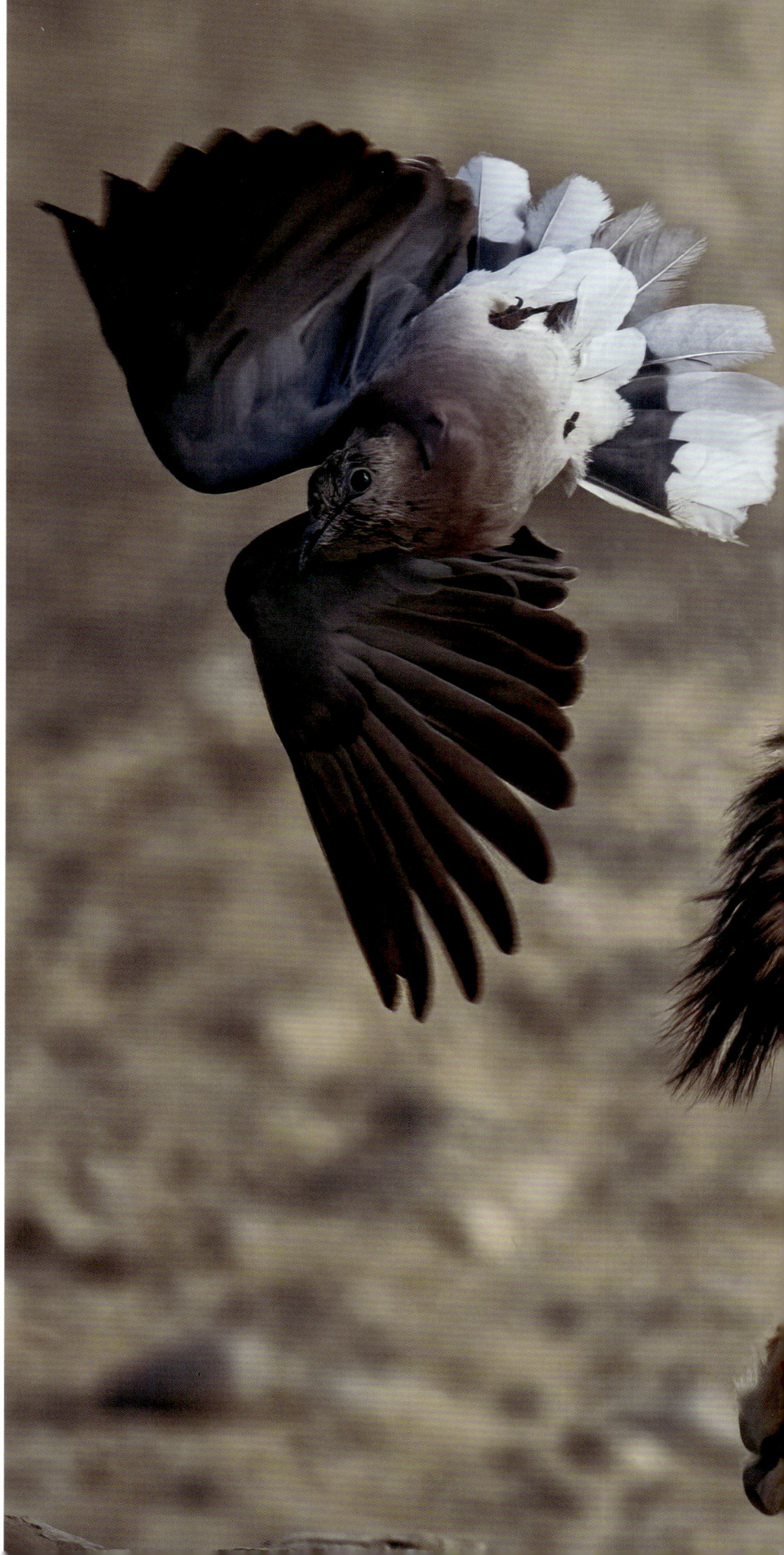

A narrow escape

Willie van Schalkwyk

SOUTH AFRICA

A thirsty dove needs just a few seconds at a waterhole to rehydrate. But it can be a risky few seconds: if the resident lanner falcons don't get you, the jackals might. This black-backed jackal and Cape turtle dove were at a waterhole in Kgalagadi Transfrontier Park, which straddles South Africa and Botswana, but the jackal wasn't there only to drink. These highly adaptable canids flourish in urban, desert, farmland, savanna and even alpine habitats. They hunt small prey alone or work together to bring down a gazelle. Willie noticed that two female jackals were working independently at the waterhole. With no cover to hide in, they had found more devious ways to get close to the doves that flew in to drink. He sensed that the jackals were deliberately ignoring the birds for much of the time, lulling them into a false sense of security perhaps, before launching into the heart of the flock to pluck out a random bird. Usually, their jaws would snap shut on thin air, but when they were successful they'd bolt their quarry straight down, feathers and all.

Canon EOS R5 + 100–500mm f4.5–7.1 lens; 1/4000 at f7.1; ISO 1600.

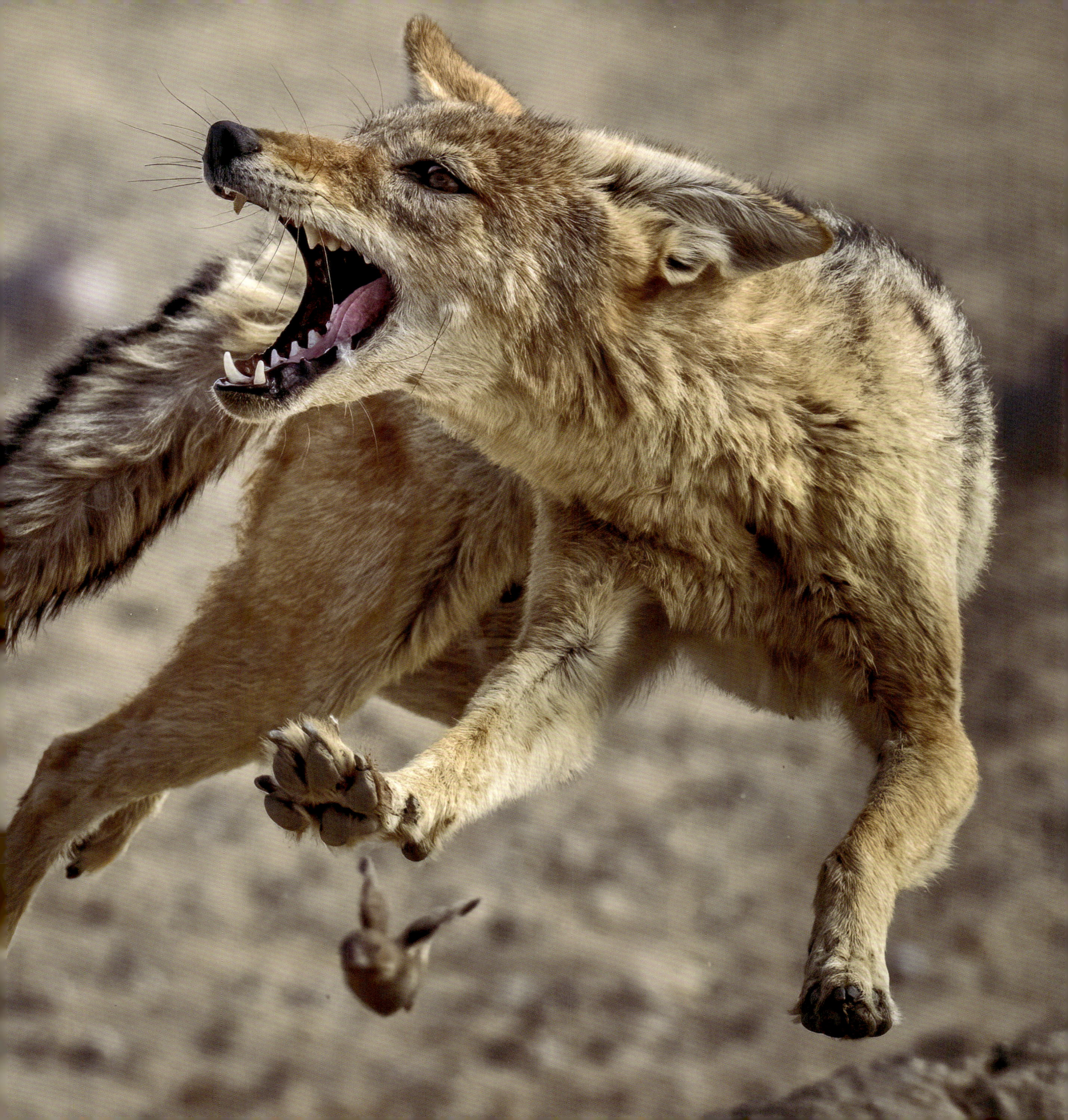

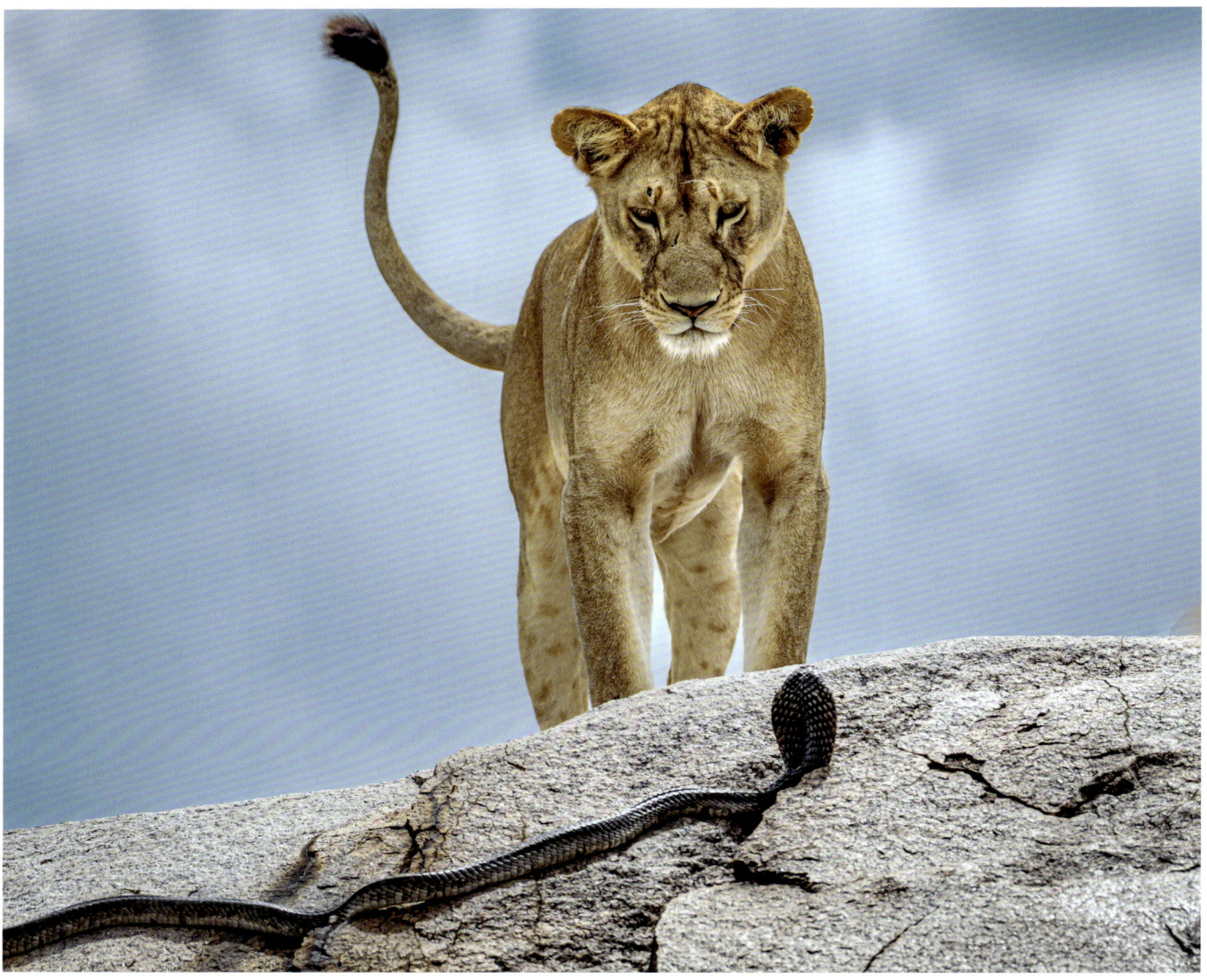

Wake-up call

Gabriella Comi

ITALY

Energy levels among the lions of Tanzania's Serengeti National Park were as low as the sun was high as Gabriella and her guide, David, drove between granite kopjes during the heat of the midday sun. They were about to move on from watching two more female lions napping on yet another kopje when David spotted some movement. What Gabriella initially thought to be a dark branch on the side of the kopje was actually an Egyptian cobra slithering its way slowly up the hot granite, directly towards the dozing cats. Within seconds, the older of the two lions was on her feet and facing down the venomous intruder. A wrong move could have serious consequences for either party, and time stood still while each assessed the options. It was the snake that flinched first, swerving to the right and following the kopje's contours to safety. The lion watched it all the way.

Fujifilm X-S10 + Tamron 150–500mm f5–6.7 lens at 288mm; 1/1600 at f5.6; ISO 250.

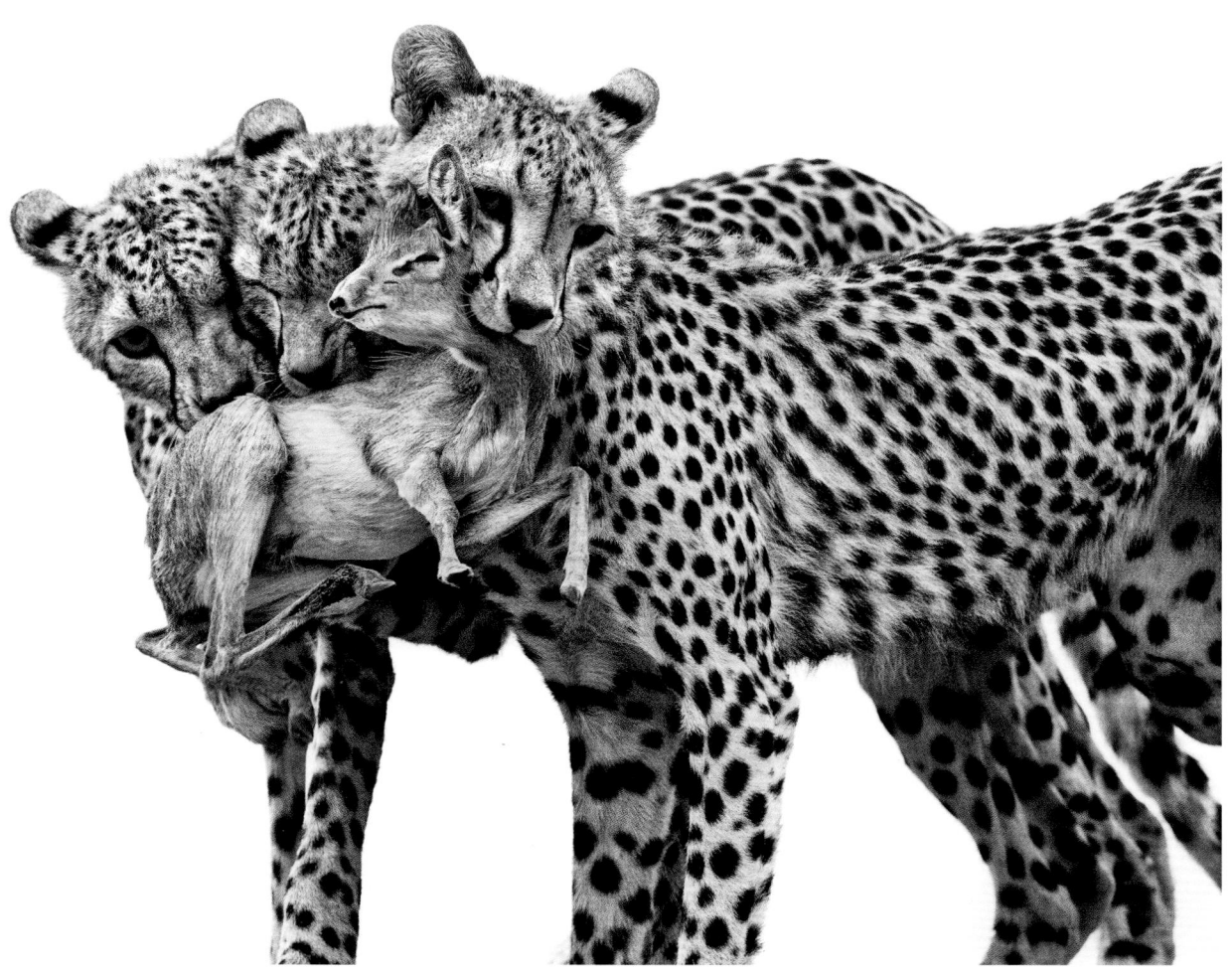

Deadly lessons

Marina Cano

SPAIN

Marina still finds this photograph hard to look at. She encountered a family group of cheetahs – an adult female and three juveniles – at Samburu National Reserve, Kenya, after they had caught the tiny antelope, a male Güenther's dik-dik. It was injured but still alive, and the siblings were using it for hunting practice while their mother looked on. Cheetah cubs participate in hunts with their mother from about one year of age. These cubs played with their victim for 15 minutes, releasing it and chasing it down repeatedly. Eventually, the dik-dik was lifted into the air and dispatched seconds after Marina took this photo, and the juveniles shared the meat between them. 'There's a kind of poetry in the precise second that's captured,' says Marina, 'the four faces together, the serene stillness in the dik-dik and the contradiction with the reality.'

Canon EOS R3 + 600mm f4 lens; 1/1250 at f8; ISO 6400.

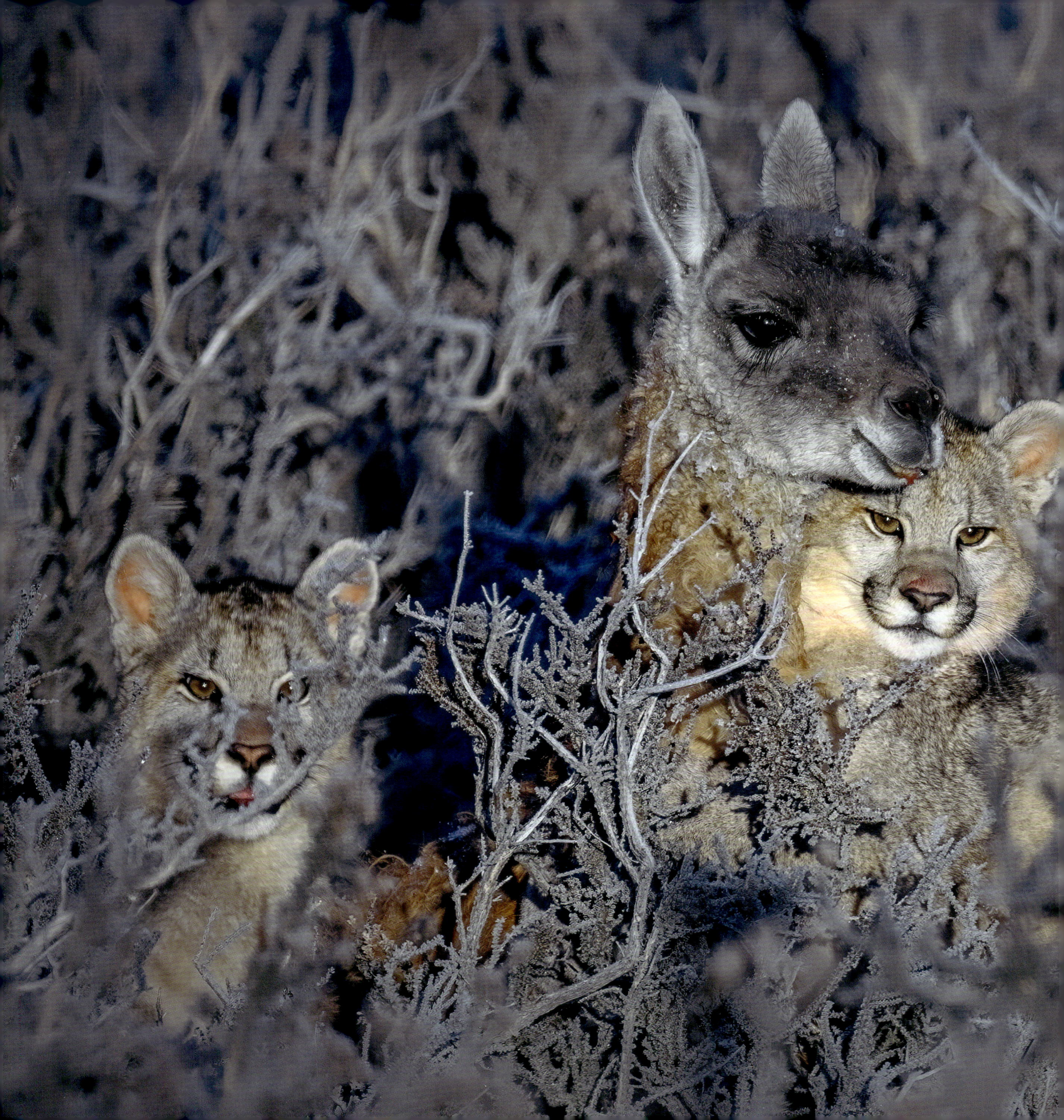

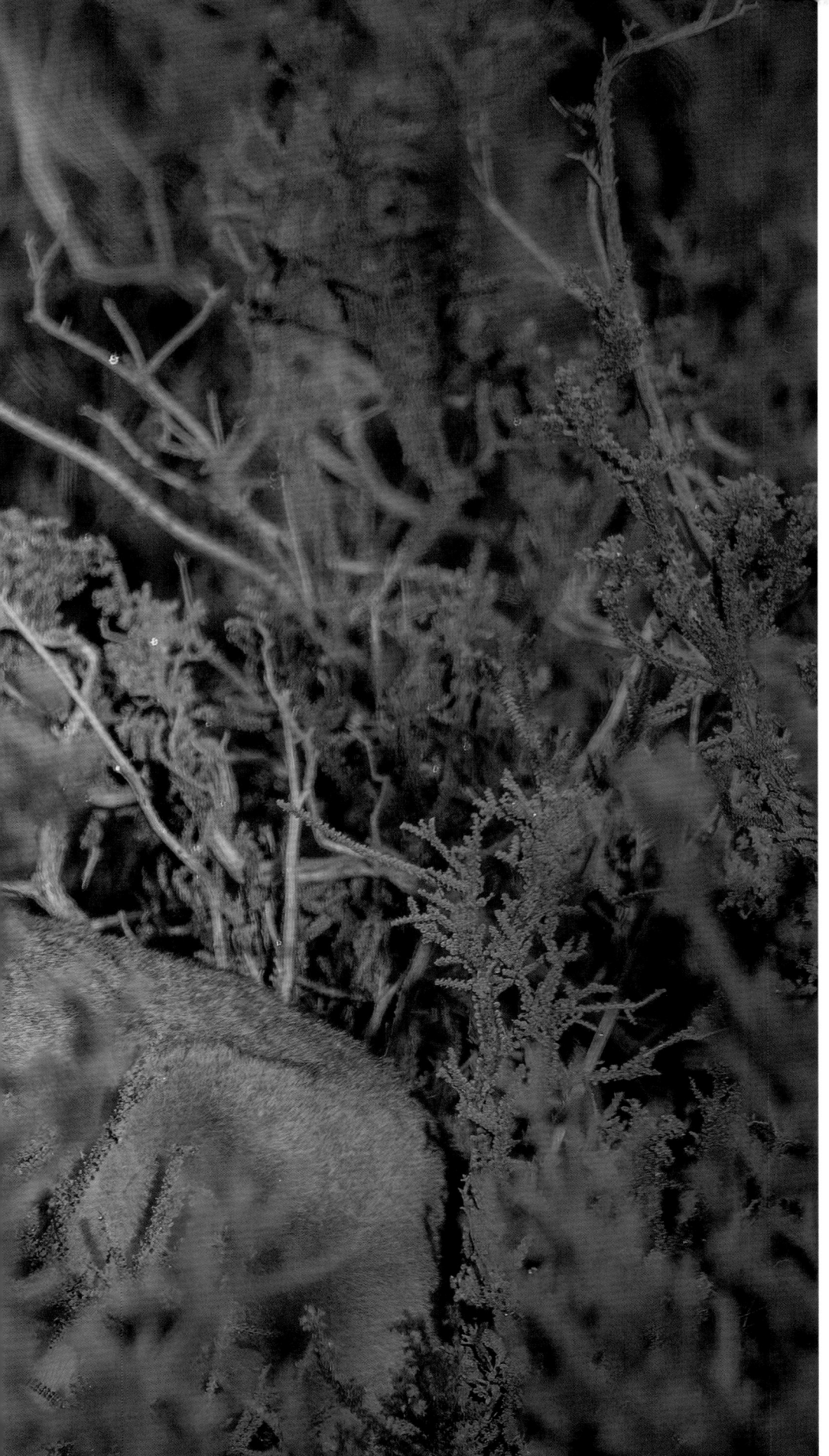

Training day

Hua Dai
CHINA

The postures and expressions might suggest warm familiarity, but don't be fooled. The fate of this camelid – most likely a young guanaco – lies with these puma cubs. Hua had been tracking a female puma and her cubs for six days through the snow in Torres del Paine National Park, Chile. The guanaco is insulated against temperature extremes by a coat of fine wool, and can survive 5,000 metres (16,400 feet) in the Andes as well as the searing heat of the Atacama Desert. But wherever guanacos may roam, so too can pumas. Hua didn't see the moment the chulengo – the name for a young guanaco – was caught, but he heard its scream, and the growls of the female summoning her cubs. When he got there, the chulengo was alive, yet unable to escape. Forty minutes later, it was bleeding profusely from multiple bites, but the cubs had failed to kill it, so the female dispatched the hapless victim herself. Afterwards, the pumas ate little of the meat. This hadn't been about dinner; it was a training exercise. The cubs would be needing more of those before they were ready to fend for themselves.

Nikon Z9 + 600mm f4 lens + 1.4x teleconverter; 1/1600 at f6.3 (+0.3 e/v); ISO 500.

Behaviour: Birds

WINNER

Synchronised fishing

Qingrong Yang

CHINA

It is part of the natural order that little fish get eaten by bigger fish. And bigger fish often get eaten by birds. But rarely does it all happen at the same time. Qingrong's fine example of photographic timing occurred at Yundang Lake near his home in Xiamen, China. The lake was once a natural marine harbour, but it was sealed off from the sea in the 1970s by waterside industrial developments and land-reclamation schemes. Isolated from the tides and currents, the lake became polluted and stagnant until an ambitious engineering project, started in the 1990s, reconnected it to the open ocean via a system of sluices. Now, at each high tide, seawater rushes into the lake, bringing with it all manner of ocean life and providing hunting opportunities for resident predators. Qingrong visits regularly to photograph the feeding frenzies. The lake's surface is patrolled by little egrets, who pounce on fish that leap from the water to escape aquatic predators. But, this is not quite the textbook food chain that it appears to be. The ladyfish in the centre is too big for the little egret to handle. It had its sights on the unfortunate smaller fish – possibly a shad or sardinella – but the ladyfish got there first and snatched it from right under the egret's beak.

Nikon Z9 + 400mm f2.8 lens; 1/2500 at f5; ISO 110.

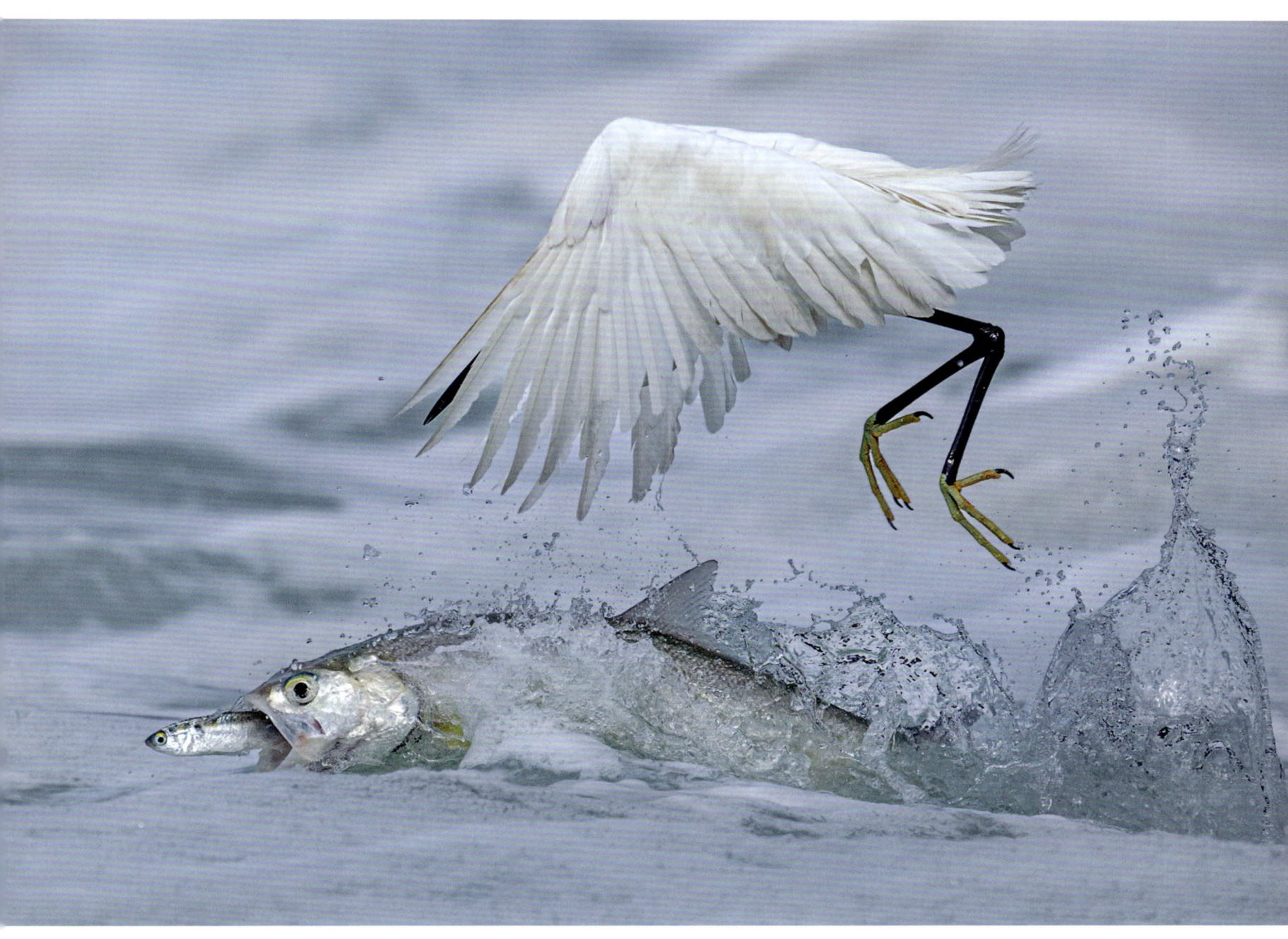

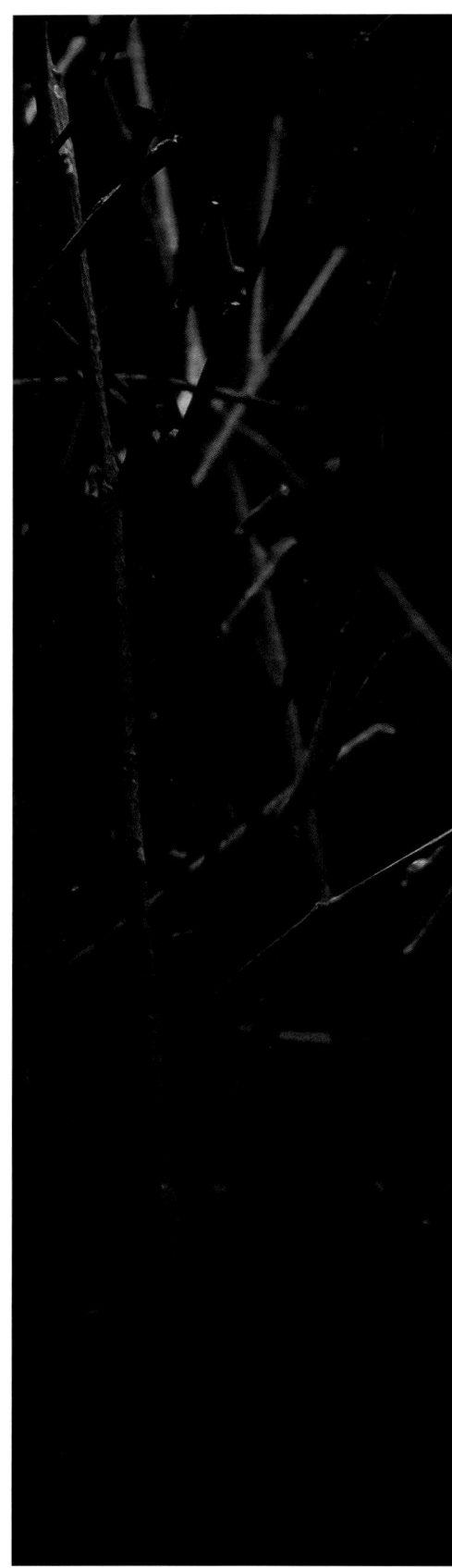

Make and mend

Georgina Steytler
AUSTRALIA

In a corner of a rainforest in Queensland, Australia, a bird with lilac-blue eyes is putting a twig back into just the right place. Male satin bowerbirds build exquisite structures of interwoven twigs, called bowers, decorated with objects collected from the forest to lure prospective mates. The more impressive the collection of blue and yellow feathers, flowers, seeds, fruits and beetle wing-cases, the more attention they get from females. Inevitably perhaps, bottle tops, drinking straws and clothes pegs feature increasingly in these displays as human settlements encroach upon their habitat. Georgina had been visiting this bower in Lamington National Park for a few days, shooting through bushes from a distance with a long lens. The male came and went, bringing sticks or fresh decorations, which he would position fastidiously, while females would drop by occasionally to inspect his efforts. There were less welcome visitors, too. Georgina took this image soon after the bower had been torn down, and its decorations pillaged by a rival male while the resident was away. Upon his return, he immediately set about repairing the damage. Georgina was outraged on his behalf, until she wondered how he had come by his collection in the first place – scientists have concluded that bowers are a key element in male sexual display and their destruction is a consequence of competition between the males.

Nikon Z8 + 400mm f4.5 lens; 1/1600 at f8; ISO 1600.

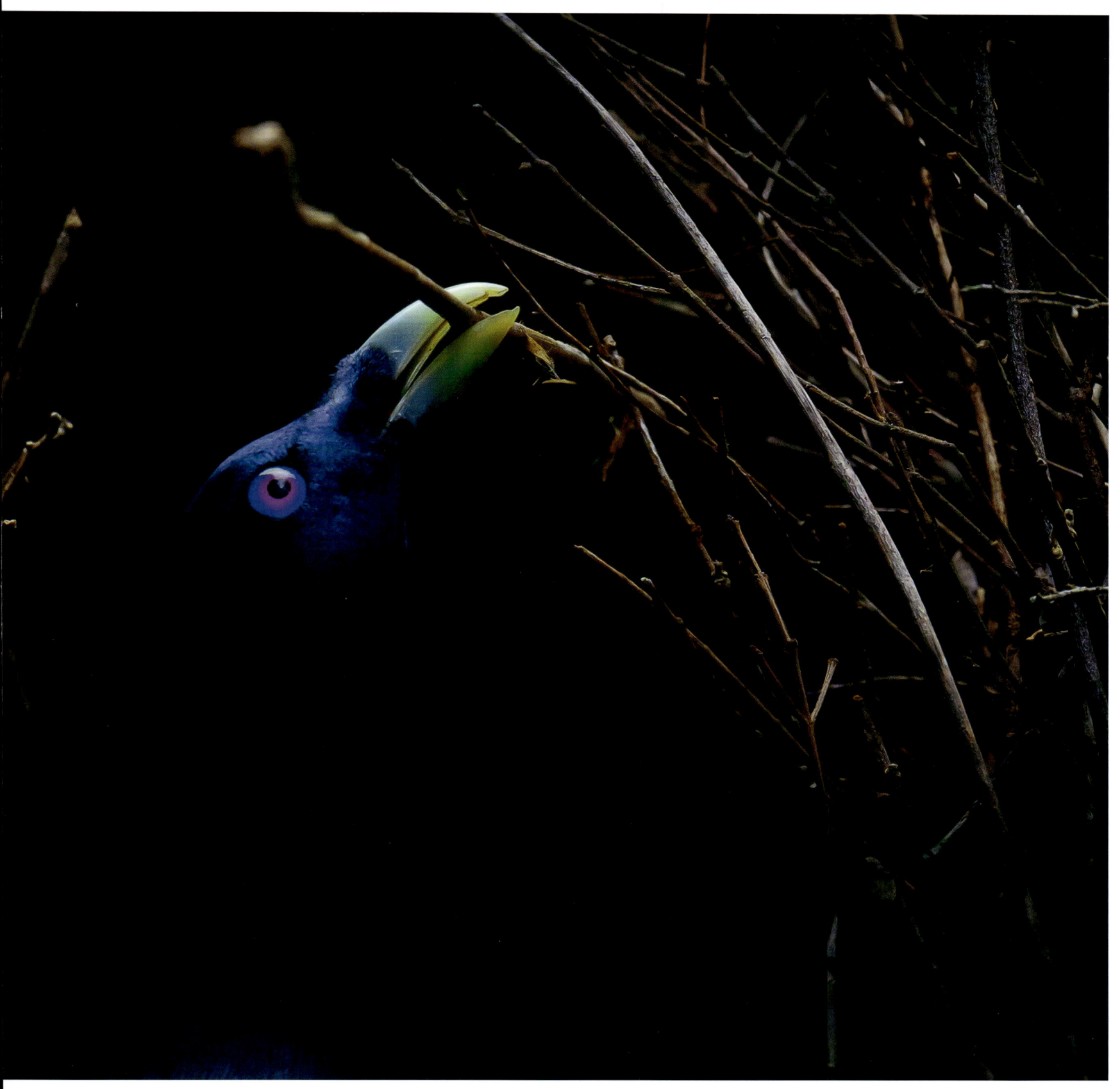

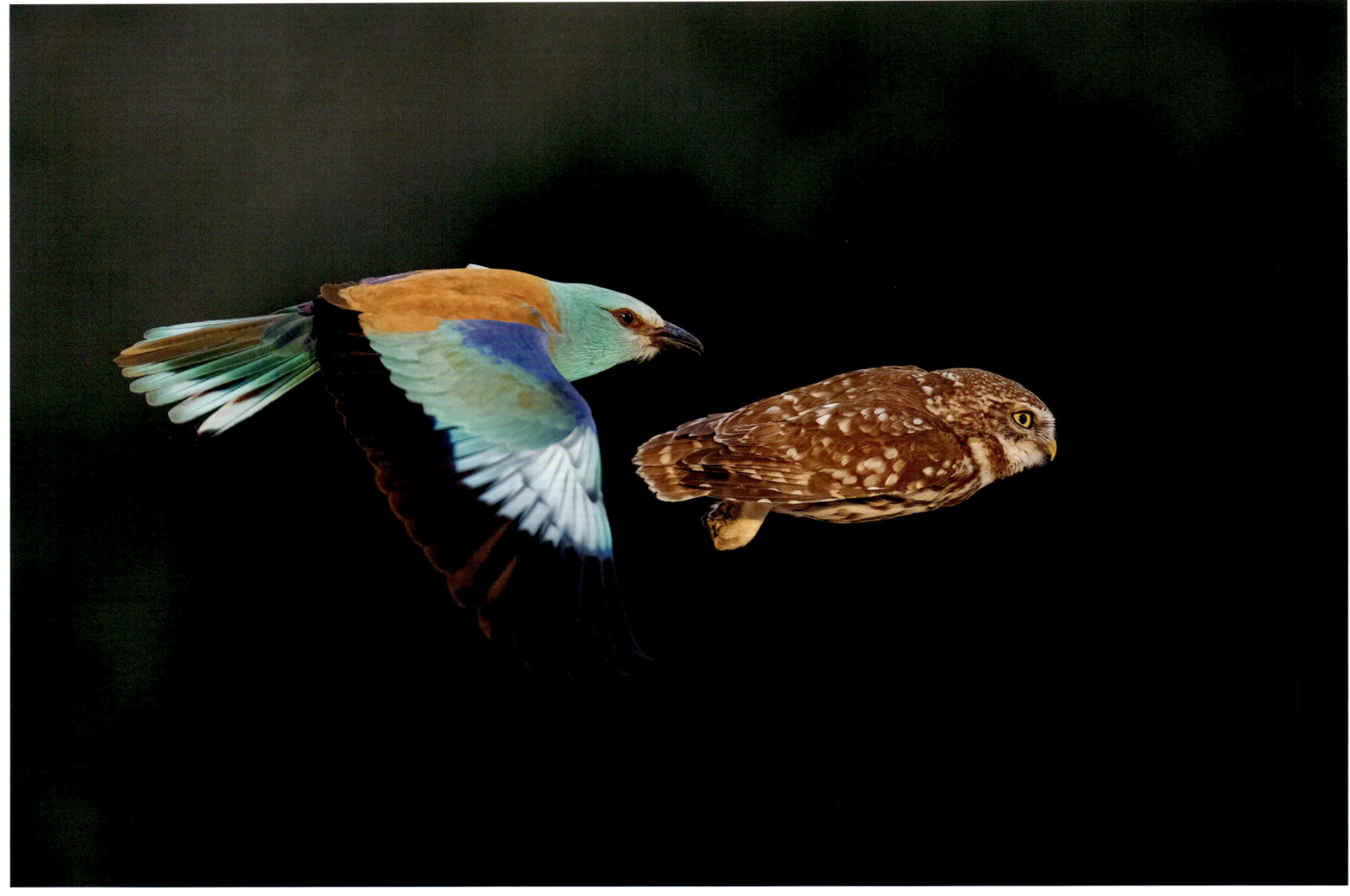

Avian tailgating

Bence Máté

HUNGARY

Even if you didn't blink, you'd likely miss this instant of high-speed action. This European roller and little owl, both males, occupied neighbouring nest boxes, and early in the breeding season they chased each other through the undergrowth. Bence had installed 200 nest boxes in former farmland he is rewilding around his home next to Kiskunság National Park, Hungary. The chases stopped once the birds had broods to tend, suggesting the behaviour is not about protecting the young; Bence reckons it is more to do with securing nest sites. To freeze the action, he mounted two cameras side by side on a tripod, each synchronized at 20 frames per second. The shutters were triggered by a remote release controlled by his foot. After 27 days in a hide, Bence captured the scene properly only once. This is it.

Canon EOS R5 + 200mm f2 lens; 1/8000 at f2; ISO 5000; Flexline twin shooter head + tripod, homemade leg-controlled remote control.

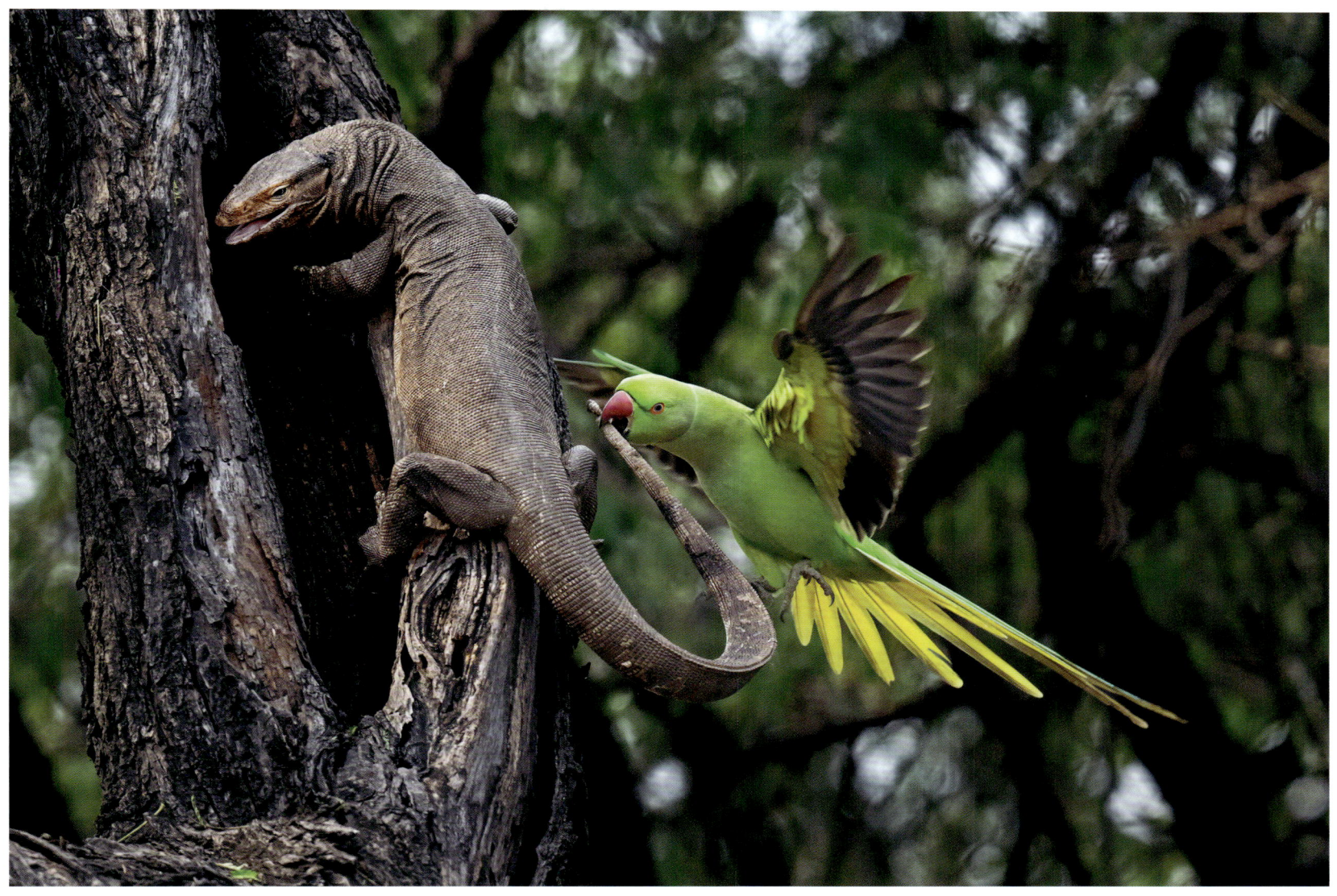

A nip to the tail

Hira Punjabi

INDIA

A beak capable of cracking nuts can surely deliver a painful nip to the fleshy tip of a reptilian tail. In Keoladeo National Park in Rajasthan, India, this Bengal monitor was investigating a tree cavity for birds' eggs or chicks, when it was attacked by the resident pair of rose-ringed parakeets. Other birds joined the assault and Hira witnessed up to 12 parakeets at a time pecking, slapping and squawking at the intruder. The resident female hadn't laid any eggs yet, but the birds maintained their onslaught for an hour before the monitor retreated. Indigenous to the Indian subcontinent and equatorial Africa, rose-ringed parakeets have been introduced around the world as pets. Feral populations now thrive in cities in Europe, North America and Japan, where they compete vigorously with local birds and bats for nest holes.

Nikon Z9 + 600mm f4 lens; 1/1250 at f8; ISO 1600.

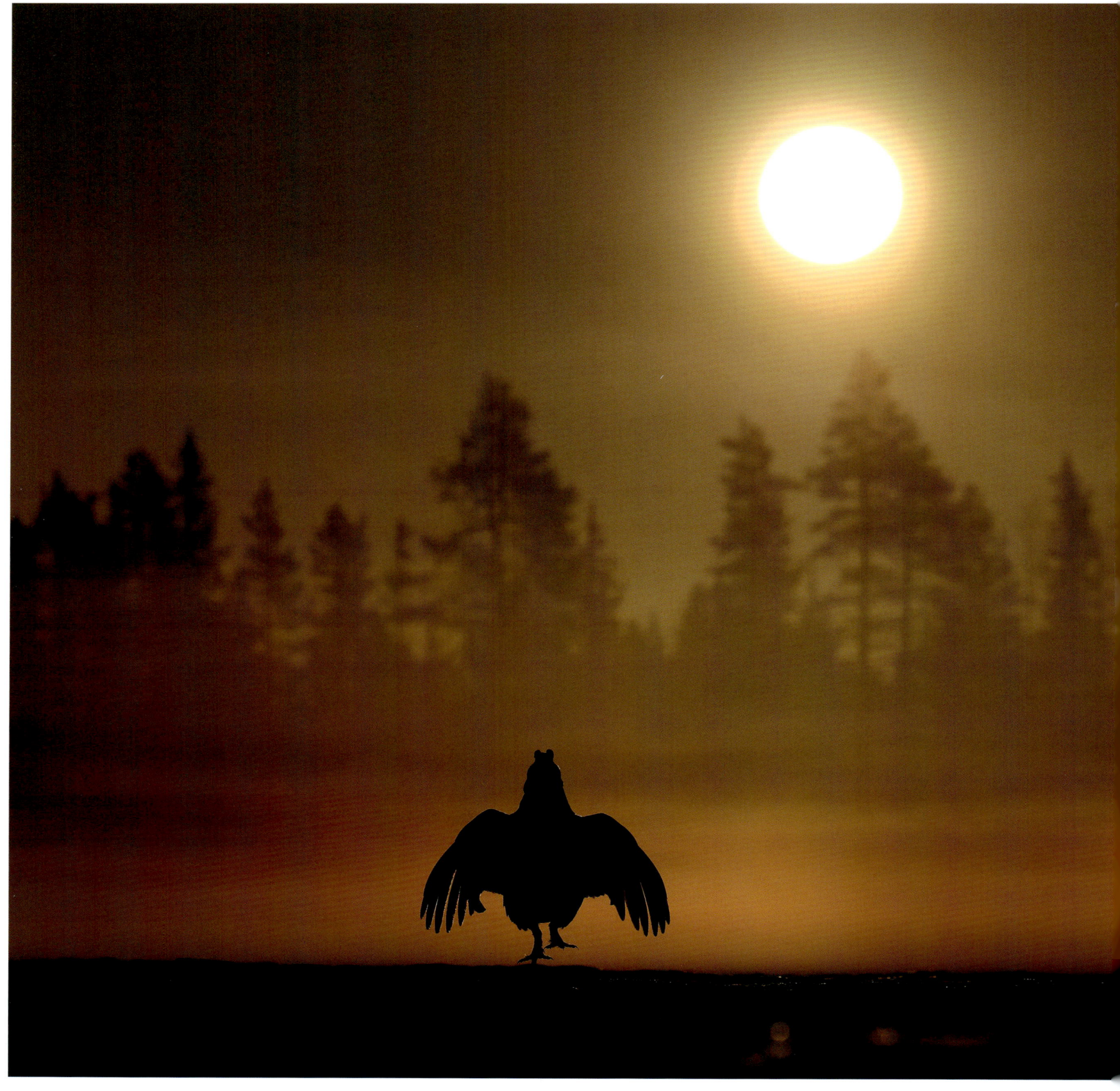

Sunrise hop

Marc Costermans
BELGIUM

A male black grouse hopping on the spot against the rising Scandinavian sun is enough to put a spring in anyone's step. Which was just what Marc needed – for five nights he had camped out in the snow to ensure he was in position at sunrise to get the picture he envisaged. A chicken-sized bird of heath, moorland and woodland edges, the black grouse occupies a vast range across northern Eurasia, although it has been declining in numbers as upland habitats are lost to forestry plantations. The males, known as blackcocks, are dressed to impress, with blue-black iridescent plumage terminating in long tail feathers that curve outwards either side of a fan of brilliant-white undertail coverts, and a scarlet crescent-shaped wattle over each eye. For a few weeks in spring, they congregate at traditional sites, called leks, to compete for dominance and to catch the eyes of the more circumspect females. About 15 blackcocks gathered at this lek near Långträsk, northern Sweden, to strut, pose, hop, coo, cackle, flap and bicker. Marc was lying on his belly in the snow when the first one arrived at 4.30am. He hoped that, finally, one of them would move in line with the sun. An hour later, this male obliged. And, just to be clear, it is facing towards his camera.

Canon EOS R6 Mark II + 100–300mm f2.8 lens + 1.4x teleconverter; 1/5000 at f13 (-1.3ev); ISO 200.

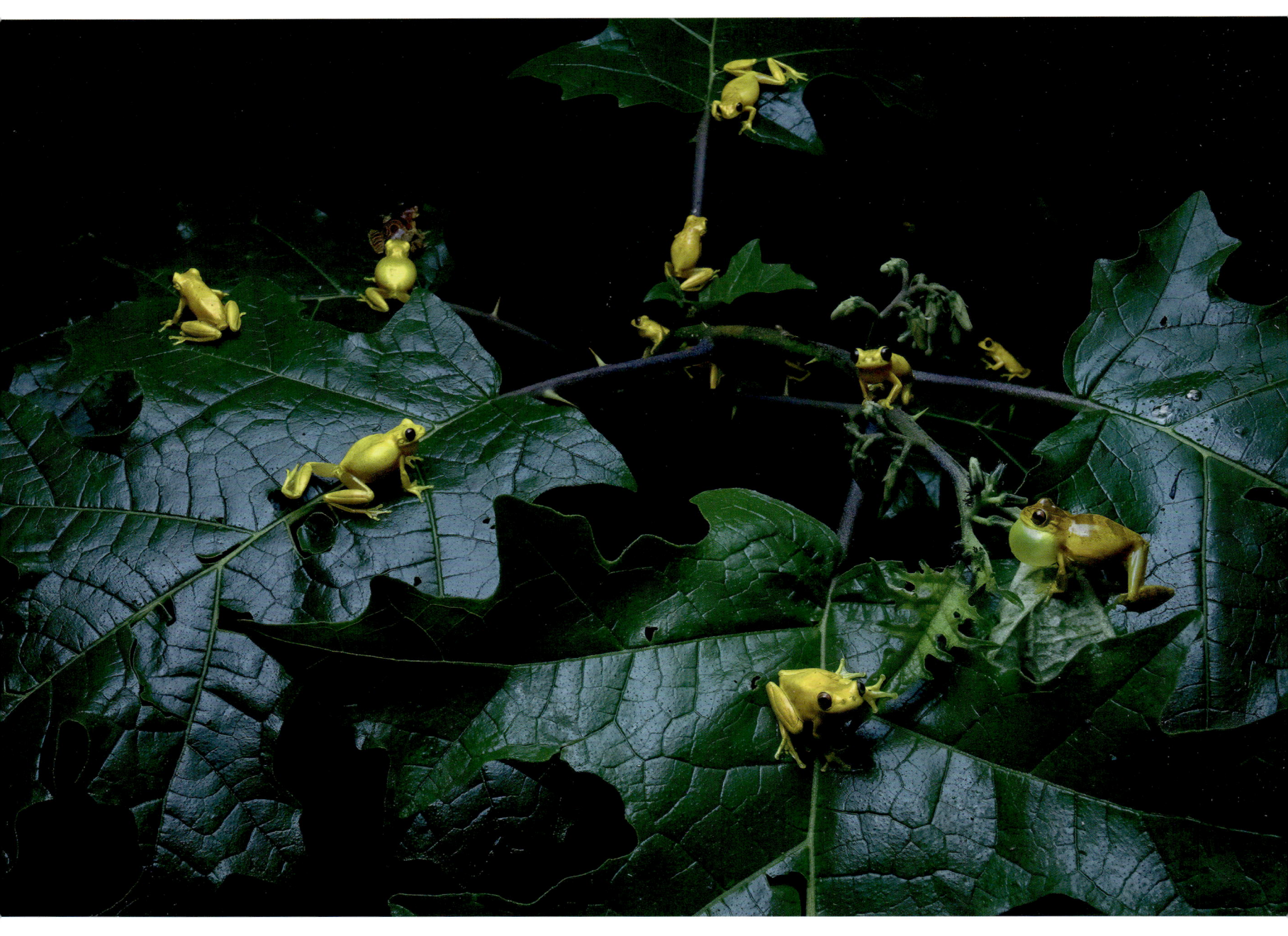

Behaviour: Amphibians and Reptiles

Frolicking frogs

Quentin Martinez

FRANCE

Every night for several weeks, Quentin trekked into the forest of Kaw Mountain, French Guiana, until he finally struck gold – a gathering of tens of thousands of lesser tree frogs in an explosive breeding event that is rarely witnessed. 'Small trees were completely covered, ponds and trails were packed and the chorus was so intense that you needed earplugs,' he says. To attract mates, male lesser tree frogs produce short, shrill calls. Predators, including snakes and invertebrates, are drawn to the bounty, but the frogs' strategy is thought to be one of safety in numbers. The chaotic spectacle usually lasts just a few hours, its timing difficult to predict but thought to be triggered by the first heavy rains of the season. This reliance on the amount and pattern of rainfall makes the frogs vulnerable to climate change, with an increasing variability of precipitation potentially shifting or disrupting their reproduction. In persistent rain, Quentin followed a flooded path to a forest clearing, where the golden frogs would lay their eggs in a temporary pool after mating. Challenged with an abundance of subject choices, he framed this small scene with a wide-angle lens, taking care to include a calling male (throat inflated on the right of the picture), and using diffused flash to highlight their metallic sheen on the dark green leaves. The event also brings together other species of frogs, including several that are almost never encountered again outside of this one night.

Canon EOS 7D Mark II + 17–40mm f4 lens at 24mm; 1/200 at f16; ISO 500; 4x Meike MK320 flashes; homemade softbox.

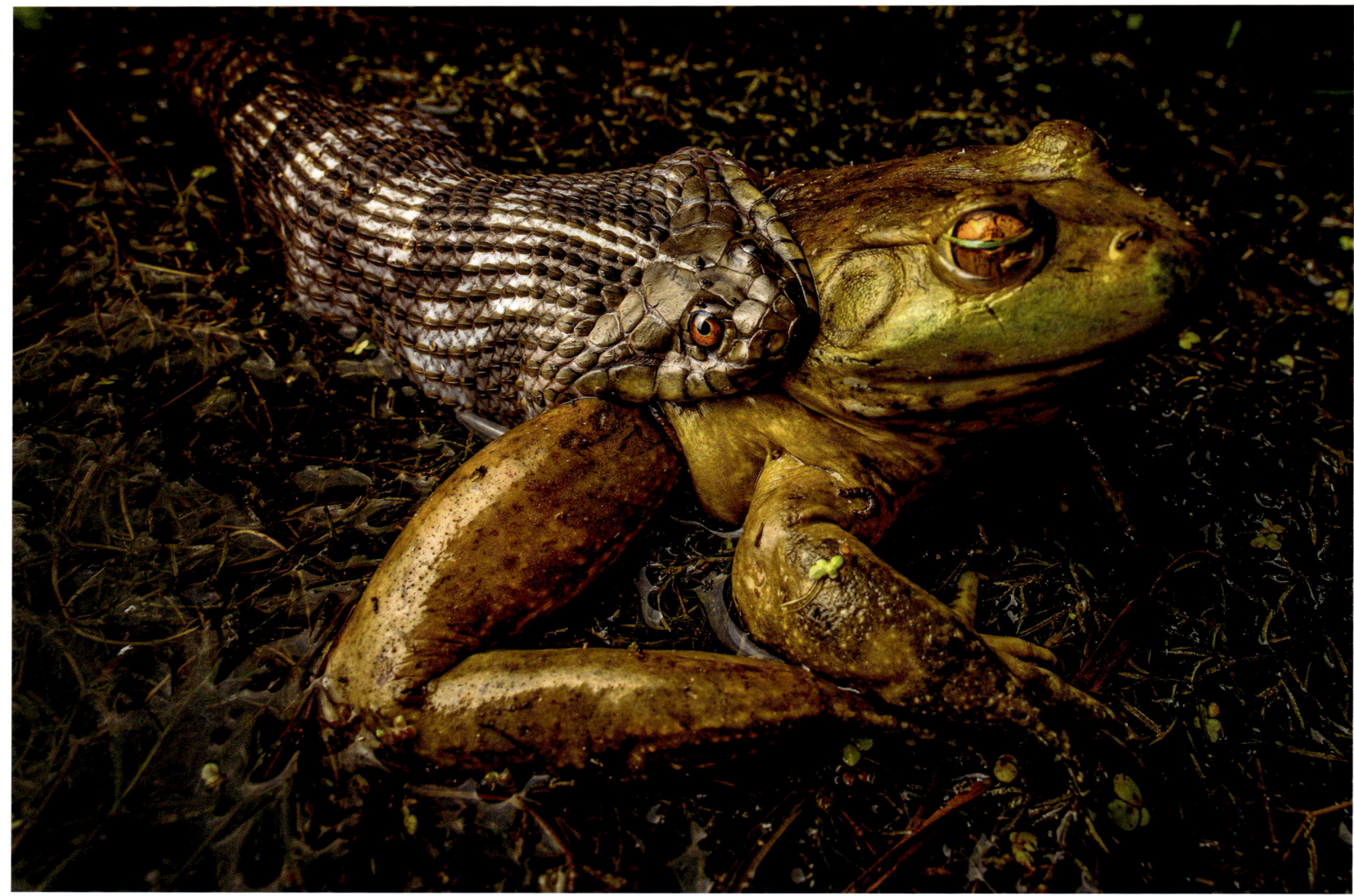

A big helping

Nick Kanakis

USA

A diamondback water snake slowly swallows an American bullfrog in Navarro County, Texas, USA. Nick sees both species regularly when night hiking on his favourite wetland, but it was unusual to witness this deadly interaction. Non-venomous and semi-aquatic, this snake is often spotted hanging from branches over water, hunting by night mainly for fish. The bullfrog is North America's largest native frog, up to 15 centimetres (6 inches) long, and has been introduced across the world. In many countries, it is regarded as a pest, preying on native species with its generalist diet, and considered by scientists to be a possible vector of pathogens. Nick diffused the flash output to illuminate the frog's burnished brass colouring, and its partly raised nictitating membrane (a translucent third eyelid), without disturbing the snake from devouring its victim.

Nikon D850 + Laowa 15mm f4 macro lens; 1/200 at f14; ISO 64; diffused off-camera flash.

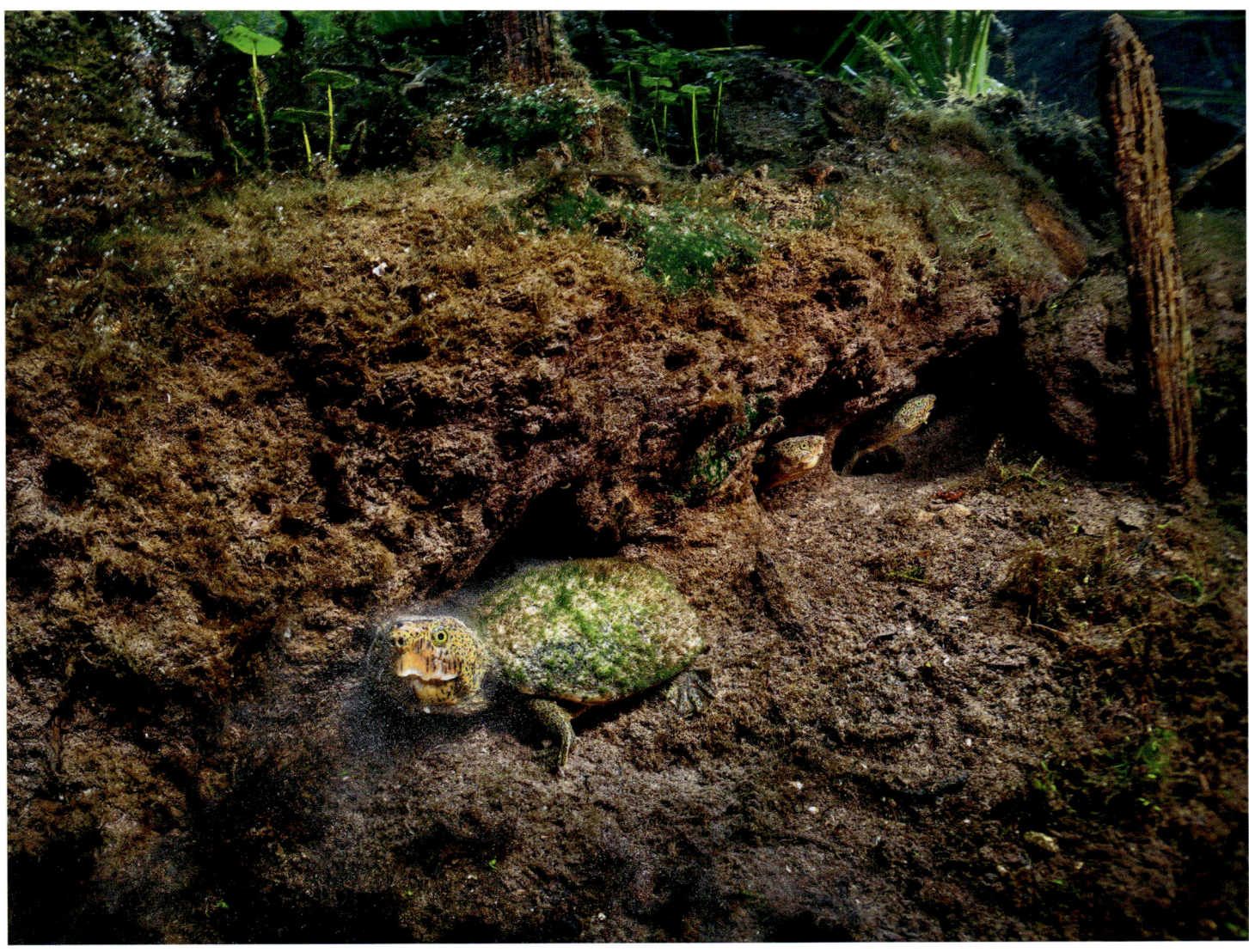

Musk turtle motel

Isaac Szabo

USA

While snorkelling in a Florida spring, Isaac rounded a submerged tree and came face to face with a loggerhead musk turtle. A trio of these small aquatic reptiles, with their characteristically large heads and webbed feet, were sheltering in holes in the soft clay bank. They have powerful jaws to crack open snails and clams but, at less than 15 centimetres (6 inches) long, become easy snacks for larger predators such as alligators. Loggerhead musk turtles are found in southeastern USA, primarily Georgia, Alabama, Louisiana, as well as Florida. They are facing loss and degradation of their habitat caused by pollution and growing demands for water extraction. Isaac moved slowly, so as not to stir up the sediment, and captured this moment before the surprised turtle disappeared inside its refuge.

Sony α7R II + Canon 60mm f2.8 lens + Nauticam EMWL lens; 1/10 at f8; ISO 160; Meikon housing; 2x Inon Z-240 strobes.

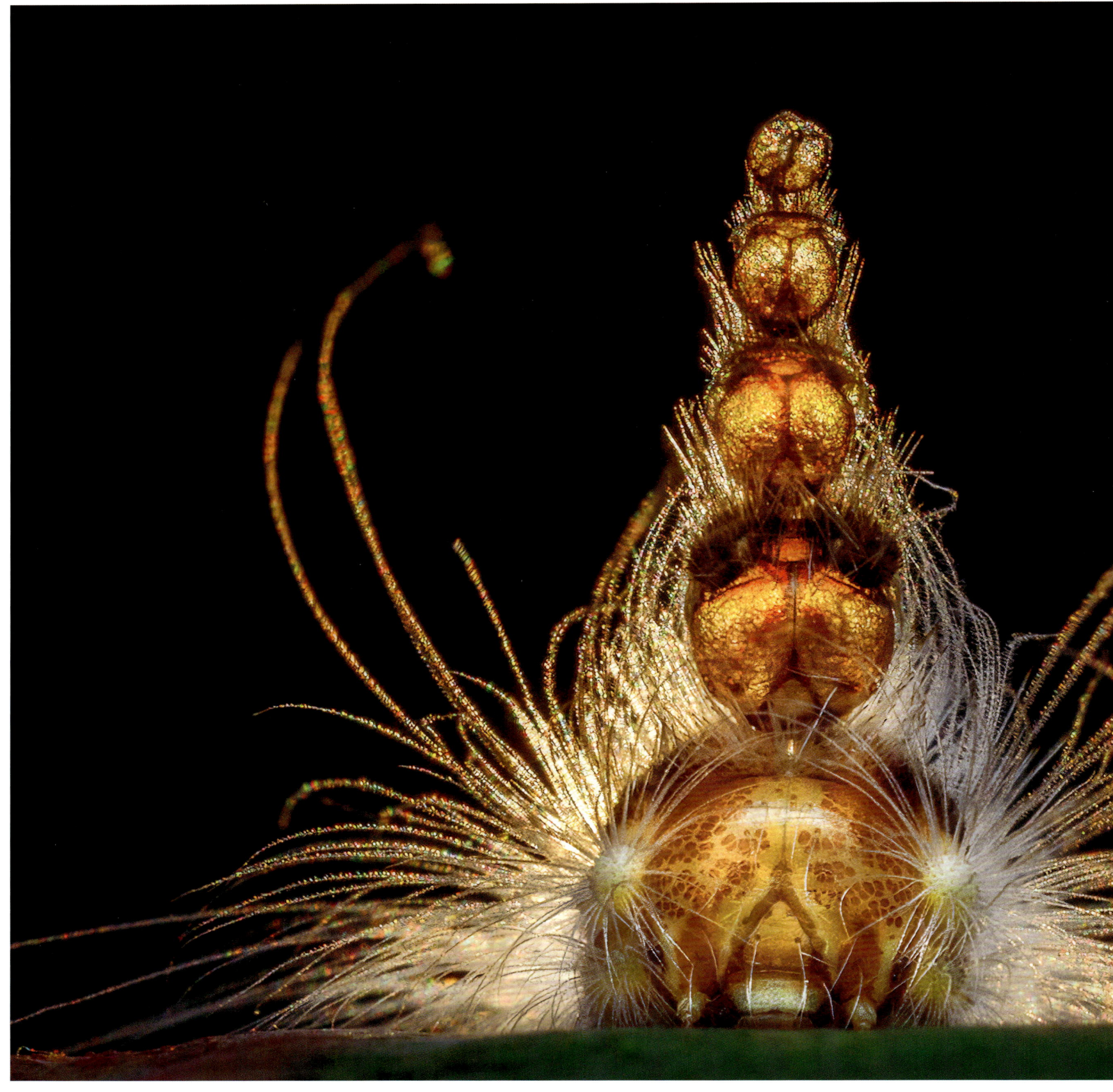

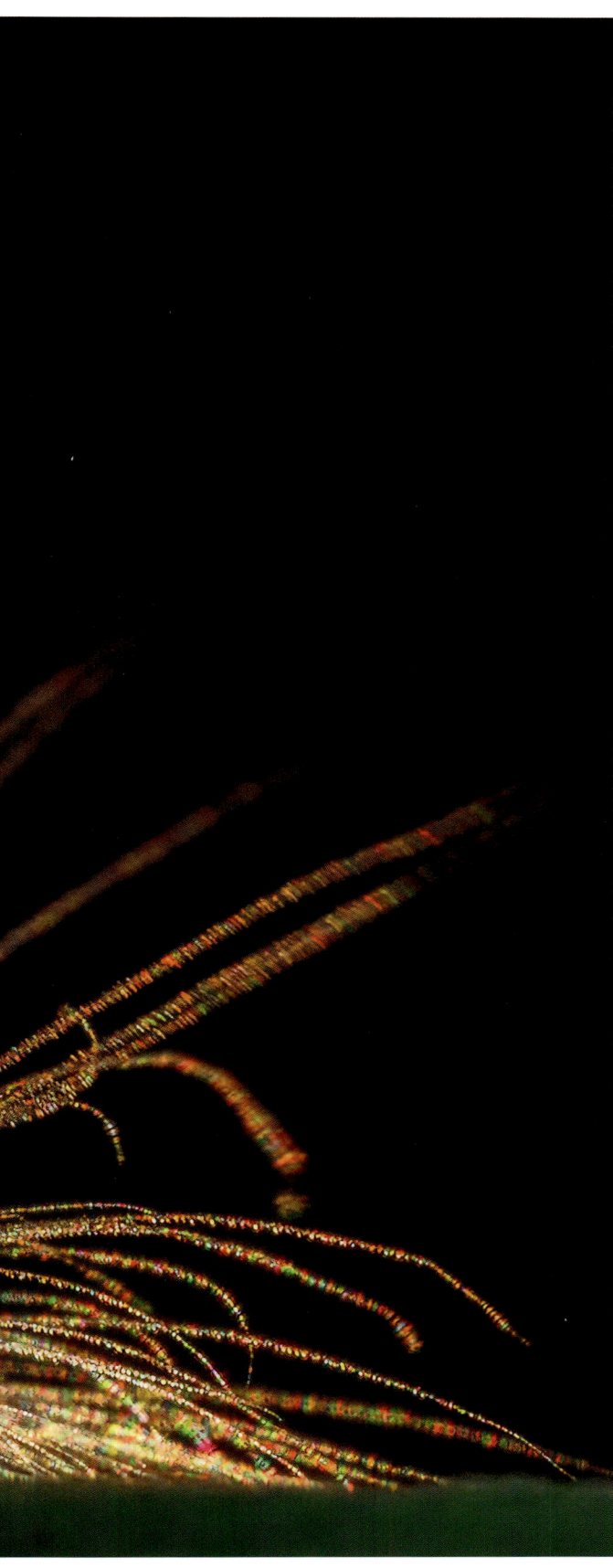

Behaviour: Invertebrates

WINNER

Mad hatterpillar

Georgina Steytler
AUSTRALIA

Sometimes, what you've been looking for everywhere turns up right on your doorstep. That was Georgina's experience in searching for the caterpillar of the gum-leaf skeletonizer moth. Native to Australia and New Zealand, the moth is named after the unconventional feeding habits of its gregarious larvae. Instead of devouring entire leaves from the edge inwards, they graze on the leaf surface, leaving behind just a ghostly leaf-shaped network of veins. Recently, an alternative name, 'mad hatterpillar', has been catching on, inspired by the larva's eccentric headgear, which is composed of the caterpillar's old head-capsules each time it sheds its skin. The structure is wielded to deflect attacks by predatory bugs – caterpillars with intact headgear are more than twice as likely to survive an encounter. Georgina had been looking out for mad hatterpillars for years. She was walking the dog behind her house in Western Australia when she noticed a stand of eucalyptus trees bearing telltale skeletal leaves. She returned that evening to photograph it, backlit by the setting sun, using fill-in flash to illuminate the living head at the bottom, before it too becomes added to the pile.

Olympus OM-D E-M1 Mark III + 90mm f3.5 lens; 1/250 at f22; ISO 500; Godox flash.

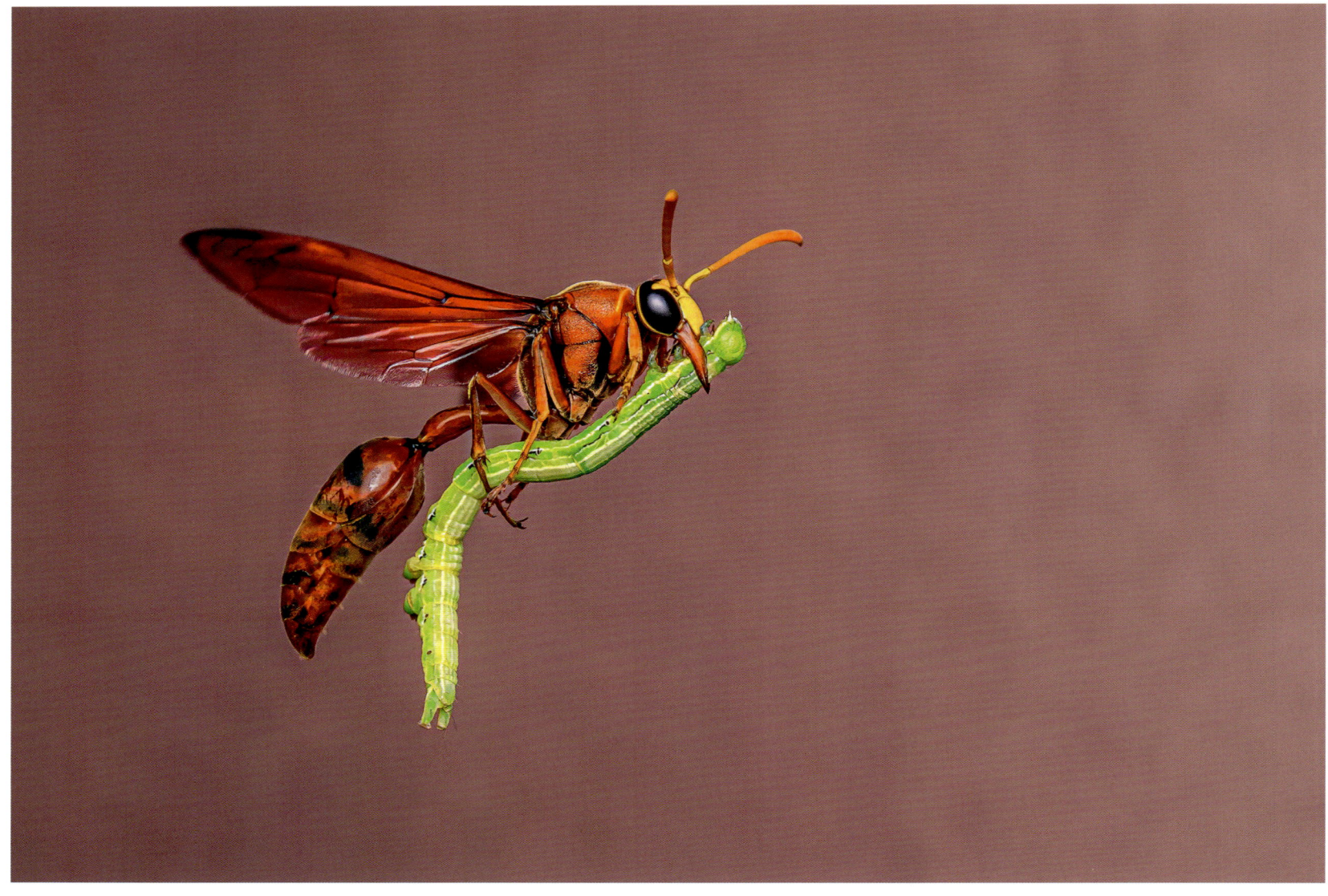

Special delivery

Bidyut Kalita

INDIA

There's something almost tender about the way this potter wasp is gripping a caterpillar in its jaws. And for good reason. It must be kept alive when stored inside a mud chamber for young wasps to feed upon once they hatch. Bidyut captured this pin-sharp image while handholding the camera, freezing the action with flash – and a modicum of post-processing. He had spotted the wasp building the chamber on a picture frame in his home in Goalpara, northeast India. It came and went several times a day, via the same door to the house, which Bidyut wedged open to allow access. Once completed, the wasp set about packing the chamber with caterpillars, which it had paralyzed with a sting. Eventually, the confined wasps broke out of their mud home as newly developed adults.

Canon EOS R6 + 85mm f2 macro lens; 1/125 at f10; ISO 500; Canon Speedlite 470EX-AI flash + Beetle macro diffuser.

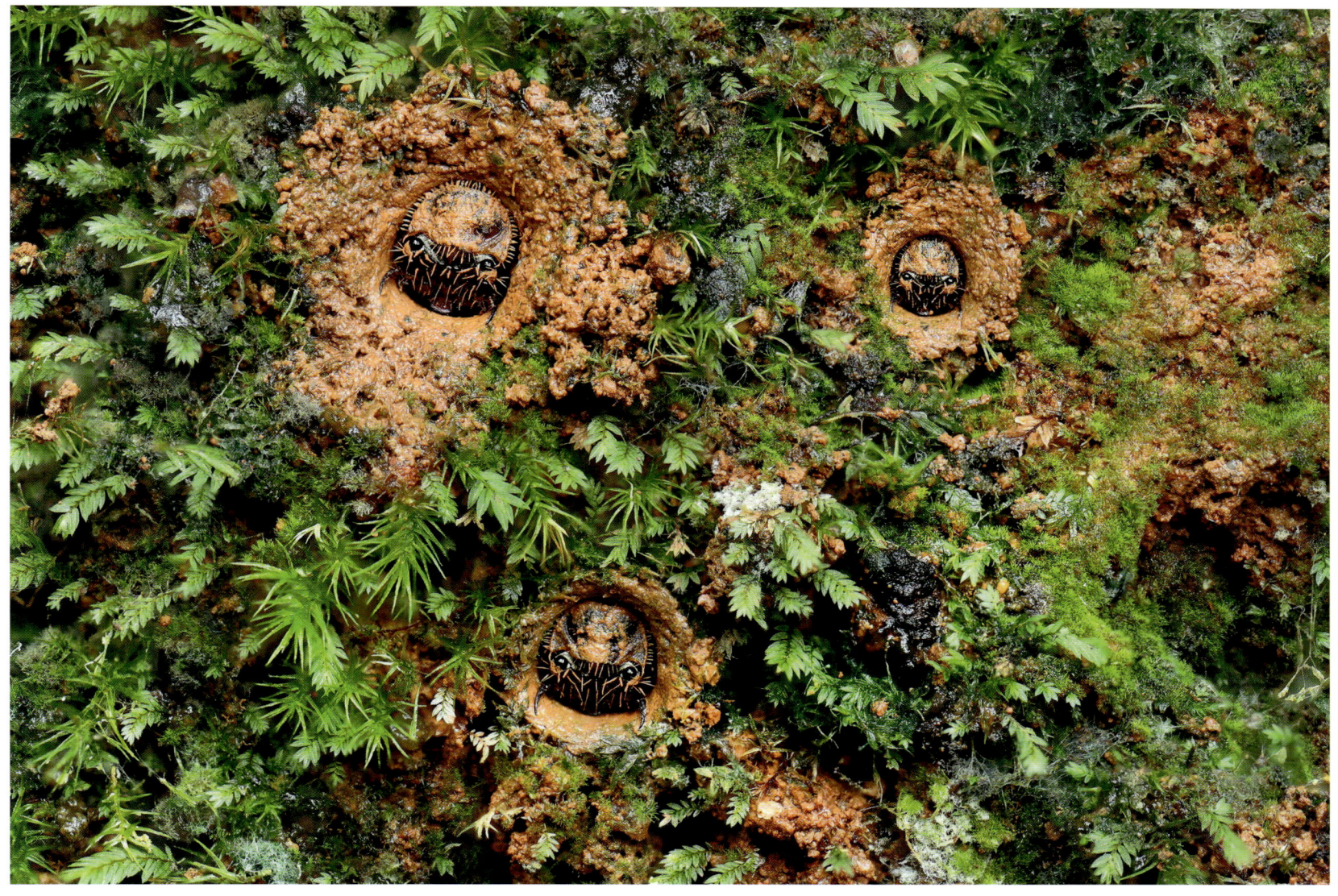

Eyes in the moss

Jithesh Pai

INDIA

With large eyes alert to any movement, and pin-sharp mandibles open wide, three tiger beetle larvae lurk in their burrows ready to seize whatever stumbles within lunging distance. Jithesh had been monitoring the mossy wall in his family's garden in Mangaluru, Karnataka, India, since he'd spotted an adult female tiger beetle pushing her eggs into the loose soil. Within days, tiny armoured larvae heads began to appear in the holes. Photographing them proved challenging, as they would retreat at the slightest movement. Keen to use only the natural light available, Jithesh ensured the sharpness of every detail by combining a stack of 70 exposures, each focused at a slightly different distance from the lens. Adult tiger beetles are voracious predators, chasing down prey at speeds of up to 2.5 metres (98 inches) per second.

Canon EOS R6 Mark II + 100mm f2.8 macro lens; 1/80 at f4; ISO 1000; focus stack of 70 images.

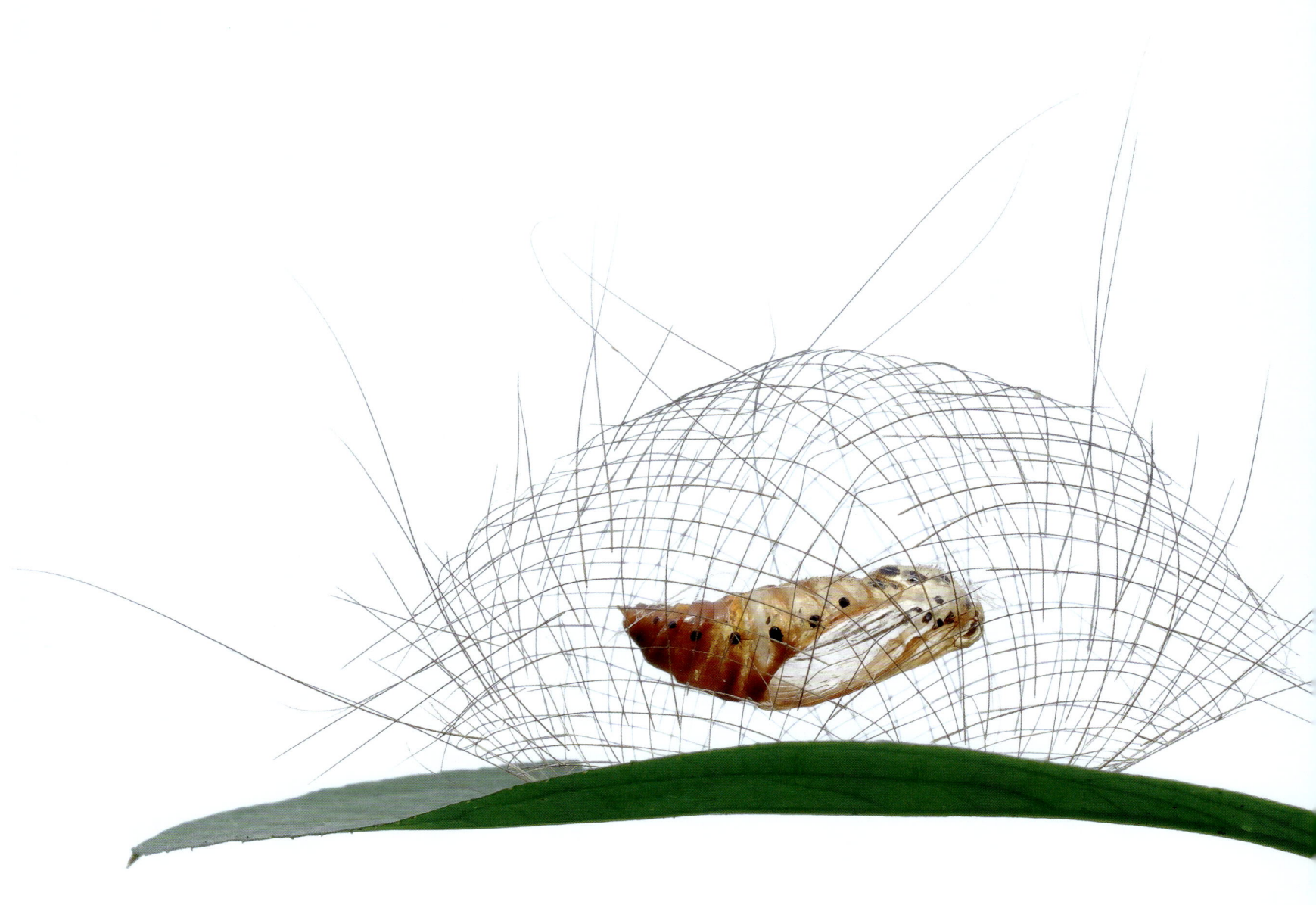

Suspended animation

Minghui Yuan

CHINA

In apparent defiance of the laws of gravity, a moth pupa hangs in mid-air within its finely constructed cocoon. Minghui spotted it while exploring Xishuangbanna Tropical Botanical Garden in China's far south, near the border with Myanmar and Laos. There were lots of cocoons about that day, in sunny spots on trees, walls and leaves. To capture the three-dimensional architectural detail, Minghui set his camera lens to its smallest aperture to maximize depth of field, and chose a cocoon that he could photograph against the plain bright sky. Despite being widespread and numerous across much of southern and eastern Asia, this species from the genus *Cyana* doesn't yet have a common name, although it is a member of a group known in China as lichen tiger moths. Large groups of striking black, white and red adults gather during the day to sip nectar from flowers. The caterpillars, which graze on the lichens, mosses and algae that encrust the trunks of trees, are exceptionally hairy to keep assailants at a safe distance. When it's time to pupate, the caterpillar chews off the hairs and recycles them as anti-predator material for building its cocoon. The gravity-defying levitation trick is achieved with the help of an invisible hammock of silken threads spun by the caterpillar just before it moults.

Fujifilm X-H2 + 80mm f2.8 macro lens; 1/105 at f22 (+1.3 e/v); ISO 640.

Death on the beach

Bence Máté

HUNGARY

It's called Bird Island for a reason. Approximately 2 kilometres (1 ¼ miles) long, this northernmost outpost of the Seychelles archipelago in the Indian Ocean is home to a surfeit of seabirds – the island's breeding-colony of sooty terns alone numbers 700,000 pairs. Bence was photographing the terns when he was distracted by a distress call from further along the beach. He saw an adult brown noddy pecking frantically at the head of a helpless chick floundering in the sand. Not yet fledged, the chick could have fallen from one of many nests in the overhanging trees. Or perhaps it was pushed; amid intense competition for nest sites, adult noddies are known to attack neighbours' unguarded chicks. But it got worse for this one. The first horned ghost crab arrived within minutes and started nipping at its wings. These scavenging omnivores, with wraparound eyes on sticks, eat anything that cannot run away. Soon after, the adult noddy abandoned the chick, which was then surrounded by about 10 crabs and dragged into bushes behind the beach, leaving nothing but tracks on the white coral sand.

Panasonic Lumix S1R II + Sigma 150–600mm f5–6.3 lens; 1/2500 at f8; ISO 3200.

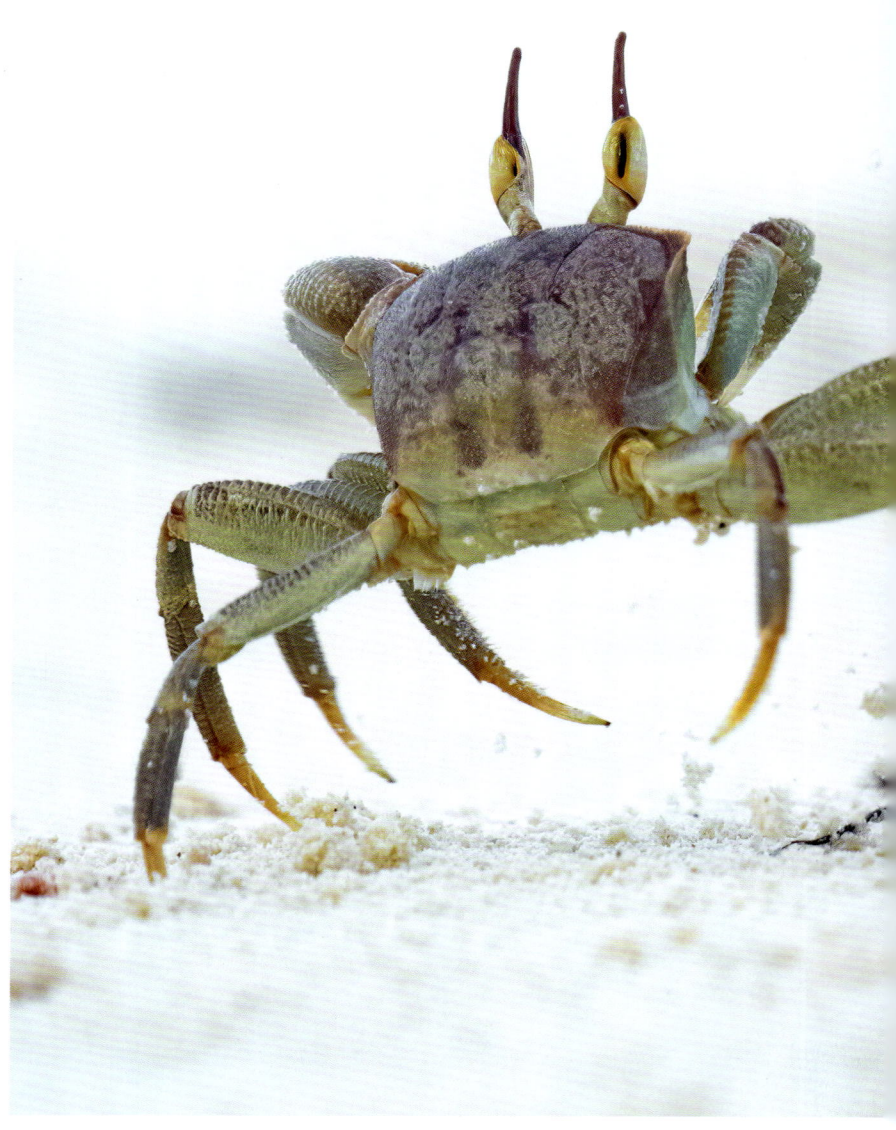

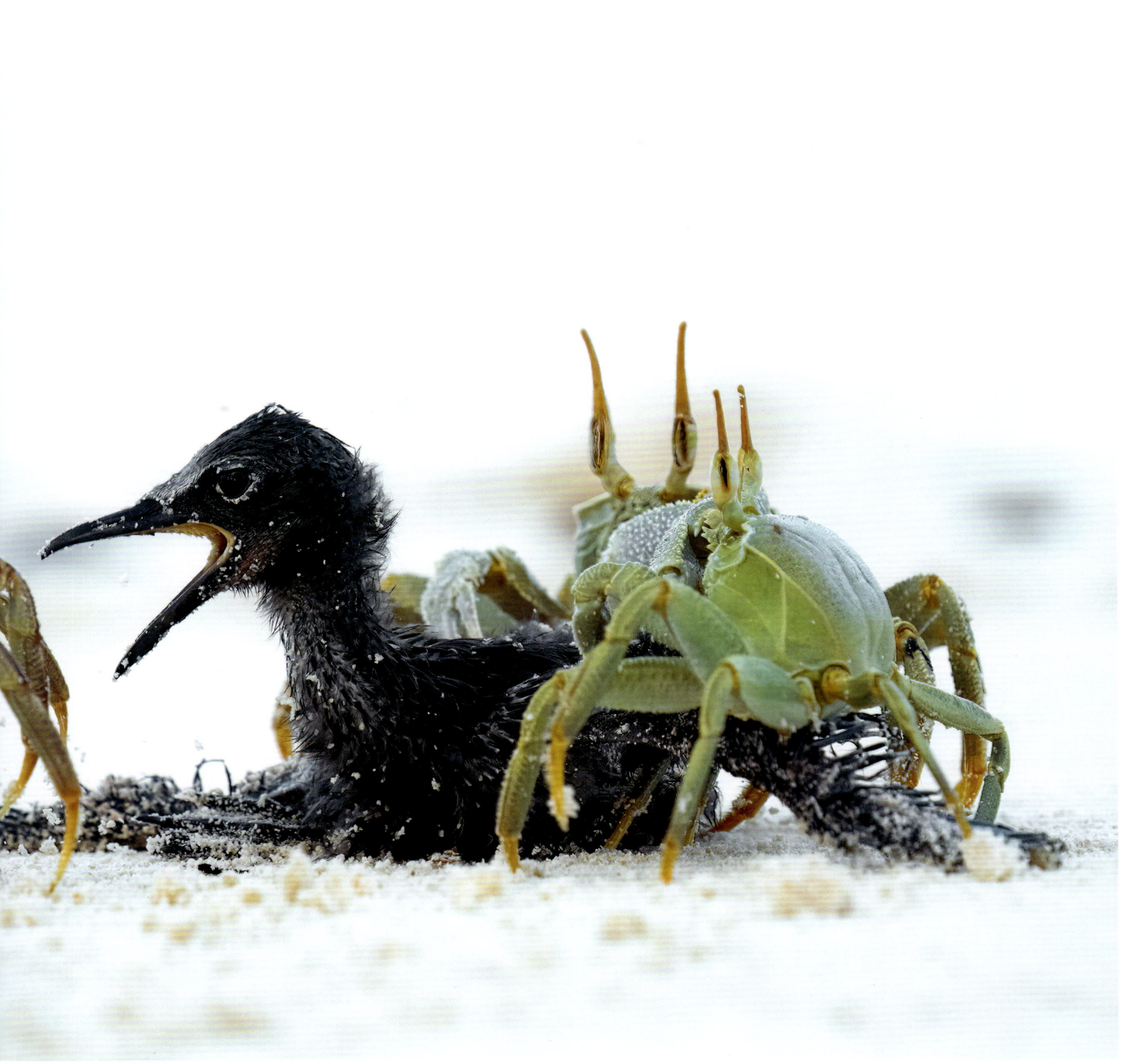

Urban Wildlife

Ghost town visitor

Wim van den Heever

SOUTH AFRICA

As sea fog rolls in from the Atlantic Ocean at night, the fleeting, almost ghostly presence of a brown hyena is caught on camera, prowling the ruins of Kolmanskop, an abandoned diamond mining settlement close to Namibia's Skeleton Coast. For nearly 10 years, Wim had visited this ghost town with the dream of photographing the rarest of all hyena species roaming these empty streets at night. With a population of fewer than 10,000 worldwide, brown hyenas are nocturnal and mostly solitary, but they were known to pass through Kolmanskop every four to six weeks on their way to scavenge carrion and prey on pups at nearby seal colonies. The buildings of Kolmanskop have been filling slowly with sand since the last inhabitants left in 1956 but, prior to the First World War, this was regarded as the richest town in Africa – following the first find in 1908, more than 1,000 kilograms (2,204 pounds) of diamonds were extracted from the surrounding desert in just six years. Wim chose this spot because it was close to where he had found hyena tracks. 'Every time I visited the ghost town I'd set up camera traps in the hope of success,' he says. 'It took me 10 years to finally get this one single image of a brown hyena in the most perfect frame imaginable.' It was a find worth more than diamonds.

Nikon D810 + 17–35mm f2.8 lens at 17mm; 15 sec at f2.8; ISO 3200; 2x Nikon SB-800 Speedlight flashes; Camtraptions motion sensor.

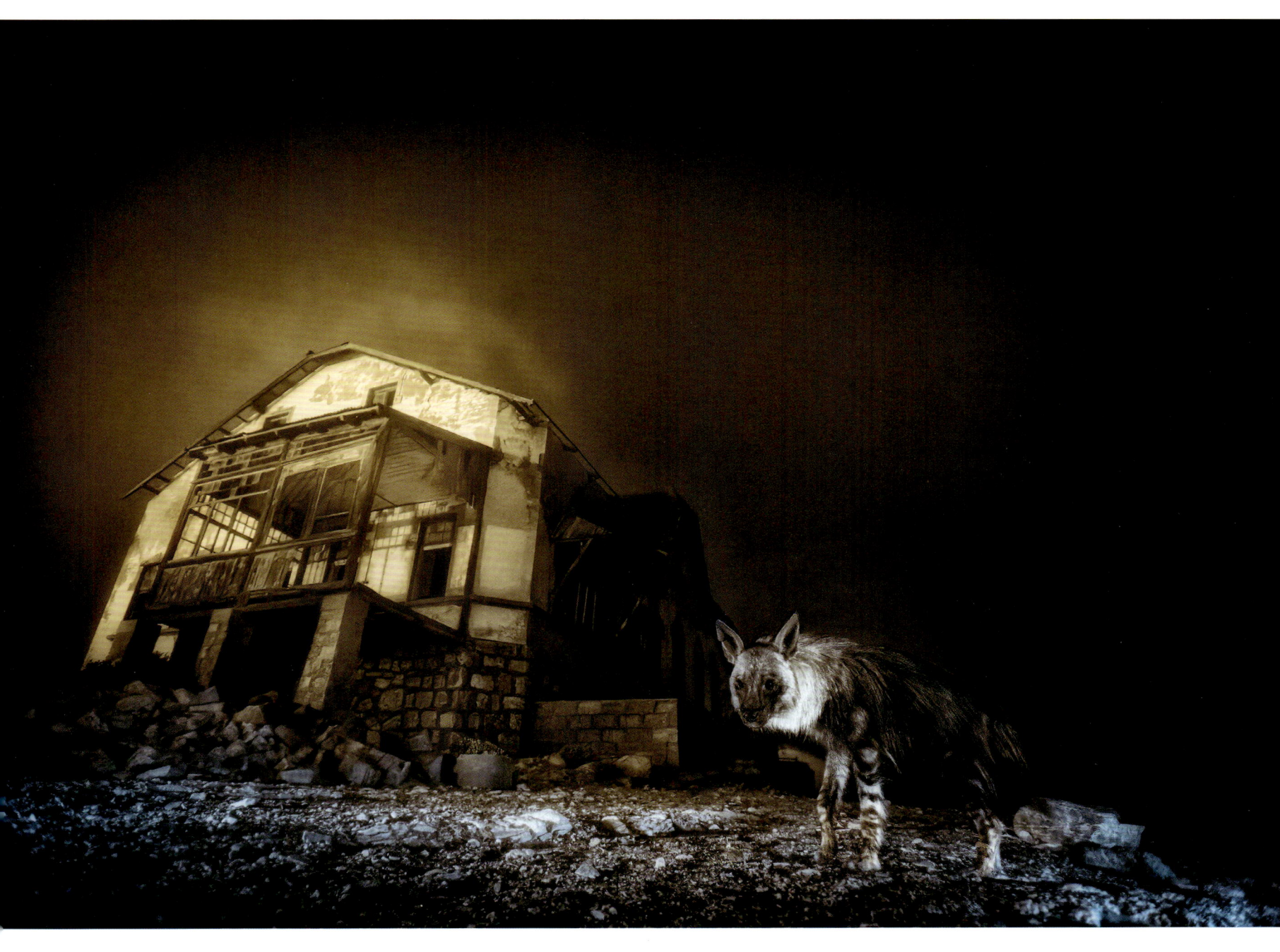

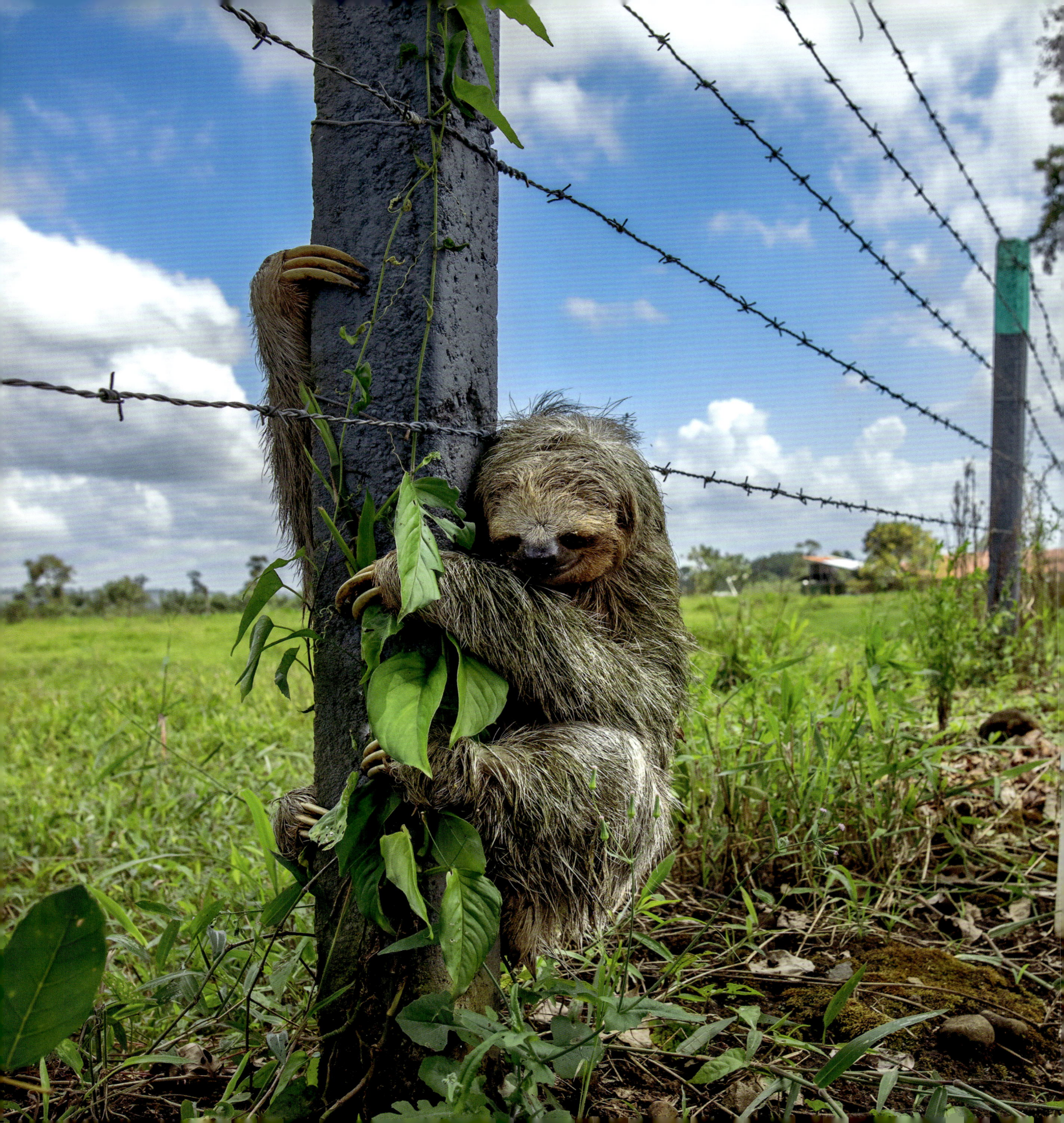

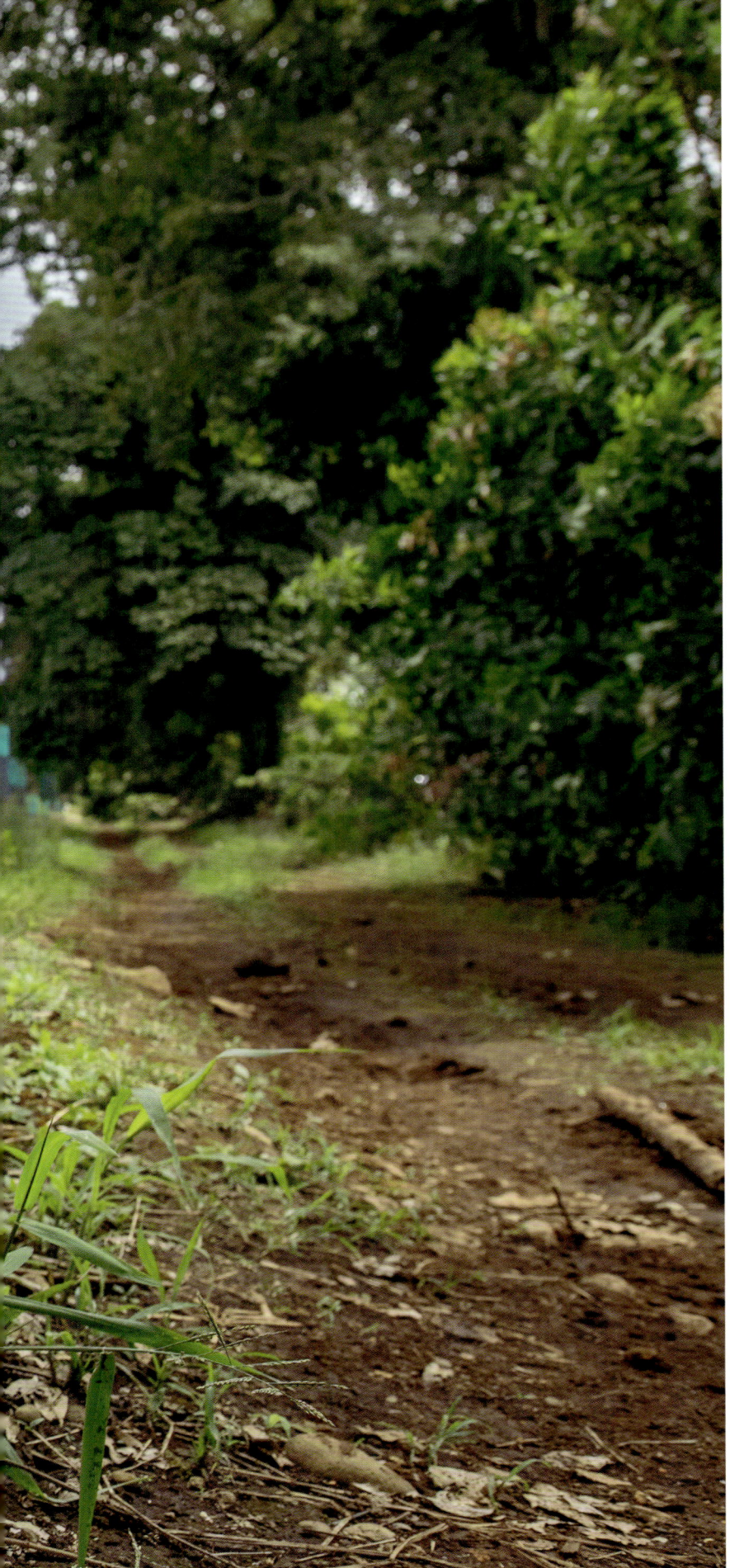

No place like home

Emmanuel Tardy

FRANCE

A concrete post on a barbed-wire fence is a poor substitute for the rainforest canopies of Costa Rica. Emmanuel was travelling to La Fortuna, near the Monteverde Cloud Forest, when he found himself stuck in a traffic jam caused by a brown-throated three-toed sloth crossing the road. The sloth eventually made its way to this post and clung tightly while onlookers observed its plight. Concerned about not adding to the animal's stress, Emmanuel patiently waited for people to leave the area before quickly taking this photo. 'It was more than 200 metres (656 feet) away from suitable habitat,' he recalls, 'a distance it would have to cover on the ground, exposing itself to numerous dangers.' Sloths have a low-nutrient diet, which leads to a reduced metabolic rate. The lack of energy means they move very slowly and usually descend the treetops only once a week, just to defecate. But fragmentation of their habitat means sloths are having to risk more ground crossings to reach the safety of the next tree. In response, the Costa Rican government is working with local NGOs to establish biological corridors with aerial bridges linking their forest homes.

Canon EOS 5D Mark IV + Sigma 24mm f1.4 lens; 1/1600 at f7.1 (+0.33 e/v); ISO 800.

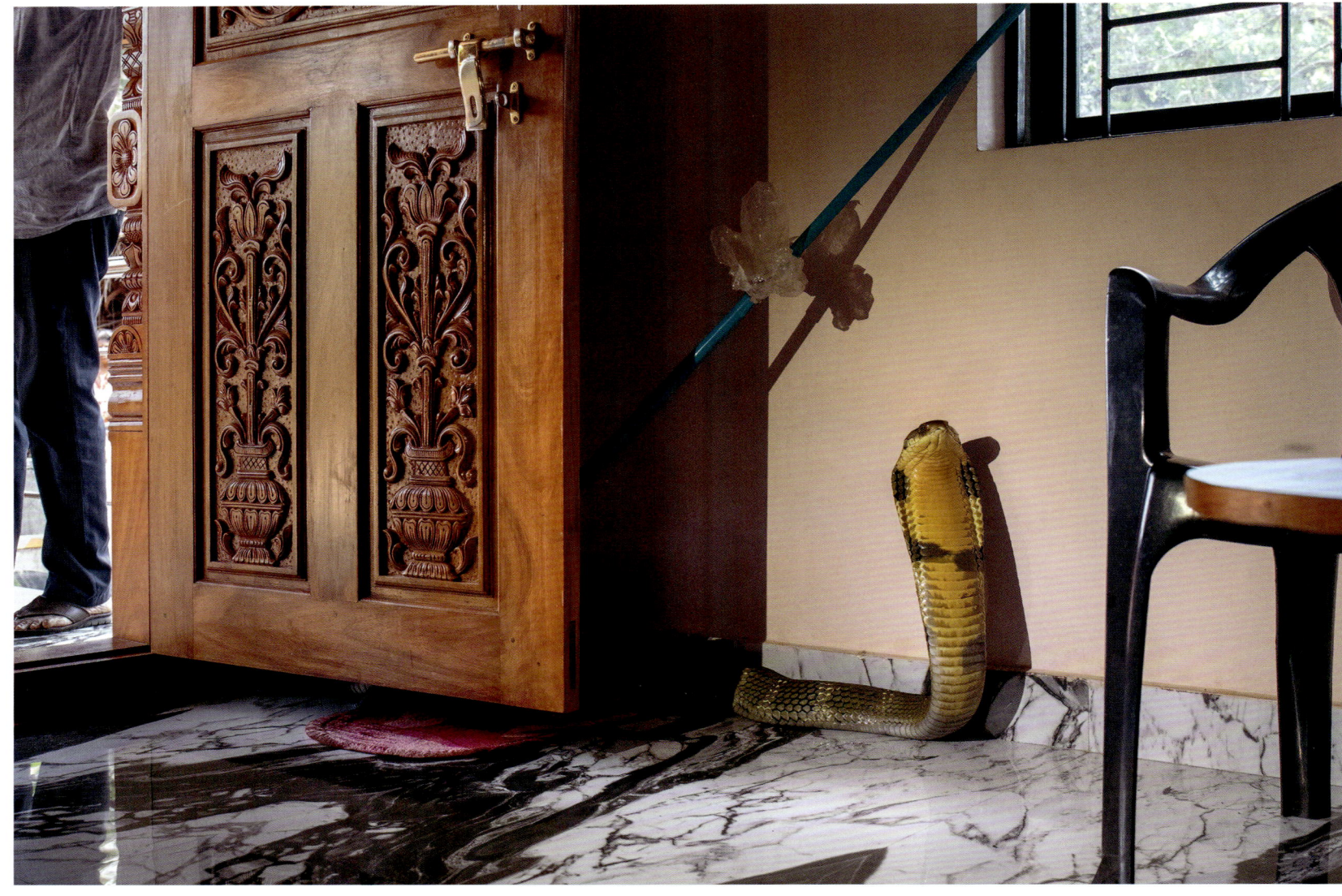

Cornered cobra

Jithesh Pai

INDIA

King cobras are the world's largest venomous snake, so being confronted with one indoors, head raised and hood extended, is an alarming sight. Jithesh came face to face with this 3.5-metre (11 ½-feet) long specimen, which had been disturbed by dogs, and had sought refuge inside a house near the Agumbe Rainforest Research Station (ARRS) in India's Western Ghats. He accompanied the ARRS rescue and release team which picked up, bagged and released the cobra into a forest 3 kilometres (2 miles) away. Until 2024, the king cobra (*Ophiophagus hannah*) was believed to be a single species found across south and southeast Asia. But, after extensive research, scientists have now concluded that this iconic reptile comprises four distinct species, one of which is this uninvited house guest – the Western Ghats king cobra (*Ophiophagus kaalinga*).

Canon EOS 77D + 24–70mm f4 lens; 1/60 at f4.5; ISO 1600; ambient light with torch light.

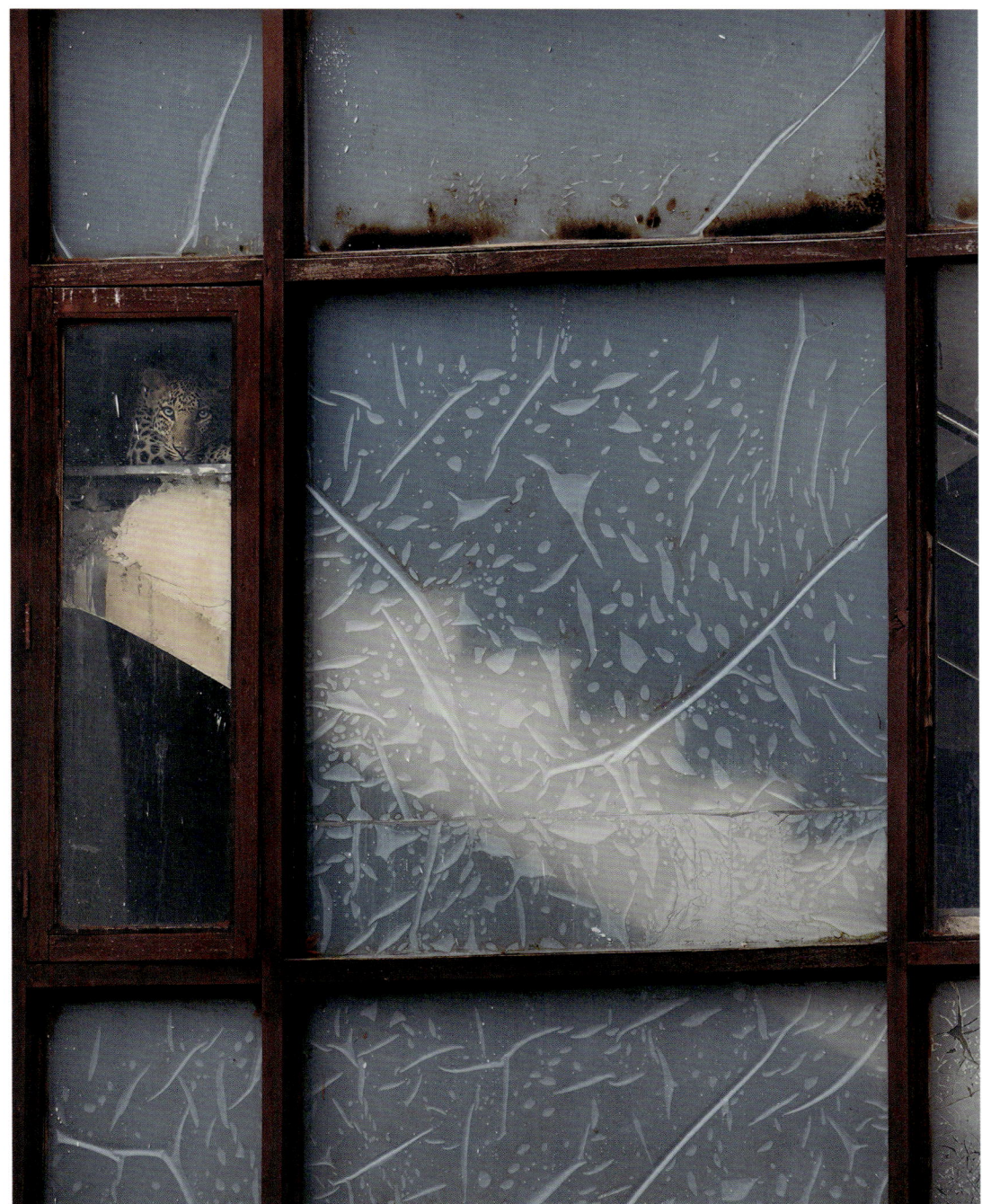

An unlikely refuge

Chaitanya Rawat
INDIA

Of the world's big cats, leopards are the most adaptable, frequenting the widest range of habitats and terrain. In India, these habitats include the fringes of urban areas. Chaitanya was alerted by a local villager to the presence of leopards passing through an abandoned resort on the outskirts of Jaipur, Rajasthan, India, and made repeated visits in the hope of seeing one for himself. He spotted this individual at nightfall, peering out of the window of a derelict building. Chaitanya believes the leopard was seeking shelter from the heat of the day, and had possibly wandered from the nearby Aravalli Mountains. According to the International Union for Conservation of Nature, populations of Indian leopards have declined by nearly 25 per cent over three generations. Fragmented habitat, loss of prey, conflict with farmers, and poaching for the illegal wildlife trade are cited as their greatest threats.

Sony α7R V + 200–600mm f5.6–6.3 lens; 1 sec at f6.3; ISO 100; tripod.

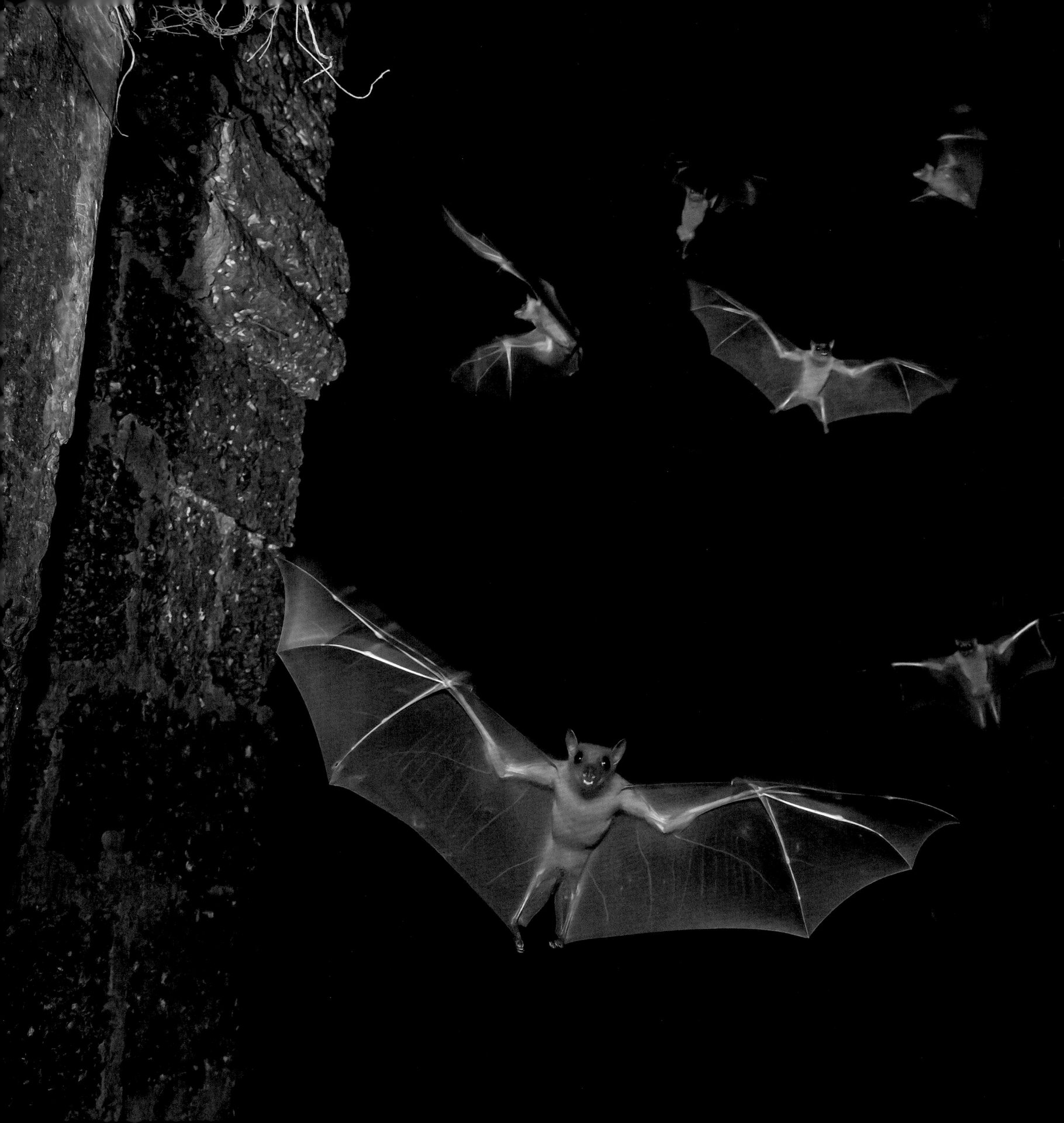

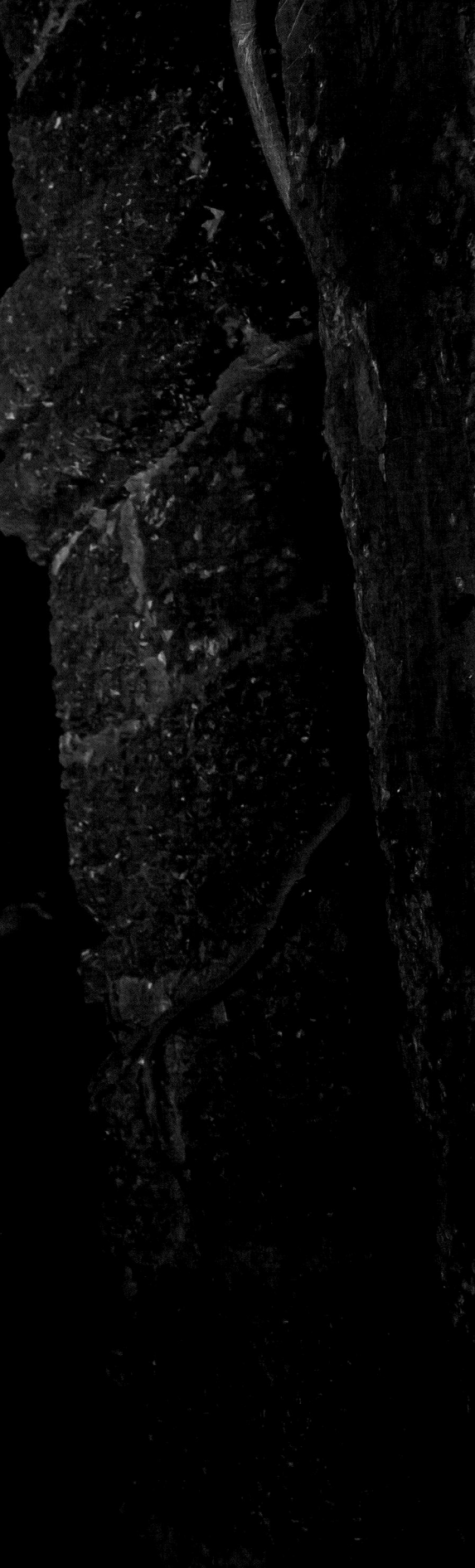

Nature reclaims its space

Sitaram Raul

INDIA

For Sitaram, this flash photograph of fruit bats leaving their roost in his home village of Banda, in Maharashtra, India, was a real shot in the dark. 'Since this is not a camera trap image, I was there amidst the chaos,' he recalls. The setting is a ruined sixteenth-century building, known locally as Ghumat (because its domed shape resembles the Goan earthenware drum of the same name), which the bats of Banda have colonized, along with scorpions, snakes, beetles, geckos and other species. But it's the 300 or so fruit bats that fly out each evening in search of food that fascinate Sitaram the most. Working in total darkness, he manually focused the lens at the distance where he guessed any of the bats might be, and relied on his flash to illuminate the scene – all while the bats were 'randomly pooping on me and the camera.' Common across southern Asia, the bats roost mostly in caves during the day, as well as deserted buildings, and occasionally supplement their fruit-based diet with fish. Sitaram says no matter how big our urban structures, once we leave them, 'eventually nature reclaims its space.'

Nikon D750 + 24–120mm f4 lens; 1/250 at f8; ISO 800; Godox TT685 flash.

Under Water

Survival purse

Ralph Pace
USA

Most fish take a quantitative approach to reproduction by casting vast numbers of eggs and sperm into the currents and leaving the outcome to chance. Sharks are different. In about 60 per cent of species, including great whites and hammerheads, embryos develop inside the female until they are born as fully formed, independent pups. The rest lay leathery, translucent egg cases, known as mermaid's purses. This one, tethered to the base of a giant kelp in Monterey Bay, California, USA, belongs to a swell shark, a broad-headed, metre-long scavenger and predator of fish and crustaceans. Swell sharks live in depths to 500 metres (1,640 feet), but more usually about 50 metres (164 feet), and swim up at night to lay their eggs in the kelp forests that fringe much of the North American coast. However, a series of marine heatwaves between 2014 and 2016 reduced kelp coverage around Monterey Bay by more than 80 per cent. Since then, the large seaweed's recovery has been hampered by an explosion in numbers of purple sea urchins, which graze on the fronds, drastically reducing the amount of fronds for swell sharks to lay their eggs. Ralph lit the egg case from behind to reveal the embryo within, its gill slits and yolk sac clearly visible. A long incubation time of up to 12 months before hatching, combined with the small numbers of offspring, means swell sharks are slow to recover from any population declines.

Nikon D850 + 28–70mm f3.5–4.5 lens; 1/125 at f14; ISO 640; Nauticam housing; 2x Sea & Sea strobes.

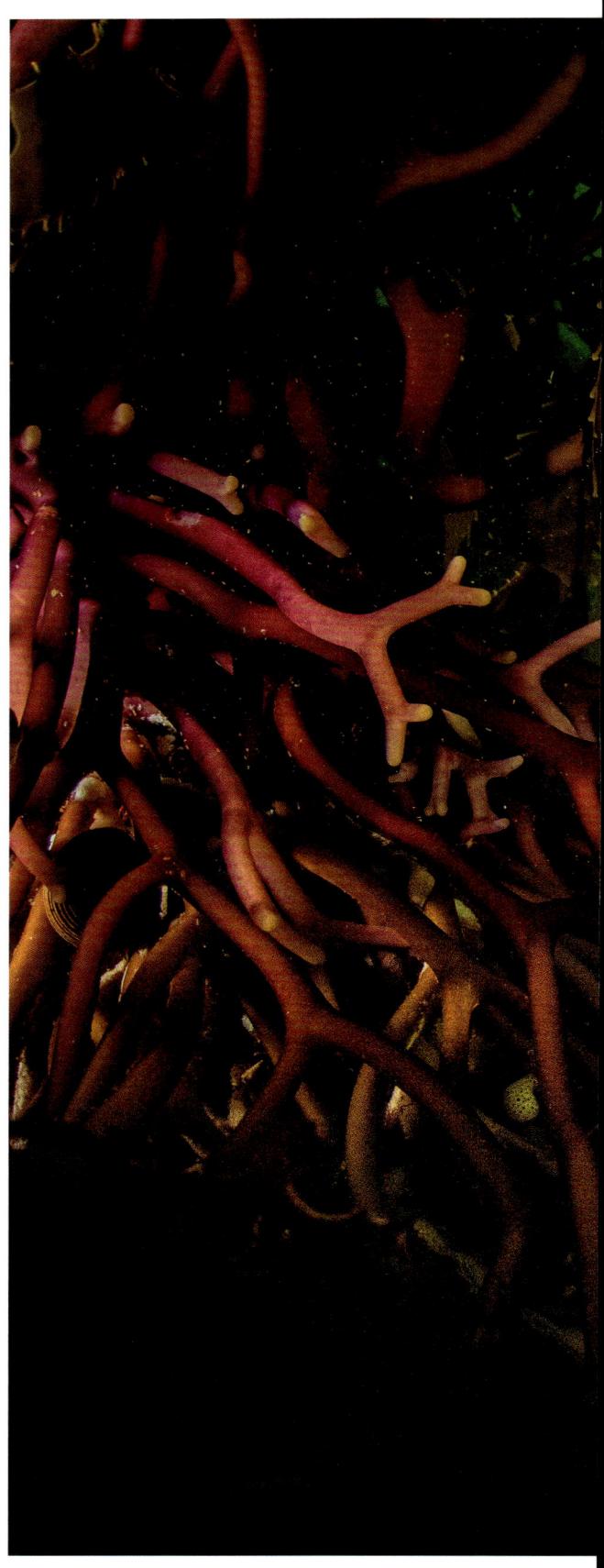

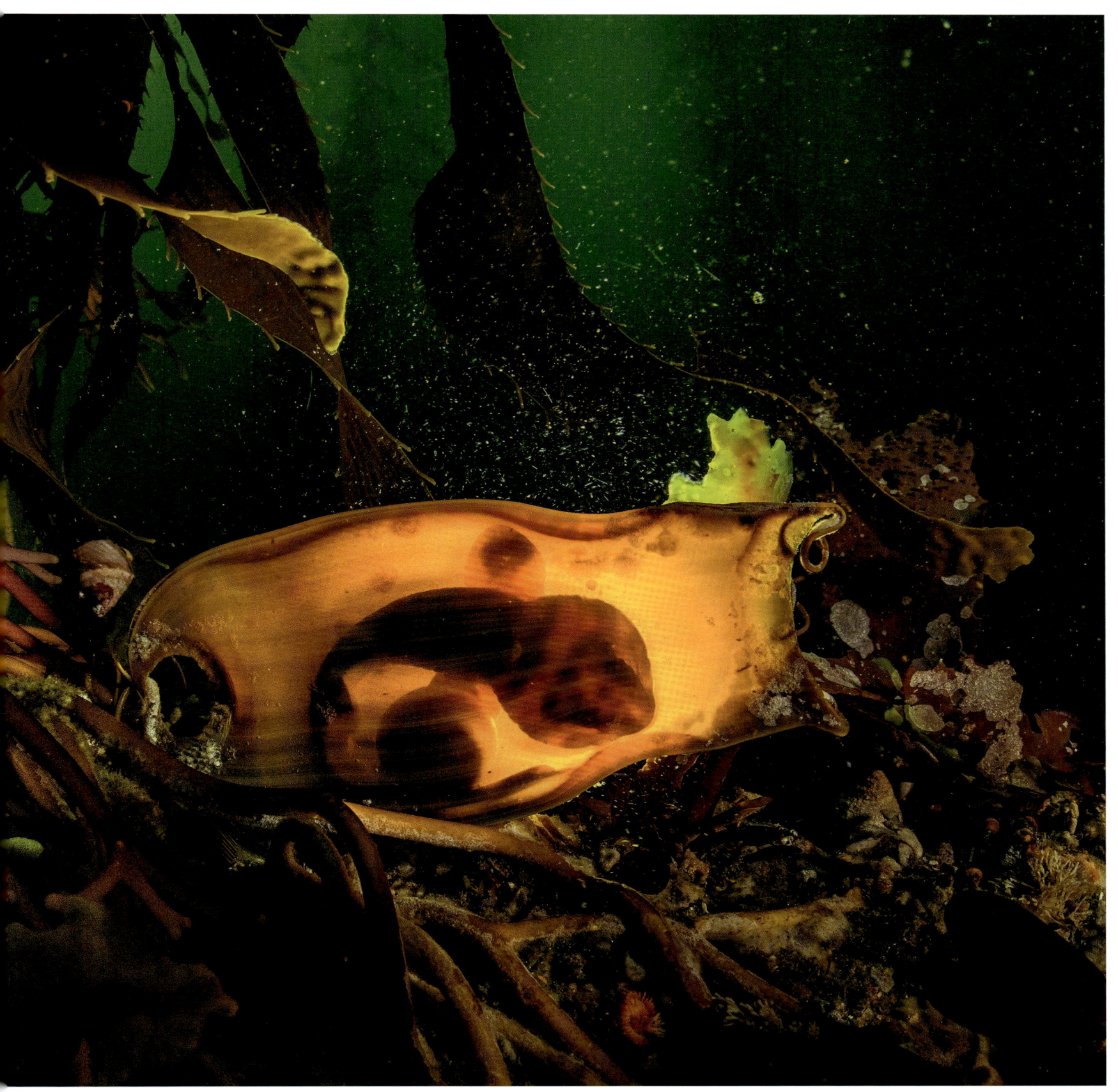

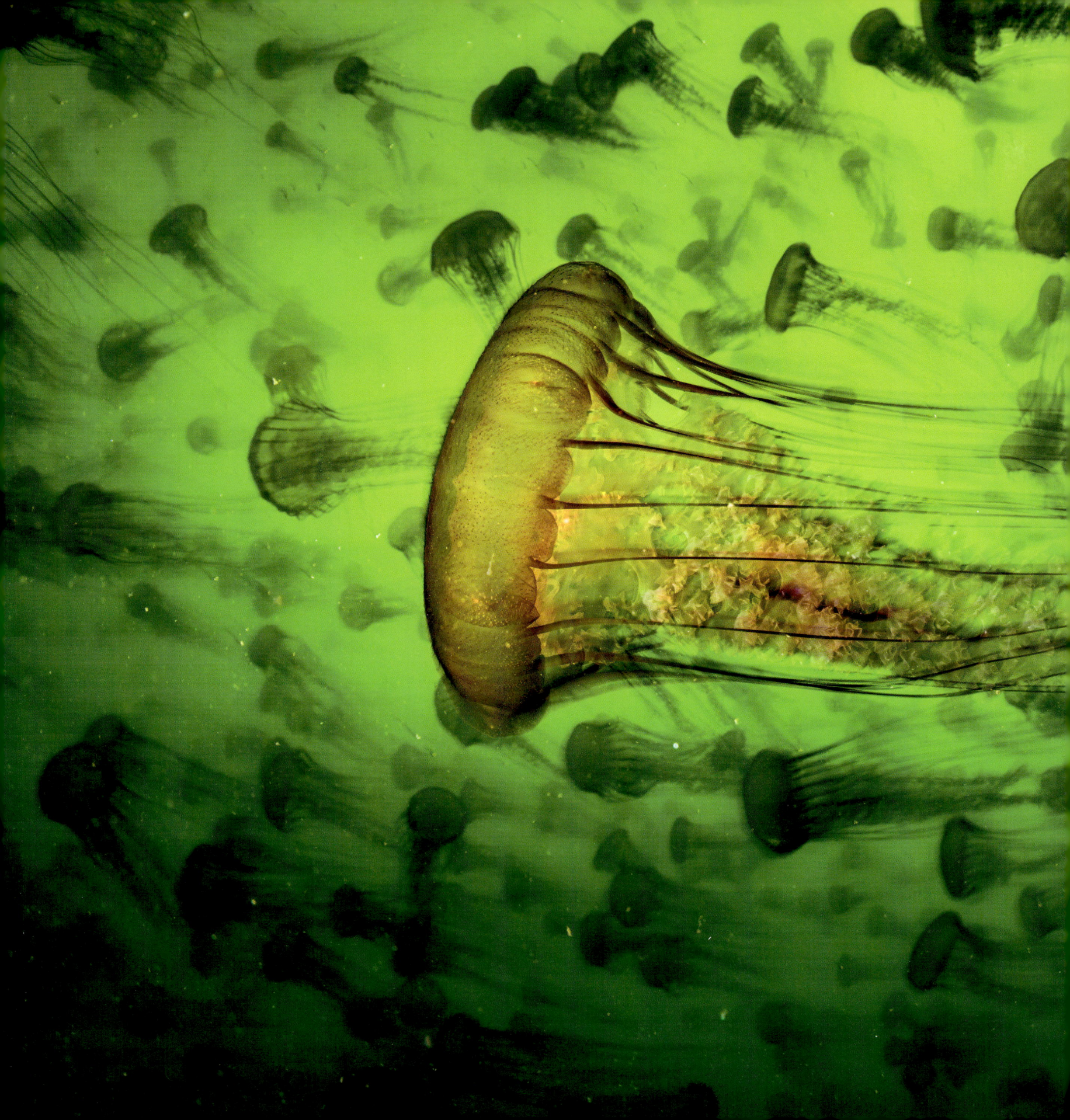

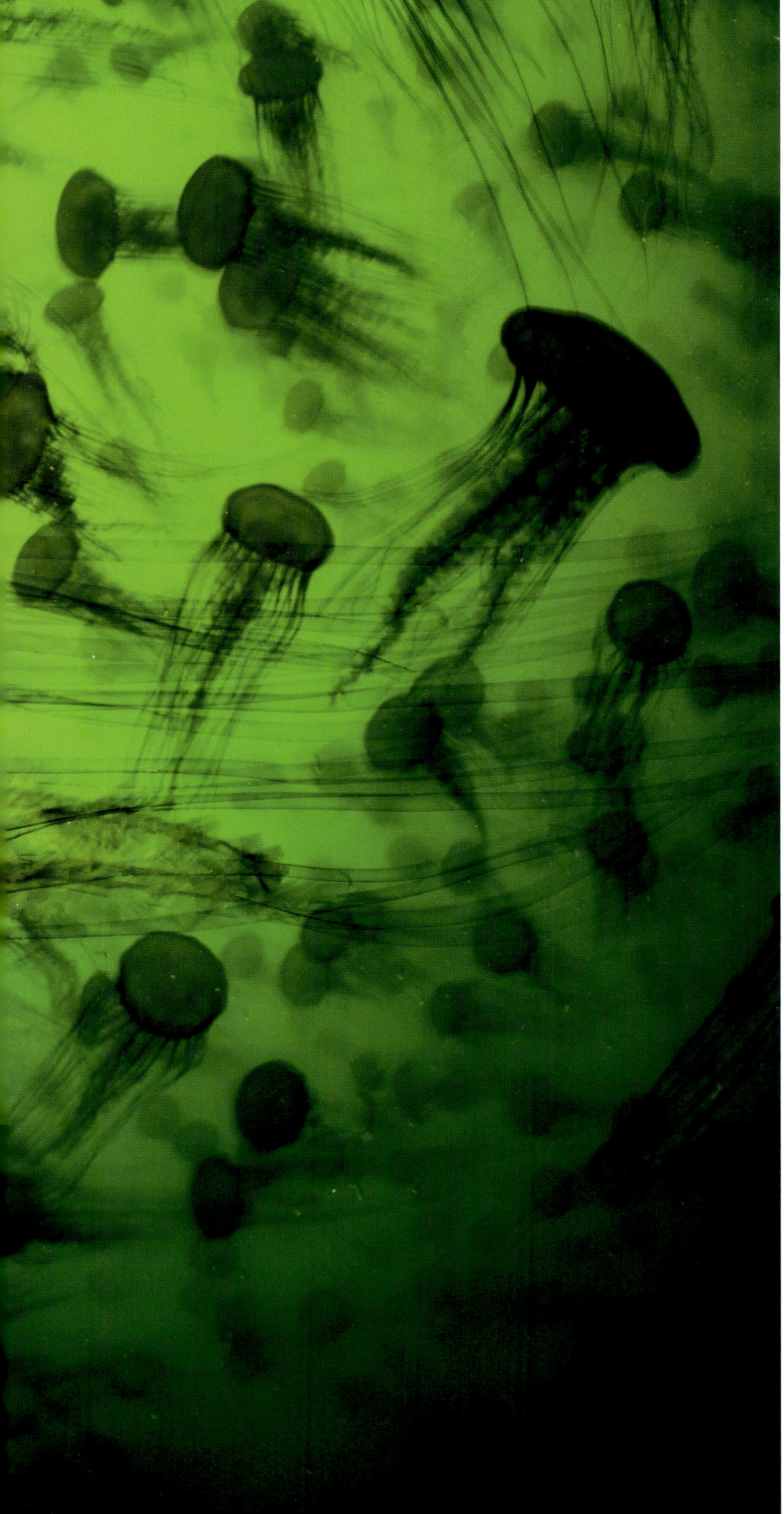

Jelly smack summer

Ralph Pace
USA

Whatever you prefer to call a mass of jellyfish – a swarm, a bloom, or a smack – Ralph was right in the middle of one. These are Pacific sea nettles. They appear in Monterey Bay most summers, arriving from deeper waters on the California Current, which flows southwards along North America's Pacific coast. Some years, they are especially numerous – Ralph has seen them form an uninterrupted swathe across the entire 40-kilometre (25-mile) breadth of the bay. A sea nettle smack can remove up to a third of the plankton from the water, and attracts predators such as leatherback turtles and ocean sunfish. Their trailing tentacles deliver a painful sting, which Ralph says is more like that of a bee than from a nettle. To protect himself, he smears petroleum jelly on any skin not covered by his wetsuit. Jellyfish are highly adaptable to warming seas, and some biologists argue that more frequent smacks are a sign of rising ocean temperatures. Anthropogenic impacts, such as nutrient run-off from agriculture and the removal of predators and competitors through overfishing, are other factors contributing to this phenomenon.

Nikon D850 + 28–70mm f3.5–4.5 lens; 1/5 at f13; ISO 125; Nauticam housing; 2x Sea & Sea strobes.

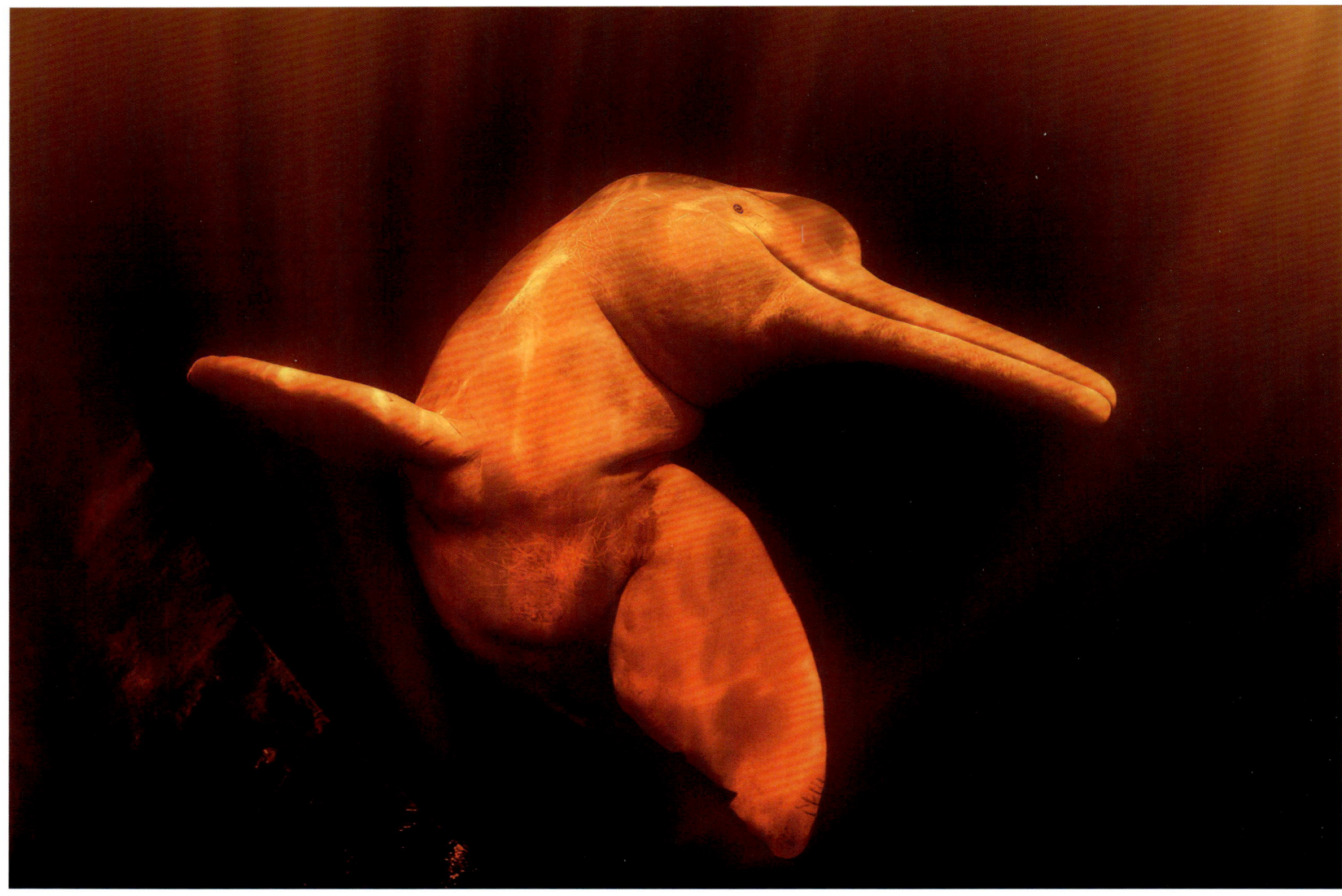

A closer look

Hussain Aga Khan

SWITZERLAND

This pink river dolphin may appear to be smiling for the camera, but not all is rosy for these freshwater cetaceans. Hussain's portrait features one of four animals present most days near one of numerous pontoons along the Rio Negro in Manaus, Brazil, providing access for tourists to feed them. Known also as a boto, or Amazon river dolphin, these wild, charismatic creatures have become a major tourist attraction, and many are dependent upon daily feeds by the paying public. With compact fins and flexible backbones, botos are built for negotiating the shallows of flooded forests and submerged tree roots. Harder to avoid are the threats from dam construction, entanglement in fishing gear and the use of boto blubber as fishing bait. Tourism might help raise interest in their conservation, but the benefits for those botos already reliant upon the handouts of paying customers remains questionable.

Canon EOS R5 + 8–15mm f4 fisheye lens; 1/125 at f6.3; ISO 2000.

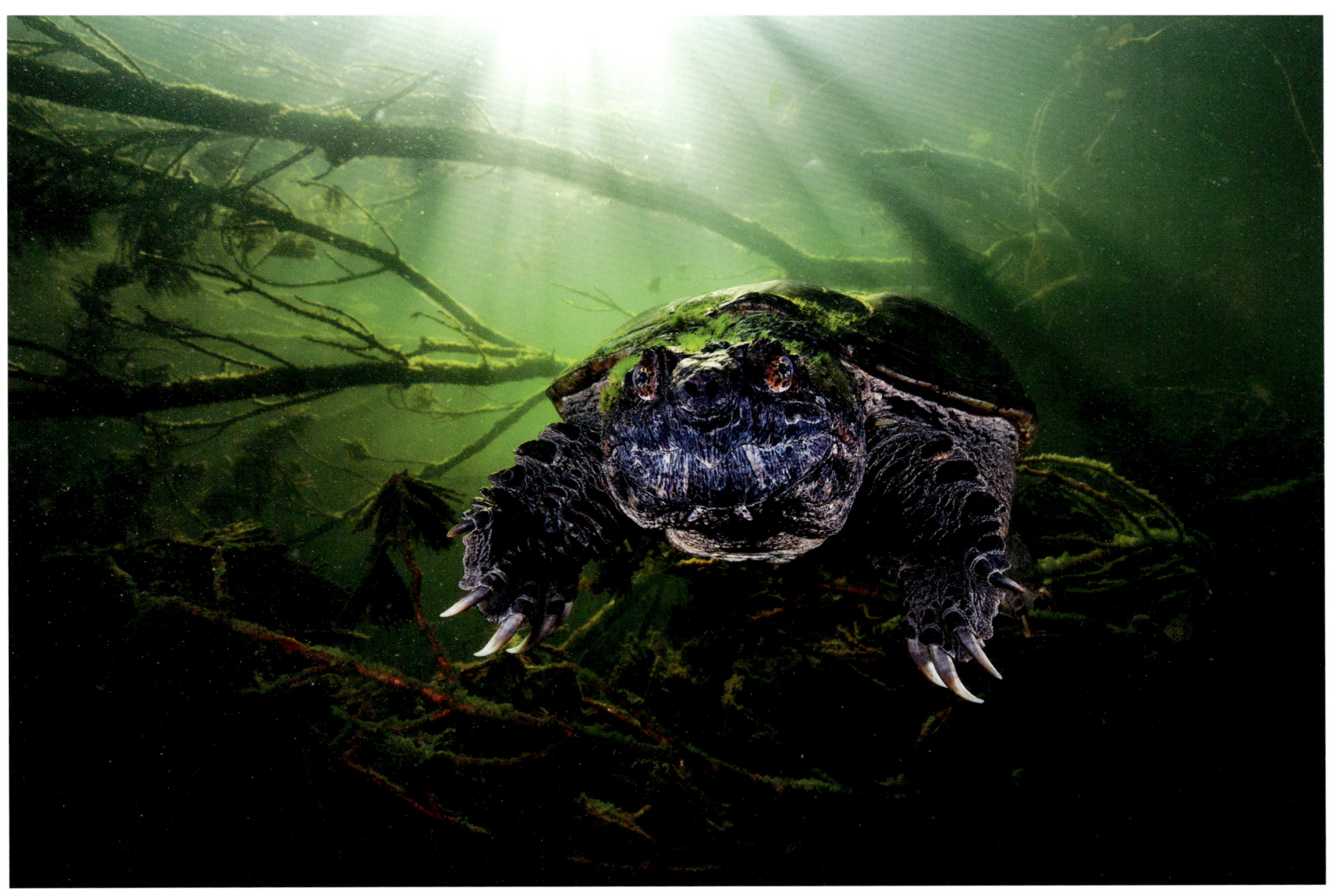

The welcoming turtle

Jake Stout

USA

Jake's experiences with common snapping turtles contrast strikingly with their fearsome reputation. Weighing up to 20 kilograms (44 pounds), these omnivorous reptiles are spread throughout North America east of the Rockies. Although some people erroneously believe the turtles capable of biting off human fingers, Jake has been photographing them in a New Hampshire lake without incident for the past four years. He finds them to be calm and inquisitive, demonstrating different personalities and behaviours. Cases of turtle-inflicted finger bites are rare and attributed to the larger alligator snapping turtle. By contrast, it is humans that pose a threat to common snapping turtles – each spring and autumn, the turtles risk car strikes while crossing roads to nest or when moving to wintering grounds.

Canon EOS 5D Mark III + 16–35mm f4 lens at 16mm; 1/125 at f11; ISO 400; Aquatica housing; 2x Sea & Sea YS-D2 strobes.

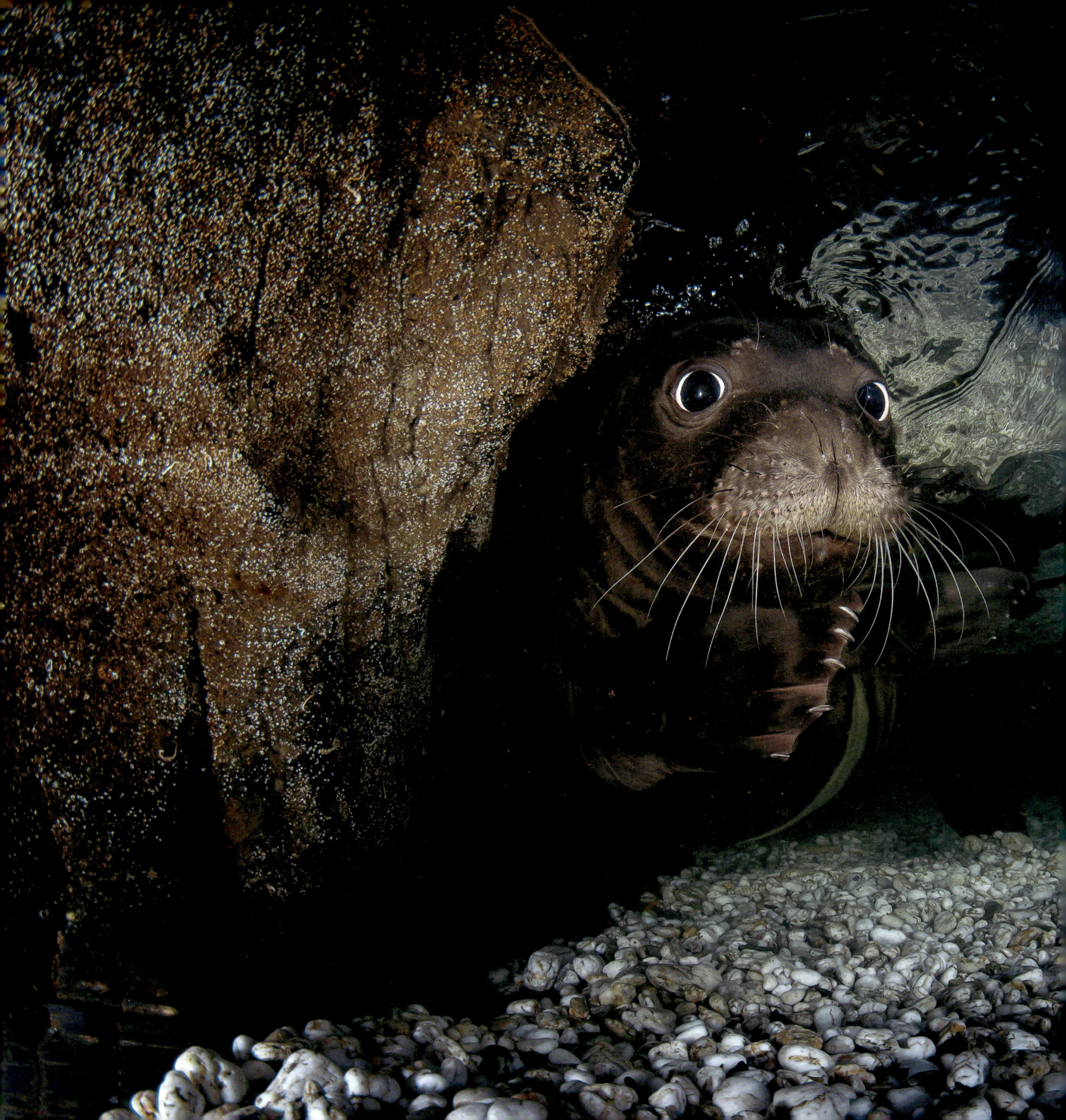

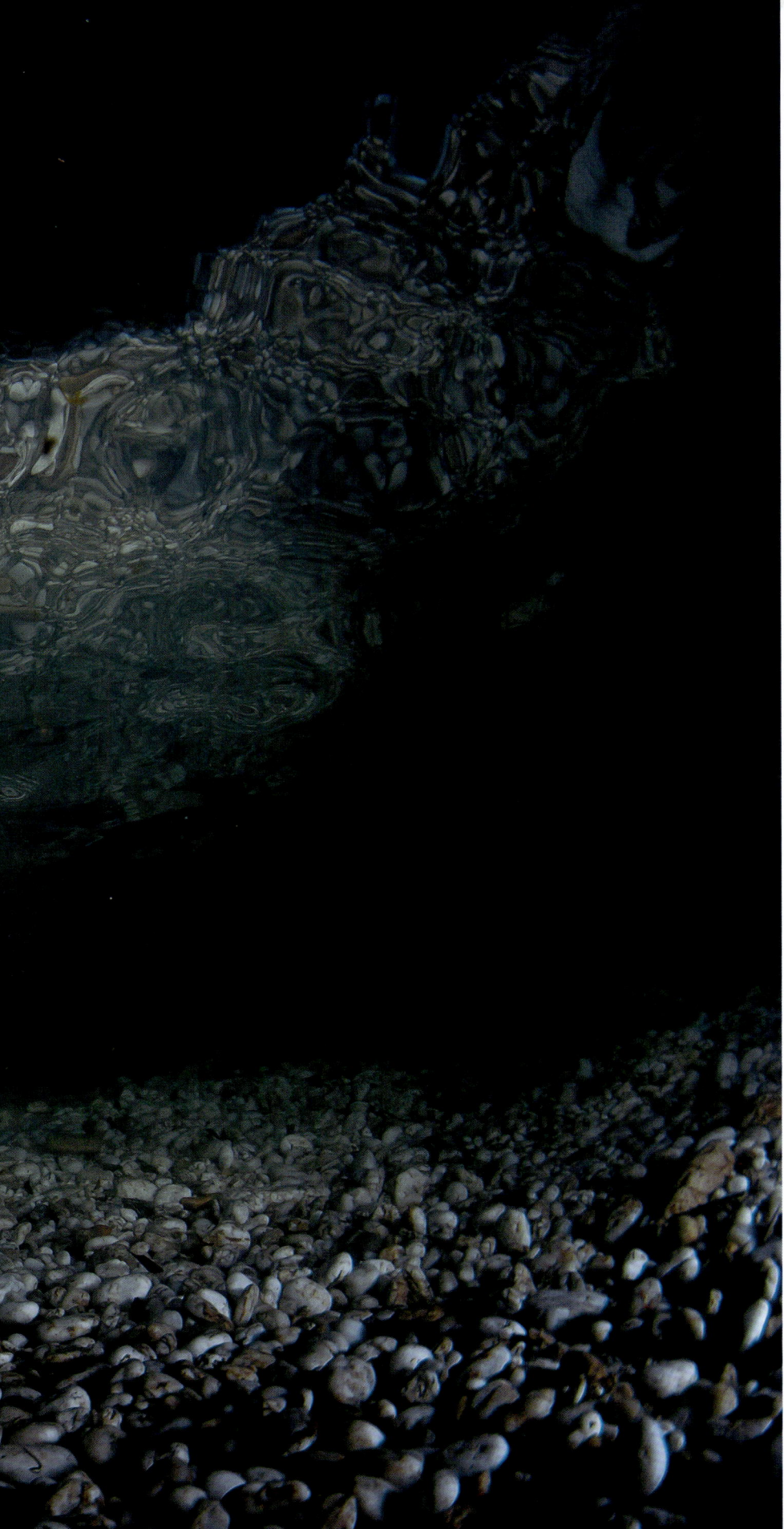

A monk's life

Greg Lecoeur

FRANCE

Wide-eyed, curious and a little wary, a Mediterranean monk seal peers from the entrance to a sea cave in Greece. Once widespread throughout the Mediterranean, Black Sea, and the Atlantic coasts of North Africa, Spain and Portugal, the species was hunted to the point of near extinction. It was listed as critically endangered in 1996, and by 2008 there were barely 350 individuals split between two viable populations, one in the eastern Mediterranean, the other in the Atlantic waters of Mauritania and Madeira. Threats to the seals include deliberate killing by fishers, accidental catch in fishing nets, and toxic algal blooms in the food chain (which caused a massive die-off in Mauritania in 1997). But conservation efforts are now reaping rewards, and Greg was documenting the work of seal biologists in Greece when he had this close encounter. Monk seal populations are increasing and even expanding in the waters of Greece and Turkey, leading to the downgrading of its status to endangered in 2015 and vulnerable in 2023. The number of mature individuals is thought to be globally more than 250, and nearly 1,000 individuals in total.

Nikon D500 + Tokina 10–17mm lens; 1/250 at f9; ISO 200; Ikelite DS161 strobe.

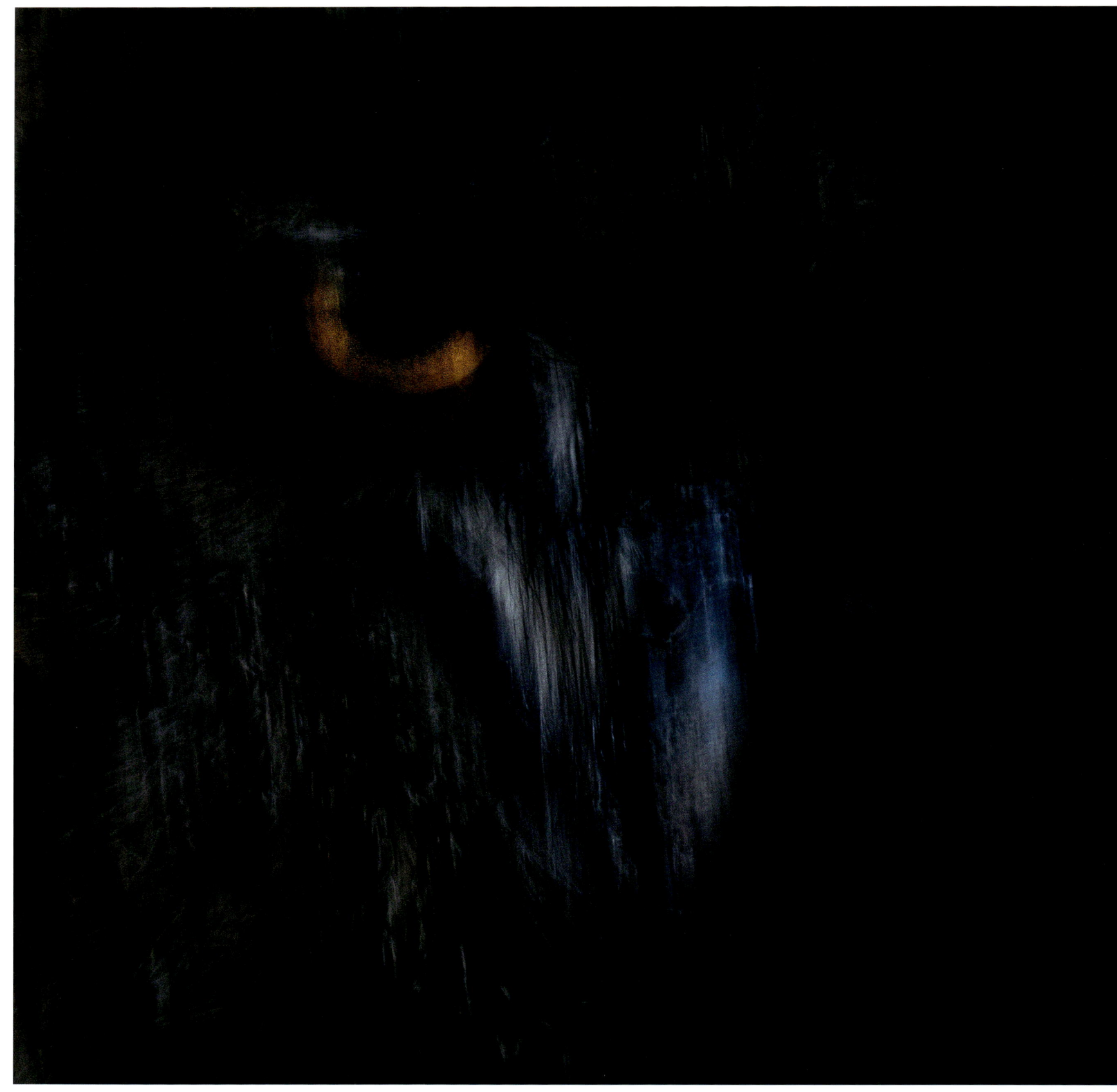

Portraits

Shadow hunter

Philipp Egger
ITALY

Philipp was climbing in the Italian Alps when he came across a nest of young Eurasian eagle owls in a rocky niche. The find was both thrilling and worrying. At about twice the weight of a buzzard and with a wingspan up to 1.8 metres (6 feet), this formidable nocturnal predator is the largest of all owls. And yet, it is highly sensitive to the slightest disturbance. Rock climbing, mountaineering and other leisure activities often take people unknowingly near nests, sometimes causing parents to abandon their brood. Philipp climbed on quickly to minimize the risk, but he also started making plans. Knowing that eagle owls return to the same nest site for years, he sought vantage points from where he could observe them undetected. Four years later, he was in position to document an entire breeding season, from the initial courtship calls through to the chicks' first efforts at solo hunting. 'They never knew I was there,' he recalls. 'The final photograph was taken from a concealed position using a tele lens with complete cover.' This ghostly, almost abstract image portrays one of three juveniles fledged that year. Philipp had planned it meticulously, right down to the deliberate wiping movement of the camera, like an artist's brushstroke, to make the owl look like a painting. What he could not have predicted was the subject's enigmatic posture, the glint in its orange eyes, and how the last light of day falls on its feathers.

Nikon Z9 + 180–600mm f5.6–6.3 lens; 1/10 at f29; ISO 320.

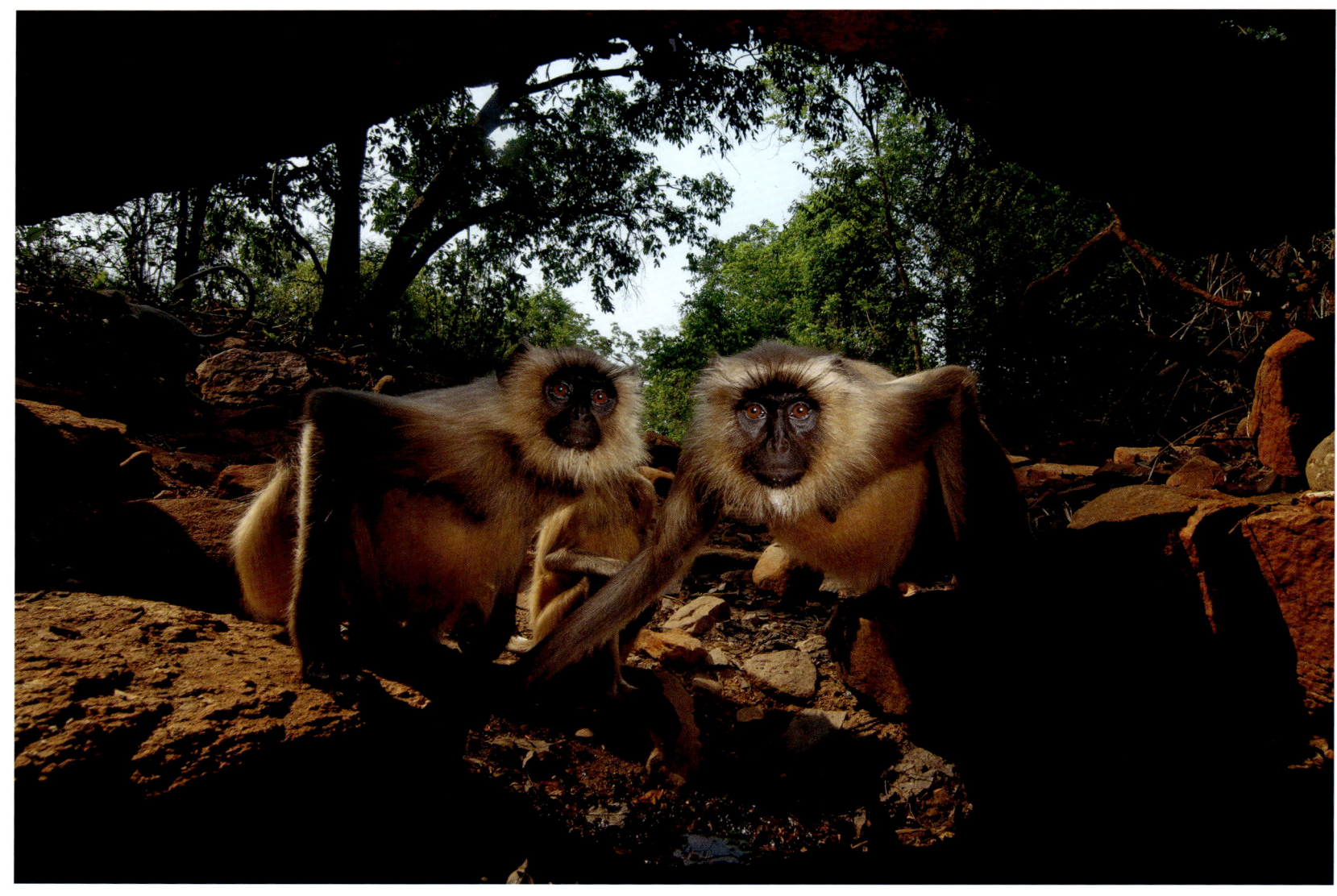

Monkey business

Nayan Khanolkar

INDIA

These langur monkeys are very observant – they discovered the camera before Nayan had a chance to switch it on. Nayan installed 10 camera traps in forests around the district of Chandrapur, India, to photograph tigers. However, much of his time over the ensuing months was spent fixing gear dismantled by the monkeys that were watching him from the trees each time he set up. Northern plains grey langurs are a familiar sight in western India, including in urban environments, where they are protected in part by their sacred status for Hindus. But relations can be fraught, especially when they raid crops or press tourists for food. Away from cities, langurs often travel with chital deer, and the two species use distinct warning calls to alert each other to approaching tigers and other intruders – including photographers.

Nikon D90 + Tokina 11–16mm f2.8 lens; 1/200 at f11; ISO 200; custom housing;
Nikon SB-900 Speedlight flash; Cognisys motion sensor.

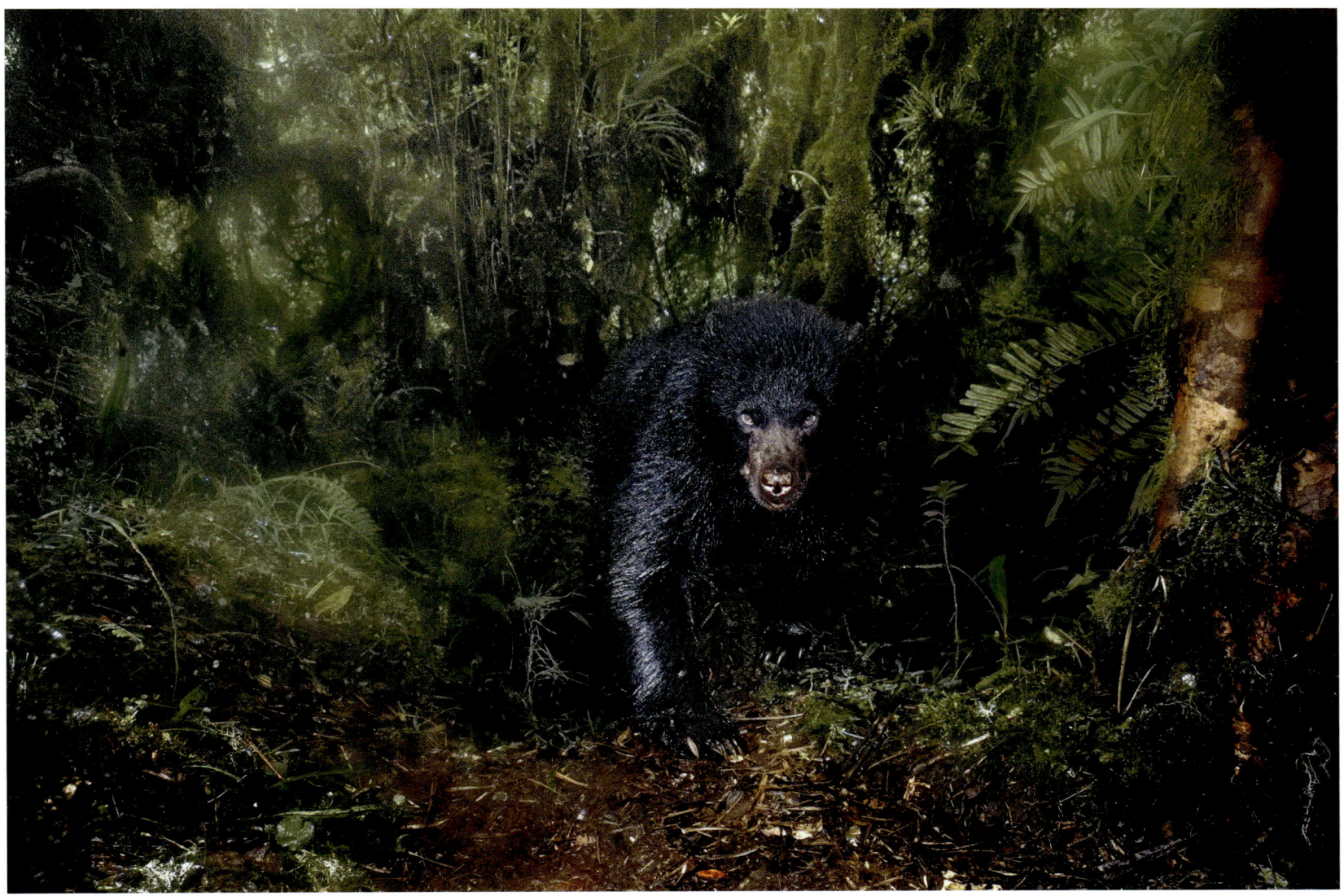

Out of the darkness

Santiago José Monroy García

COLOMBIA

On viewing the images from the camera trap he had set in the Ecopalacio Nature Reserve near Colombia's Chingaza National Park, Santiago recognized the face immediately. Local guides had named this male Andean bear Nariz de Calavera (Skull Nose), inspired by the distinctive markings on its muzzle. Also known as spectacled bears, they range across much of the tropical Andes and are South America's only native ursid. The bears are opportunistic feeders, eating mostly plants, but sometimes prey on mammals, including cattle, bringing them into conflict with farmers. Mature Andean bears number fewer than 10,000 individuals. Fortunately for Santiago, rain splashed the lens in just the right places to convey the humidity of the forests without blotting out the bear's intense stare.

Nikon D7200 + 18–55mm f3.5 lens; 1/80 at f11; ISO 800; 2x Camtraptions Z Pro flashes; Camtraptions housing + motion sensor.

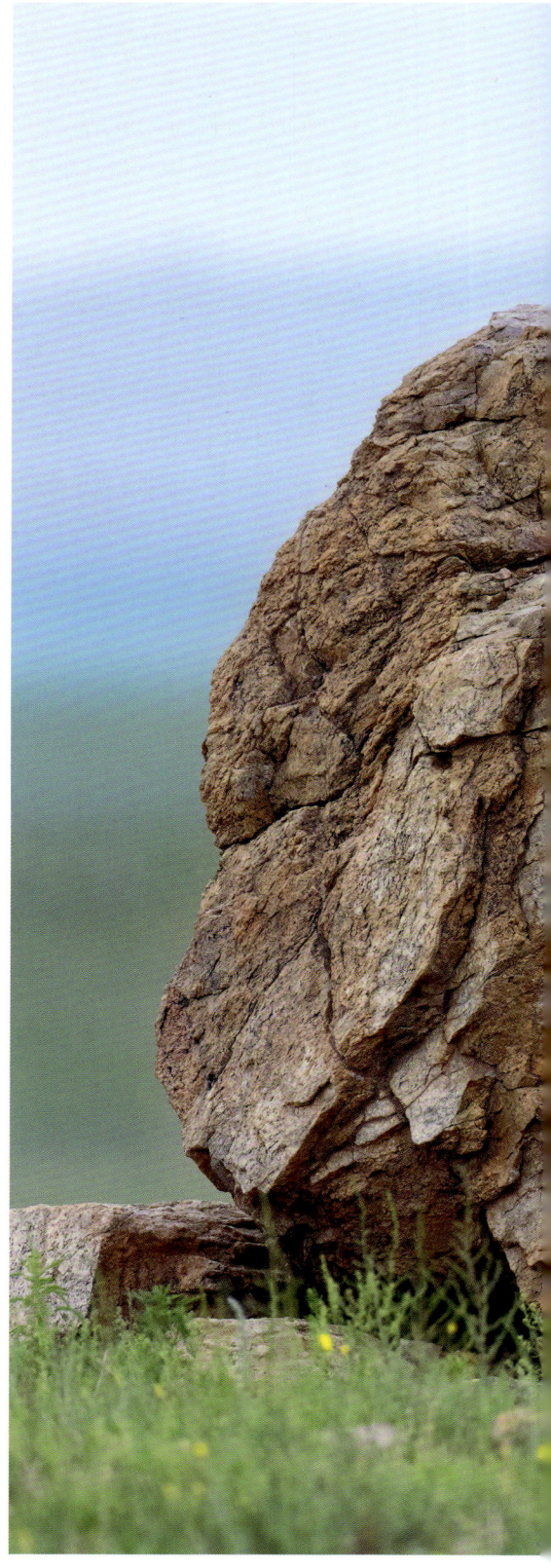

Kitten rock

Amit Eshel

ISRAEL

It is unusual to see two Pallas's cats together, let alone six. These stocky felines, about the size of a domestic cat, are solitary animals, roaming vast areas of central Asian grass and scrublands in search of pika and small rodents. But come spring, their range shrinks, revolving around a single breeding den in a rocky crevice, abandoned marmot burrow or tree cavity. Litters are rarely bigger than this, and Amit spent a week in his hide on Mongolia's eastern steppe to photograph the kittens whenever they emerged from the safety of the den at dawn and dusk. Pallas's cats are hunted in turn by foxes, wolves and raptors. They are not built for speed, so rely instead on being neither seen nor heard. Even the kittens' communal play is quiet and unobtrusive.

Canon EOS R5 + 200–400mm f4 lens + 1.4x teleconverter; 1/250 at f8; ISO 6400.

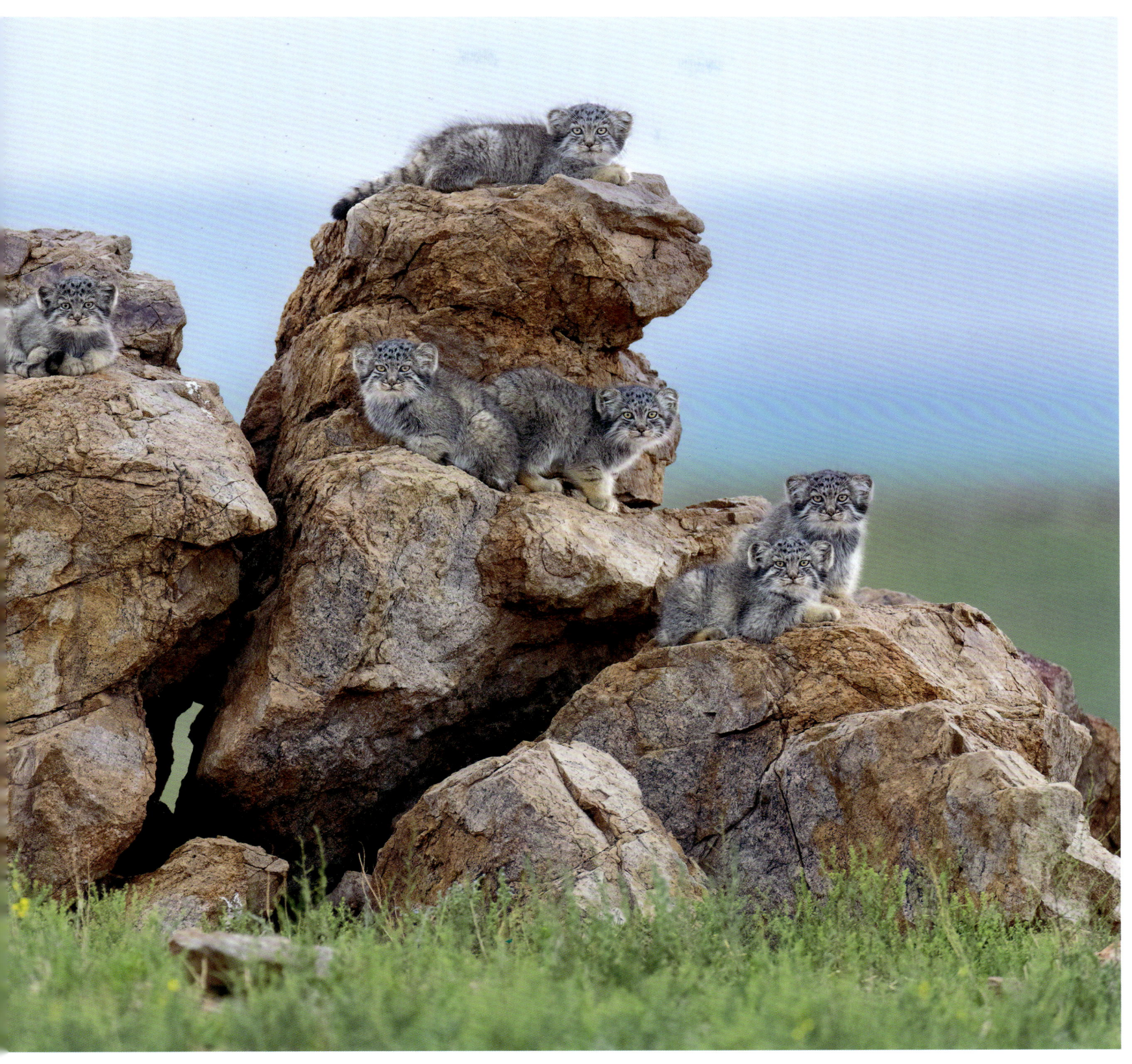

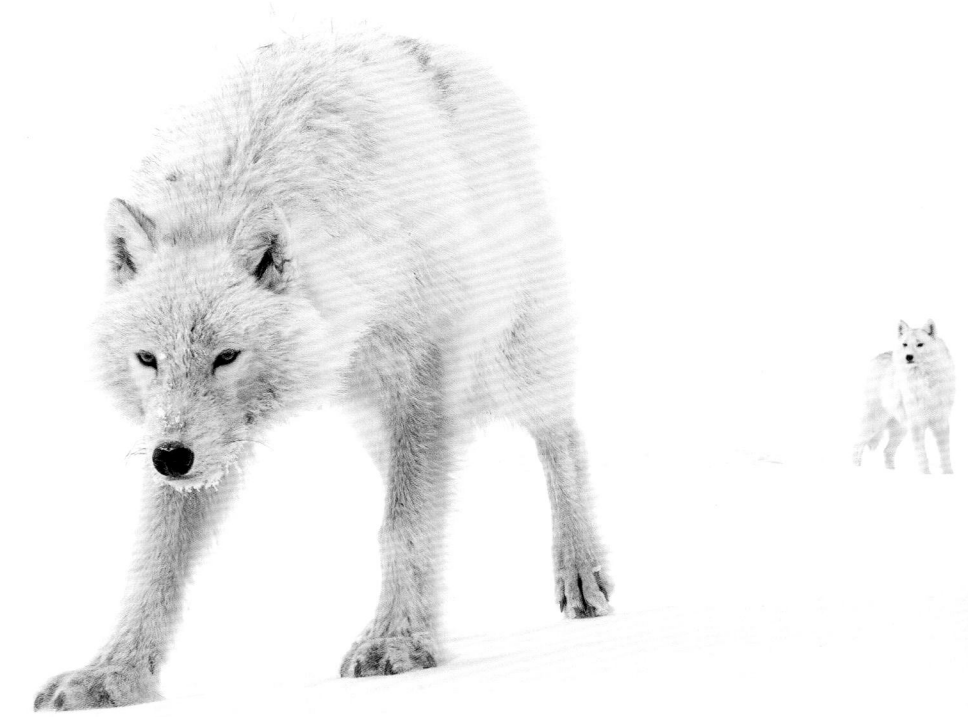

Inside the pack

Amit Eshel

ISRAEL

Amit had waited a long time to fulfil his dream of photographing the Arctic wolves of Ellesmere Island. Then, one day, they were so close he could smell their breath. Restricted to Canada's most northerly territories and northern Greenland, Arctic wolves are a snow-white subspecies of the grey wolf. These are pack animals that hunt hares, caribou, musk oxen and seals, yet have not learned to distrust humans. Amit had to find them first; Ellesmere is about the same size as the island of Great Britain, but home to barely 150 people. With territories covering 2,590 square kilometres (1,000 square miles), Arctic wolf packs are spread thinly. On his first expedition, Amit didn't see any. By day 12 of his second trip, he'd experienced -35°C (-31°F) and seen musk oxen, Arctic foxes, snowy owls and ringed seals, but no wolves. And then, one appeared in the distance, followed by another eight. Arctic wolves have a reputation for inquisitiveness and they came closer than Amit anticipated as he lay on the ice. The result is a low-angled view of the pack – one that holds no fear of their human observer.

Canon EOS R5 + 24–105mm f4 lens; 1/1250 at f11; ISO 2000.

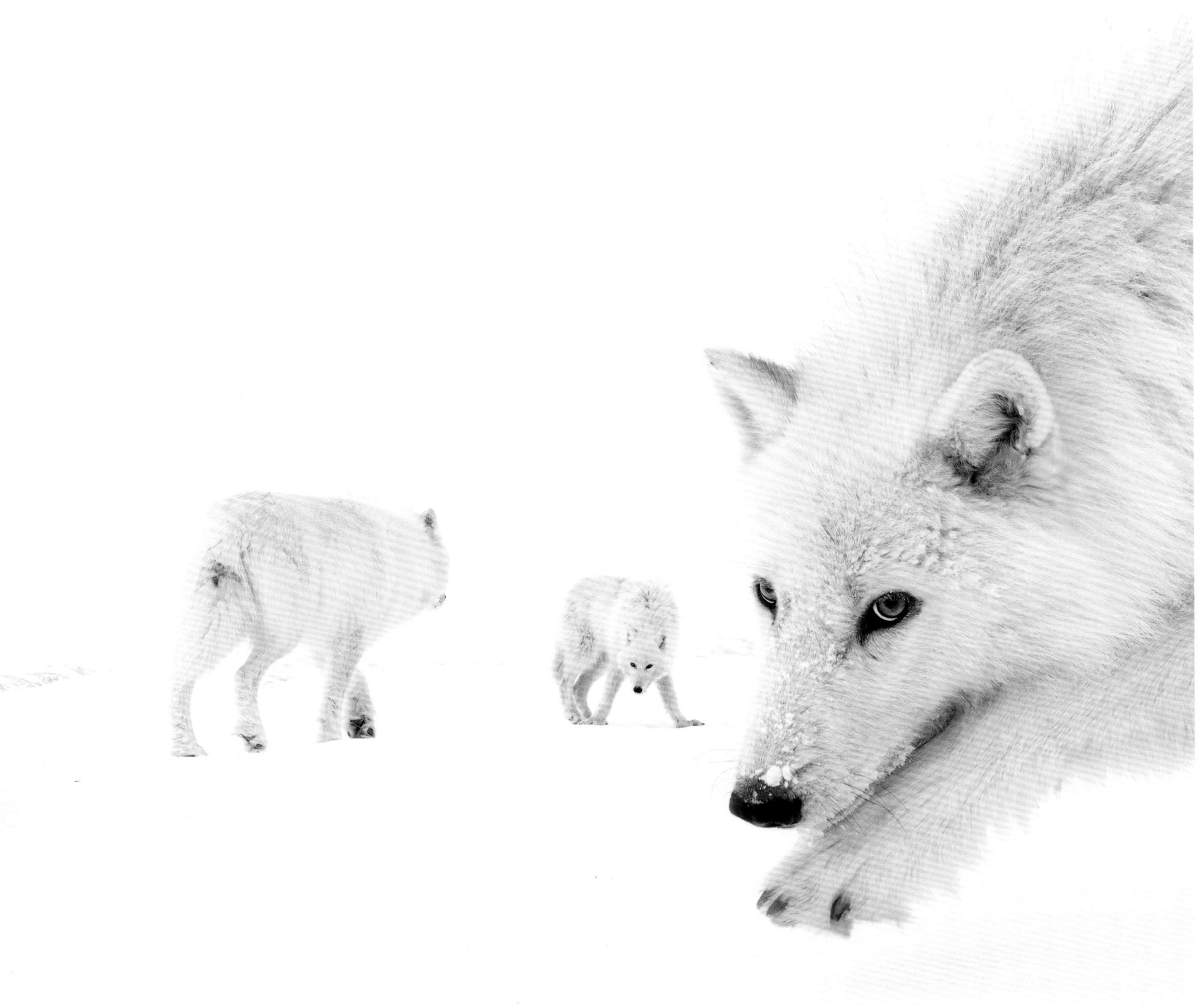

Natural Artistry

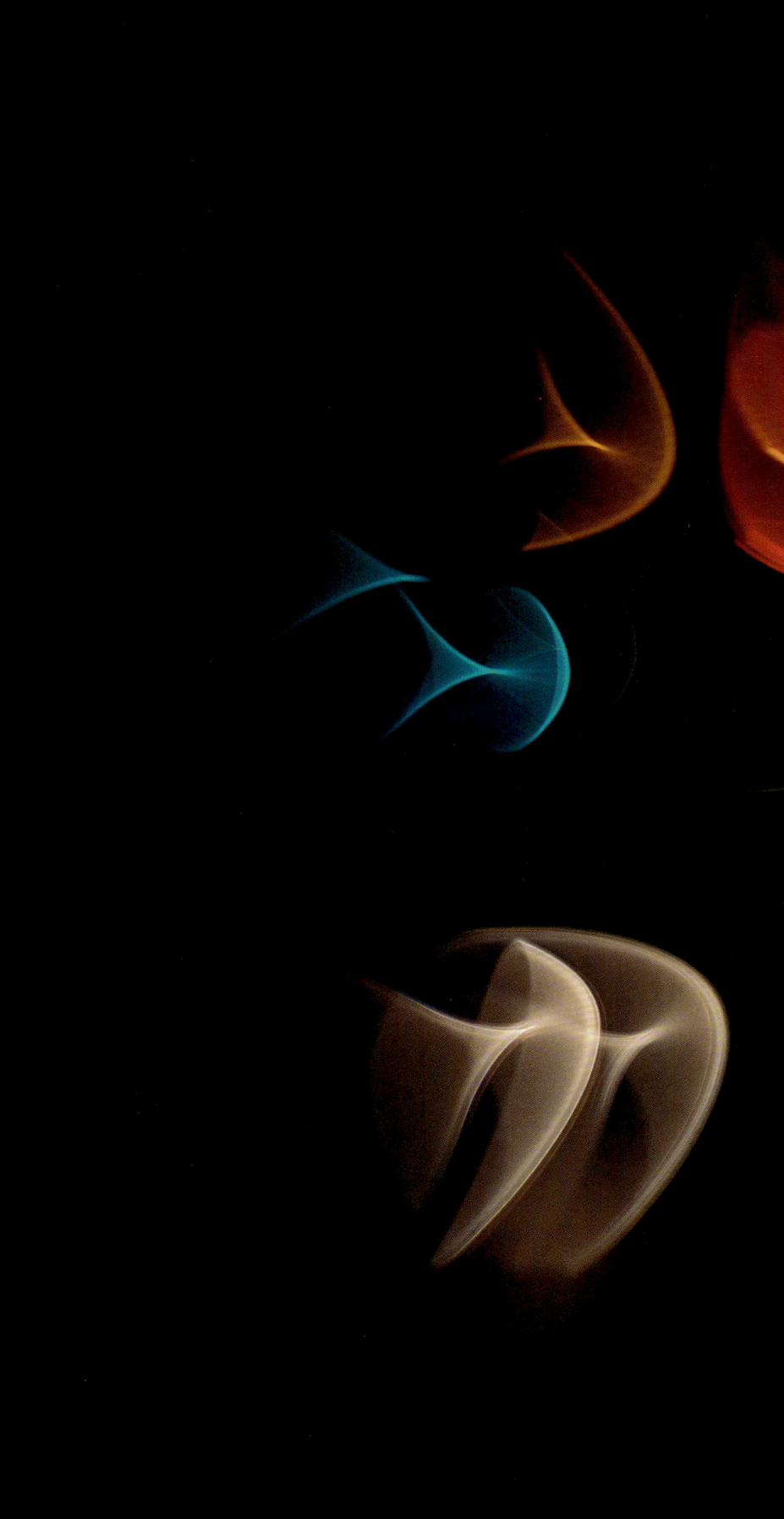

WINNER

Caught in the headlights

Simone Baumeister
GERMANY

Silhouetted by lights from the cars below, an orb weaver spider waits for insects to stumble into its web on the railings of a pedestrian bridge over a busy road junction in Ibbenbüren, northwest Germany. Orb weavers are among the most widely distributed spider families and occupy various habitats, including numerous human-made urban structures – many species have a distinctive flattened body that enables them to hide in crevices. They are numerous also near artificial lights, which attract large numbers of insects at night. To achieve the kaleidoscopic effect, Simone dismantled an old analogue lens and reversed one of the six glass elements inside before reassembling it. This optical reconfiguration distorted and blurred the image towards the edges, leaving only the centre point sharply focused. By cropping the image afterwards, Simone was able to move the spider slightly out of the centre of the picture. A spider's web functions as a sense organ, gathering sound from an area many times greater than the spider itself and transmitting the vibrations (including that of its captured prey) to its legs – very useful in a habitat as noisy as a bridge.

Canon EOS R5 + Carl Zeiss Jena Pancolar 50mm f1.8 lens + 16mm extension tube; 1/250 at f2.8 (–1.33 e/v); ISO 1250.

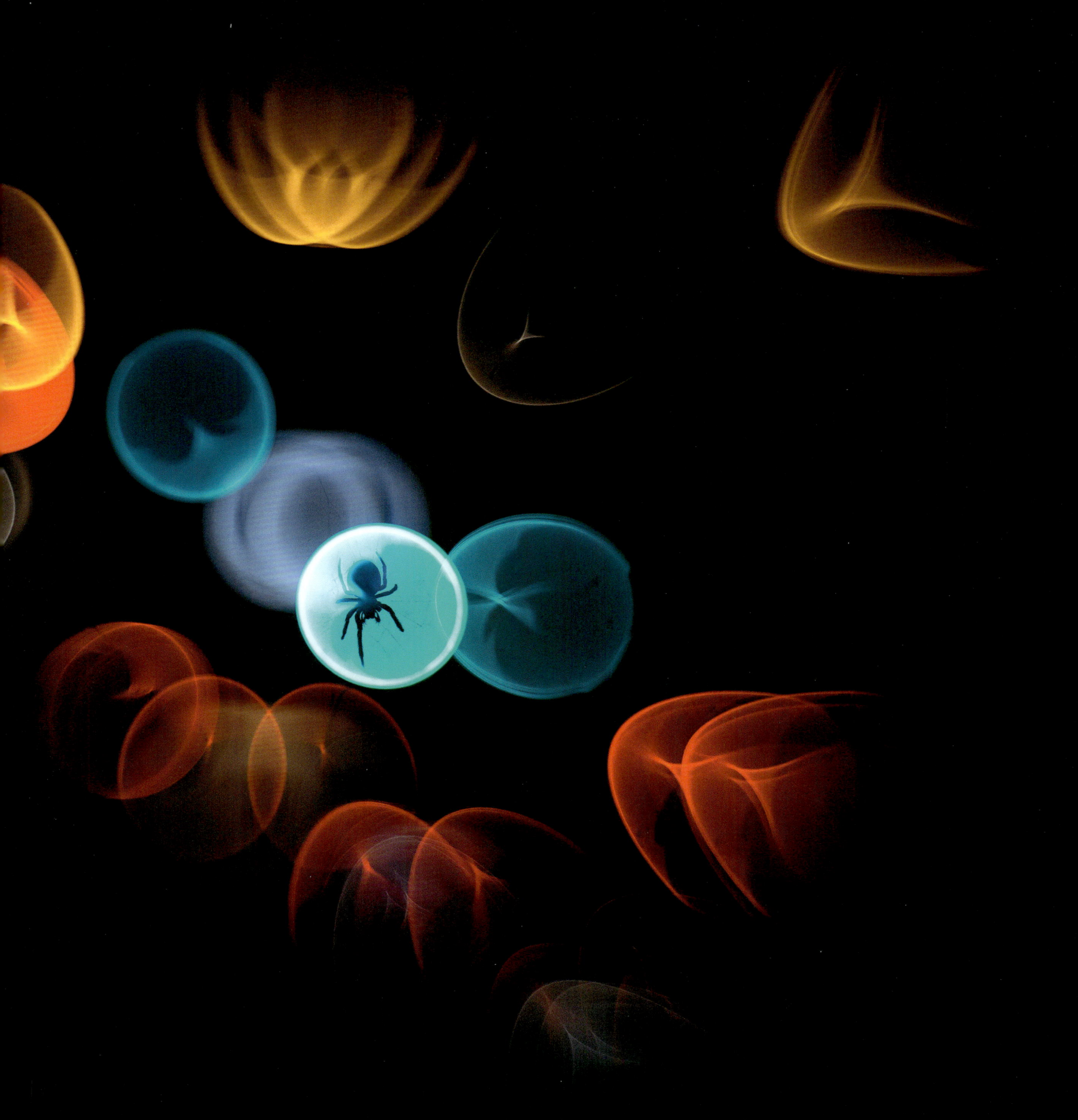

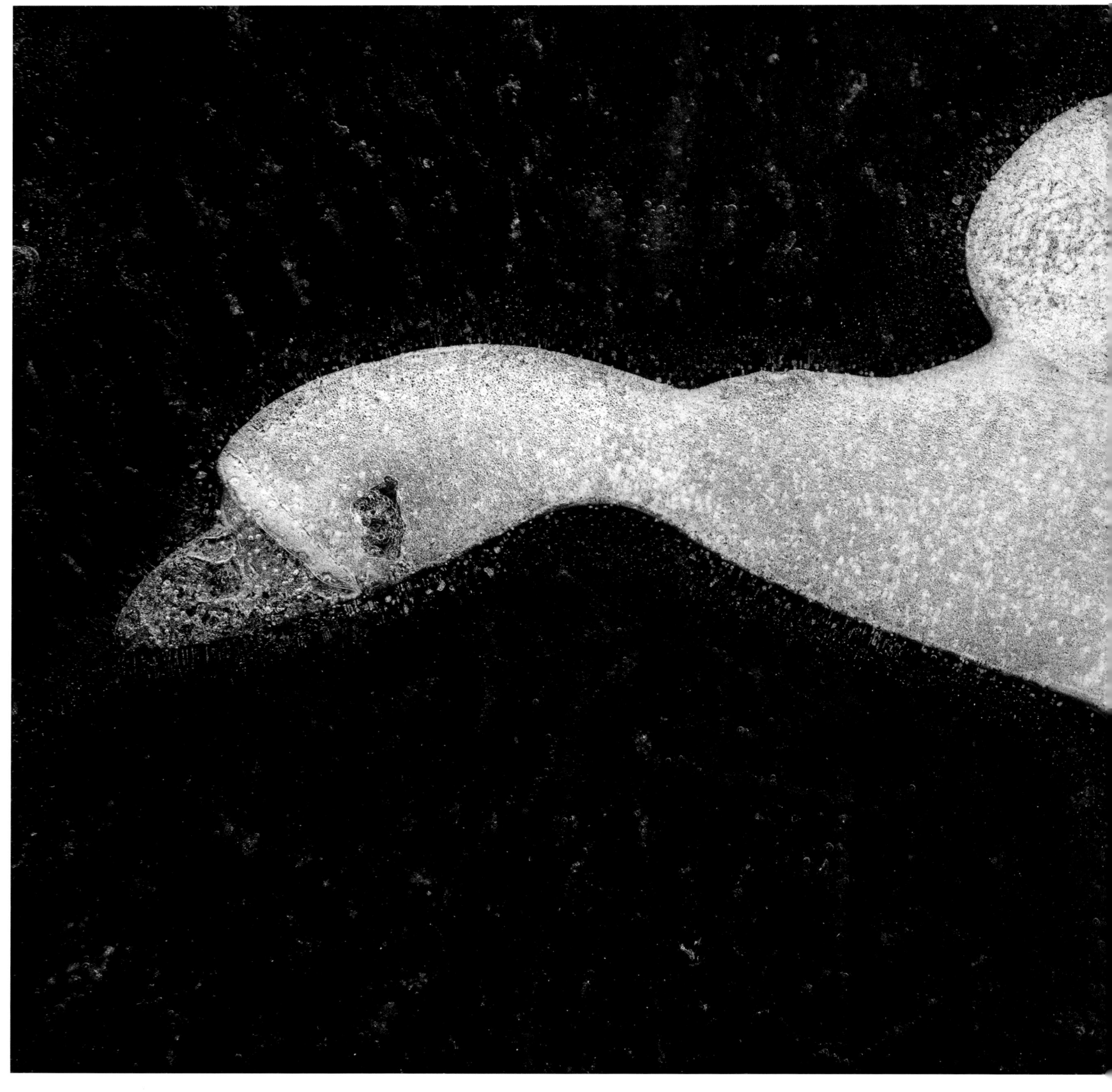

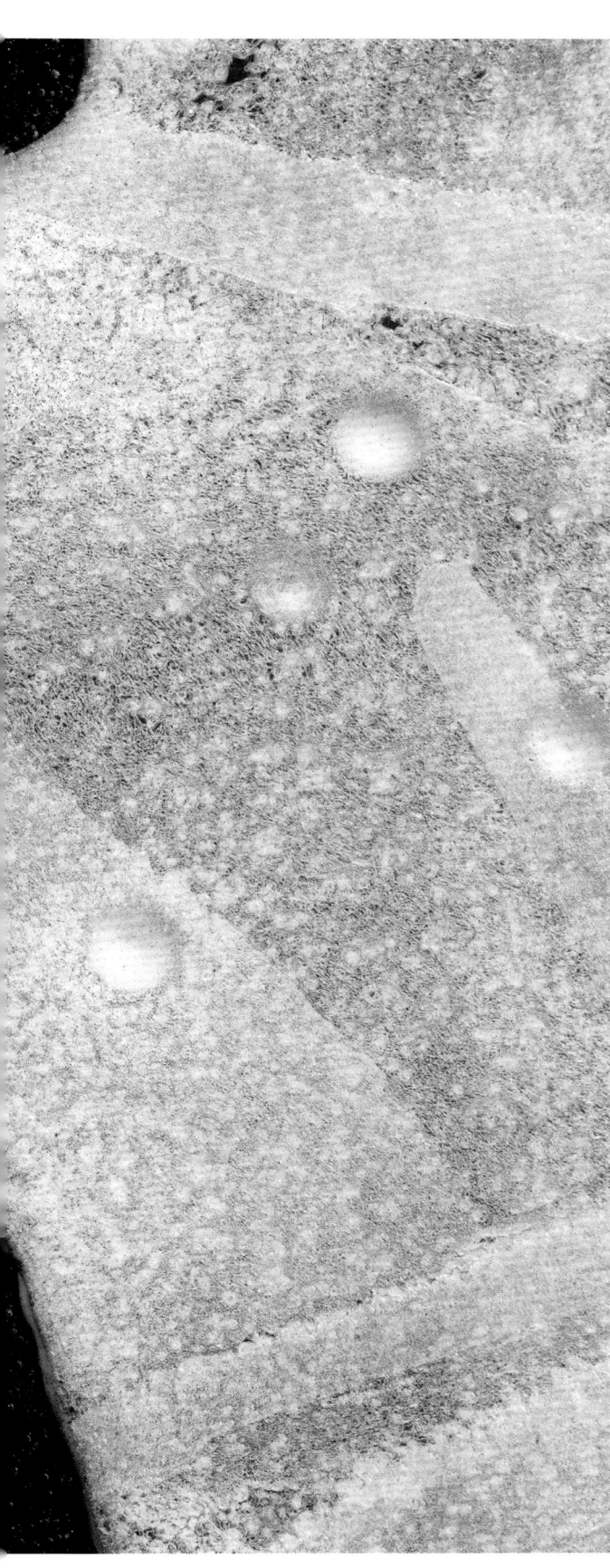

The frozen swan

Fortunato Gatto

ITALY

Just as no two snowflakes are exactly the same, neither are two frozen puddles. Depending on the precise conditions in which it froze, ice can take on a multitude of forms. Its molecules can arrange themselves into a variety of crystalline structures. It may freeze as a single block, as a coalescence of individual crystals or, if freeze-thaw cycles are involved, in distinct layers. Its appearance will vary according to how quickly it froze, what else is dissolved in it, the moisture content of the surrounding air, and the quantity and size of any trapped bubbles. The result is that ice can be powdery or angular, smooth or textured, uniform or complex, cracked or flawless, milky white, jet black or completely transparent. These contrasting qualities can occur together in close proximity, as was the case in the puddle that Fortunato chanced upon in a bog in the south of Iceland. Fortunato calls it a 'meta-image', in which nature itself provides both the canvas and the artwork. It's only when seen through human eyes, though, that it becomes a swan.

Canon EOS 5D Mark IV + 24–70mm f4 lens; 1/50 at f13; ISO 100; polarizing filter; Leofoto tripod.

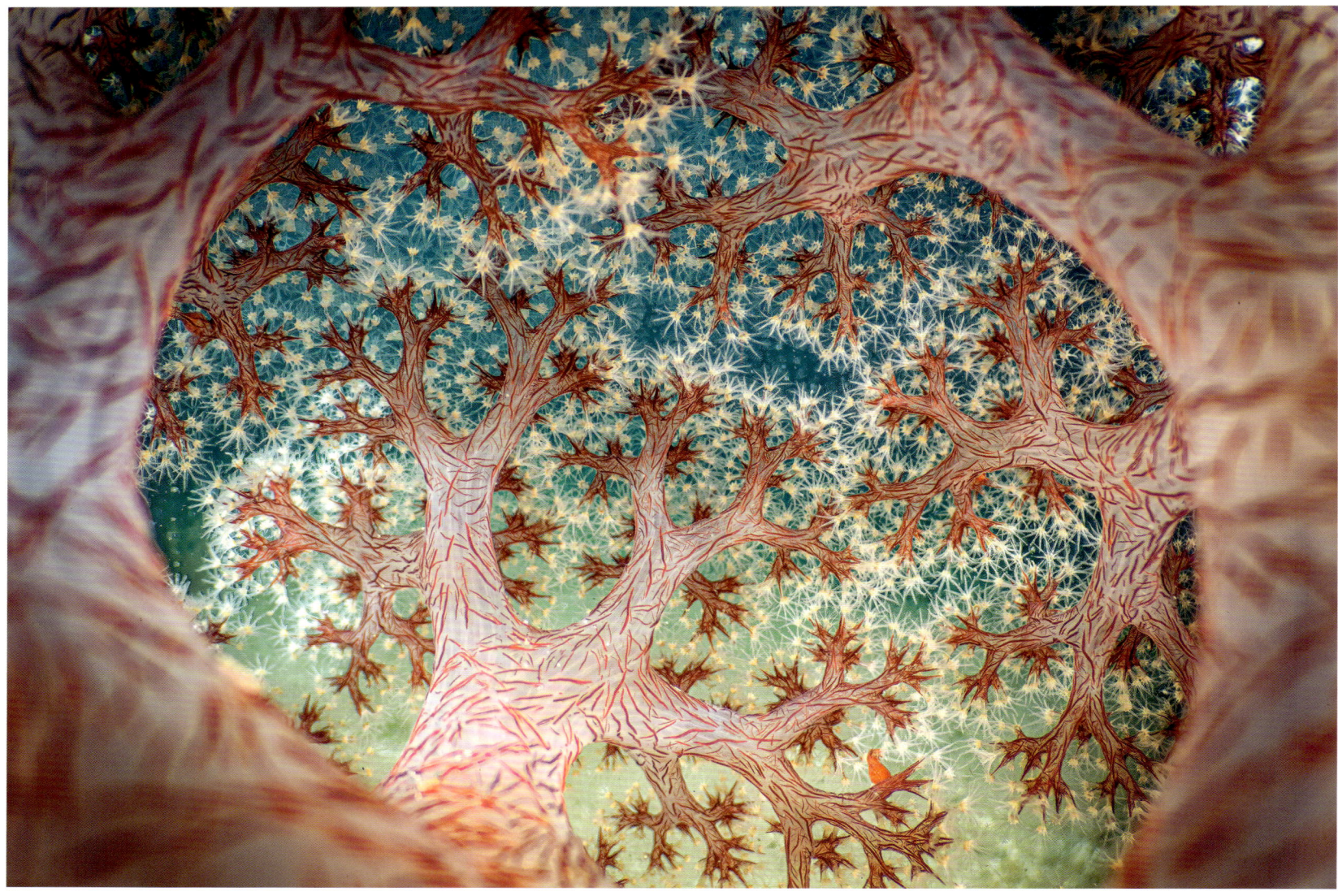

Fractal forest

Ross Gudgeon
AUSTRALIA

This image could pass for an impressionistic grove of olive trees painted against a starry sky. There's even what looks like a bird perched on one of the lower branches at the bottom of the picture. But these twisting limbs belong to an animal, a soft coral named *Dendronephthya*, known generically as cauliflower coral, that Ross found rooted to the sea-bed 20 metres (65 feet) below the Lembeh Strait off the Indonesian island of Sulawesi. Its finest twigs are tipped with myriad clonal polyps, their stinging tentacles trawling for tiny waterborne prey. Ross's camera was fitted with an extended macro wide lens (EMWL), an underwater version of a probe that allows the photographer to carefully thread the lens between the branches to reveal the exquisite structure from the inside out, and backlit with two flashes.

Sony α7R IV + 90mm f2.8 macro lens + Nauticam EMWL 160° lens; 1/100 at f9; ISO 400; 2x Retra Pro flashes; Nauticam NA– α7R IV housing.

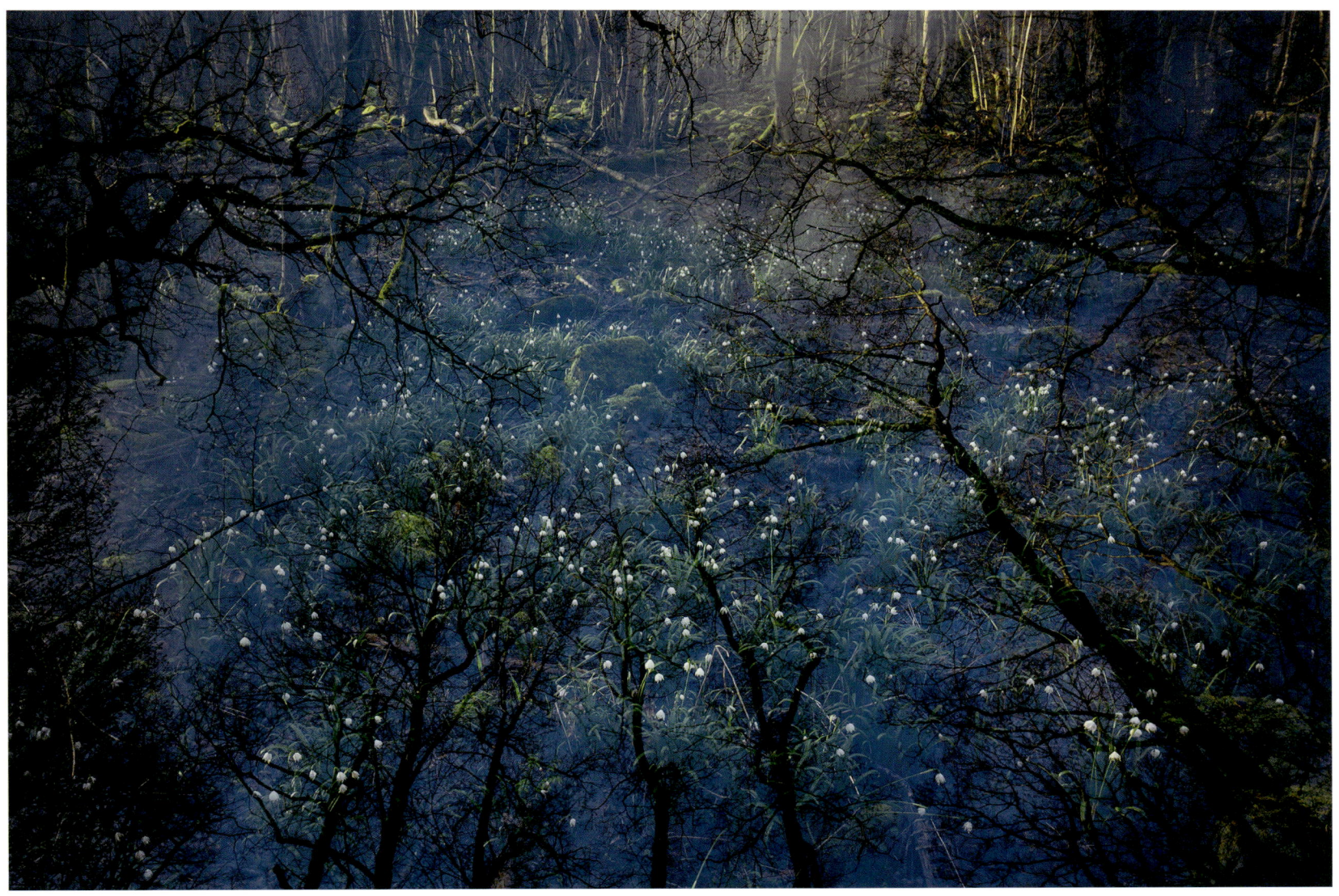

Spring snowflake morning

Thomas Schwarze

GERMANY

If it's hard to tell whether we are looking up to the sky or down to the ground, it might be because this image gives us both views simultaneously. For the first few seconds of this long exposure, Thomas's camera was trained on the woodland floor and its carpet of spring snowflake flowers. Partway through, he tilted it upwards towards the canopy to superimpose the two viewpoints. The leafy crowns in the foreground, looking like watery reflections, belong to the distant tree trunks illuminated by the early morning sun. The woodland, near the small German town of Elkenroth, possesses what Thomas describes as a 'dense energy'. His photograph is a manipulation of objective reality, but it is arguably a more accurate representation of what it might be like to be there.

Nikon Z6 + 24–70mm f4 lens; 13 sec at f13; ISO 400; neutral density filter; Sirui W-2204 tripod.

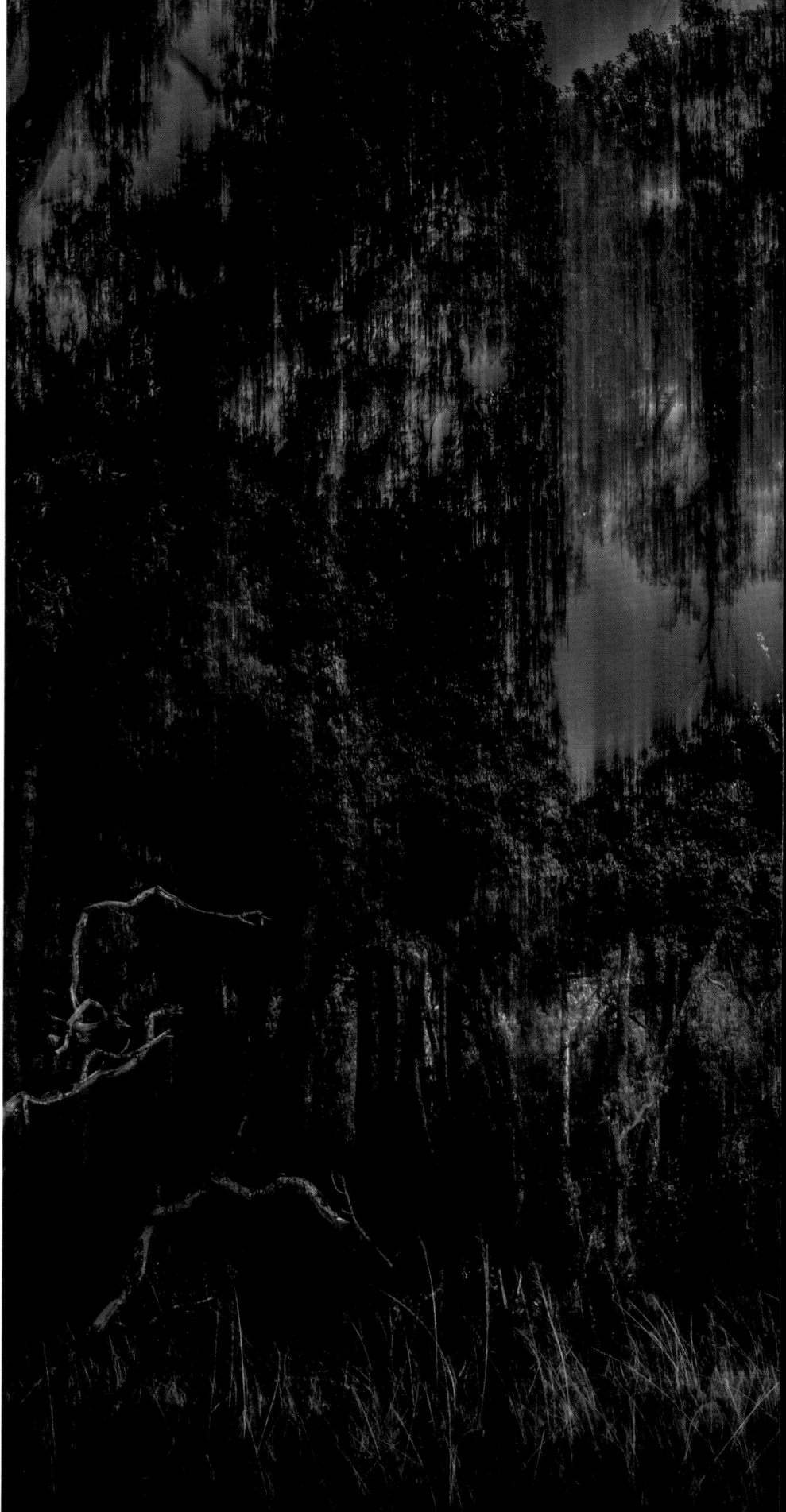

Oasis of calm

Rahul Sachdev

INDIA

August is a lively month in Kenya's Maasai Mara. It is the time of the great migration, when over a million wildebeest and hundreds of thousands of zebras and Thomson's gazelles make their way here from neighbouring Tanzania. Rahul had been photographing groups crossing the perilous waters of the Mara River, frequented by hungry crocodiles. But there are places where it is possible to escape the action, and this bull elephant found a quiet spot amongst the greenheart trees of a riverside woodland. African savanna elephants number around 400,000 individuals spread between 24 of Africa's 54 sovereign states. Habitat fragmentation, poaching for ivory and conflicts with farmers means they now occupy just 15 per cent of their historic pre-agricultural range. Earlier, Rahul had watched marabou storks hunting around a large grassland fire, picking off animals flushed by the flames. Later that evening, all was calm in the lush woodland. A slight movement of the camera during this exposure adds a dreamlike quality to the image and blurs the boundary between animal and habitat. Only the elephant's brilliant-white tusks appear pin sharp.

Canon EOS R5 + 100–500mm f4.5–7.1 lens; 1/5 at f32 (-1e/v); ISO 100.

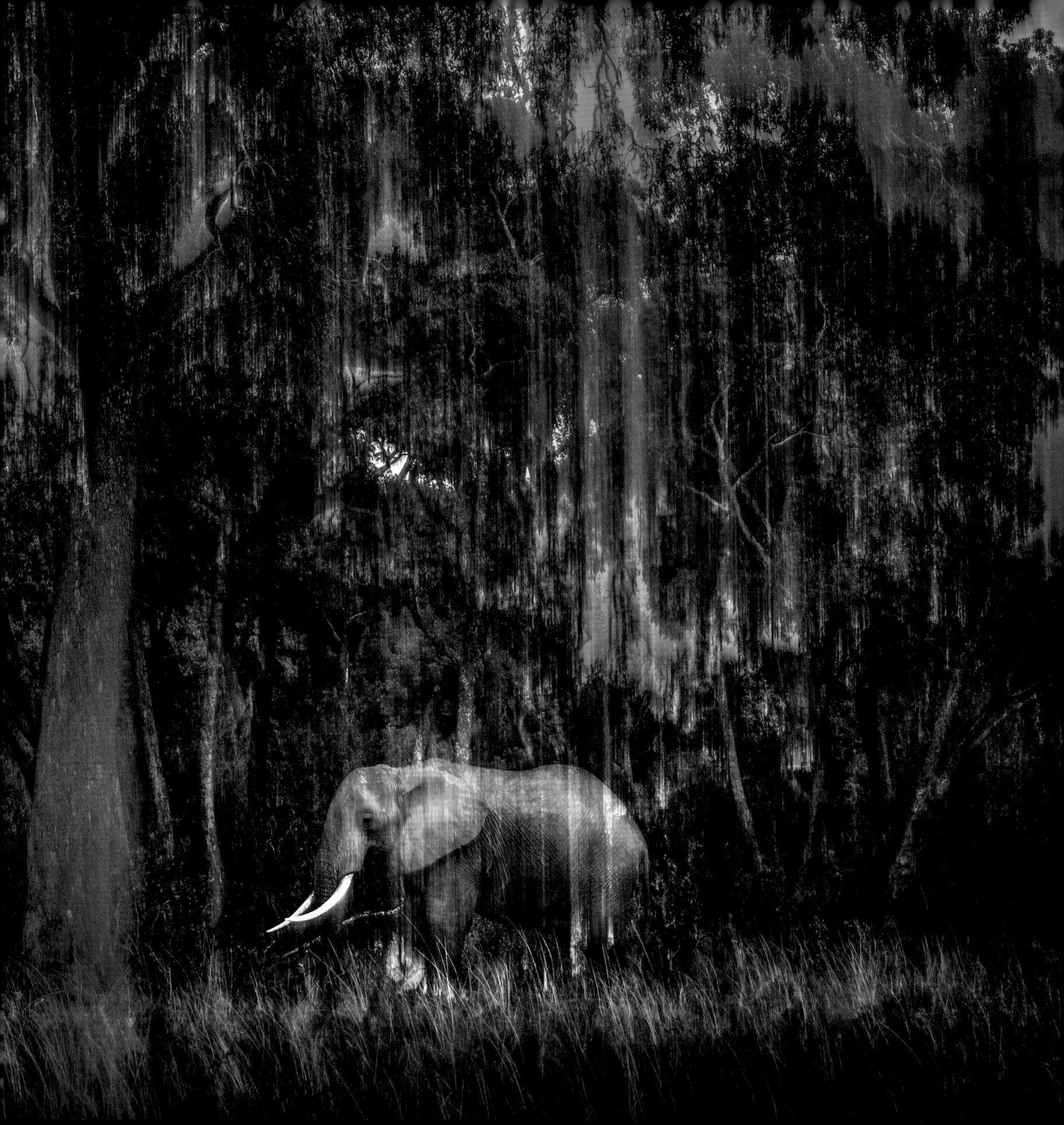

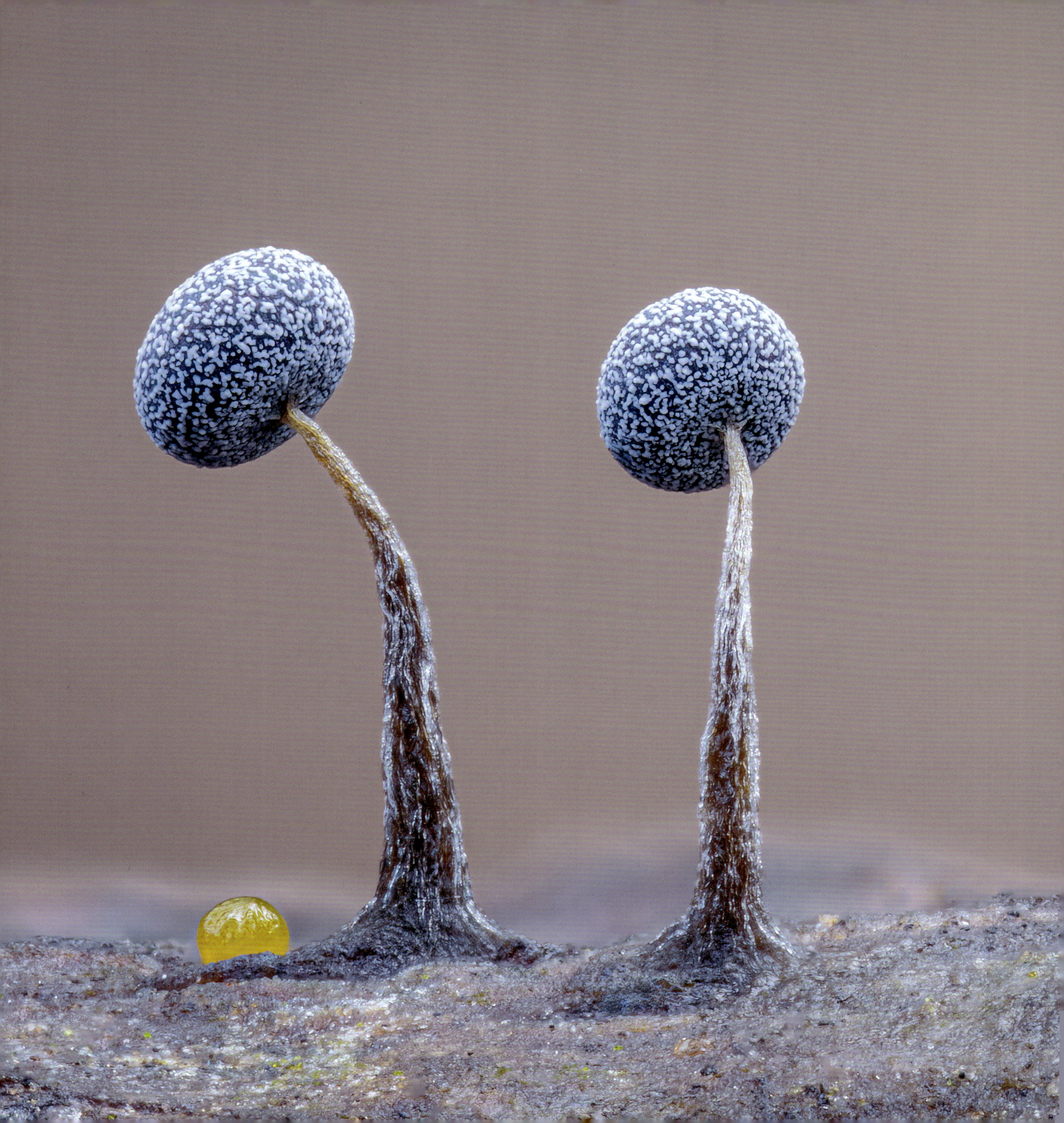

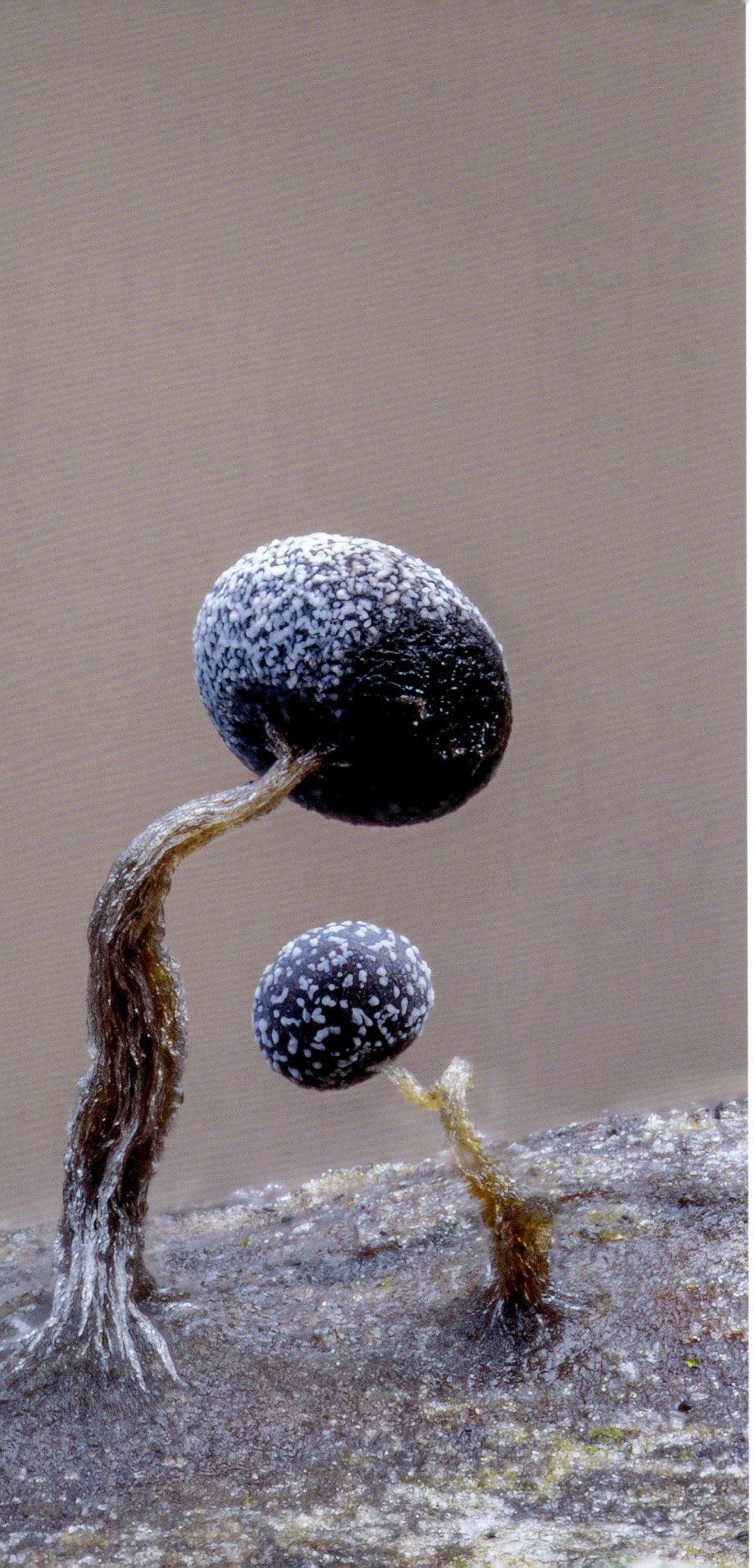

Slime family portrait

Kutub Uddin

BANGLADESH/UK

Some life forms are so otherworldly that it's hard to say whether they are animal or vegetable. These are neither, although they share similarities with both. Nor are they fungi, although there is a passing resemblance. Rather, the slime moulds in this row are members of an ancient lineage that evolved independently before the animal kingdom even existed. A slime mould is a society of mobile single-celled, amoeba-like organisms that lead separate lives until they come together and work as one to find food and reproduce. This communal phase of the life cycle is a shape-shifting entity, called a plasmodium, that flows over rotting vegetation, mopping up microorganisms and nutrients as it goes. These sticky spheres, 1–2 millimetres (less than a twelfth of an inch) in diameter, are the reproductive parts of a species named *Physarum album*, which Kutub found on a fallen beech tree in Slindon Wood, West Sussex, UK. Soon, they will open like flowers to release the spores within. Kutub's study of a little-known branch of the evolutionary tree also works as a fantasy landscape (with a tiny yellow insect egg next to one of the slime moulds), but he prefers to describe the scene as a bizarre family portrait.

Canon EOS R5 + 65mm f2.8 1–5x macro lens; 0.6 sec at f5.6; ISO 200; focus stack of 78 images.

Oceans:
The Bigger Picture

WINNER

The feast

Audun Rikardsen

NORWAY

During the winter polar night in northern Norway, when the sun doesn't rise above the horizon, Atlantic herring migrate to Kvænangen fjord for two to three months, before continuing to their spawning grounds off the coast. Following the fish are hordes of gulls, whales and much of Norway's herring fleet, all hunting for the same resource within a restricted area. In the darkness, the sound of the boats signals to the birds that dinner is served; and the message has spread, with more gulls turning up each year to feast around the boats. In the chaos, many drown in or around the purse seine nets suspended like curtains from the water's surface to encircle fish. A purse seine net used in these fjords is commonly 800 metres (½ mile) in length and can reach up to 180 metres (600 feet) in depth. The high density of birds also facilitates the spread of diseases, such as avian flu. The flocks mainly comprise glaucous, great black-backed and European herring gulls, with some lesser black-backed and common gulls, and black-legged kittiwakes. The fishing industry, marine scientists and nature managers are trying to find solutions to reduce these fishery bycatch interactions that are killing hundreds of thousands of seabirds annually worldwide.

Canon EOS R5 + 15–35mm f2.8 lens at 15mm; 1/200 at f4.5; ISO 10,000; Canon Speedlite 600EX II flash; LED torch.

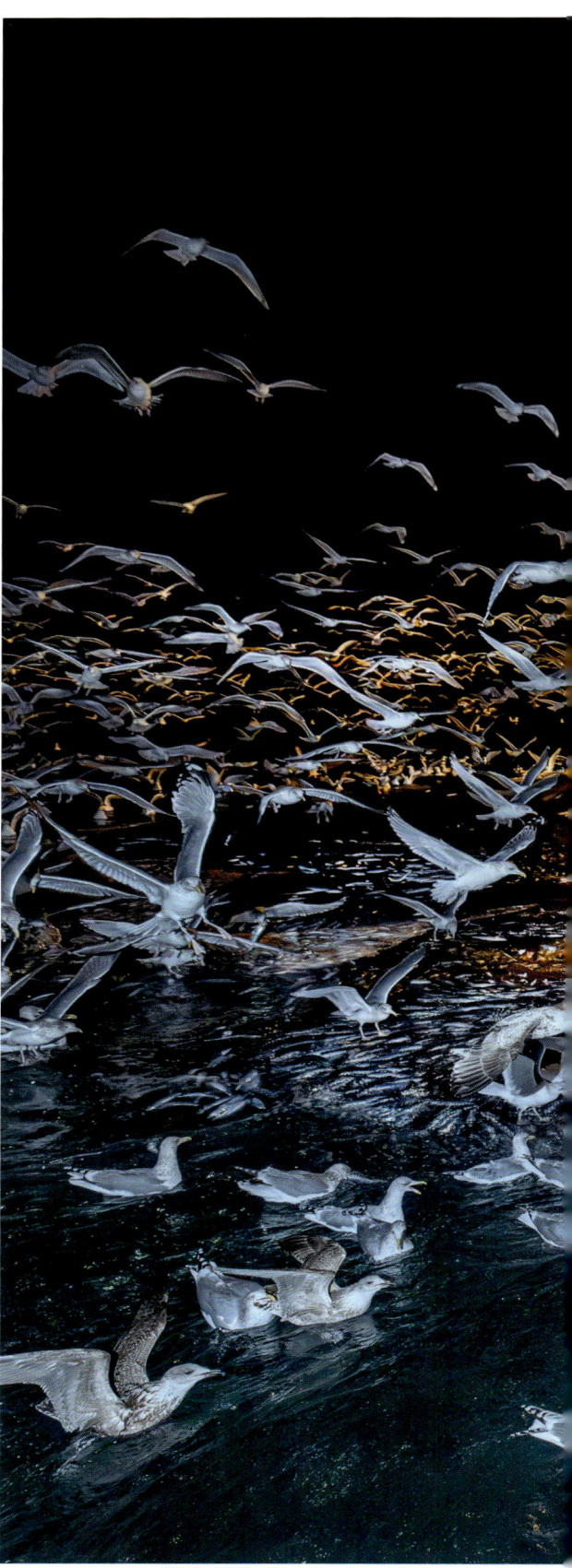

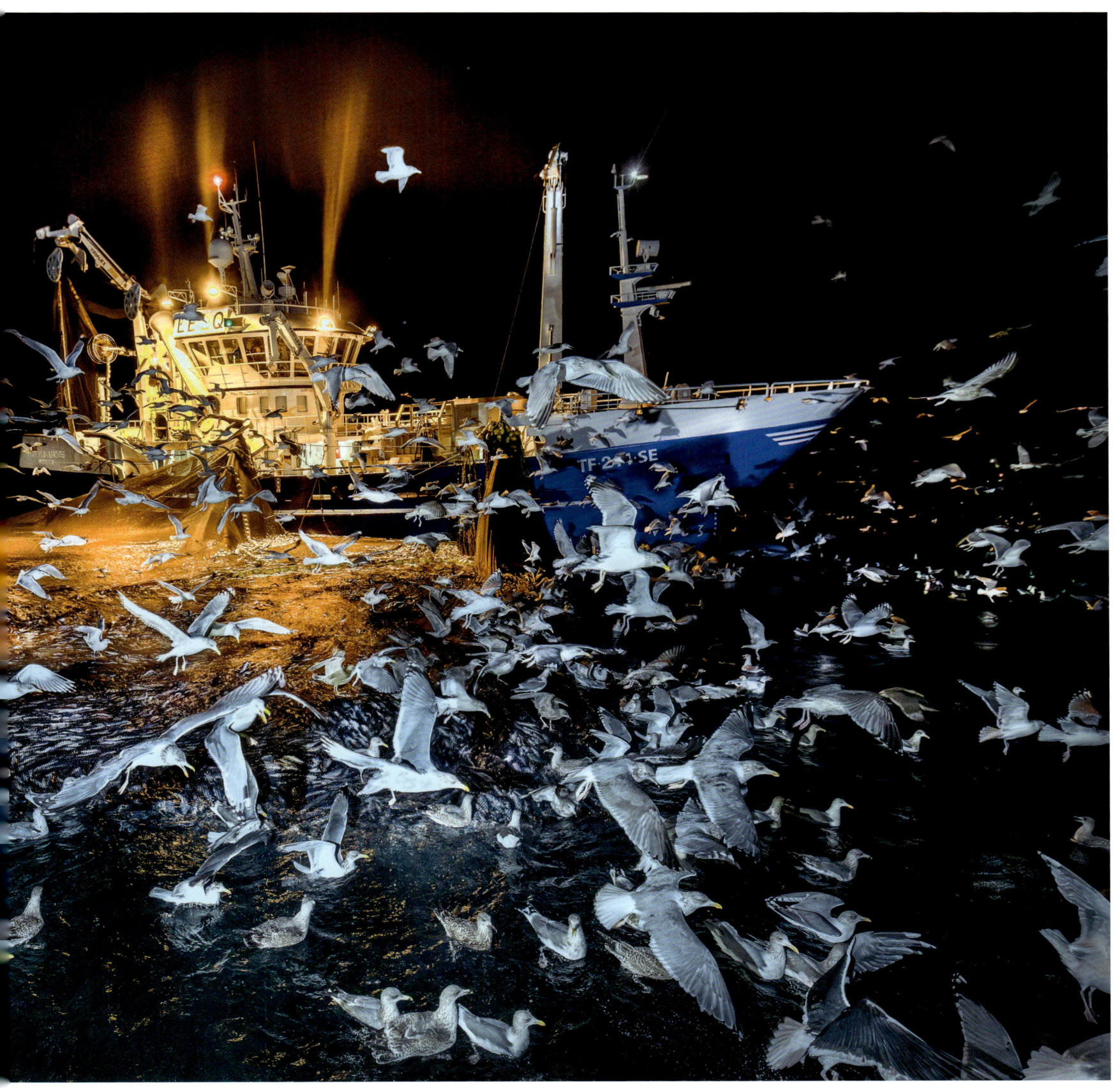

Undersea harvest

Anna Boyiazis

USA

Seaweed farmers Maua Mkubwa (standing) and Maua Mdogo nurture their undersea farm in the Indian Ocean off Paje, Zanzibar, within the Menai Bay Conservation Area, the archipelago's largest marine-protected area. As members of the female-led, community-based Mwani (Swahili for seaweed) Zanzibar co-operative, they sustainably harvest a red alga in the genus *Eucheuma*, known as eucheumatoid seaweeds. These are used to create handmade skincare for international markets. This recent initiative is empowering local women and improving the livelihoods of families traditionally reliant on fishing – now facing depleted stocks due to climate change, overfishing and destructive practices. Seaweed cultivation does not require common farming inputs such as fresh water, pesticides or fertilizers. Using a technique known as off-bottom (peg and line), seaweed seedlings are tied at short intervals to durable nylon ropes 3–5 metres (10–16 feet) long with strands of nylon twine. The ropes are then strung between wooden posts in shallow water, where they can be easily accessed at low tide, as seen here in Anna's photograph. Seaweed farming also has environmental benefits: the fronds absorb carbon dioxide in photosynthesis and take up nitrogen and phosphorus, and act as a water purifier by reducing acidification and removing some pollutants. All this, while providing precious habitat for marine life too.

Nikon Z9 + 24–70mm f2.8 lens at 38mm; 1/160 at f22 (-0.3 e/v); ISO 400.

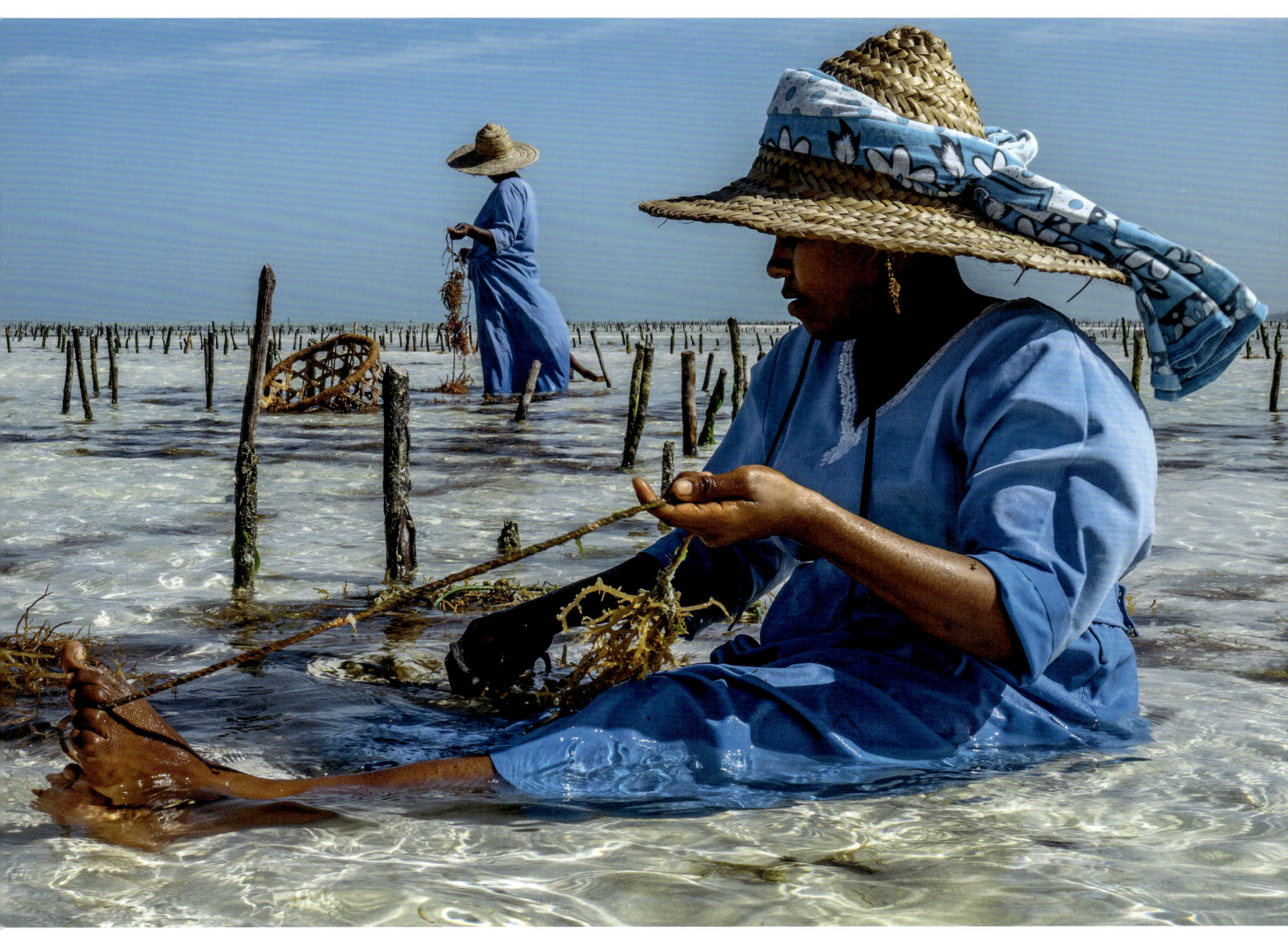

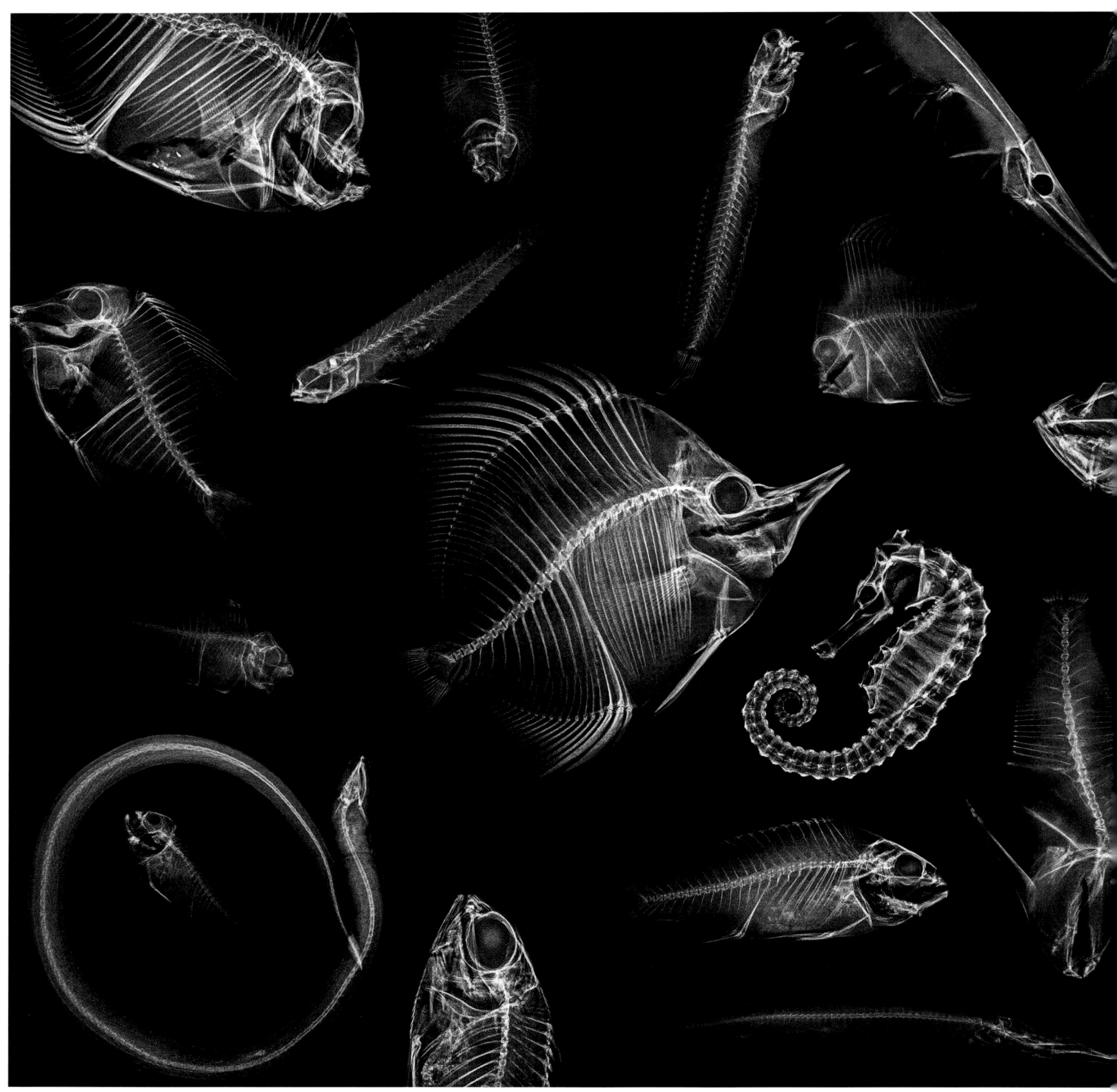

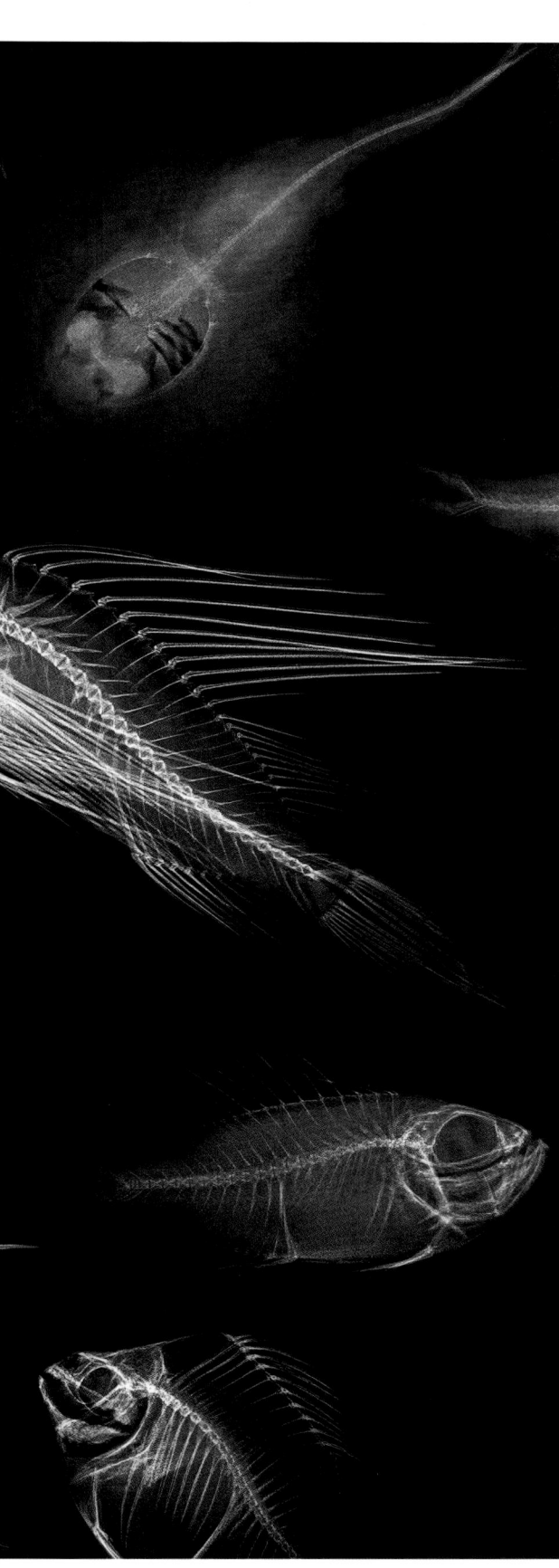

Baring the bones

Sirachai Arunrugstichai

THAILAND

The skeletal beauty of more than 20 different families of tropical fish is laid bare by X-ray imaging at Chulalongkorn University, Bangkok, Thailand. 'My aim was to visualize the potential loss of marine biodiversity, particularly from coral reef ecosystems, so I exposed the skeletons to symbolize death,' explains Sirachai. Warm-water coral reefs are home to a quarter of all marine life, including more than 7,000 fish species, but remain one of the most vulnerable marine ecosystems. They are threatened especially by ocean warming (leading to mass coral bleaching and mortality), ocean acidification, destructive fishing practices, pollution and development. According to the Intergovernmental Panel on Climate Change, the majority of these reefs are projected to disappear even if global warming is limited to 1.5°C. Sirachai's array of preserved specimens comprises coral reef species mostly from the Indo-West Pacific: from the copperband butterflyfish (centre), with its elongated snout for plucking invertebrates from crevices, to the venomous lionfish (to its right), and the snake eel (bottom left), encircling a clown anemonefish. The powder blue surgeonfish (far left, second down) depends exclusively on coral reef habitat, as do most surgeonfish species. The seahorse is probably a three-spot seahorse, threatened primarily by fisheries bycatch and habitat damage, but also as one of the most traded seahorse species for use in traditional Chinese medicine.

Poskom PXM-40BT hybrid battery-powered portable X-ray unit + Mars1417X wireless digital flat panel detector.

Animals in
Their Environment

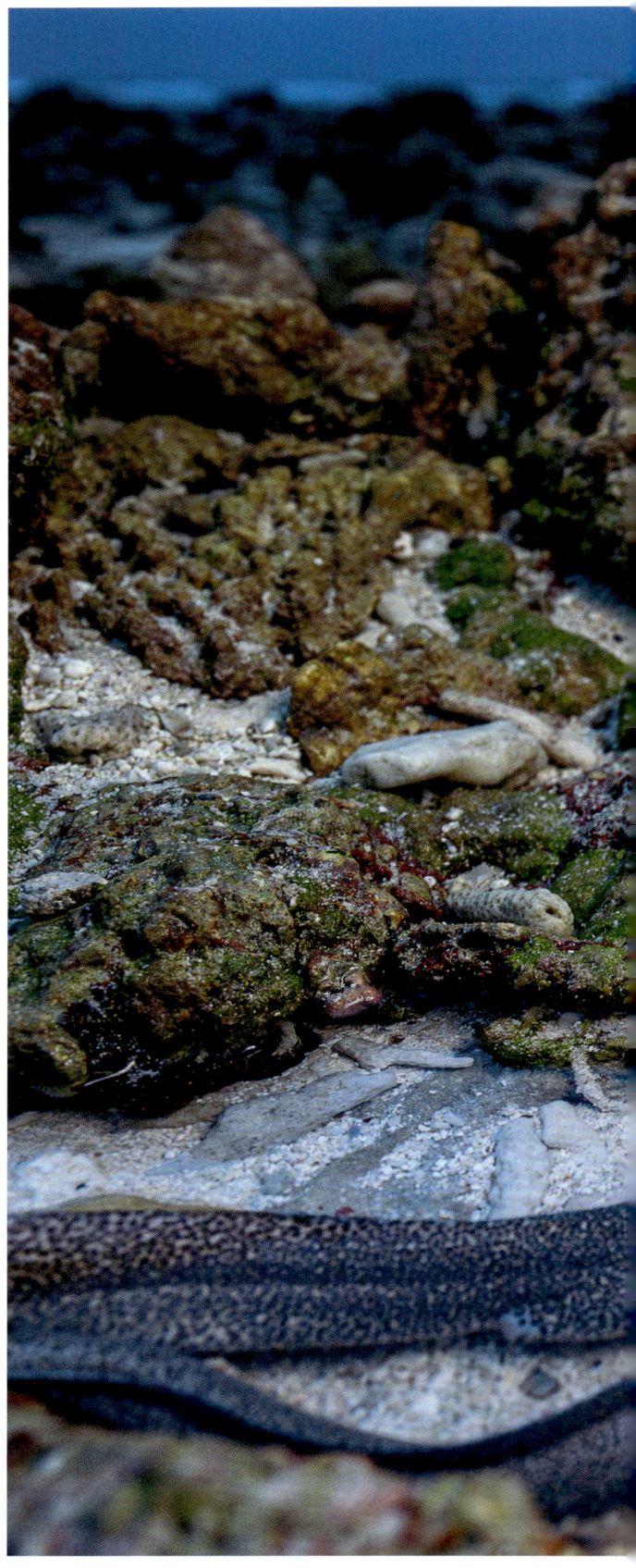

Like an eel out of water

Shane Gross
CANADA

Contrary to first impressions, this peppered moray eel is not stranded out of water. In fact, it is a species well adapted to the intertidal zone because it can hunt both above and below the surface, sometimes staying out of water for more than 30 seconds. Shane captured this behaviour on D'Arros Island in the outer coral archipelago of the Seychelles. It took him numerous attempts over several weeks to work out how best to capture this rarely photographed phenomenon. Initially, he found the eels were elusive and shy, and rapidly dispersed when he approached. Having worked out that they were scavenging for carrion using their keen sense of smell, he looked for dead fish, sat very still a few metres away and waited for their approach. Soon, these three eels overcame any fear of his presence. Shane was in the Seychelles to document its marine wildlife following the designation of 13 Marine Protected Areas, including D'Arros, covering 400,000 square kilometres (154,440 square miles) around the islands. Through a 'debt-for-nature' deal, some of the Seychelles' foreign debt was written off in return for the government enacting measures to protect biodiversity. As a result, the proportion of marine areas where commercial activities such as fishing or mining are now banned or regulated has risen to 30 per cent – in line with international goals.

Nikon Z6 + 24–70mm lens at 24mm; 1/250 at f5.6; ISO 2500; Godox AD400 Pro flash with 24-inch diffuser; light stand.

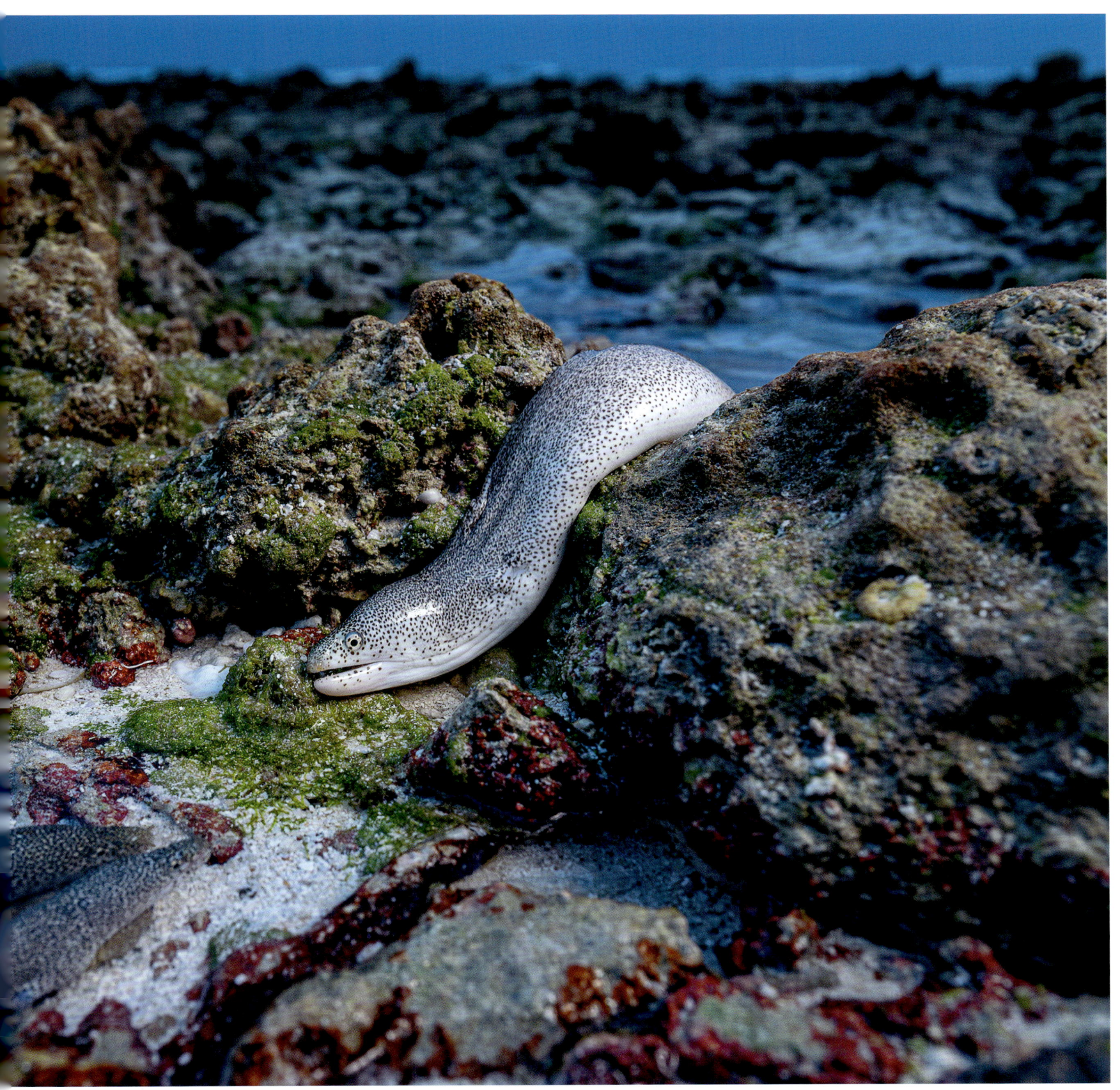

Ice edge journey

Bertie Gregory

UK

A large group of fledgling emperor penguin chicks resemble a crowd leaving a football match, as they make their way along an ice shelf high above the sea. After being left by their parents a month earlier, their need to feed was too strong to ignore, and they had to find a way for their first dip into the icy ocean. Bertie spent two months with the colony in Atka Bay, Antarctica, and witnessed most chicks using snow ramps to descend to sea level, but this group missed the easy way down. He used his drone to follow them to a part of the shelf where there was clear water 15 metres (49 feet) below them. Then they leapt in. 'Because this behaviour had never been filmed before, I wanted to make 100 per cent [sure] the drone noise was not affecting their decisions,' he says. Only when Bertie was certain of their direction did he move the drone closer to the penguins. Scientists say the continuing decline of sea ice in Antarctica may force more emperor penguins to breed on ice shelves, making this behaviour more common in the future.

DJI Mavic 3 Pro + Hasselblad L2D-20c 24mm f2.8 lens; 1/50 at f3.5; ISO 100.

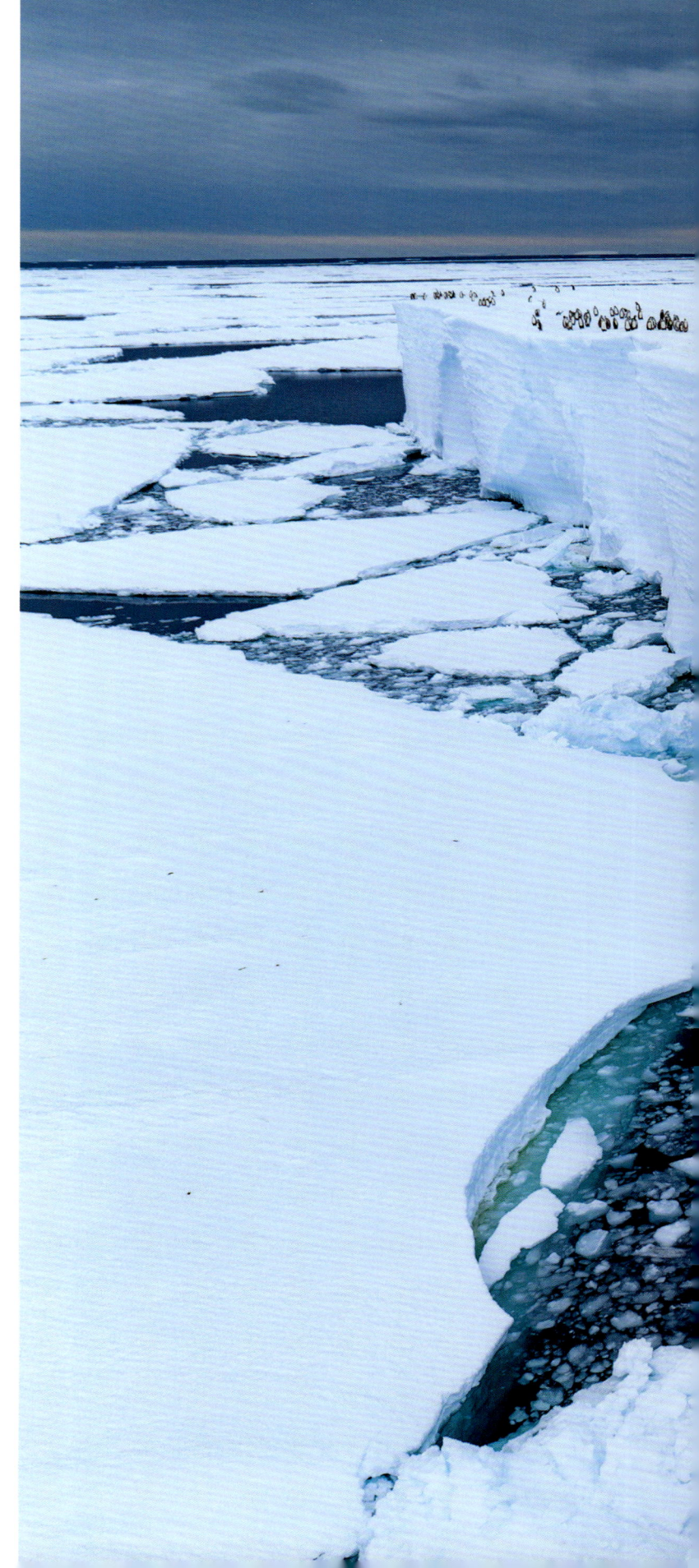

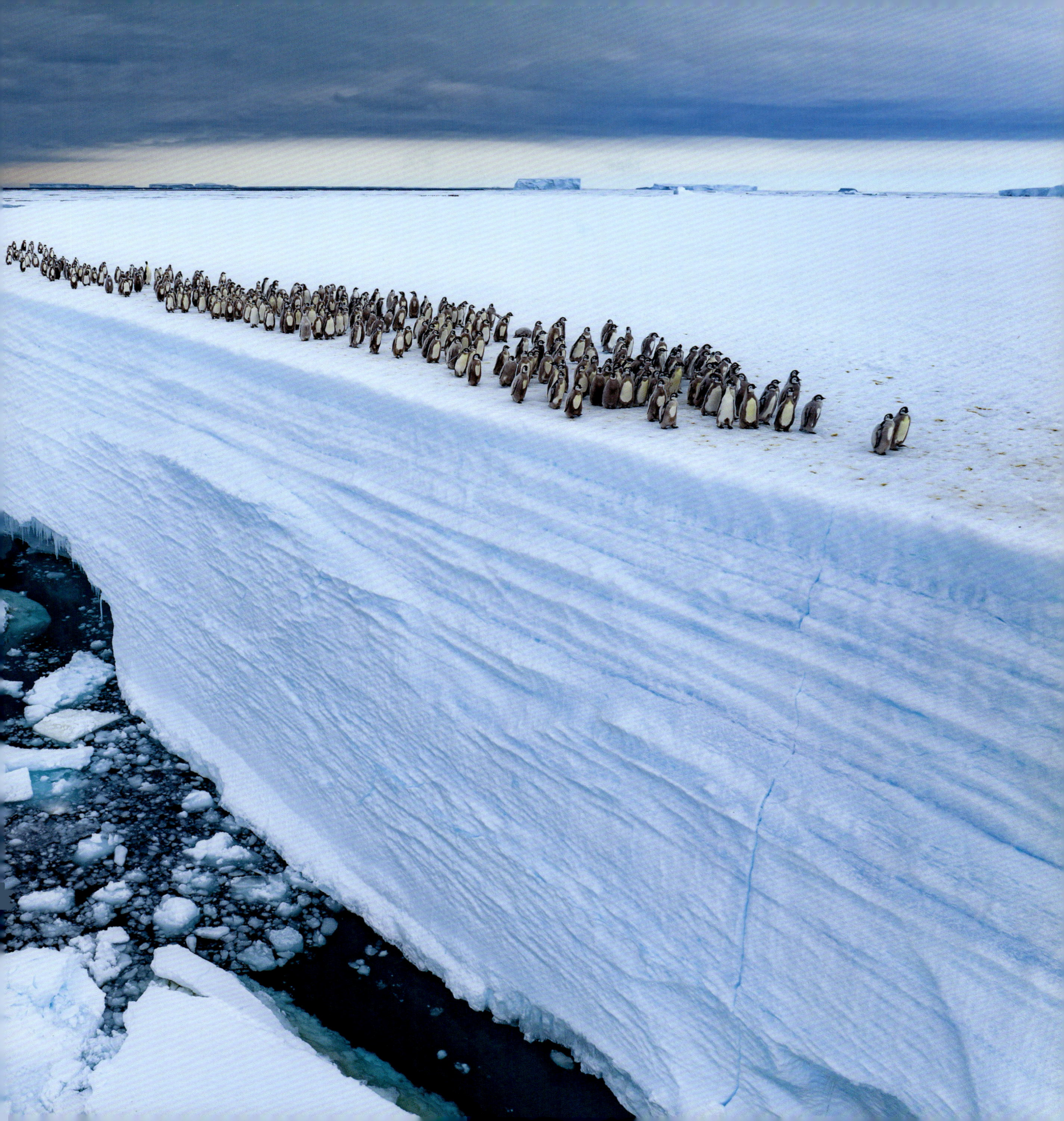

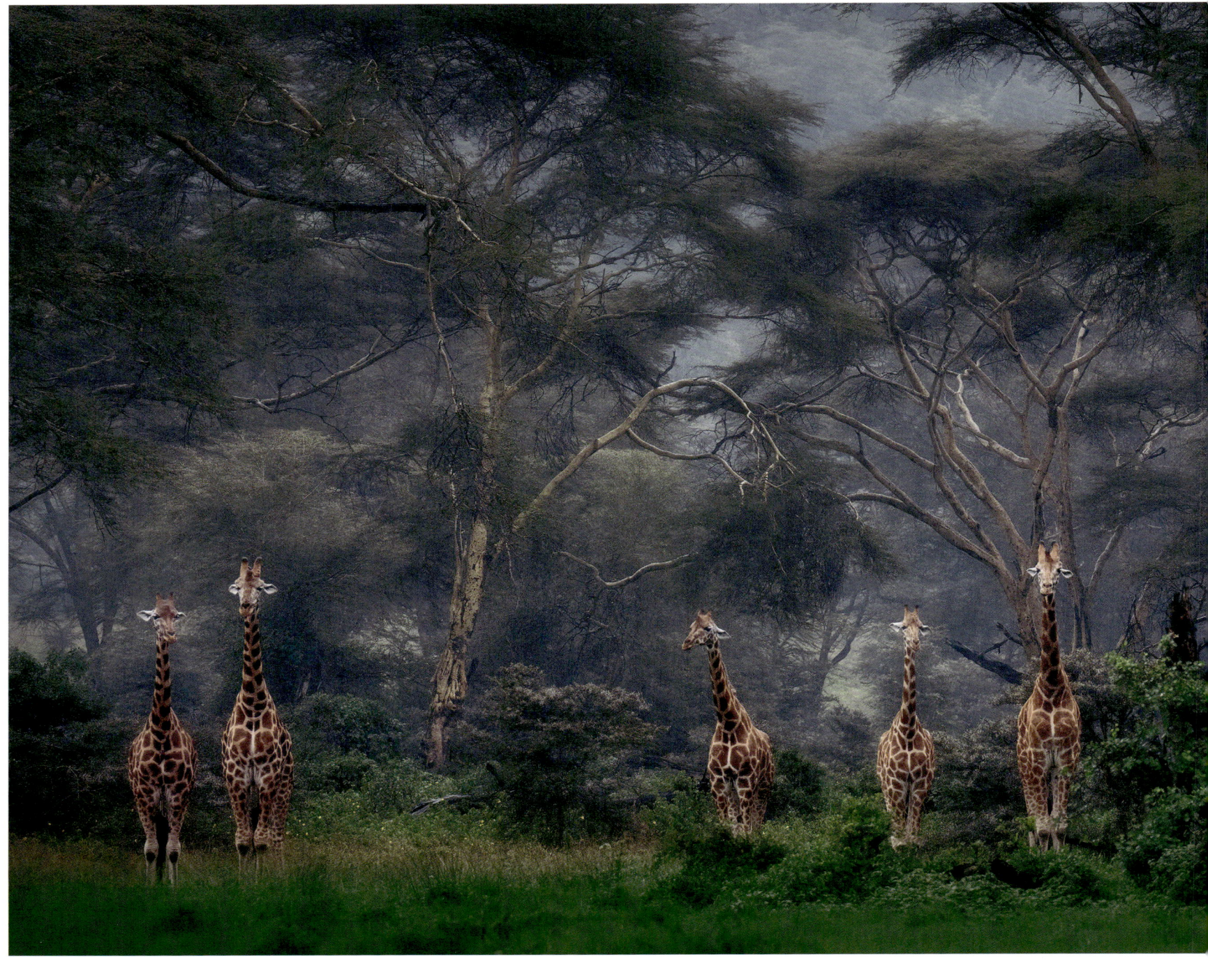

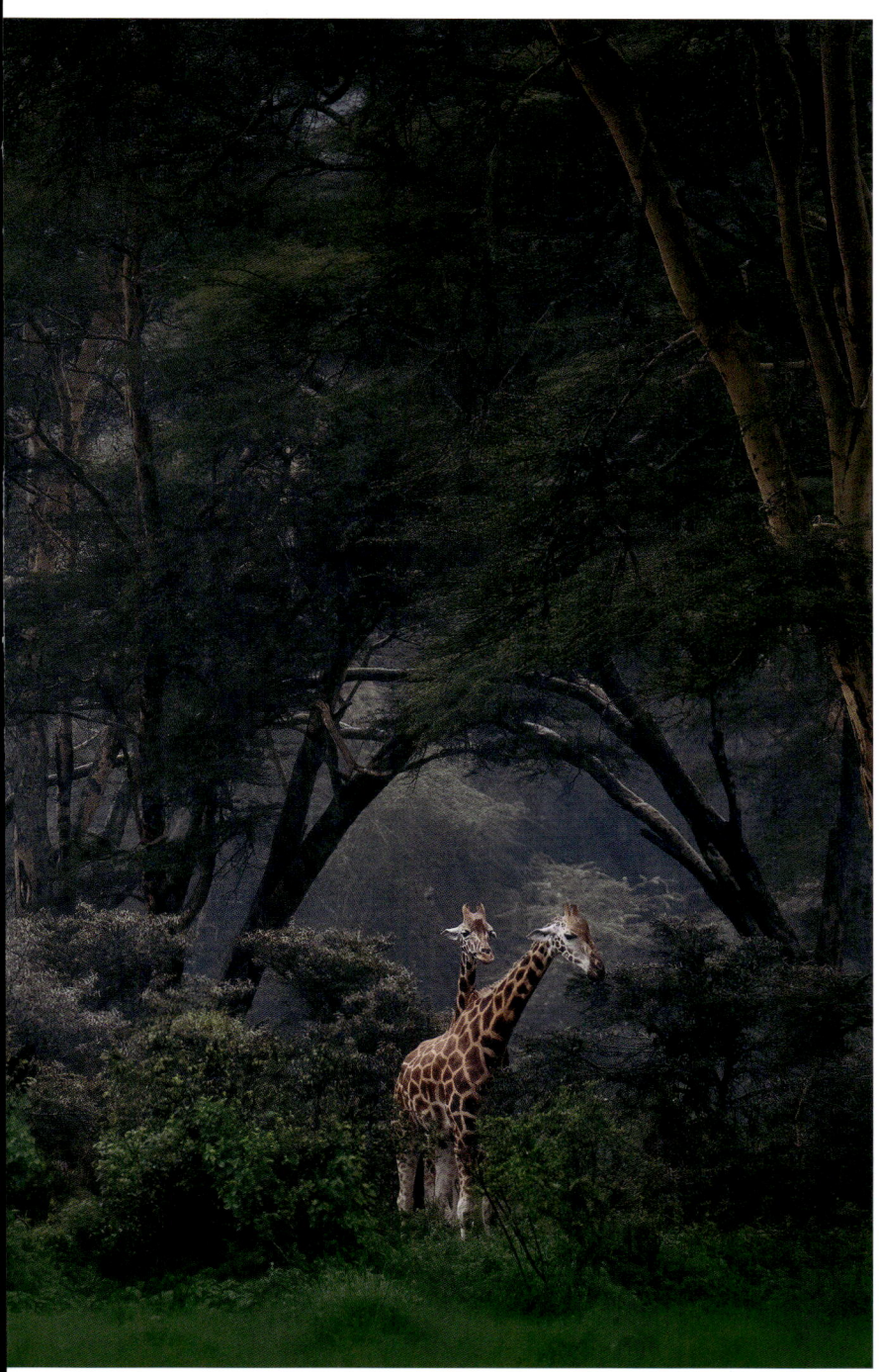

The calm after the storm

Roberto Marchegiani
ITALY

For Roberto, these giraffes emerged from the forest in Lake Nakuru National Park in southwest Kenya at exactly the right moment. A heavy downpour had just turned to much lighter rain, creating a fine mist in the background that lends the photo an ethereal quality. These are Baringo giraffes, a rare subspecies restricted to parts of Kenya, Uganda and South Sudan. The Kenyan population only exists today because some were reintroduced to Lake Nakuru in 1977 after it had been extirpated from the country because of poaching, agricultural expansion and habitat destruction. Today, there are an estimated 65 in the park's nearly 190 square kilometres (73 square miles). Overall numbers in Kenya and Uganda today are estimated at 2,000. Baringo giraffes differ from their close cousins in having five ossicones (or horns) instead of the usual two, and fewer serrated orange-brown patches on their coat, with creamier channels inbetween. Also, Baringo giraffes have no spots on the lower part of their legs, giving the impression they are wearing white socks.

Sony α7R III + 70–200mm f2.8 lens; 1/400 at f/5.6; 1SO 1600.

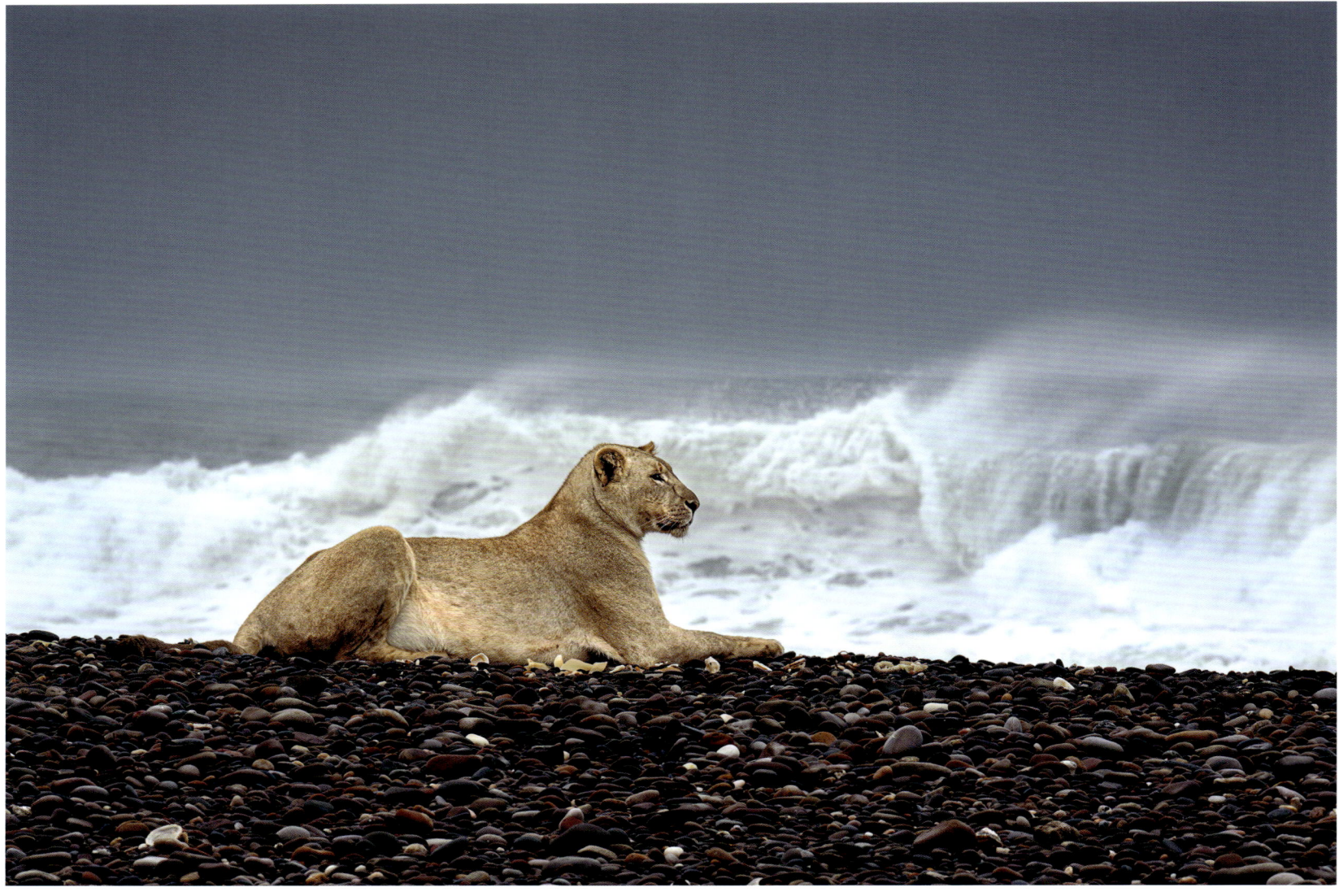

Ocean lion

Griet Van Malderen

BELGIUM

Sitting on a stony shore with the wind whipping the waves into huge rollers, this female lion is one of only six currently known to prey on seals on Namibia's Skeleton Coast. She is guarding a Cape fur seal carcass (out of sight) found during the night, and is one of an estimated 80 lions that live in this extreme environment, where the Namib Desert meets the Atlantic Ocean. In the 1980s, these lions almost died out, victims of persecution by farmers, but they began returning to the area in the early 2000s. When a drought in 2015 wiped out huge numbers of zebras, springboks and ostriches, the big cats began targeting coastal prey, mostly marine birds. Three years later, scientists working for the Desert Lion Conservation Trust spotted lionesses hunting fur seals, a behaviour that hadn't been observed in four decades.

Fujifilm GFX100 II + 500mm f5.6 lens; 1/320 at f26 (–1.33 e/v); ISO 500.

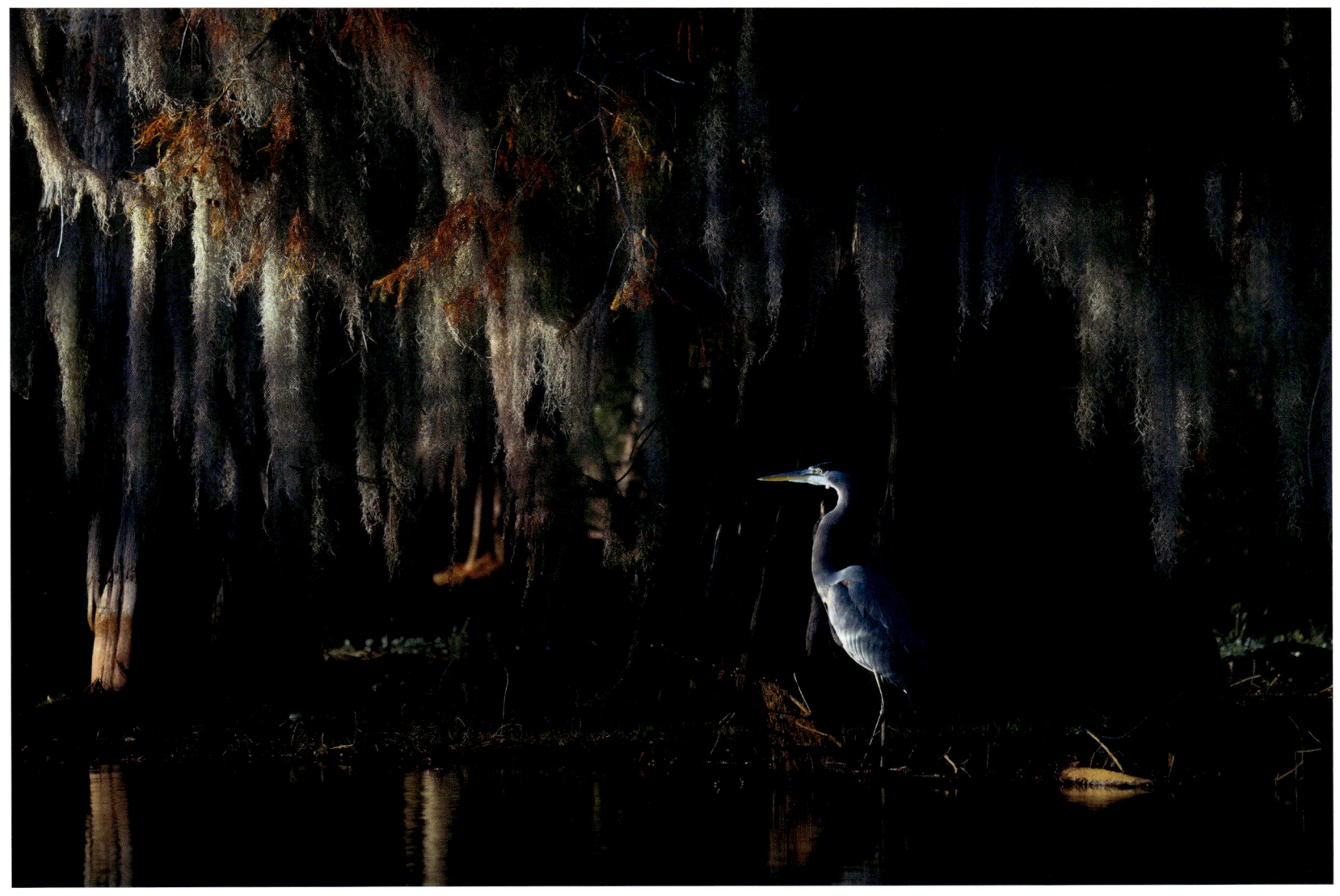

Shadowlands

Roberto Marchegiani

ITALY

A great blue heron stands perfectly still in the shadows while hunting for fish and other prey along the edge of Lake Martin in Louisiana, USA. Roberto was aboard a small boat, which enabled him to navigate the narrow channels and lake edges amongst the cypress trees in one of Louisiana's most picturesque wetlands. In his photo, the low sun illuminates the statuesque heron and luxuriant Spanish moss hanging from the cypress branches on the edge of the swamp. Lurking in these waters are alligators, great white egrets, roseate spoonbills and other waders. As well as providing vital wildlife habitat, Lake Martin performs other ecological functions such as slowing down and filter-cleaning the waters entering the Gulf of Mexico, thereby helping oysters and other aquatic species to flourish downstream.

Sony α1 + 200–600mm f5.6–6.3 lens at 284mm; 1/640 at f6.3; ISO 800.

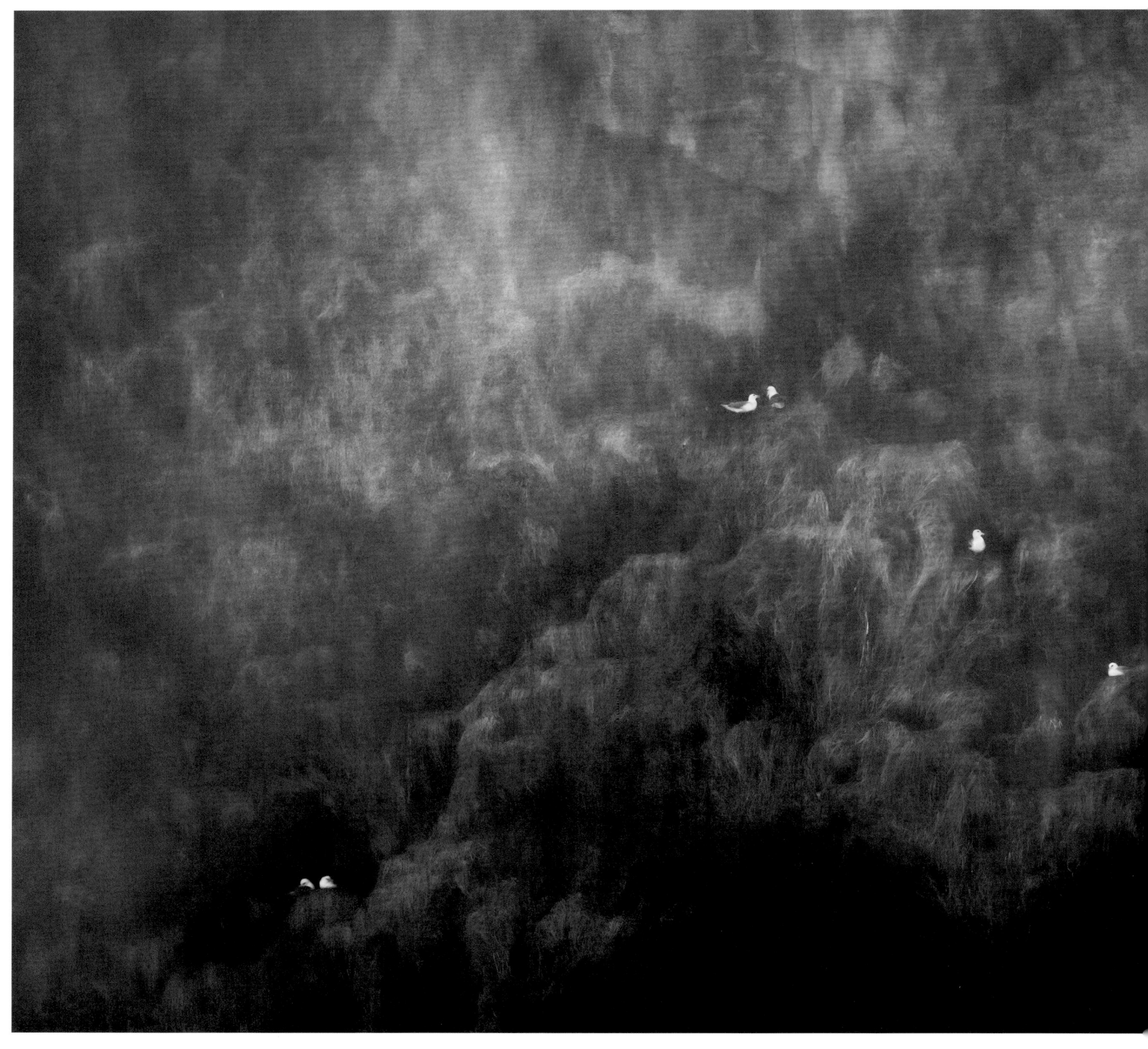

Legends of the falls

Stefan Gerrits
FINLAND

According to Nordic legend, there lies a Viking hoard of gold beneath the falls of Skógafoss in southern Iceland. More easily found is the natural treasure of northern fulmars, which fly across the 60-metre (197-feet) high waterfall to nest in the nearby cliffs. On the day Stefan visited, a strong, blustery wind created a constant veil of spray that hid the birds from view, while also covering his camera lens with fine water drops. Eventually, enough gaps appeared in the misty curtain to allow him to capture this scene. Sometimes described as Europe's mini-albatrosses, fulmars are widespread across northern latitudes around the world, with a global population estimated at 20 million individuals. They typically breed on cliffs and rock faces, and sometimes on houses along the seafront of towns. When not breeding, they lead largely solitary lives – like albatrosses – on the open ocean, feeding on sand eels, squid, crustaceans and discarded fish from commercial boats.

Canon EOS R5 + 500mm f4 lens; 1/2500 at f4.5 (-4/3 e/v); ISO 250.

Wetlands: The Bigger Picture

Vanishing pond

Sebastian Frölich

GERMANY

Gas bubbles, probably of carbon dioxide and methane, rise slowly through algae in a shallow pond in the Platzertal, one of the last remaining, intact high peat bogs in the Austrian Alps. Only the tiny springtail – estimated by Sebastian to be just 1 millimetre ($\frac{1}{25}$ inch) long – that ran across the algae gives this image a sense of scale. That's it on the right-hand side of the picture. Springtails are commonly found in moist environments in very large numbers and possess an appendage, called a furcula, that propels them upwards and forwards like a spring to escape from predators. But it is facing a far greater threat: the prospect of a hydropower storage facility that will turn most of this high valley ecosystem into a vast reservoir, thereby disturbing and releasing much of the carbon stored in the bogs. According to WWF, Austria has lost 90 per cent of its peat bogs, and only 10 per cent of what remains is in good condition. The company behind the project says the additional storage capacity at Platzertal will help Europe meet its energy targets. Sebastian was in the Platzertal to record the landscape and wildlife affected by the proposed development.

Nikon Z7 + 105mm f2.8 lens; 1/800 at f9 (–1.67 e/v); ISO 400.

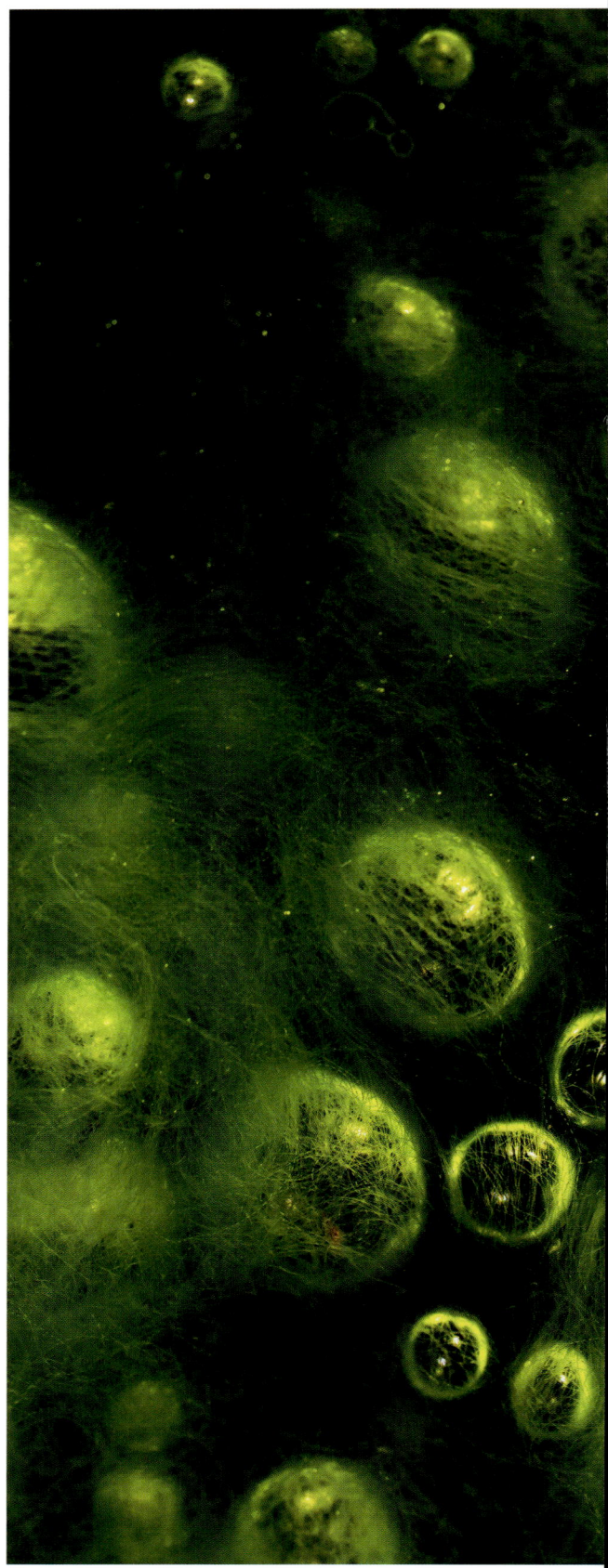

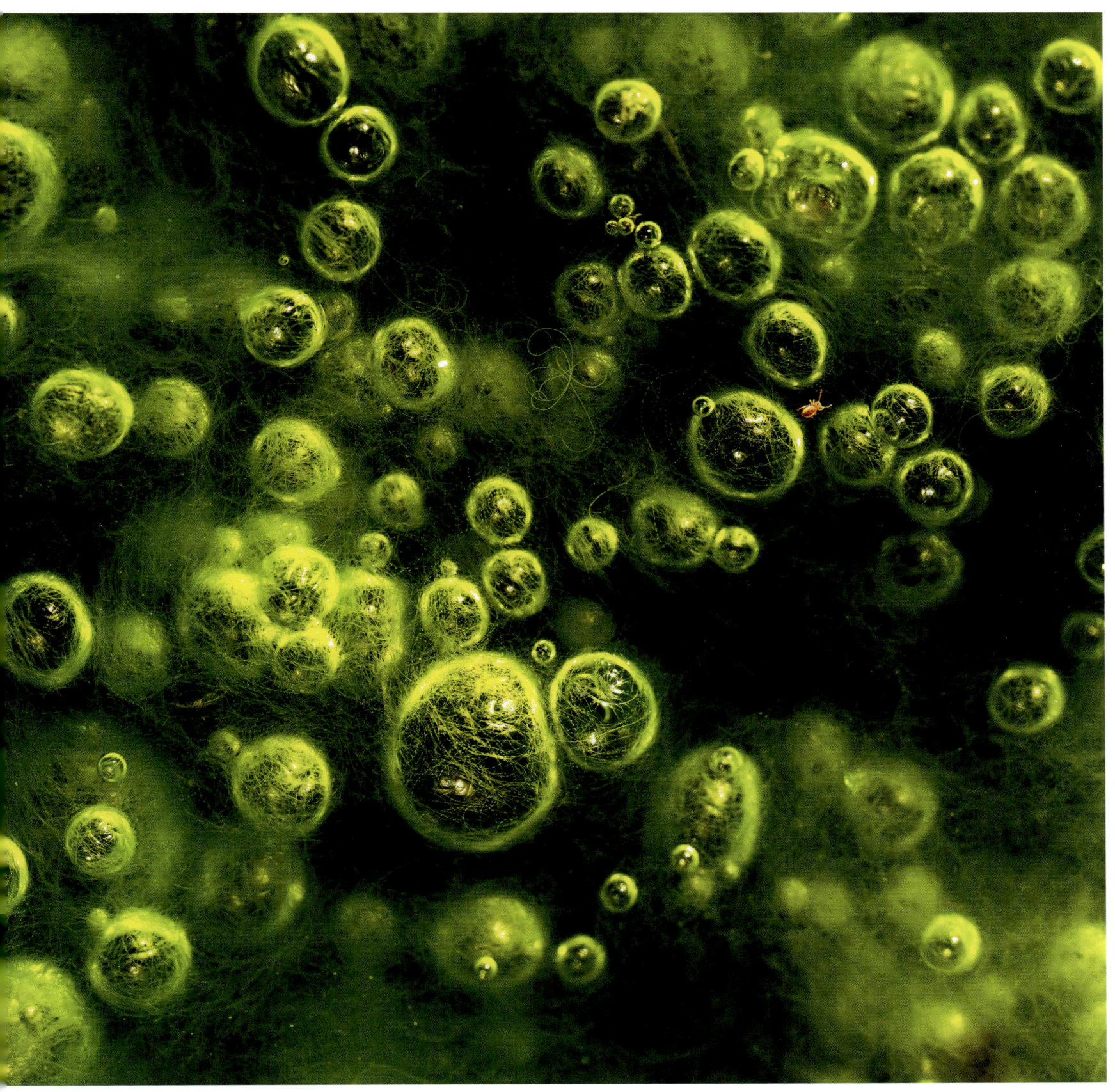

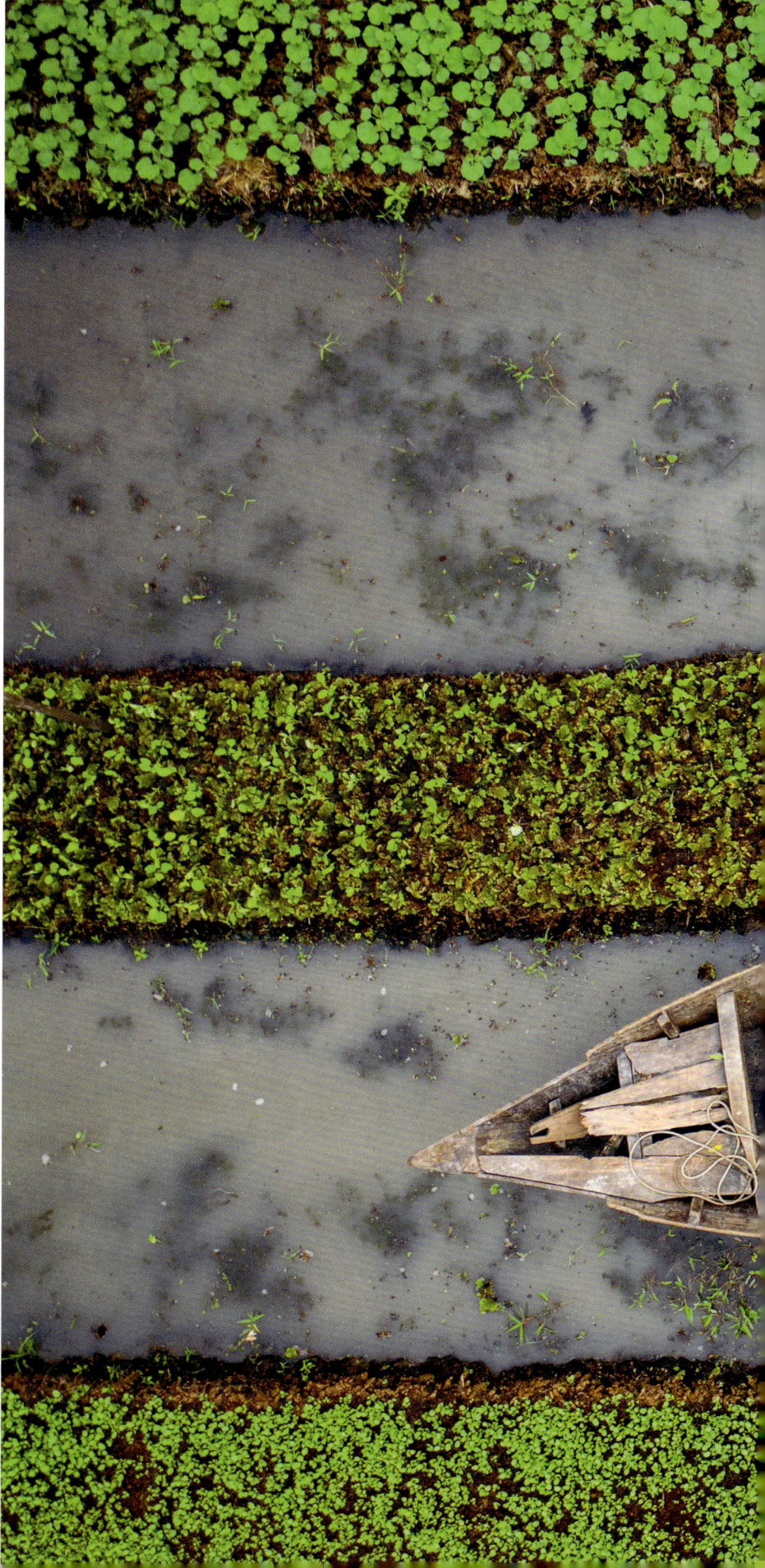

Floating food farms

Azim Khan Ronnie

BANGLADESH/FRANCE

Floating gardens in southern Bangladesh are an innovative way for farmers to grow hundreds of different varieties of vegetables such as beans, pumpkins, aubergines and cauliflowers in areas affected by seasonal flooding. First, a floating raft is made out of water hyacinths and rice paddy stalks, which are packed together and mixed with cow dung and river silt, and left to rot to create a rich, organic bed. Then, as seen here in Azim's photo, vegetable seedlings are planted into this floating bed, which rises and falls with the water levels of a lake or river. These strips of floating vegetable beds can be anywhere from 6 to 60 metres (20 to 197 feet) long. This traditional form of agriculture is being revived to counter the greater occurrences of flooding in the country, caused by rising sea levels. With a predicted income of $140 per 100 square metres (1,076 square feet), floating gardens can help reduce poverty while also providing a more sustainable way to grow food. As well as in Bangladesh, this form of agriculture is also practiced in Kerala, southern India.

DJI Mavic 2 Pro + Hasselblad L1D-20c 28mm f2.8 lens; 1/1600 at f5.6; ISO 100.

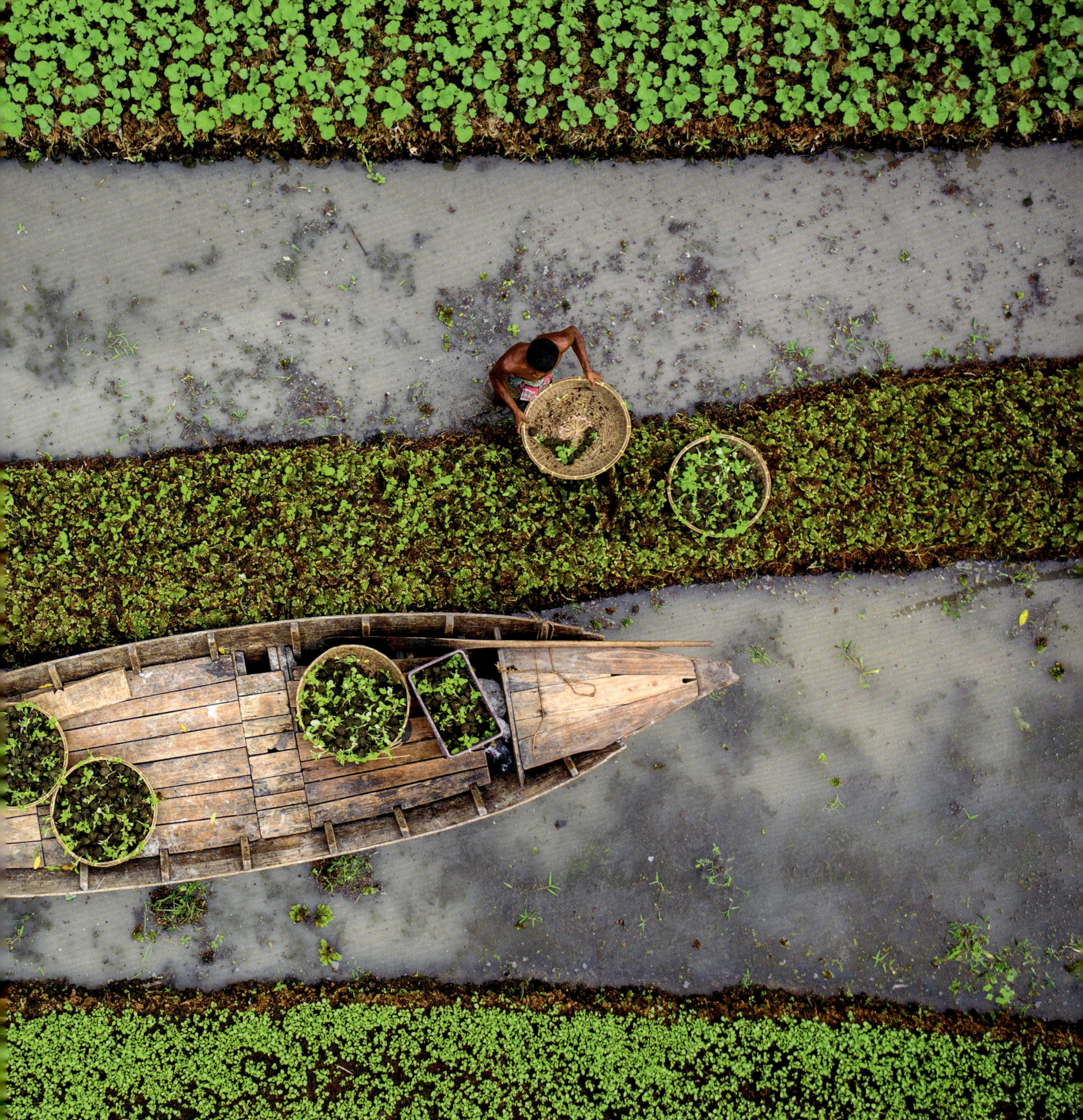

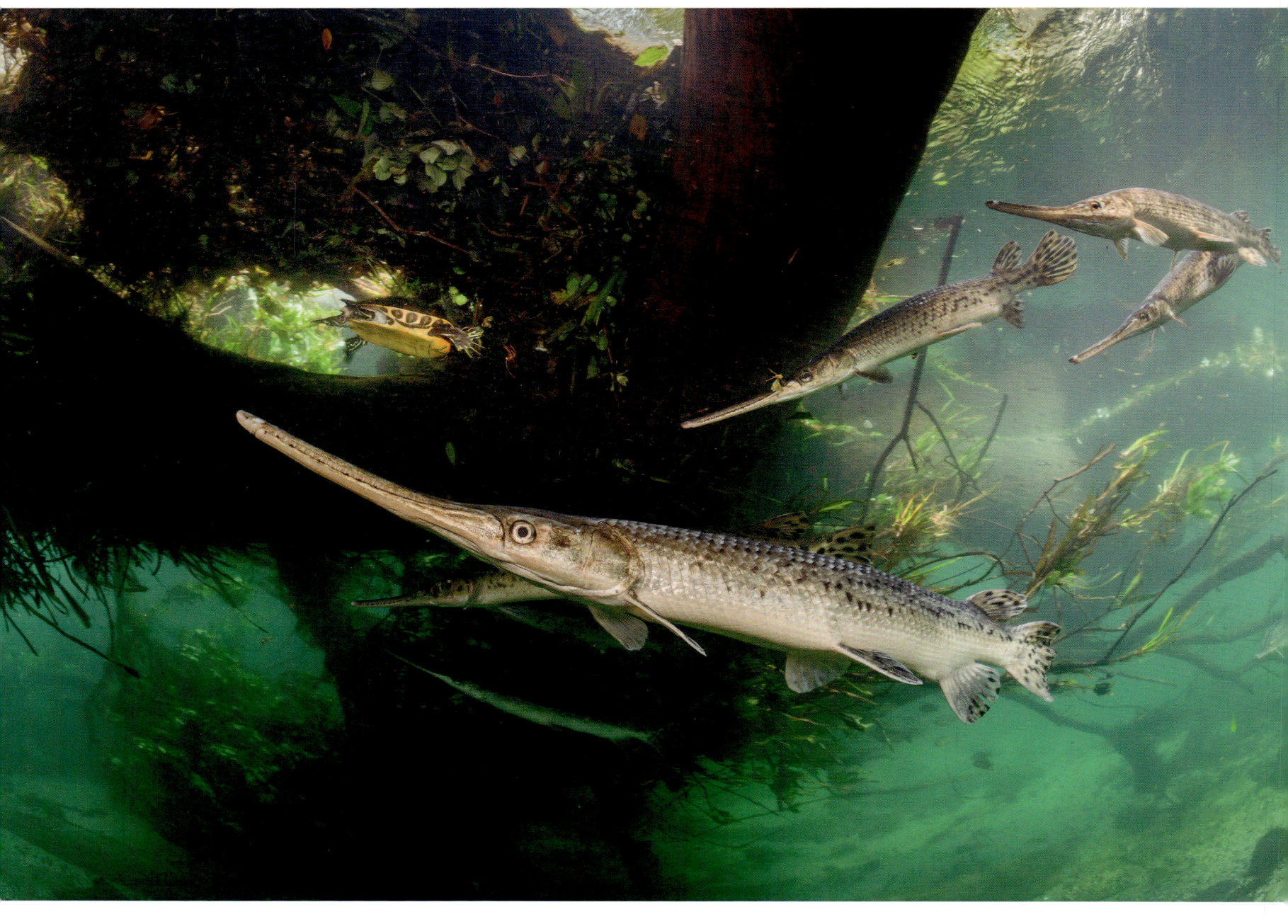

Fragile river of life

Isaac Szabo

USA

In a scene that could have taken place over 70 million years ago, an adult female longnose gar is chased by several males intent upon mating with her. Fossils of this group of primitive-looking, armoured fish date back to the Cretaceous Period. Today, this species can be found from northern Mexico to the North American Great Lakes and St Lawrence River in Canada. Isaac was snorkelling a river in Columbia County, Florida, one of more than 1,000 waterways fed by the southern state's freshwater springs. These rivers are renowned for their clarity and are home to iconic wildlife such as manatees and the river cooter turtle, also seen here. But abstraction for agriculture and human drinking water has reduced the flow of many rivers and springs, while increased levels of nitrogen from fertilizer run-off and discharges of human and animal waste have led to excessive growth of algae that crowds out other aquatic plants. Sustaining the aquifers from which the springs receive their water is important, not just for wildlife, but also for supplying drinking water to nearly half of Florida's population. Longnose gar feed on smaller fish and some invertebrates; their snout is lined with sharp, pointed teeth for easy catching and tearing of prey. When fully grown, they can reach nearly 2 metres (6 ½ feet) in length and have very few natural predators other than humans.

Sony α7R II + Nikonos RS 13mm f2.8 lens; 1/30 at f8; ISO 200; Inon Z-240 strobes.

Clouds of gold

Jassen Todorov

USA

While flying his single-engine Piper Warrior above San Francisco Bay, USA, Jassen photographed the clouds reflecting in salt ponds that cover nearly 5,000 hectares (12,355 acres) of the bay. For centuries, the Ohlone Indigenous Americans collected salt from the naturally occurring tidal pools, but the process was industrialized in the nineteenth century when European settlers filled in and built dykes around the wetlands. At their peak, salt ponds covered about 14,600 hectares (36,000 acres), but the bay lost about 85 per cent of this natural and wildlife-rich habitat as a result of the dykes being built. Since 2003, the South Bay Salt Pond Restoration Project has acquired 6,000 hectares (nearly 15,000 acres) from the multinational food corporation Cargill, which continues to harvest about half a million tons of sea salt annually. Through the careful removal of levees, the project is reintroducing tidal flow and reviving ecosystems where salt-tolerant plants and wildlife, including steelhead trout and American avocets, can once again flourish. Jassen regularly flies over the bay, never tiring of the changing colours in the ponds. On this occasion, he says, 'the light during the golden hour, at sunset was magnificent.'

Nikon D810 + 70–200mm f2.8 lens at 70mm; 1/400 at f2.8; ISO 280.

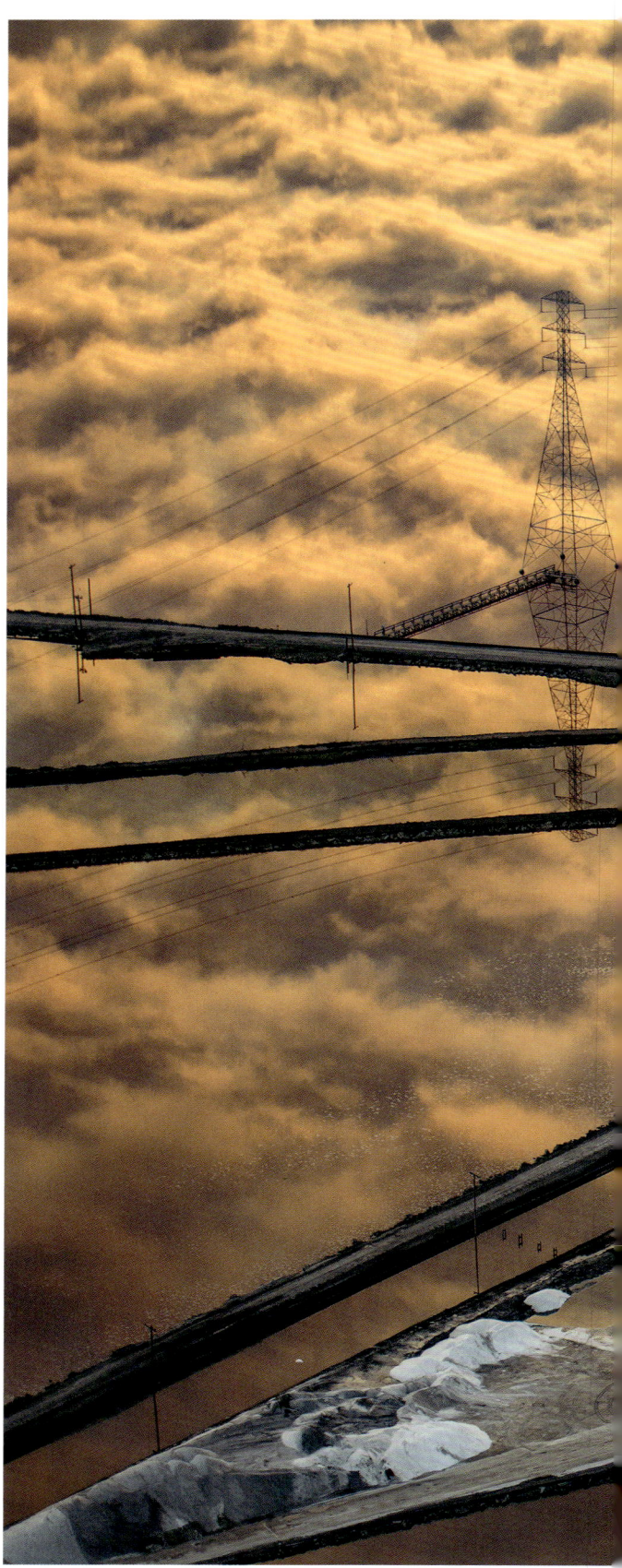

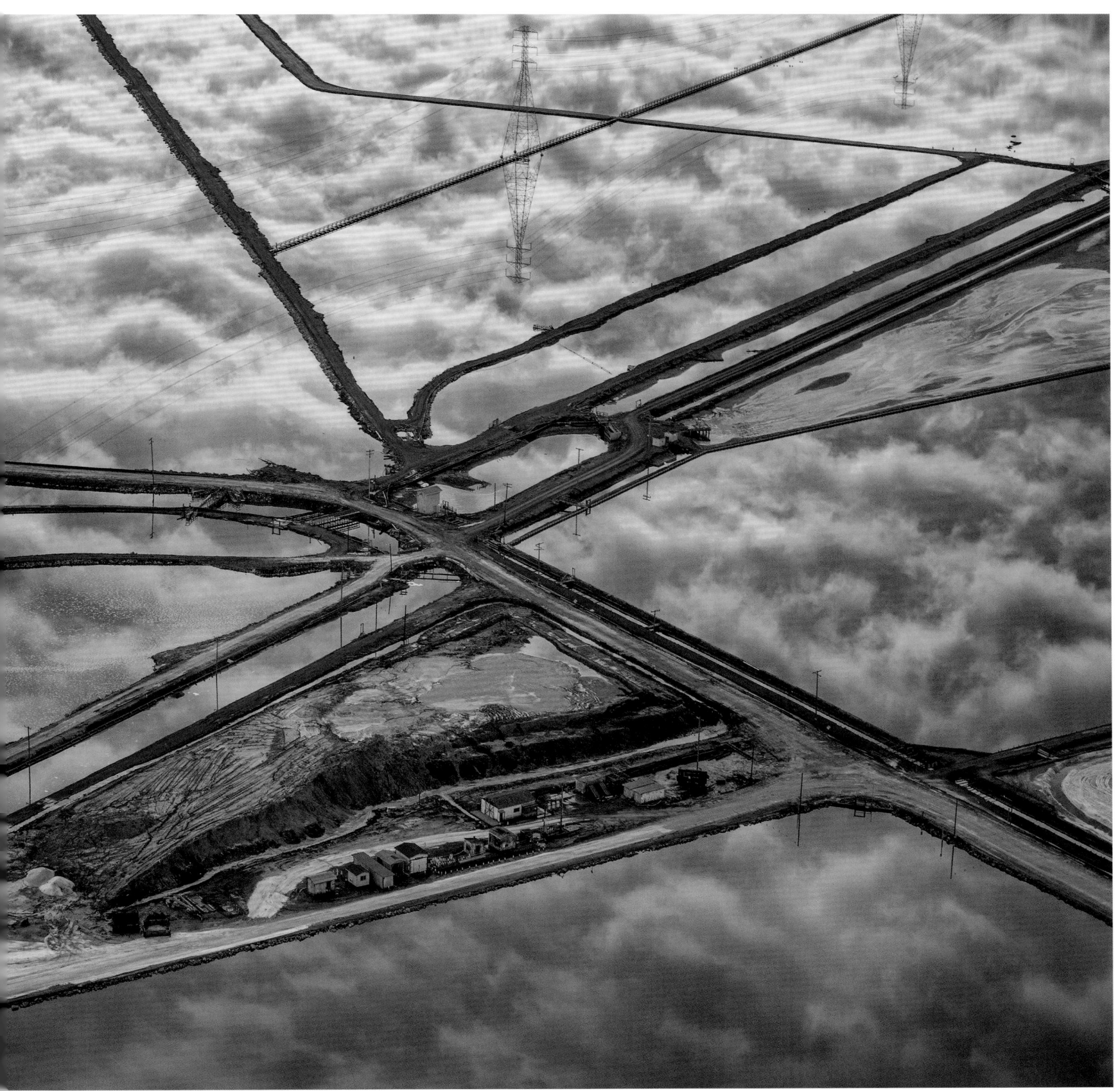

Plants and Fungi

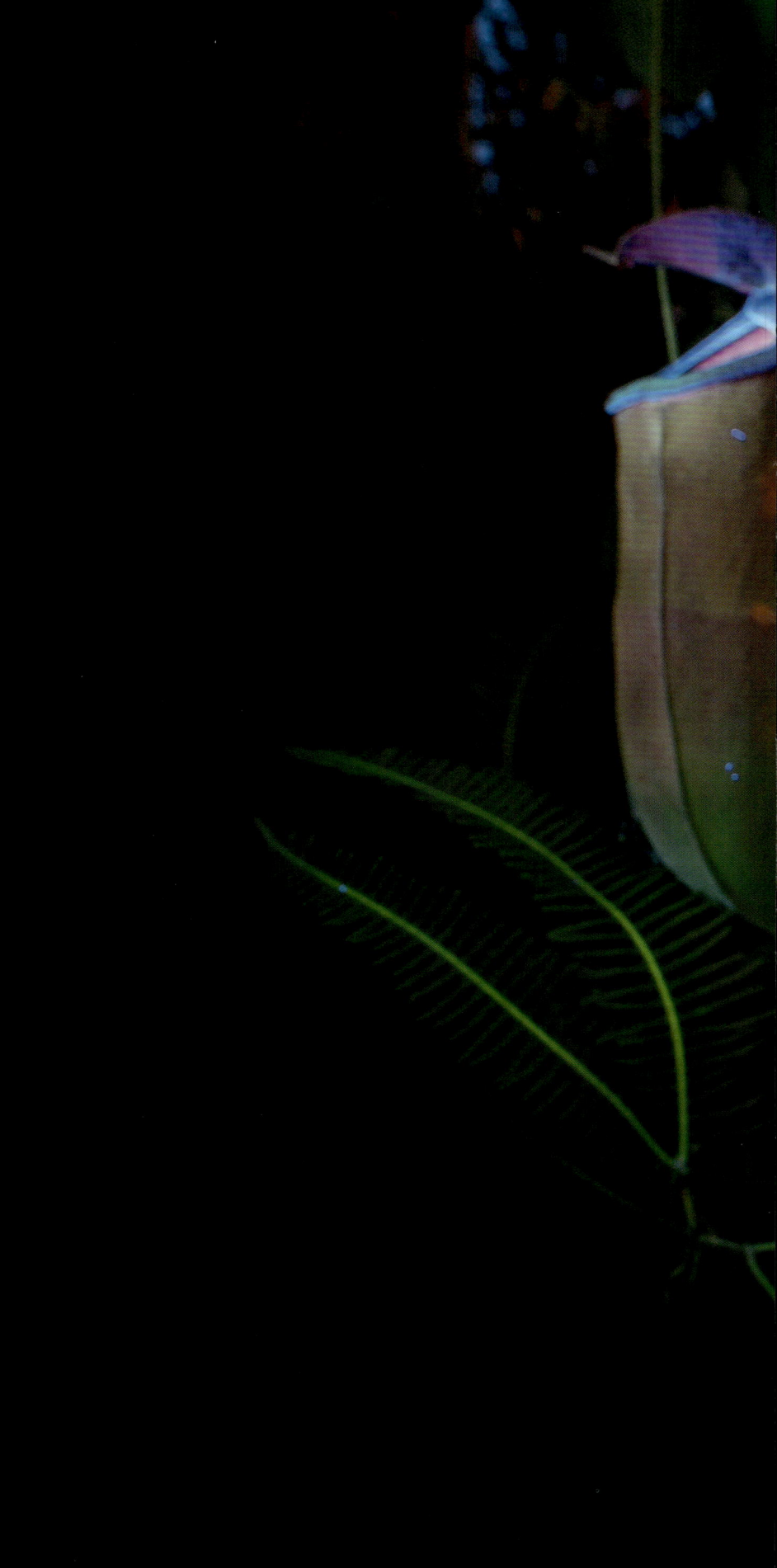

Deadly allure

Chien Lee

MALAYSIA

A pitcher plant is the last thing some insects will ever see. These carnivorous plants use colour, scent and nectar to lure their prey to a floundering death in the pools of digestive juices at the bottom of their bucket-like leaves. Some, including this tropical pitcher plant, a common species in Sarawak, Malaysian Borneo, reflect ultraviolet (UV) light as part of their display, especially around the slippery lip of each trap and the underside of the lid, the very spots where insects are most vulnerable to falling in. However, unlike insects, humans cannot see UV unaided. So, to reveal how a pitcher plant might appear to an insect, Chien utilized a phenomenon called fluorescence, whereby the tissues that reflect UV also absorb some of it and re-emit it at visible blue wavelengths. He accentuated the effect by using a long exposure and a UV torch. It's an image achievable only at night because during the day the colours would be swamped by sunlight. Once the sun set, Chien had a working window of barely five minutes before the ambient light illuminating the backdrop disappeared completely.

Nikon Z9 + Laowa 15mm f4 macro lens; 30 sec at f16; ISO 100; Convoy C8 ultraviolet torch.

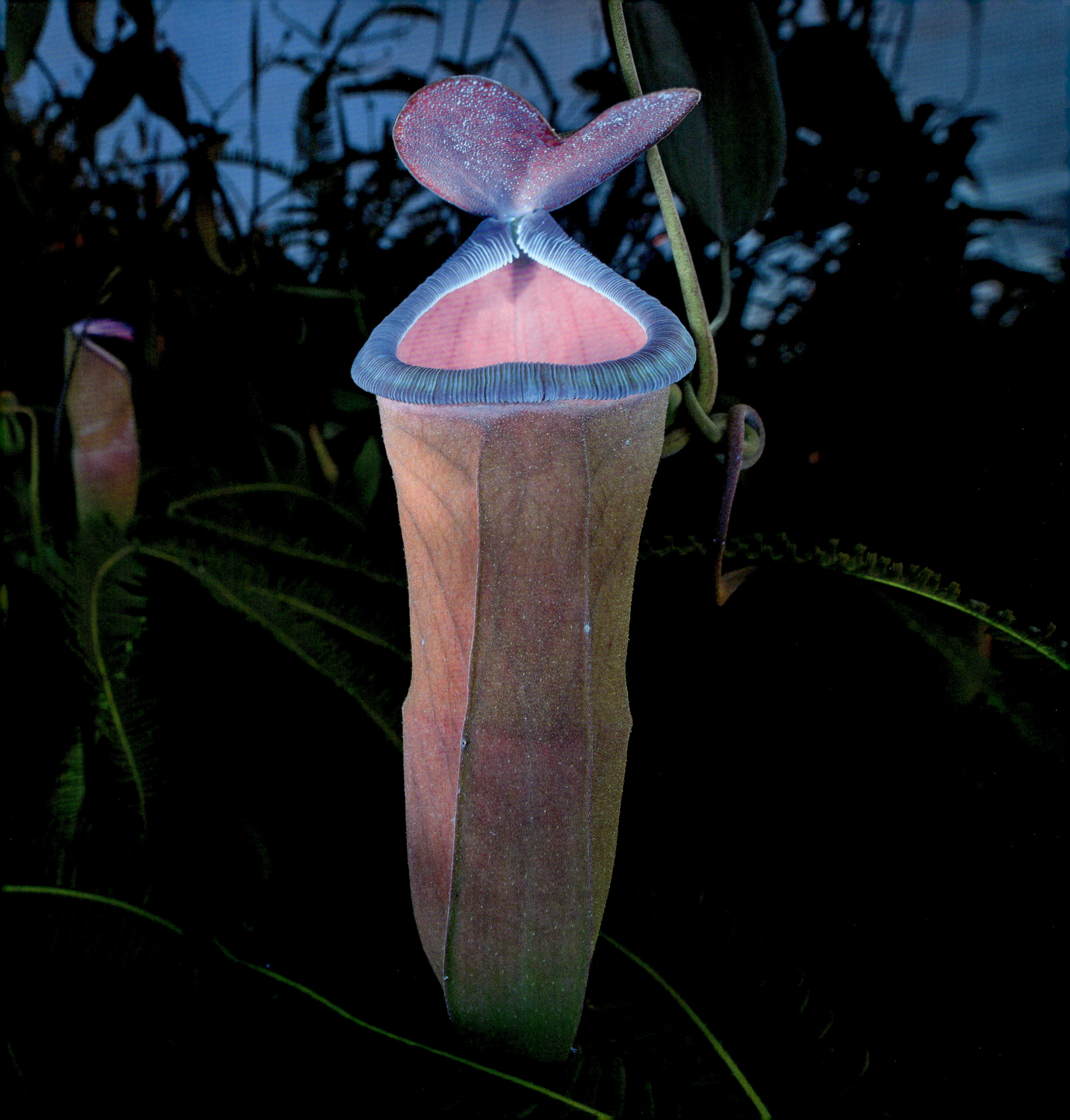

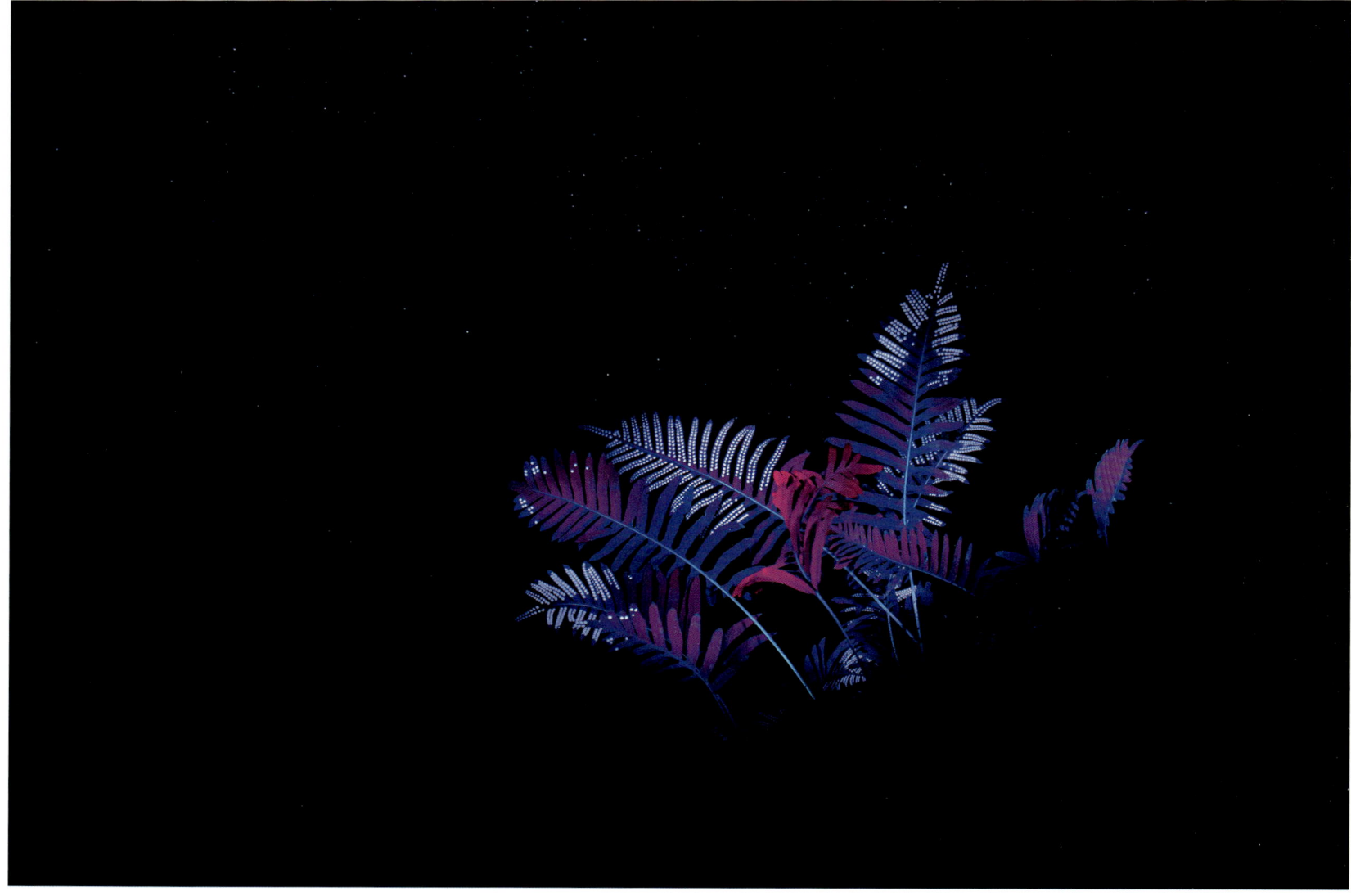

Celestial spores

Juan Cuetos

SPAIN

In recent years, Juan has packed an ultraviolet (UV) torch whenever he goes out at night. Motivated by an urge to find unconventional ways to portray familiar species, he has discovered that the UV torch can reveal frogs, insects, sea anemones, and ferns such as this southern *Polypodium vulgare* in a new light. Juan encountered this native of western Europe and the Mediterranean in a woodland in Cantabria, northern Spain, its tissues reflecting the UV light at wavelengths visible to human eyes: a subtle blend of violets and blues. The spore capsules, or sori, arranged in rows on the underside of the fronds, are part of the fern's reproductive lifecycle and especially reflective to UV light. Indeed, they appear as bright as the stars that fill the night sky – like spores floating off on a breeze.

Nikon D500 + 10mm f2.8 lens; 21 sec at f5.6; ISO 400; ultraviolet torch; remote trigger; tripod.

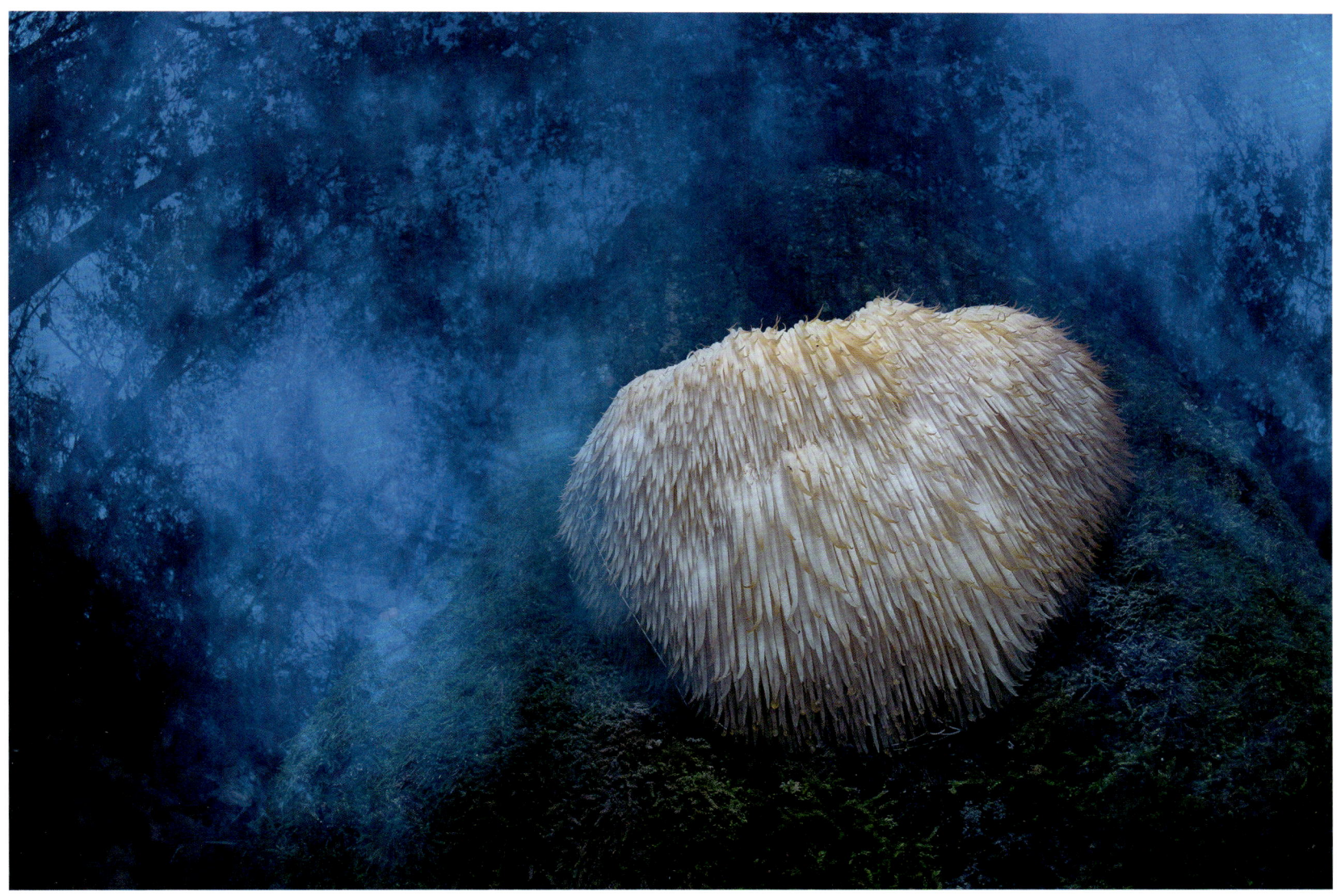

Strange beauty

Imre Potyó

HUNGARY

The bearded hedgehog fungus is hard to miss but rarely seen. Deforestation and the selective removal of the older trees on which it feeds have contributed to its scarcity in Europe. Also known as the lion's mane fungus, it is more common in North America and East Asia. In Japan, where it is called yamabushitake, it is cultivated for culinary use and hailed for its health benefits. Imre found this mighty specimen, 30 centimetres (12 inches) in diameter, cascading down the trunk of a turkey oak in the Börzsöny Mountains of northern Hungary. During a 30-second exposure, just before nightfall, Imre fired the flash manually several times to illuminate the mushroom from different angles, before shaking the camera slightly to blur the woodland canopy.

Nikon D7200 + 10.5mm f2.8 fisheye lens; 30 sec at f16; ISO 250; Nikon SB-800 Speedlight flash + diffuser; tripod.

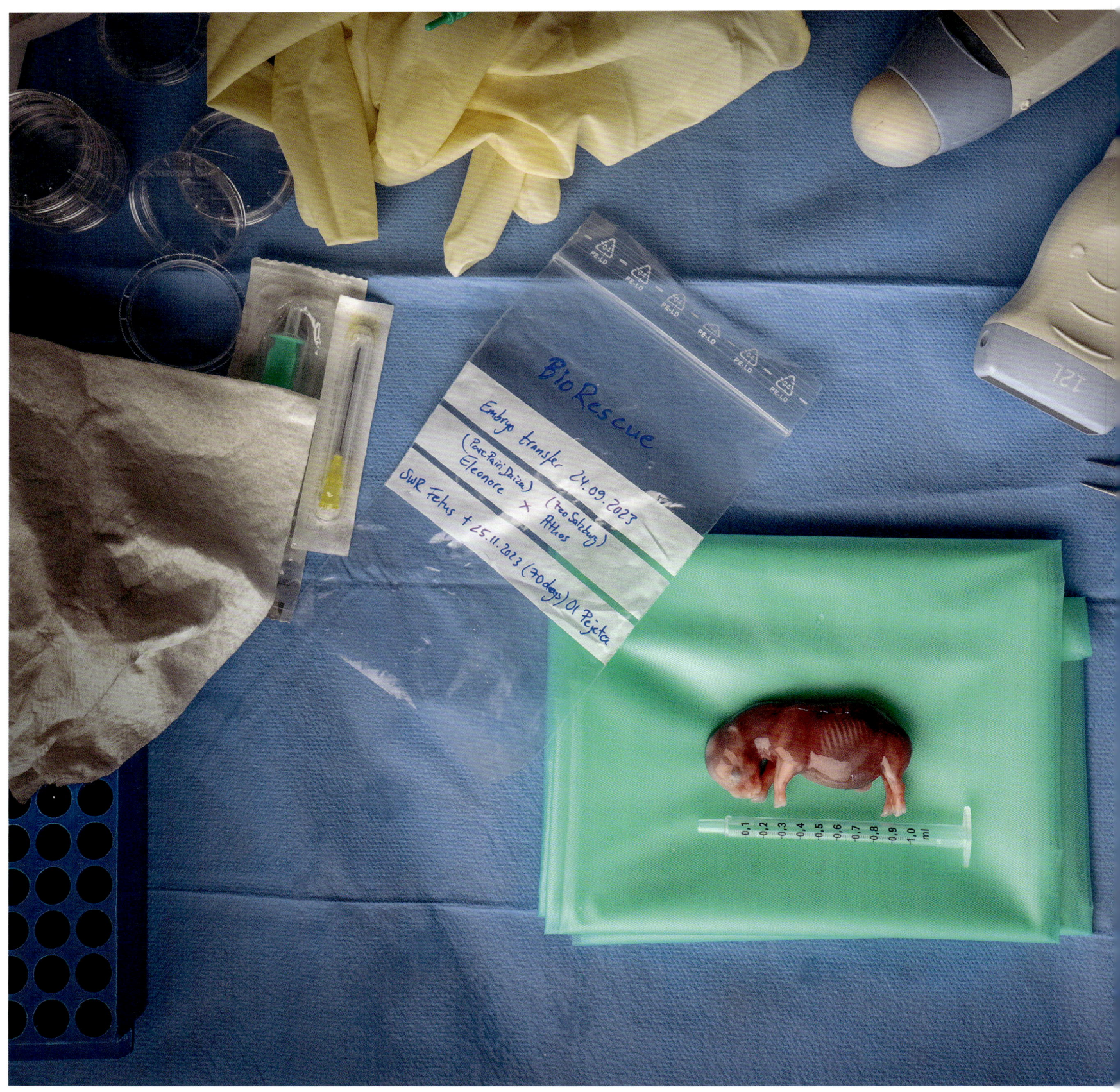

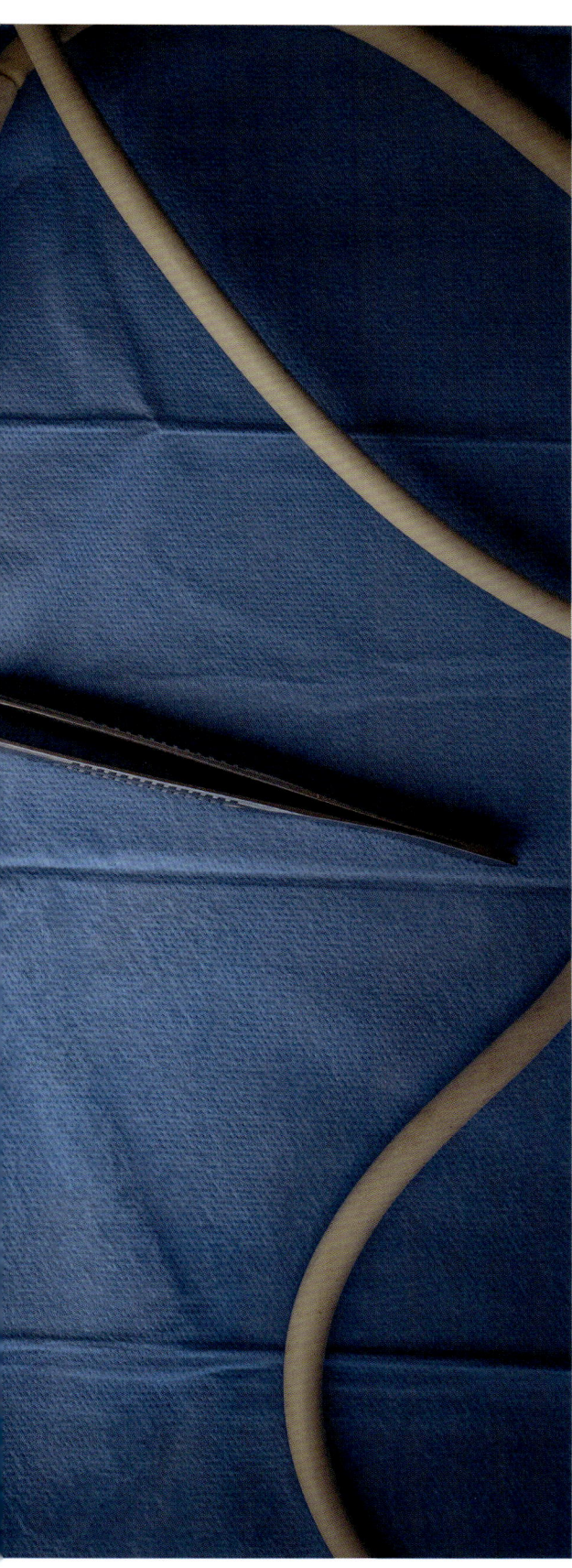

Photojournalism

How to save a species

Jon A. Juárez

SPAIN

Out of loss there remains hope. This tiny rhino foetus, which was unable to survive because of an infection, might yet prove instrumental in scientists' efforts to save the northern white rhino from extinction. Just 6.4 centimetres (2 ½ inches) long, this southern white rhino foetus is the first evidence that embryos of any rhino species created through in-vitro fertilization (IVF), can be transferred into a surrogate mother. With an estimated 17,000 individuals, the southern white rhino remains the most populous of the world's five rhino species. However, in 2015 only three northern white rhinos (a subspecies) remained: one male and two females. That year, a group of scientists led by Professor Thomas Hildebrandt, launched a plan to save them using assisted reproductive technologies. The last male, Sudan, died in 2018. A year later, the team began extracting egg cells from the last females, Najin and Fatu. They have since created over 30 frozen embryos using semen previously taken from two other late male northern white rhinos. Due to the high risks of the procedure, the team made their first IVF transfer using southern white rhinos. This foetus was the result of that successful transfer into a surrogate mother: both parents (sperm and oocyte) and surrogate mother were southern white rhinos. However, both mother and baby died due to a bacterial infection unrelated to the embryo-transfer procedure. Despite this setback, the team – now called BioRescue Project – is taking the next crucial steps towards their goal of transferring the first northern white rhino embryo.

Nikon Z9 + 24–120mm f4 lens at 24mm; 1/400 at 7.1; ISO 1600; LED light panel.

Orphan of the road

Fernando Faciole

BRAZIL

An orphaned giant anteater pup follows its carer after an evening feed in a rehabilitation centre in Belo Horizonte, Brazil. Its mother was hit and killed by a vehicle, a fate that befalls hundreds of anteaters every year, due in part to their poor eyesight. In one three-year study, 761 dead anteaters were found along 2,000 kilometres (1,240 miles) of roads in the state of Mato Grosso do Sul. Fernando visited different rehabilitation centres in search of giant anteater pups to shed light on the impact of road collisions. Replicating an anteater's strictly insectivorous diet in rehabilitation is challenging, and only half the individuals taken into care will be returned to the wild, with many either dying in captivity or simply not demonstrating sufficient independence to be released. The Anteaters and Highways project of the Wild Animal Conservation Institute (ICAS) is developing mitigation strategies to reduce anteater deaths on Brazil's roads. Studies suggest that fencing collision hotspot areas that divert wildlife to underpasses might be the best solution, as well as engaging with truck drivers and local communities about how to reduce the risk of animal collisions. The International Union for Conservation of Nature says habitat loss and fragmentation, road kills and wildfires are contributing to declining giant anteater numbers throughout Central and South America.

Nikon D850 + 24–70mm f/2.8 lens at 28mm; 0.8 sec at f/22; ISO 31; Nikon Speedlight flash with Greica CT-16 transmitter/receiver.

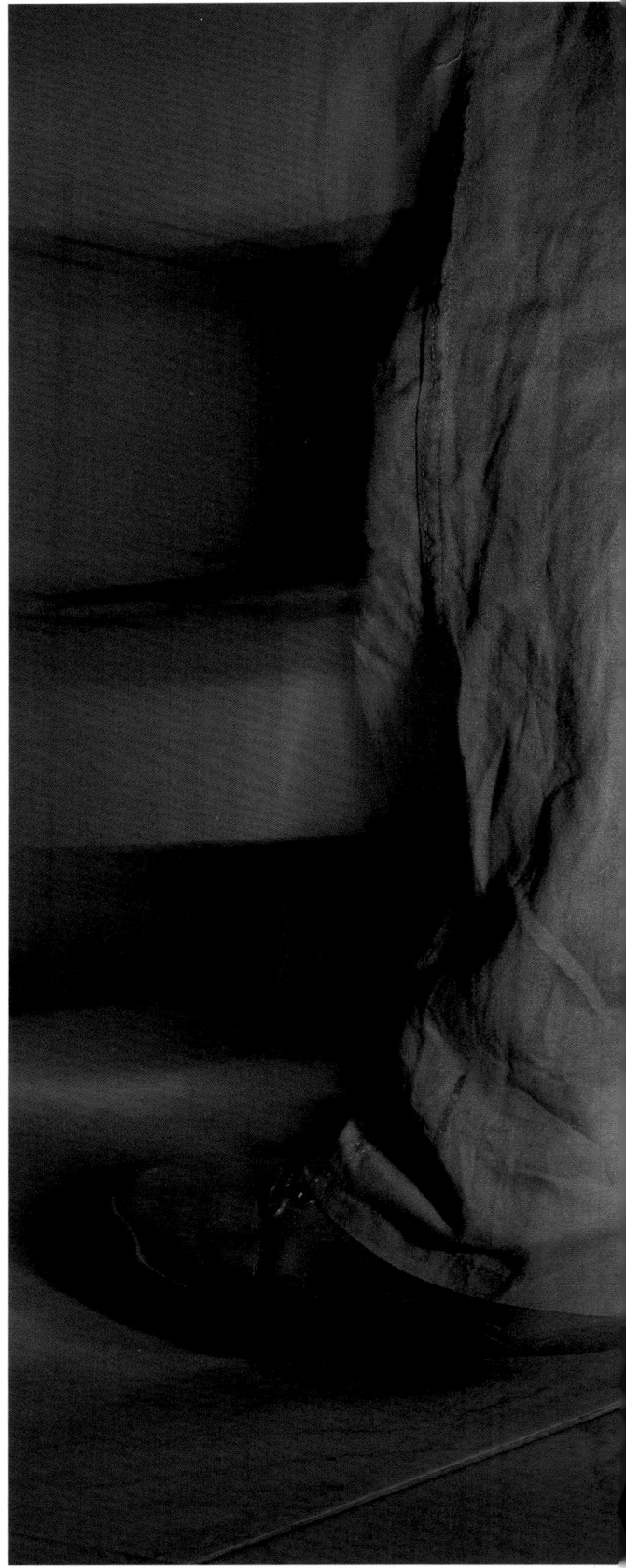

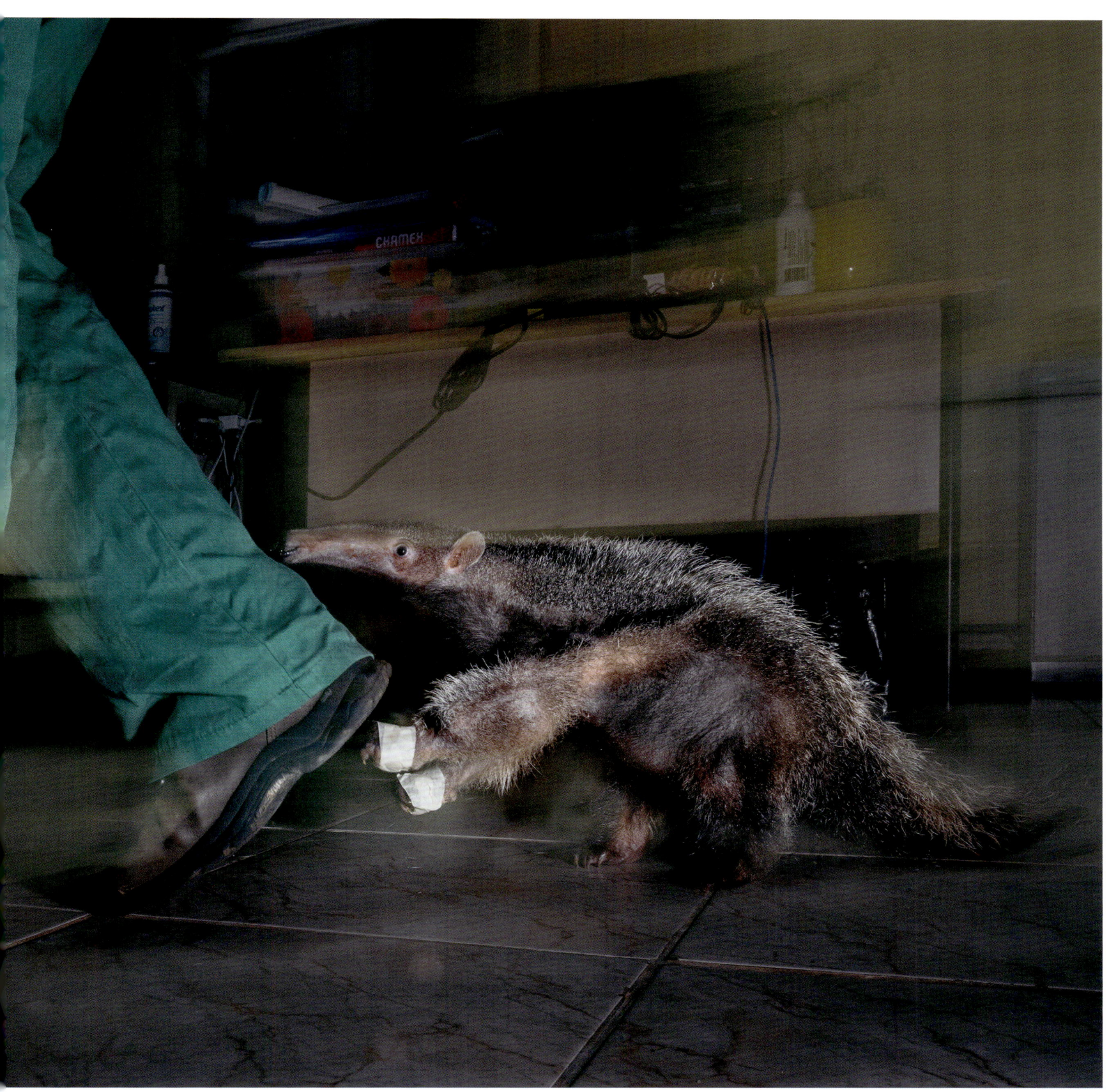

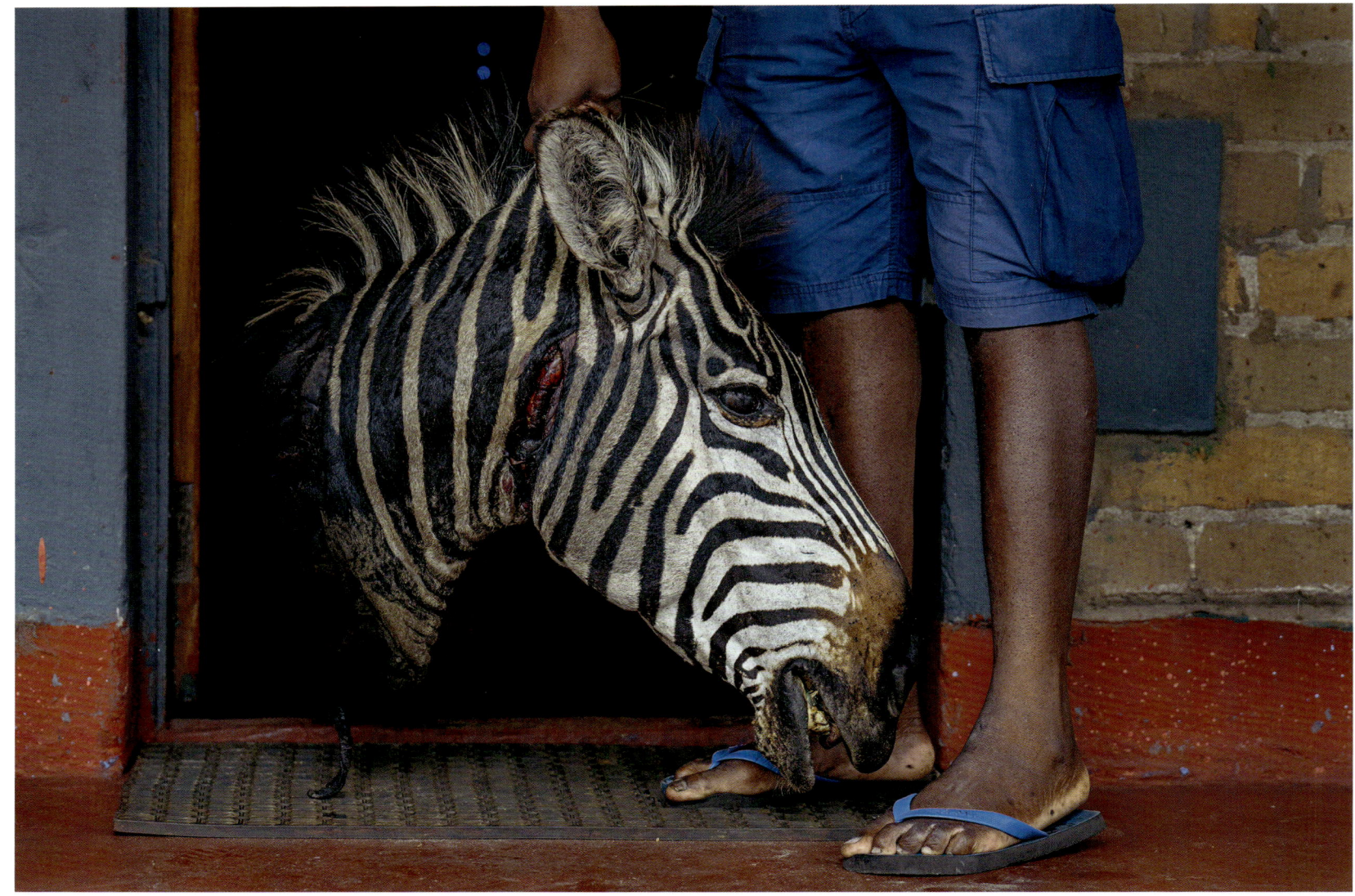

Hard evidence

Marcus Westberg

SWEDEN/PORTUGAL

The trade in elephant ivory and rhino horn generates much of the publicity about illegal wildlife poaching, but this head of a plains zebra is a reminder that demand for wild-caught meat is another reason for the deaths of many wild animals. Marcus was on assignment in Zambia when the zebra, which had been caught in a snare and killed inside a protected area, was brought into a small town – along with the suspected poachers – and presented to the magistrate as evidence. Crop failures caused by two years of severe drought, and the resulting food shortage, led to a sharp increase in the hunting of wild animals. According to Wildlife Crime Prevention Zambia, the popularity of wild-caught meat is driven also by wealthy, urban diners for its perceived health benefits and luxury status. An estimated 1,140 tons of wild animals are consumed in Zambia's capital city, Lusaka, each year.

Sony α1 + 70–200mm f2.8 lens at 88mm; 1/125 at f4.5; ISO 250.

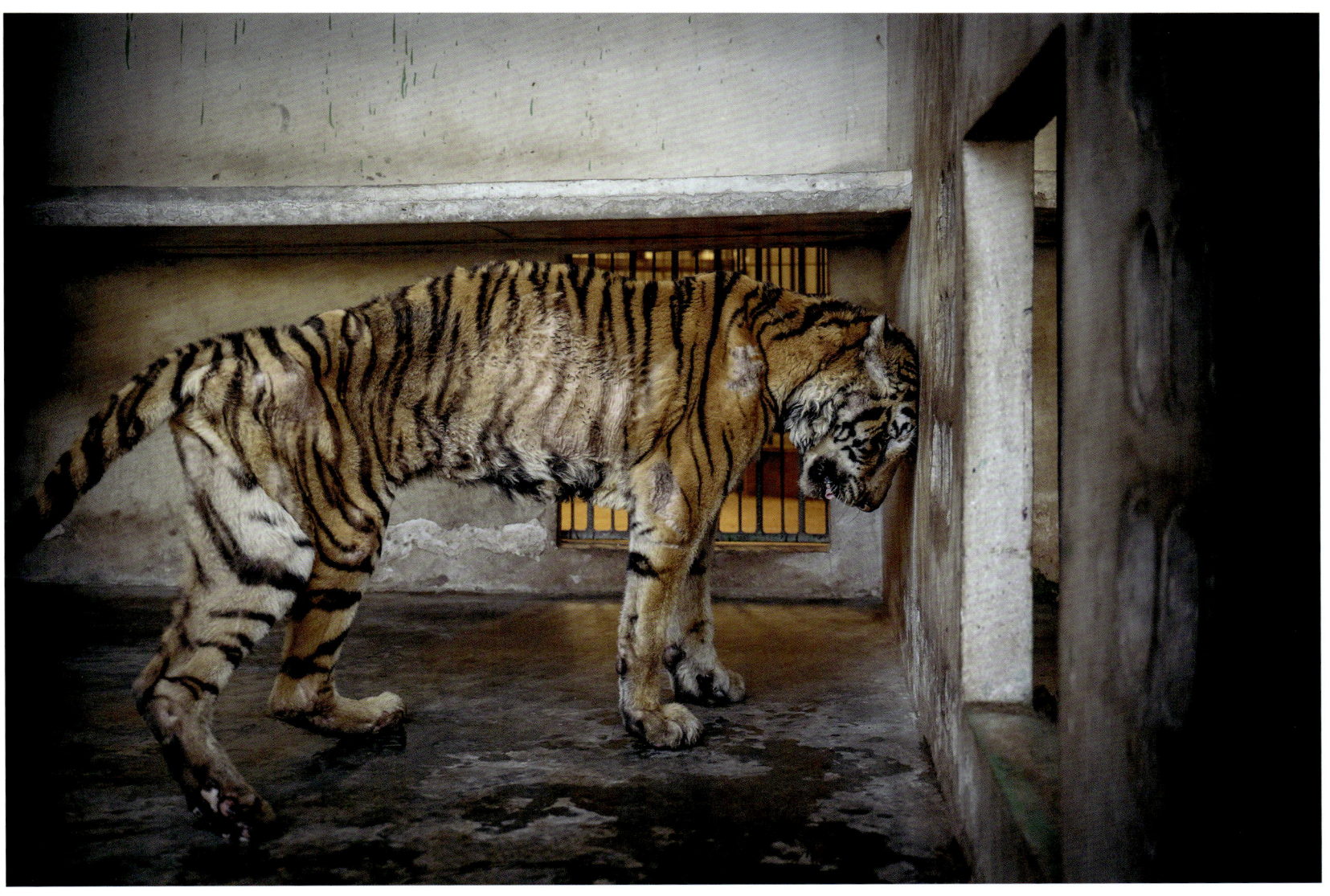

Skin and bones

Amy Jones
UK

Painfully thin and with fur rubbed through to the skin, this female Indochinese tiger was kept in a cage on a tiger farm in northern Thailand for more than 20 years. She was used for intensive breeding of cubs that were doomed to be petted by tourists, raised to maturity and ultimately slaughtered for the illegal trade in tiger skins, teeth, claws, meat and bones. Amy witnessed the emaciated cat's rescue (along with another 11 tigers and three leopards) by a wildlife NGO and watched her struggle to walk the short distance to the vehicle that transported her to a sanctuary. However, she lived only another nine months. According to WWF, nearly 9,000 tigers are held in farms throughout Southeast Asia, including 1,600 in Thailand. In stark contrast, the International Union for Conservation of Nature says the global wild population of tigers is estimated to be just 3,140 mature individuals.

Nikon Z9 + 24–70mm f2.8 lens at 40mm; 1/250 at f3.2; ISO 1400.

Toxic tip

Lakshitha Karunarathna

SRI LANKA

Much of Sri Lanka's waste is dumped into open rubbish tips, many of which are accessible to the island's Asian elephants, as this aerial photo by Lakshitha starkly reveals. According to one report, an estimated 20 elephants died over an eight-year period at a single site in the eastern district of Ampara after consuming indigestible food wrappers and other plastic items. Studies have shown toxic substances produced by food decomposing in polythene bags prove fatal once consumed by the pachyderms. Sri Lanka's Department of Wildlife Conservation says there are 54 open garbage dumps in the country, which remain accessible to elephants, despite government pledges to erect electric fences to deter them. However, some scientists say elephants will turn to crop raiding if kept out of waste dumps, leading to greater human-wildlife conflict – already a major issue for the island nation's estimated 5,000 elephants. Lakshitha has been documenting human–elephant conflict in Sri Lanka for over three years. This image is the result of months of meticulous observation at two open rubbish tips, where herds have been foraging.

DJI Mavic 3 Pro + Hasselblad L2D-20c 24mm f2.8 lens; 1/320 at f4 (0 e/v); ISO 200.

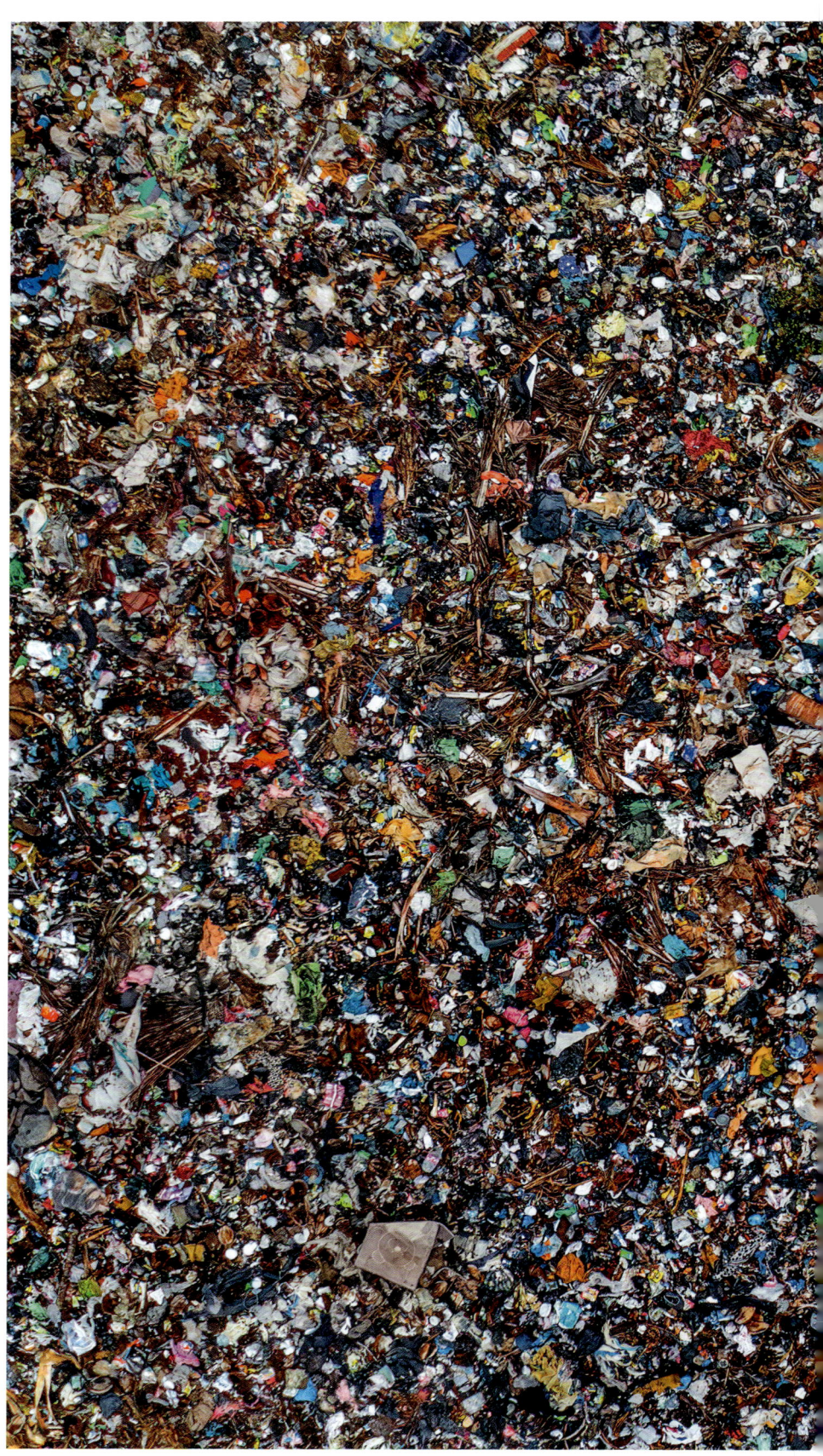

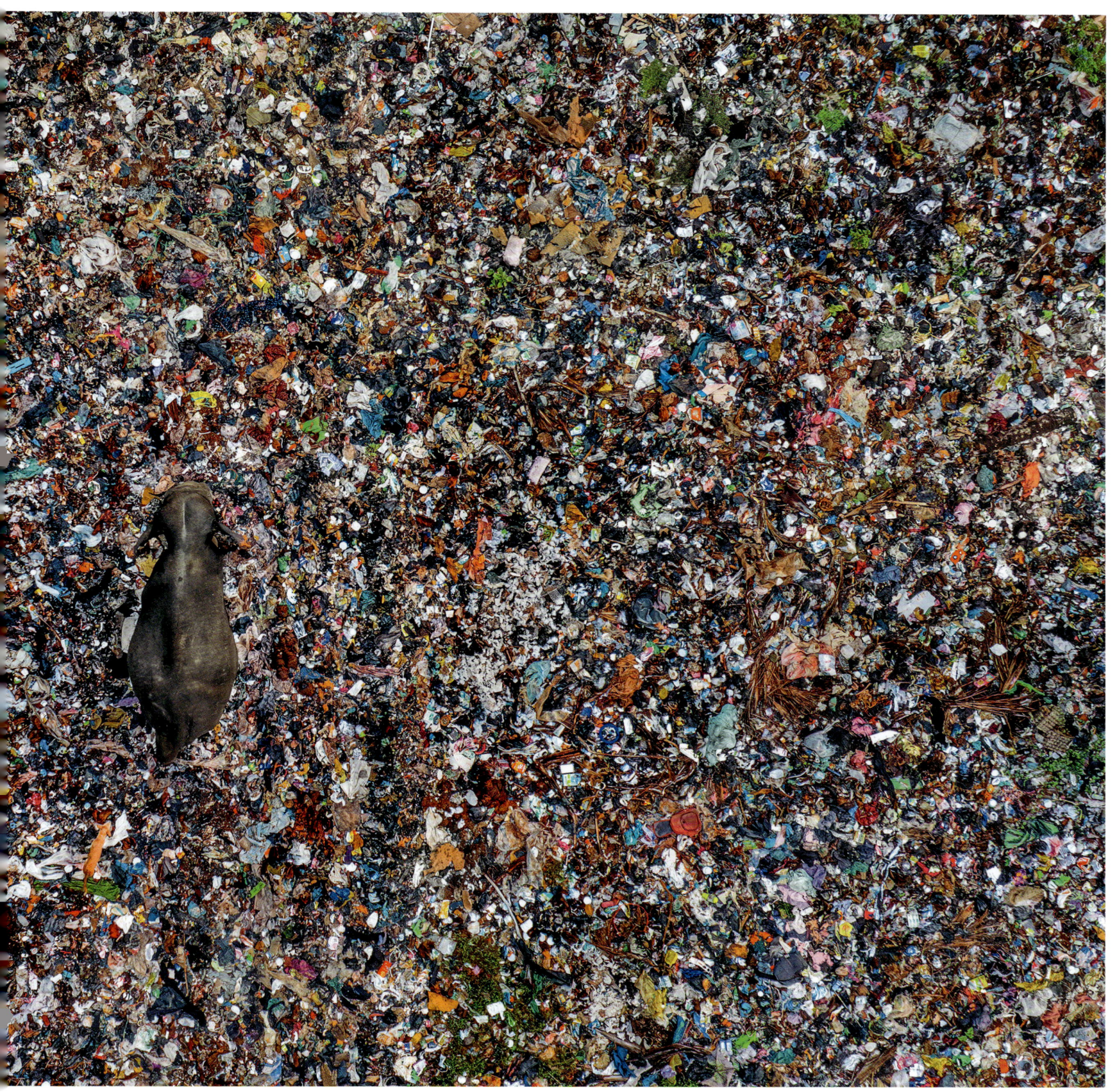

Photojournalist Story Award

The award is given for a story told in just six images, which are judged on their storytelling power as a whole, as well as for their individual quality.

Javier Aznar González de Rueda
SPAIN

End of the round-up

For centuries, rattlesnakes have been viewed in vastly different ways across the American continent. Hunted and harassed into the dark corners of our imagination, they evoke a mix of fascination and fear. This portfolio by Javier Aznar González de Rueda explores the complex relationship humans have with rattlesnakes, particularly in the American West. Killing them for a bounty started in the seventeenth century, but annual rattlesnake round-ups – whereby hunters compete to bring back the greatest poundage of snakes, which are then killed – only started in the 1930s. Today, these competitions are losing their appeal; some have changed into educational festivals where snakes are handled and not killed. But in some states the anti-rattler sentiment lives on. Javier's pictures challenge that perspective by urging respect and protection for these misunderstood creatures.

Rattled

To raise their body temperature so they can hunt and digest, rattlesnakes often bask on warm roads when the air cools. This northern black-tailed rattlesnake was spotted at night outside Fort Davis, in western Texas, USA, and then moved to prevent it from being run over. Although venomous, it only raises and rattles its tail when feeling threatened; in this instance, the perceived threat was not from Javier while taking this photo, but from the snake handler who had rescued it from the road. The rattle is made of interlocking scales, which the snake adds to each time it moults. Muscle contractions cause the scales to click together, resulting in the rattling sound. Despite their fearsome reputation, rattlesnakes do not seek out humans to attack. Most bites occur when people stumble across them or make deliberate attempts to handle one. Rattlesnakes play a vital role in ecosystems by controlling populations of rodents, their main prey, and other small mammals.

Sony α7R IV + 20mm f1.8 lens: 54 sec at f14; ISO 500; Profoto B10 flash; Profoto Air Remote; tripod.

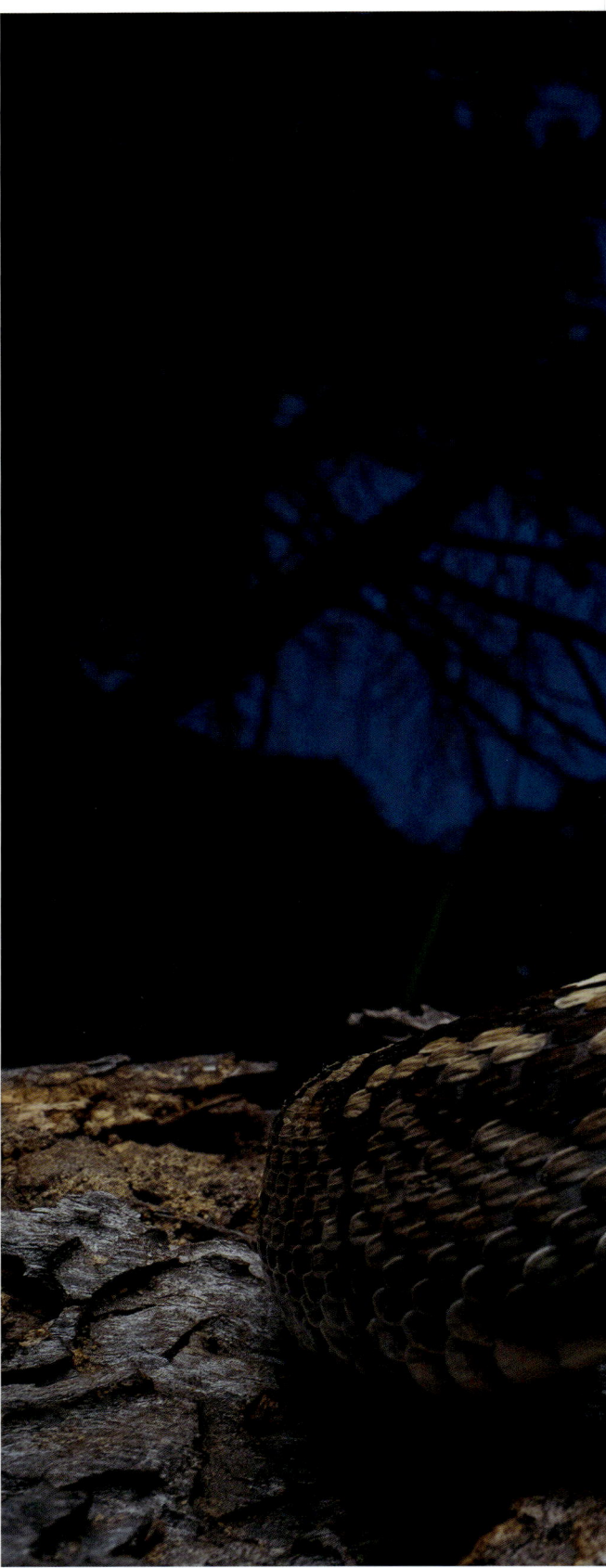

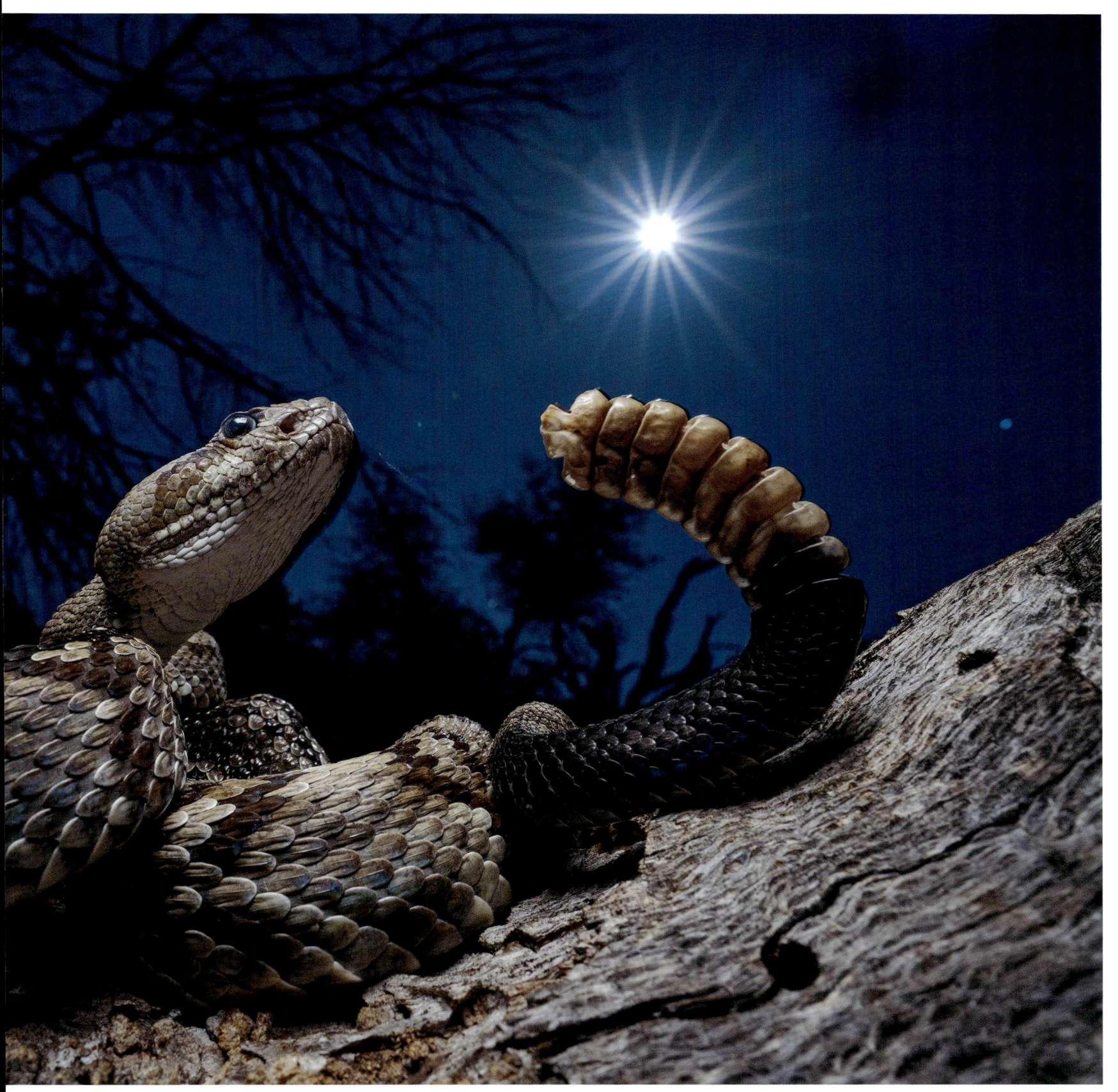

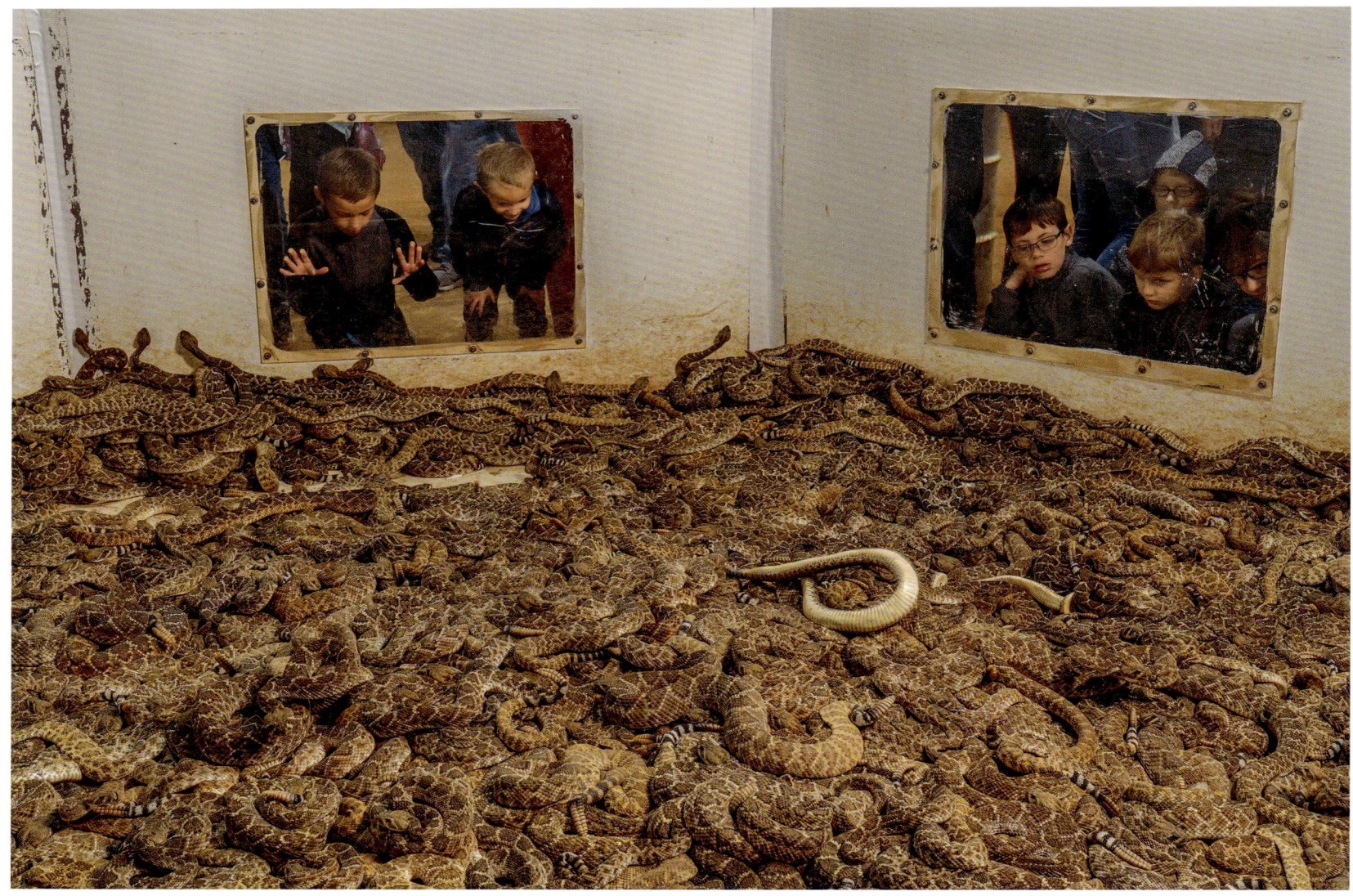

Seething pit

Children gaze intently at hundreds of western diamond-backed rattlesnakes thrown into a pit at the annual rattlesnake round-up in Sweetwater, Texas, USA. Many of the snakes will later die from decapitation by machete, while others succumb to asphyxiation from the weight of this writhing mass within the pit. The round-up, which began in 1958, is organized by the local branch of the United States Junior Chamber (aka Jaycees) youth leadership organization. In 2025, it reported that 1,600 kilograms (3,527 pounds) of rattlesnakes were brought to the event by competitors vying for cash prizes awarded to the most snakes captured, as measured by weight. Conservationists are critical of the methods used to catch the snakes – many are driven from their rock shelters using petrol fumes, causing harm to other animal species that shelter with the snakes. After measuring, sexing, and extracting venom, the snakes are then killed for their skins, which are sold along with the meat and some organs. Organizers say round-ups are necessary to reduce the risk posed to humans and livestock by the venomous reptiles.

Sony α7R III + 24–70mm f2.8 lens at 44mm: 1/30 at f10; ISO 4000.

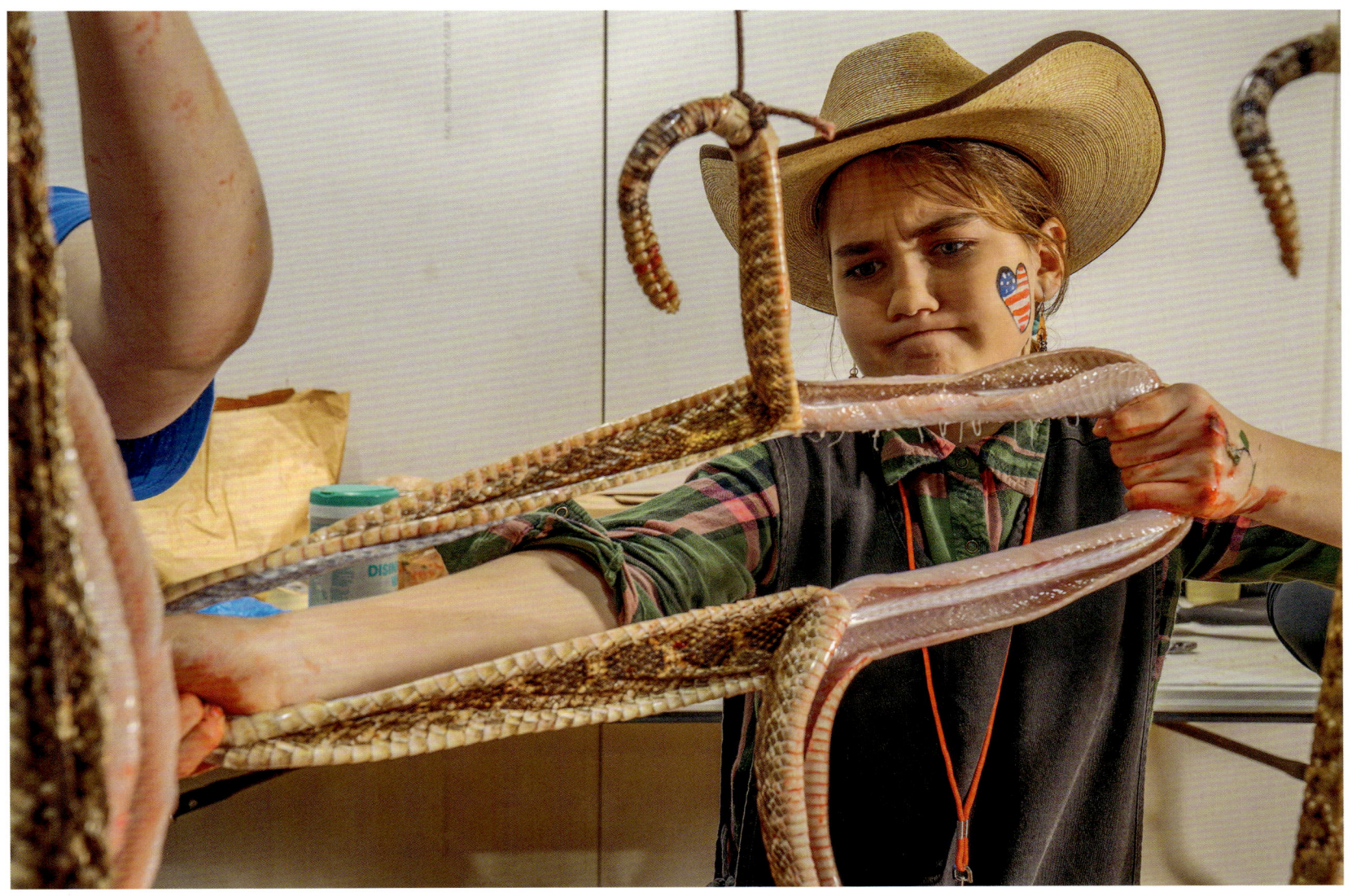

Snake-skinning

A teenager skins a western diamond-backed rattlesnake at the annual Sweetwater round-up. The snake had been decapitated and then hung up by its tail. While taking this photo, Javier remembered a nauseating smell filled the air and blood spattered from the snake as the skin was ripped off. The skin and meat were later sold, but critics say many snake bodies are simply dumped. Rattlesnake round-ups are thought to have started in Oklahoma in 1939, and soon spread to other parts of the USA. Today, they are partly justified as fundraisers for local community groups and charities, but round-ups are on the decline in many American states. In 1980, Texas had a reported 40 rattlesnake round-ups a year; today there are just five. In Georgia, the last deadly rattlesnake round-up was in 2022, and it has now changed to an educational format, in which visitors learn about rattlesnakes without any being killed. According to the Center for Biological Diversity, there are more deaths in the United States each year from dog bites, lightning strikes and bee stings than from snake bites.

Sony α7R IV + 24–70mm f2.8 lens at 44mm; 1/160 at f7.1; ISO 3200; flash.

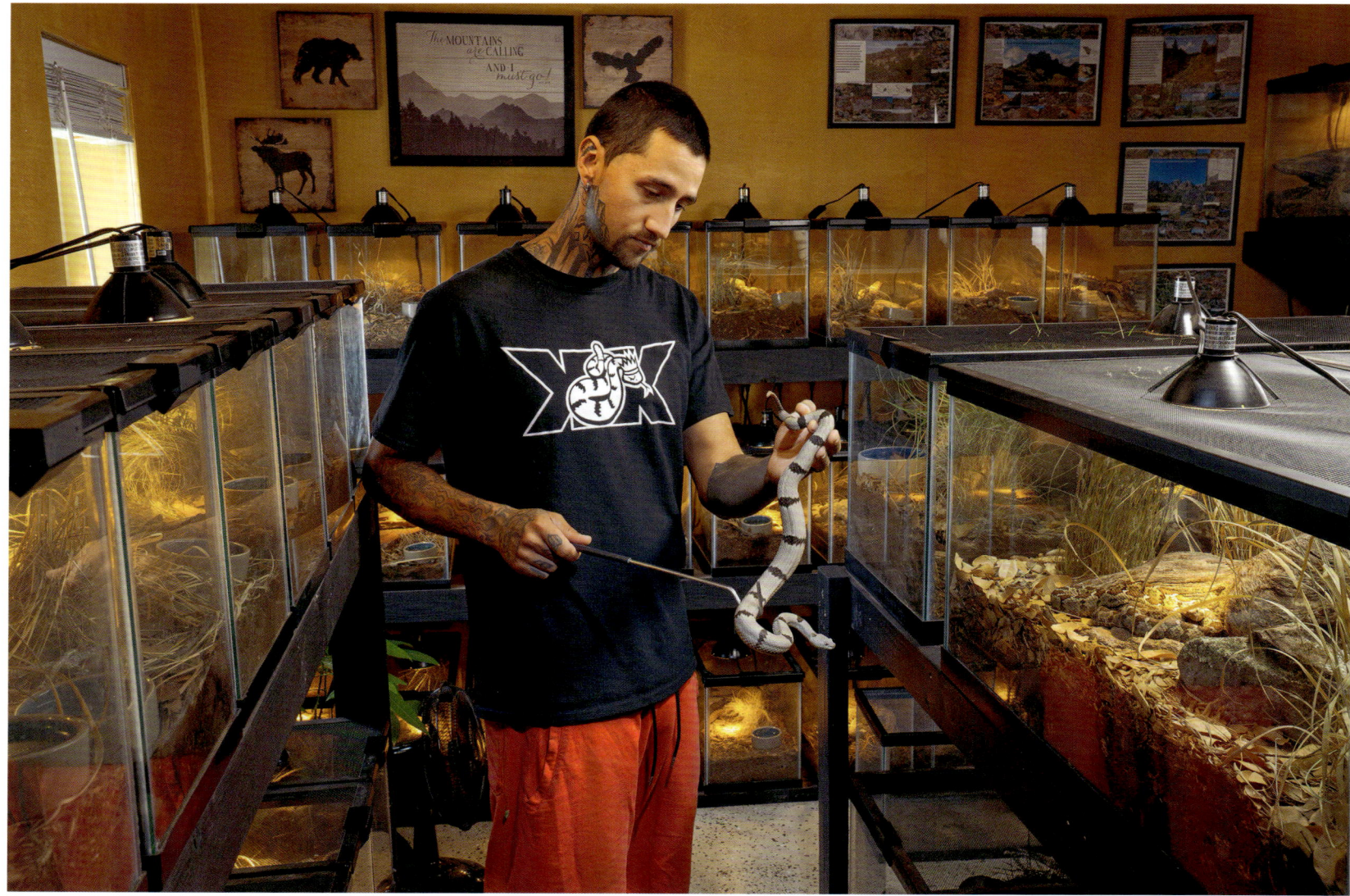

The collector

Kyle Vargas discovered he had a passion for rattlesnakes at a young age, and he's been keeping them ever since. Here, he holds a banded rock rattlesnake, a species native to the southern USA and Mexico where it lives in arid areas up to nearly 3,000 metres (9,840 feet) above sea level. Kyle has about 400 individual snakes in his collection from about 20 different species. Unlike many other enthusiasts, his specimens are kept in vivaria stocked with plants, soil and wood from their indigenous habitats. Though he rarely takes snakes from the wild, Kyle says it is only ever under permit. Keeping rattlesnakes in captivity is not permitted in every US state, and the Smithsonian Institution has identified the pet trade as a conservation threat to many snake species. In the wild, banded rock rattlers feed on small mammals, lizards, invertebrates and birds. The species is considered common across much of its range but faces threats from urban development and industrial mining, as well as collection for the pet trade.

Sony α7R IV + 24–70mm f2.8 lens at 36mm; 1/15 at f13; ISO 2000; Profoto B10 flash.

From venom to medicine

Drops of deadly venom drip inside a glass as an eastern diamond-backed rattlesnake is milked in a laboratory in Wisconsin, USA. To get this close, Javier waited until the snake was properly held in the hand and its fangs exposed, and for good reason – this is the largest venomous snake in North America, reaching 2.4 metres (8 feet) in length and weighing up to 4.6 kilograms (10 pounds). While its very toxic venom is mostly used to manufacture anti-venom for treating snakebites, scientists are hopeful that it can be used for treating other medical conditions. For example, rattlesnake venom has been identified as having a potential role in treating chronic, neuropathic pain. Other rattlesnake venoms have been shown to inhibit the growth of some cancer cells, and to prevent platelet aggregation, thereby having the potential to treat thrombosis.

Sony α1 + 90mm f2.8 macro lens: 1/350 at f16; ISO 200; 2 x Profoto B10 flashes.

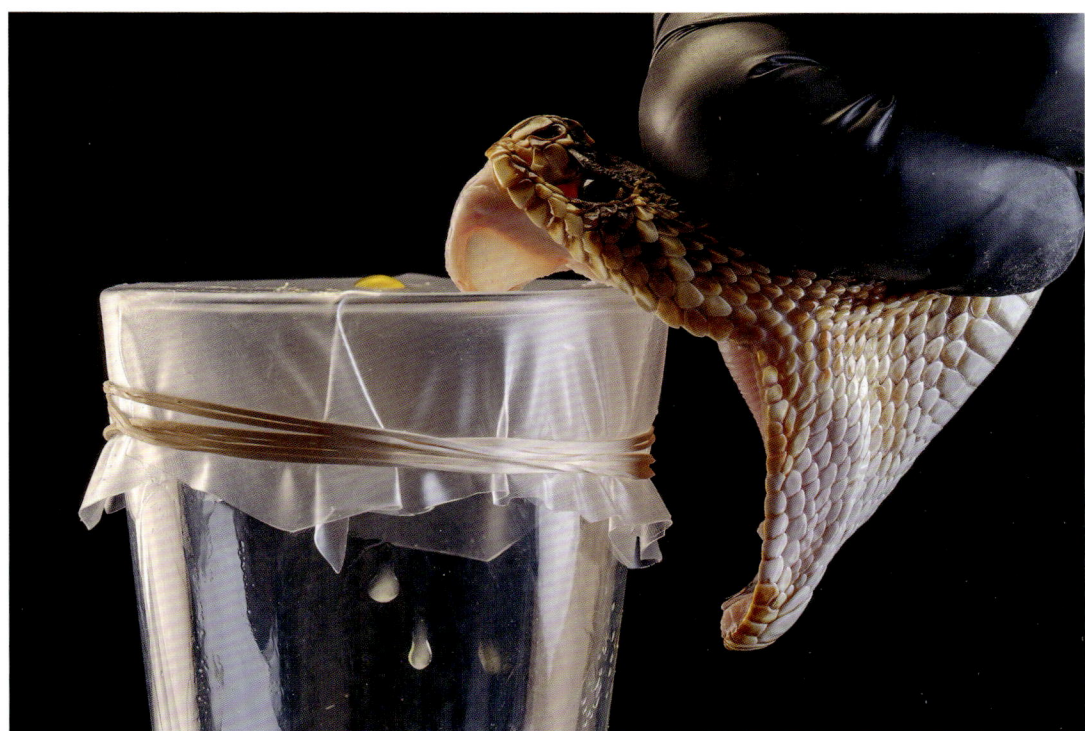

Education outreach

Stacy Foster presents a timber rattlesnake to visitors at the annual Morris Township Volunteer Fire Company rattlesnake round-up in Pennsylvania, USA. Unlike the Sweetwater event, no snakes are killed on site, but hunters holding a venomous snake permit can bring their catches to compete for a trophy awarded to the heaviest specimen. In the round-up's earlier years, snakes were killed and eaten. Now, it is an educational event, where organizers talk about the importance of rattlesnakes to the ecosystem and allow visitors to touch them. Although the organizers intend for any captured snakes to be returned to the wild, it is up to the hunters to decide. Similar non-lethal round-ups occur in other US states. In Georgia, the Claxton Rattlesnake and Wildlife Festival took on its present incarnation in 2012, and is supported by the state's Department of Natural Resources and Georgia Southern University.

Sony α7R III + 28mm f2 lens; 1/80 at f10; ISO 1600.

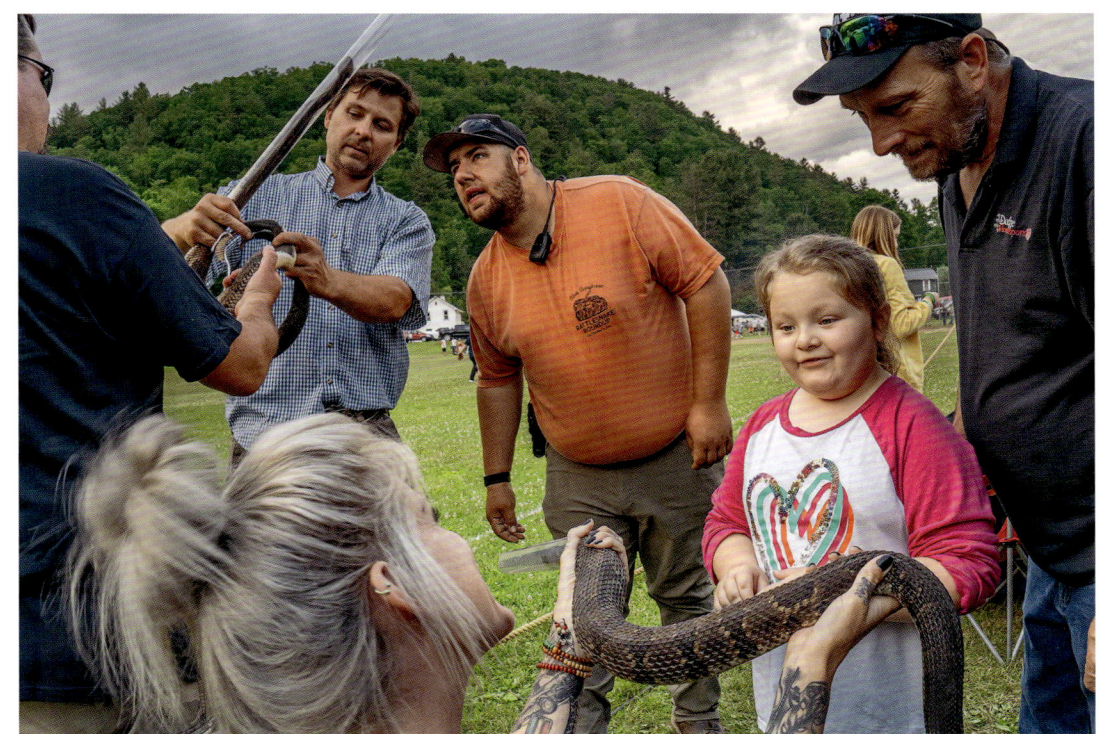

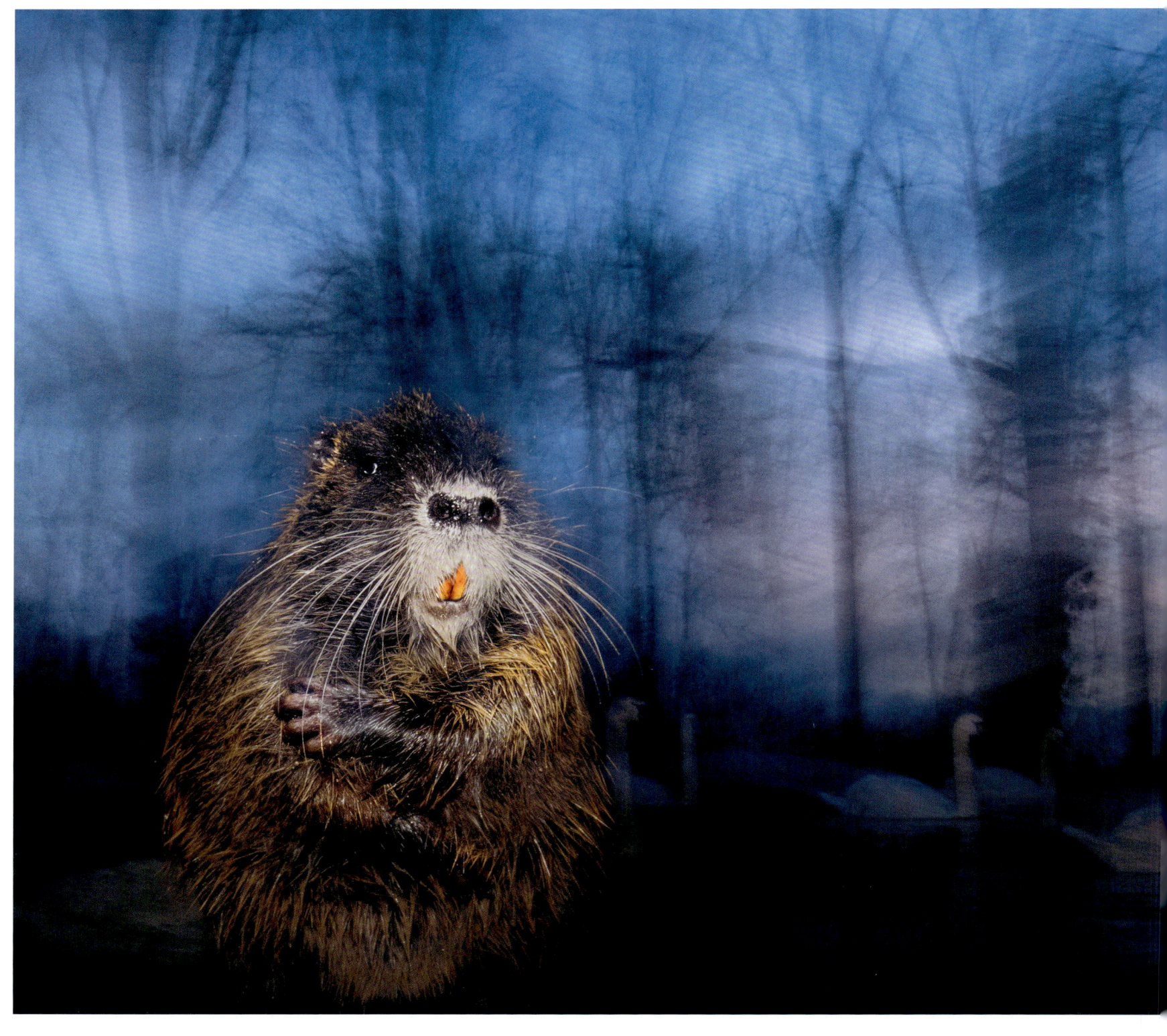

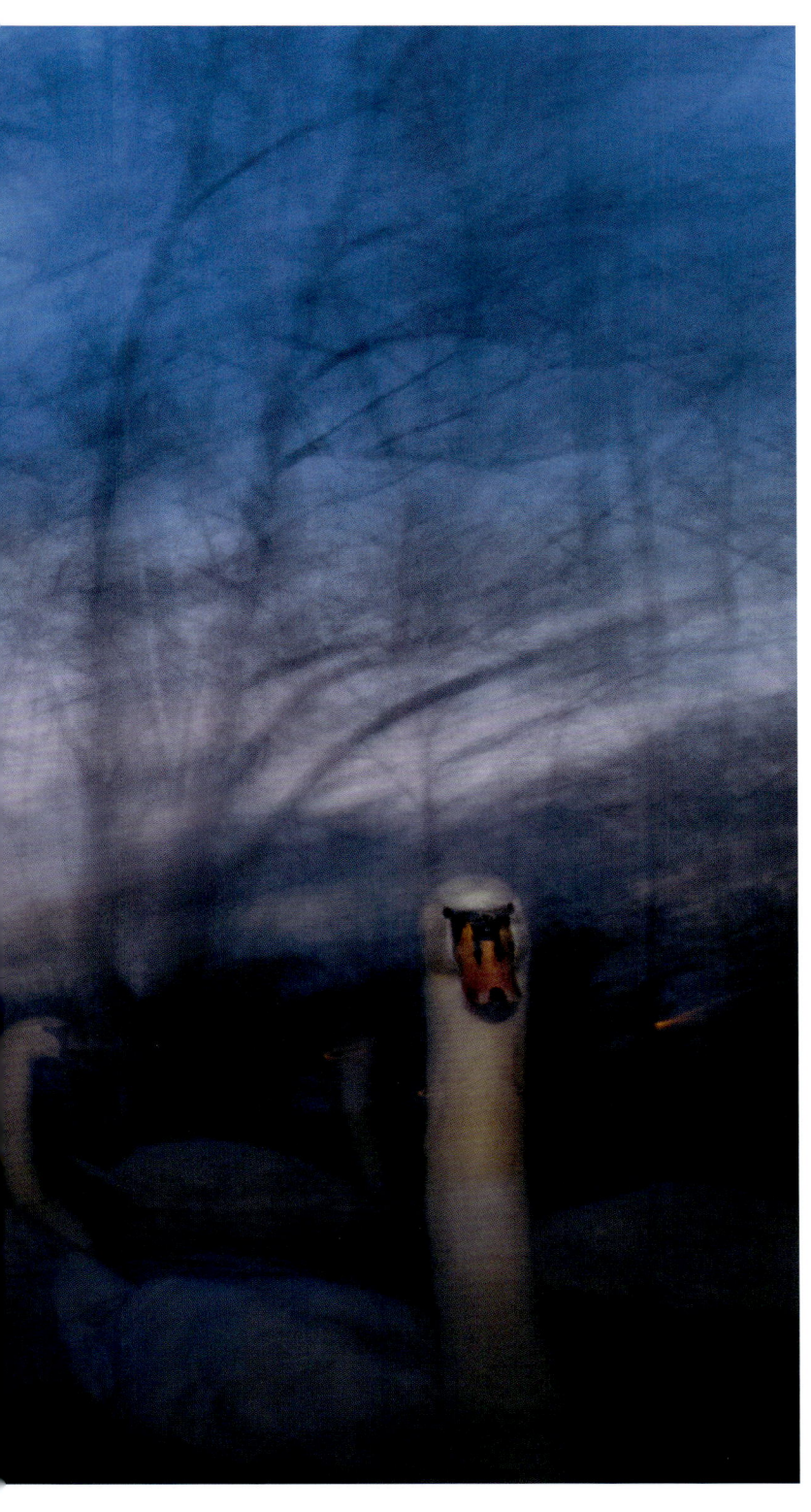

Rising Star
Portfolio Award

The award seeks to inspire and encourage photographers aged 18 to 26 and is given for a portfolio of work comprising six photographs.

Luca Lorenz
GERMANY

Watchful moments

Luca's first love was birds. His childhood ambition was to find out everything there was to know about them. This inspired him to collect feathers, learn their songs and calls, and spend long hours alone in the parks around his home on the outskirts of Berlin, just watching and following his instincts. Aged 11, he realized he'd like to share what he felt and saw with family and friends, so he began saving for a camera. Aged 13, he bought one. Now 19, Luca doesn't take pictures only of birds – well, most of the time.

Meet the neighbours

Luca was photographing mute swans on an urban lake in the German city of Bonn one evening when he was photobombed by a coypu, a large South American rodent. Coypus (also known as nutrias) are orange-toothed wetland specialists that look like a very big rat or a small beaver. Shipped around the world for the fur trade, they have established feral populations in North America, Russia, the Middle East, Africa and Japan, as well as Europe, where they are considered a pest in many countries. Luca was intrigued by its interactions with the swans. They were clearly on familiar terms. The coypu swam straight for the middle of the group of floating birds, who nipped at it, almost playfully. Luca employed a soft flash to brighten and sharply focus the coypu's face, and made a long exposure to capture the dying light of sunset.

Nikon D850 + Tamron 15–30mm f2.8 lens at 15mm; 1/2 at f22; ISO 1000; Nikon Speedlight SB-28 flash.

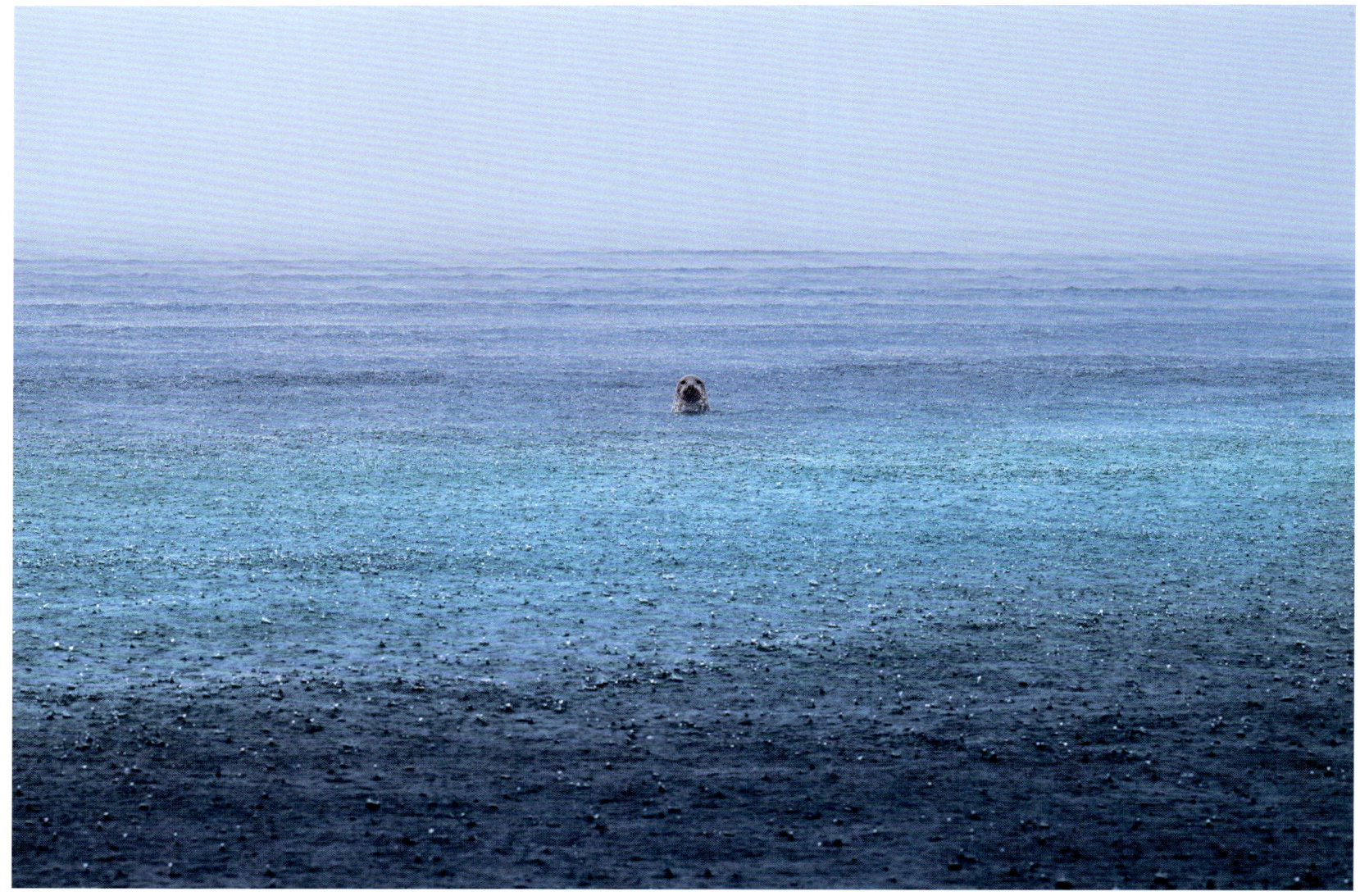

Seal serenity

You're never far from the beach on Heligoland, a tiny archipelago 46 kilometres (29 miles) from Germany's North Sea coast. When the heavens opened, Luca was out with his camera on the larger of the two islands. He is fascinated by how animals respond to rain. Some are invigorated, others just sit it out. At the beach, he was pleased to see harbour seals (also known as common seals), popping up unpredictably to draw breath between dives. 'They kept poking their heads out of the water of the North Sea, which was surprisingly calm at the time,' he recalls. Harbour seals are found throughout coastal waters of the northern hemisphere, from temperate to polar regions. For this photograph, Luca minimized the lens aperture to ensure that the full expanse of the sea was in focus and framed an inquisitive seal dead centre. The turquoise stripe across the water, created by a sandbar beneath the surface, was a bonus, as was the seamless transition between sea and cloud in the distance. Luca likes the idea that the seals enjoy the patter of raindrops on their head as much as he does.

Nikon Z8 + 180–600mm f5.6–6.3 lens at 180mm; 1/200 at f18; ISO 1600.

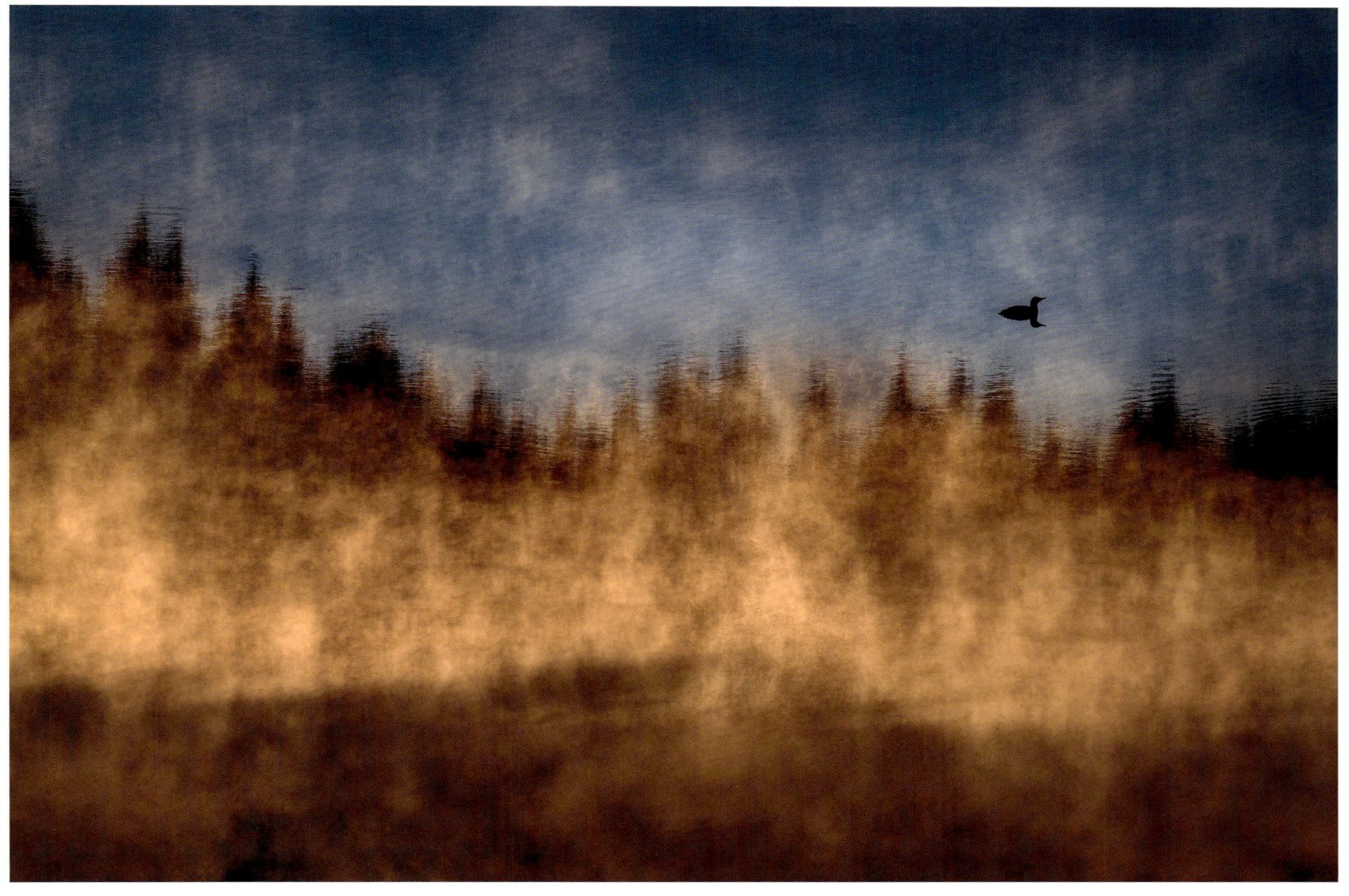

Reflected glory

Conditions were perfect when Luca arrived at this lake shore at 3am to ensure he didn't miss the first rays of sunlight on the water. A delicate mist hung over the mirror-like surface. But as dawn broke, there were no red-throated divers to be seen. He need not have worried. Luca heard their goose-like flight calls before he saw them. They circled the lake several times before landing, and immediately began their eerie, mewing contact calls. 'I can't even describe how much I love that sound,' he says. Luca visits Tiveden National Park, Sweden, with family every summer and knows the lake well. Red-throated divers are long-lived, monogamous birds that occupy a vast range across North America (where they are called red-throated loons) and northern Eurasia. They spend winters at sea. Luca rotated the original image through 180 degrees to bring the mirrored pines and spruces into an upright position and create a more harmonious and balanced composition overall. The result is a glorious morning, whichever way you look at it.

Nikon Z8 + 180–600mm f5.6–6.3 lens at 180mm; 1/200 at f32; ISO 500.

Dawn watch

A redstart singing from the neighbour's chimney inspired Luca to head out at dawn to a wooded park close to home in the north of Berlin. He was lying down flat on the dewy grass for a better perspective on one of the park's ubiquitous blackbirds, which had just pulled an earthworm from the soil. Suddenly, four fallow deer emerged from the background mist and stopped to assess the situation. Though thriving in woods and parks across western Europe, where they have been introduced, fallow deer have almost disappeared from their native range in Turkey. As Luca framed the scene, the blackbird paused between him and the fallow deer, 'and we all watched each other'. Time stood still and he caught the moment. The mist sapped most of the colour from the scene, so he simplified the image by converting it to black and white.

Nikon Z6 + 200–500mm f5.6 lens at 500mm; 1/400 at f5.6; ISO 8000.

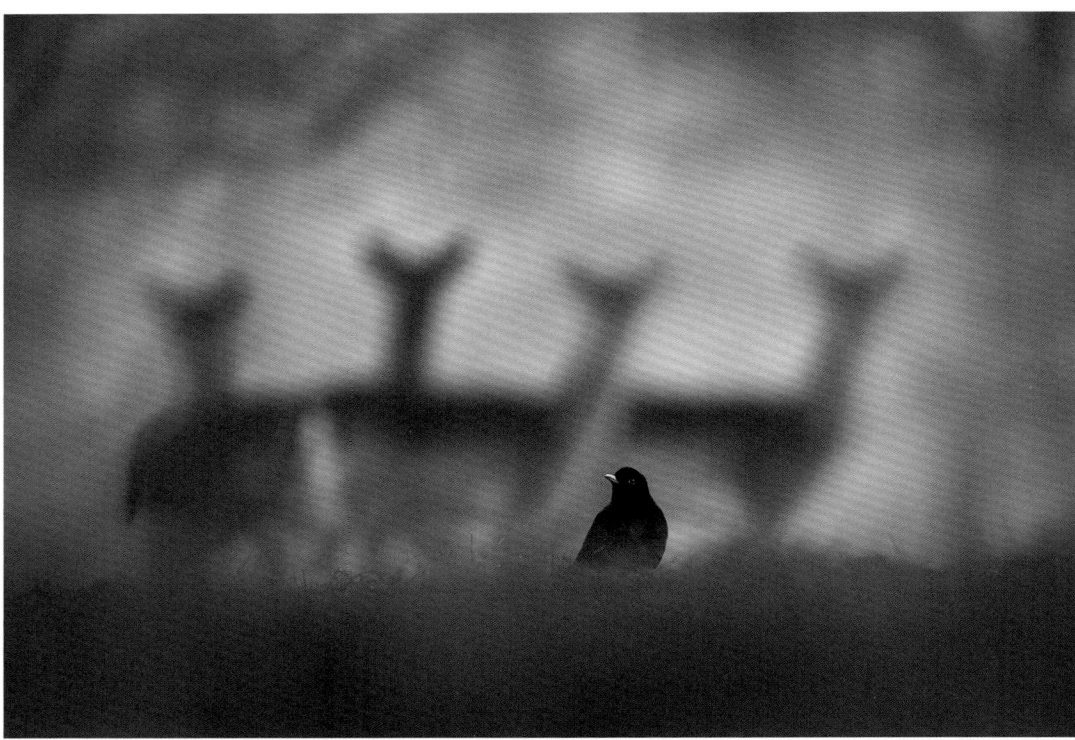

Sole survivor

It was a fateful day not only for the mouse, but also for this male Eurasian pygmy owl and his brood. For 10 days, from dawn to dusk, Luca had been watching a tree hole in a forest near Nürnberg, Germany, where the male and his mate were nesting. A few days in, the female vanished, taken, Luca suspects, by a tawny owl or hawk, which also frequent this area. The male continued alone to feed the brood, and a week later, the chicks – still flightless and dependent – emerged from the hollow to roost in the branches for the first time. The next morning, they too were gone. The now agitated male, clutching their breakfast in his claws, called for them incessantly, but to no avail.

Nikon Z8 + 180–600mm f5.6–6.3 lens at 600mm; 1/125 at f6.3; ISO 2500.

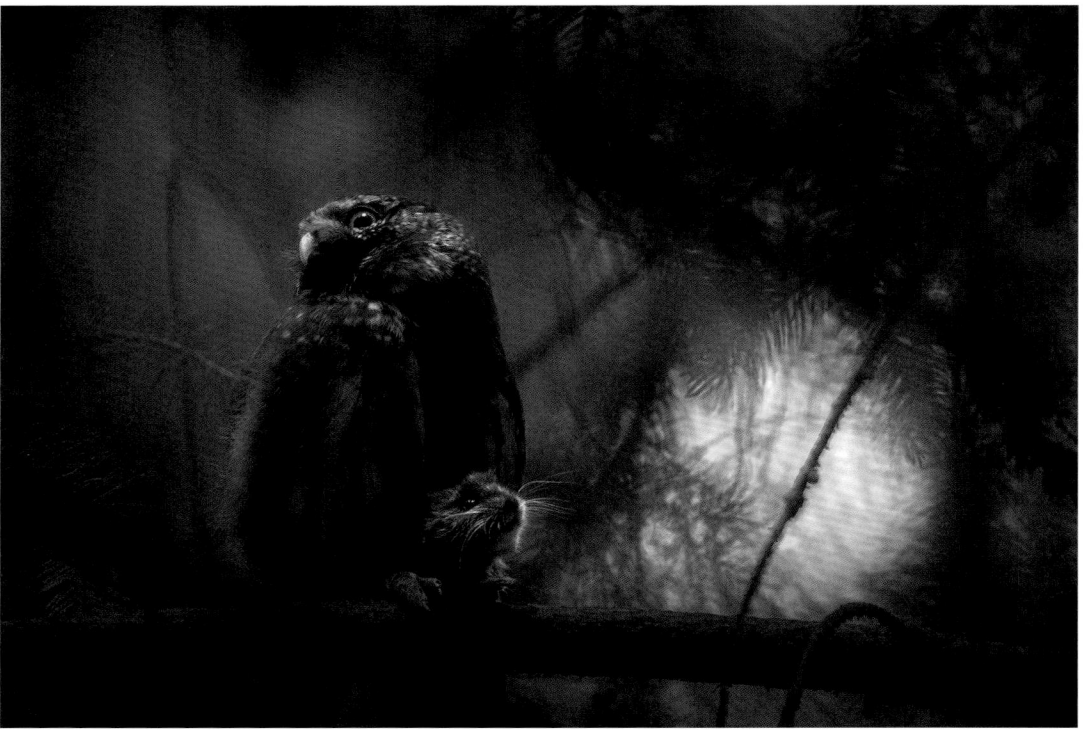

Small but mighty

Staking out a Eurasian pygmy owl nest hole involves the photographer experiencing long periods of doing nothing, broken only by infrequent bursts of activity when the bird makes a brief appearance. At less than half the weight of a little owl, which is itself renowned for its diminutive stature, the pygmy owl is the smallest owl in Europe. This tiny, secretive predator hunts by sight and sound and strikes silently. Breeding pairs divide the labour rigorously: females incubate; males provide. Males visit the nest only to bring small rodents and songbirds, while females only leave it to receive the offerings. In the depths of this German forest, handovers took place high in the trees, so photographic opportunities were few, until the female, a blue tit gripped in its talons, gave Luca four minutes of its precious time on the forest floor before retreating to the nest. This unusual composition in black and white makes the most of the background silhouettes, which Luca felt suited a bird that lives amongst the shadows.

Nikon D850 + 200–500mm f5.6 lens at 500mm; 1/80 at f5.6; ISO 4000.

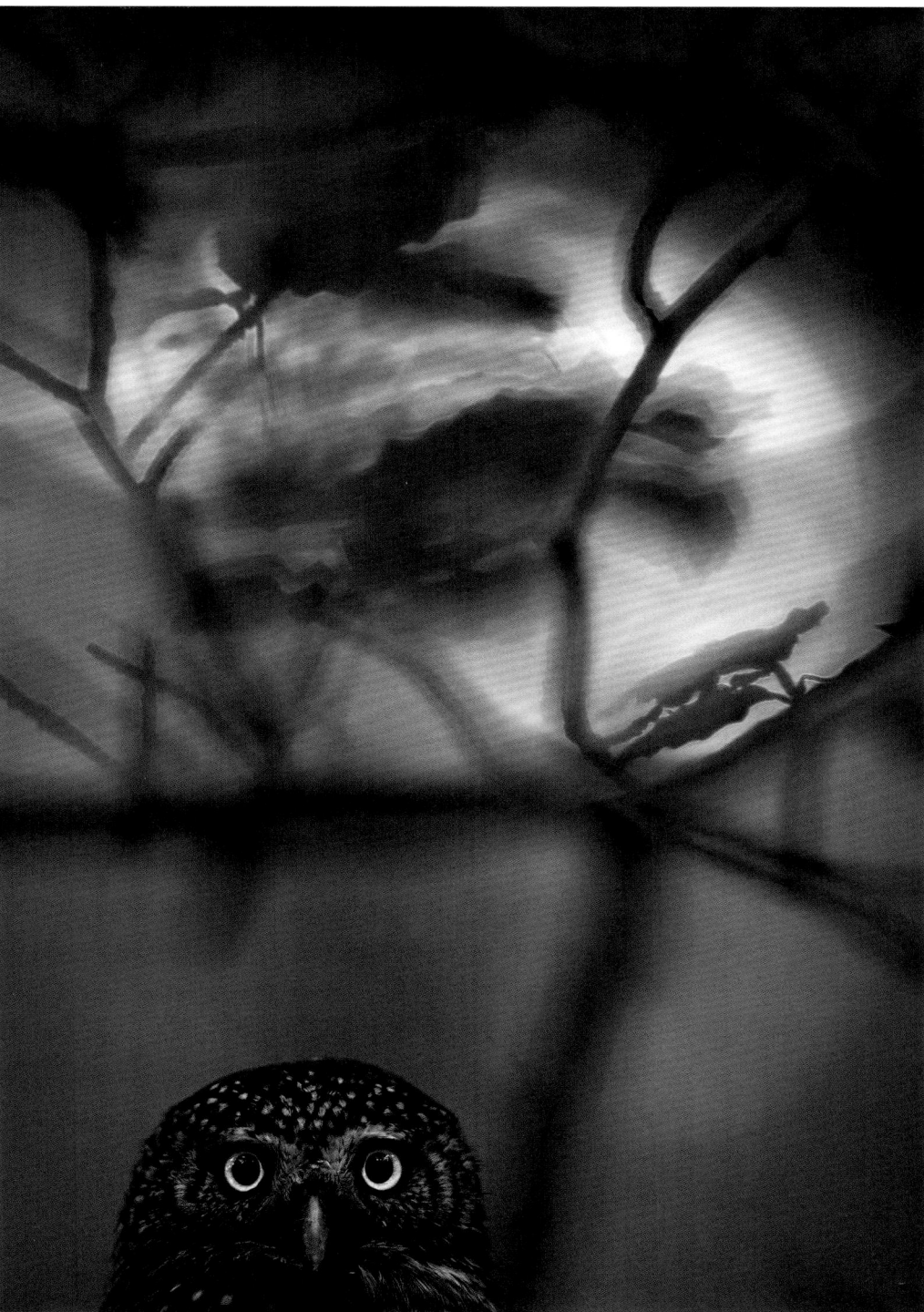

Portfolio Award

The award is given for six of the photographer's best images that complement each other through a creative style, or a focus on a particular topic, but do not need to tell a story.

WINNER

Alexey Kharitonov
ISRAEL/RUSSIA

Visions of the north

Alexey's artistic exploration of remote parts of the Russian North, Russian Far East and Siberia transports us over undisturbed taiga and Arctic tundra landscapes as summer rapidly turns to winter. Using drones registered with the Russian Federal Air Transport Agency, and flying at altitudes of 68–216 metres (224–709 feet), he picked out details in these vast terrains, capturing their wild beauty in striking compositions that invite interpretation. Beyond this visual feast, however, lie anthropogenic threats, not least a pressing vulnerability to climate change.

Ice motifs

In the Leningrad region of northwest Russia, autumn recedes to winter in early November, creating scenes that change by the hour. This lake, among the marshes of Svetlyachkovskoye swamp, had recently frozen over, the ice catching a light coat of freshly fallen snow. Then patches began to melt, and spider-like cracks crept across dark, snow-free circles. This region falls within the broad circumpolar taiga belt – Earth's largest land biome, comprising nearly 30 per cent of global forest cover. It embraces some 1,800 lakes, 50,000 kilometres (31,000 miles) of rivers, and extensive boreal forests threatened by legal and illegal logging. The proximity of the swamp to the Baltic Sea and Atlantic weather systems means that winters here are relatively warm.

DJI Mavic 3 Classic + Hasselblad L2D-20c 24mm f2.8 lens; 1/25 at f2.8 (-0.7 e/v); ISO 100.

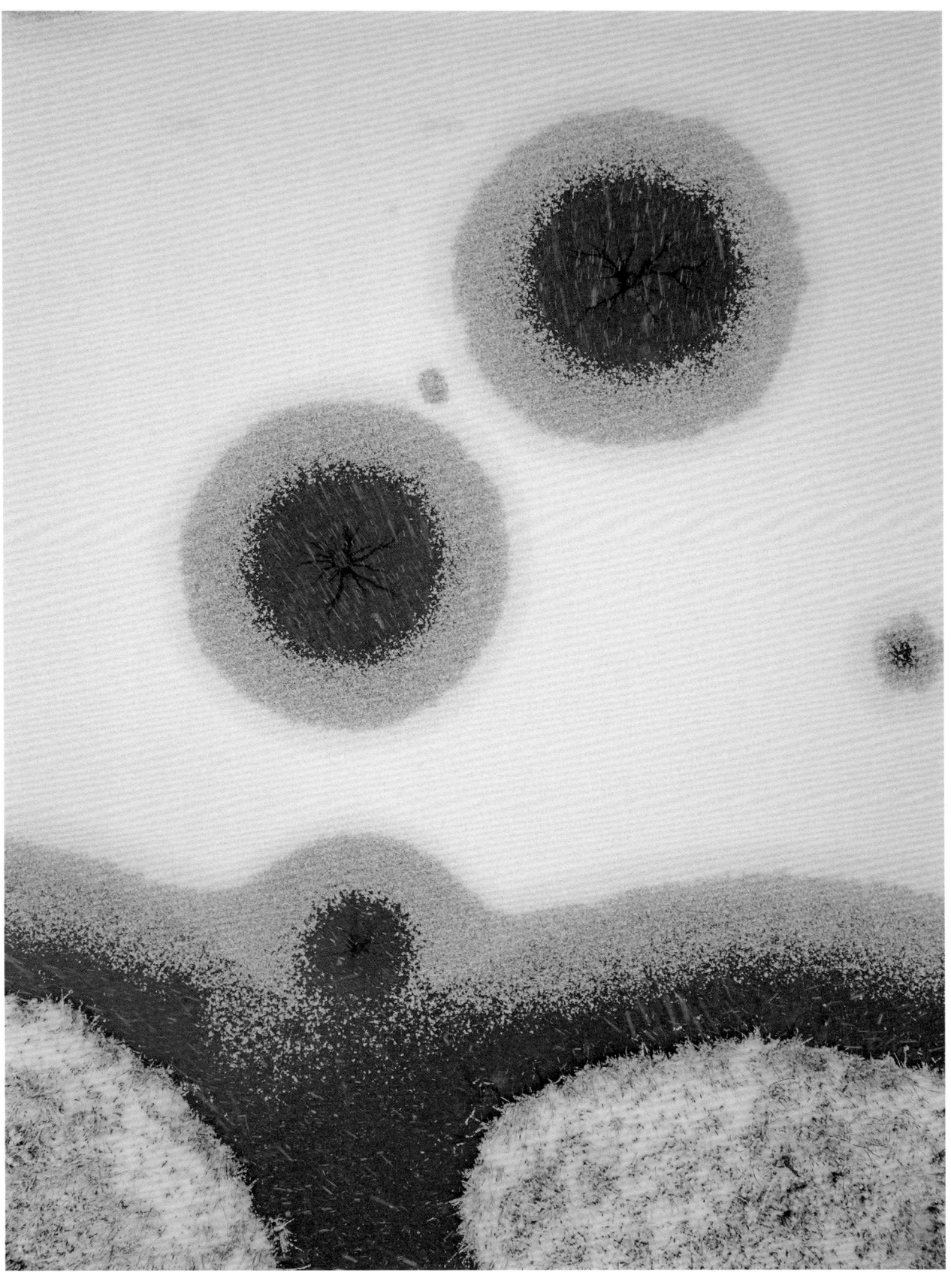

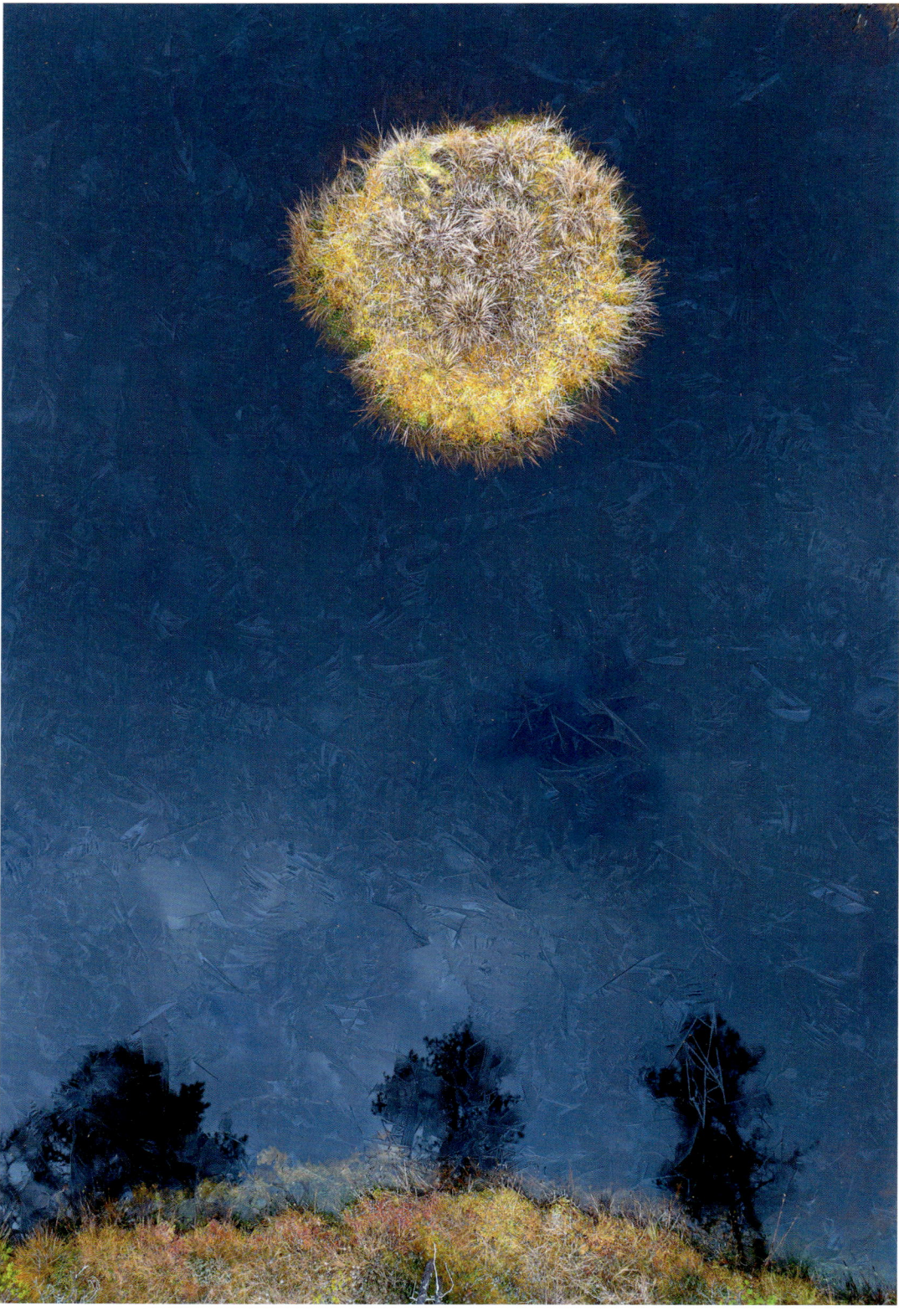

Taiga moon

From the air, a new world comes into view above the marshes of the Boloto Ozernoe nature reserve, to a fanciful realm that reminded Alexey of Van Gogh's painting, Starry Night. Alexey is drawn back repeatedly to this taiga landscape, in the Leningrad region of northwest Russia, every visit offering fresh opportunities. November brought the first frost in the rapid transition to winter. The ground was carpeted with peat-forming sphagnum mosses, while cold-resistant trees offered shelter for elusive elk and wild boar. Boloto Ozernoe's beauty is fragile: the reserve is relatively small – barely 1,000 hectares (2,470 acres) – and close to new roads and holiday home developments. Alexey launched his drone from an isthmus between a mosaic of small lakes, framing his picture around a dry grassy hummock encircled by ice, reflected pine silhouettes and the autumn glow of sphagnum moss.

DJI Mavic 3 Classic + Hasselblad L2D-20c 24mm f2.8 lens; 1/120 at f2.8 (-1.7 e/v); ISO 110.

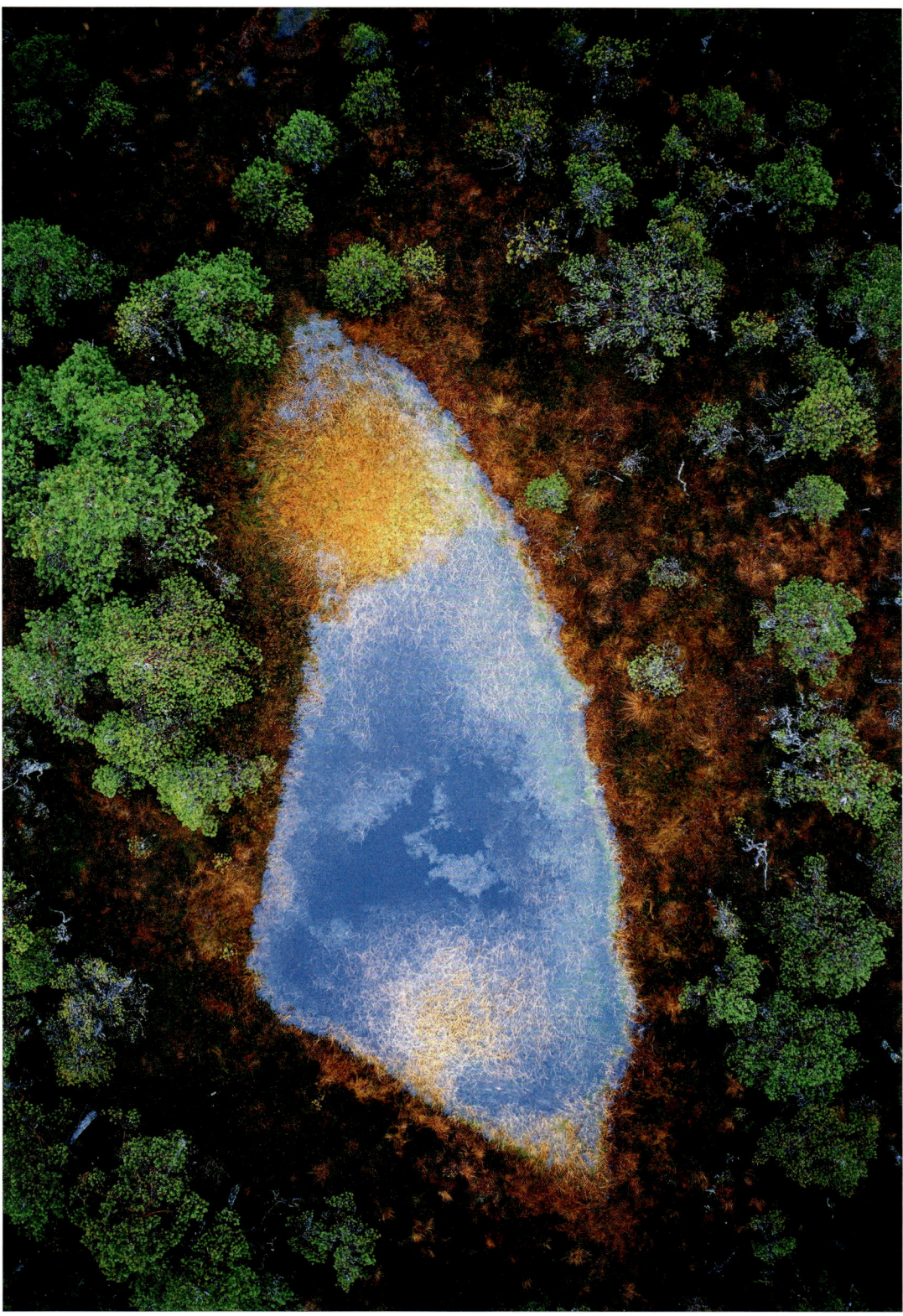

Piece of sky

In the drizzle of a grey November twilight over Bolshoe Znamenskoe swamp in Russia's Leningrad region, Alexey flew his drone one last time before heading home. His reward was a sudden break in the clouds: a fragment of blue reflected in a small lake and a grassy hummock posing as the sun, together conjuring a window to a brighter world. The swamp around the lake was dotted with pines, among the few tree species (including spruce, larch, fir and birch) comprising the vast Russian taiga. These forests help mitigate climate change by absorbing carbon dioxide from the atmosphere. Beneath them, huge amounts of carbon are locked in peat that remains frozen within permafrost. Temperature records show that global warming is more pronounced in northern latitudes, contributing to the melting of permafrost, changes in tree growth and increases in wildfires.

DJI Mavic 2 + Hasselblad L1D–20c 28mm f2.8 lens; 1/15 at f2.8 (–0.3 e/v); ISO 500.

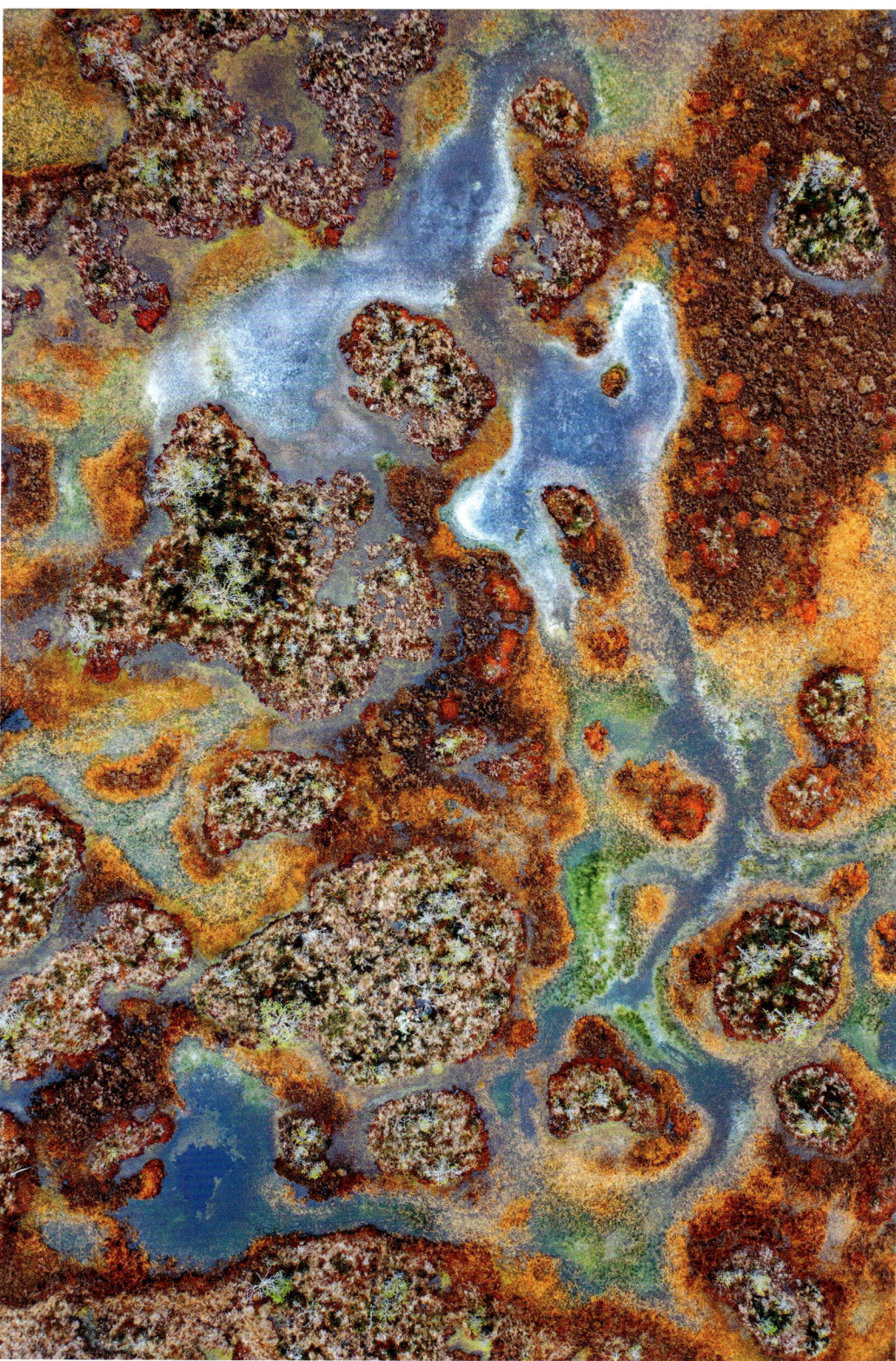

Taiga tapestry

A kaleidoscope of colours carpets the Mukhinskoye swamp under a grey November sky in northwest Russia. The patterns change from year to year, making every picture unique. The blue of small lakes and channels, fringed with white ice, is set against green and yellow grass and widespread sphagnum mosses, turned vibrant orange and red in the brief autumn. The dense sphagnum mats comprise a multitude of individual plants, and their spongy forms and slow rate of decay gradually builds a carbon-rich layer of peat. Studies suggest that Russia holds almost half the northern hemisphere's terrestrial carbon, with about 60 per cent locked in peat that is frozen within permafrost.

DJI Mavic 2 Pro + Hasselblad L1D-20c 28mm f2.8 lens; 1/30 at f2.8 (-0.3 e/v); ISO 100.

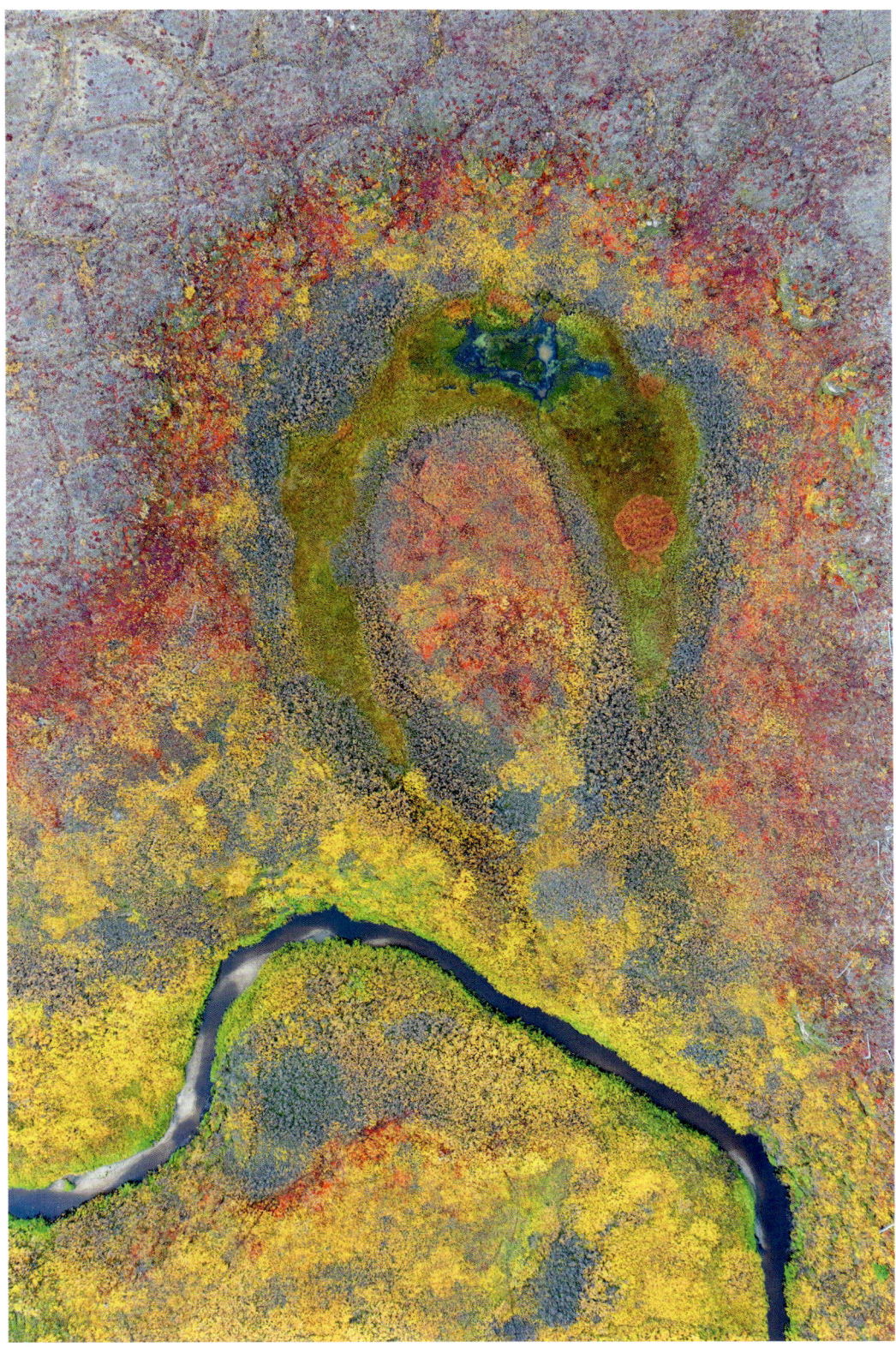

Autumn icon

Autumn in the Arctic tundra of Polar Yakutia, northeast Siberia, is fleeting; its rich colours last just a couple of weeks from the end of August. Alexey captured possibly the first drone pictures of this remote landscape during a 180-kilometre (112-mile) motorboat trip through uninhabited territory along the Taymylyr River. Waterways edged with bright green grass gave way to golden shrubs and a landscape sprinkled with the crimson blaze of alpine bearberry and bog blueberry. Where undisturbed by Yakutia's expanding mining industry, this vast region supports more than 500 species each of mosses, lichens and fungi. It also provides important breeding grounds for many migratory birds, including Siberian cranes, eider and Bewick's swans. Alexey says when he first saw this picture while flying his drone, it reminded him of a religious icon of a barely recognizable saint.

DJI Mavic 2 Pro + Hasselblad L1D-20c 28mm f2.8 lens; 1/50 at f3.5 (−0.3 e/v); ISO 100.

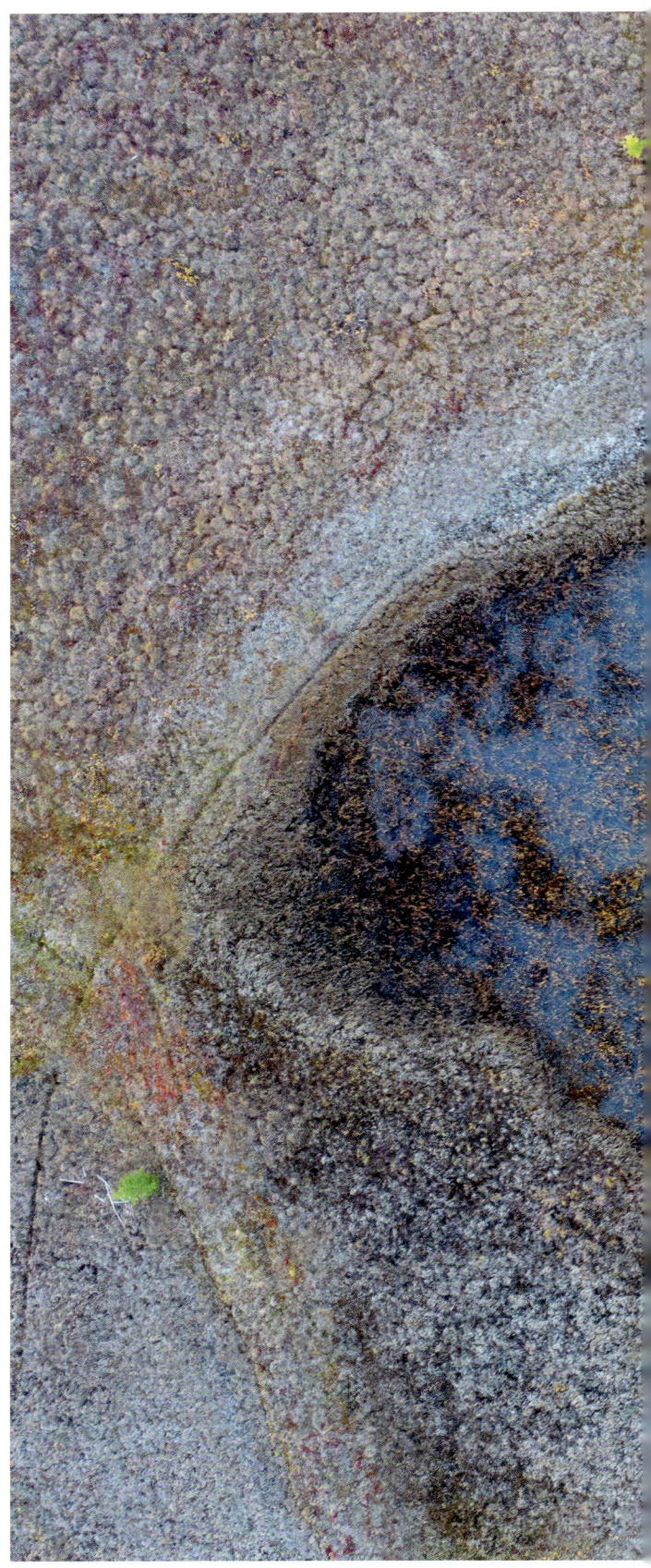

Eye of the tundra

When ice-rich permafrost below ground thaws, a striking thermokarst landscape can form with a large depression (known in Arctic Russia as an alas) on the surface. These often develop into swampy lakes. Alases are numerous – 16,000 have been recorded in Russia's Central Yakutia region – and evolve into unique ecosystems. Alexey discovered this 30-metre-wide (100 feet) thermokarst lake in the Olenyok valley of Polar Yakutia. Nearly half of the vast Yakutia region is within the Arctic Circle, and almost entirely within the permafrost zone. Here, autumn arrives by the end of August. The deciduous larches were already yellowing, and low-growing shrubs flamed orange and red, while pendant grass and other plants clung to the margins of the blue-eyed lake. Looking to the future, Arctic temperatures are rising roughly twice as fast as the global average. Meteorological studies predict that melting permafrost will accelerate, causing ground instability to buildings and transport links, and triggering the release of stored carbon.

DJI Mavic 2 Pro + Hasselblad L1D-20c 28mm f2.8 lens; 1/30 at f2.8 (-0.7 e/v); ISO 320.

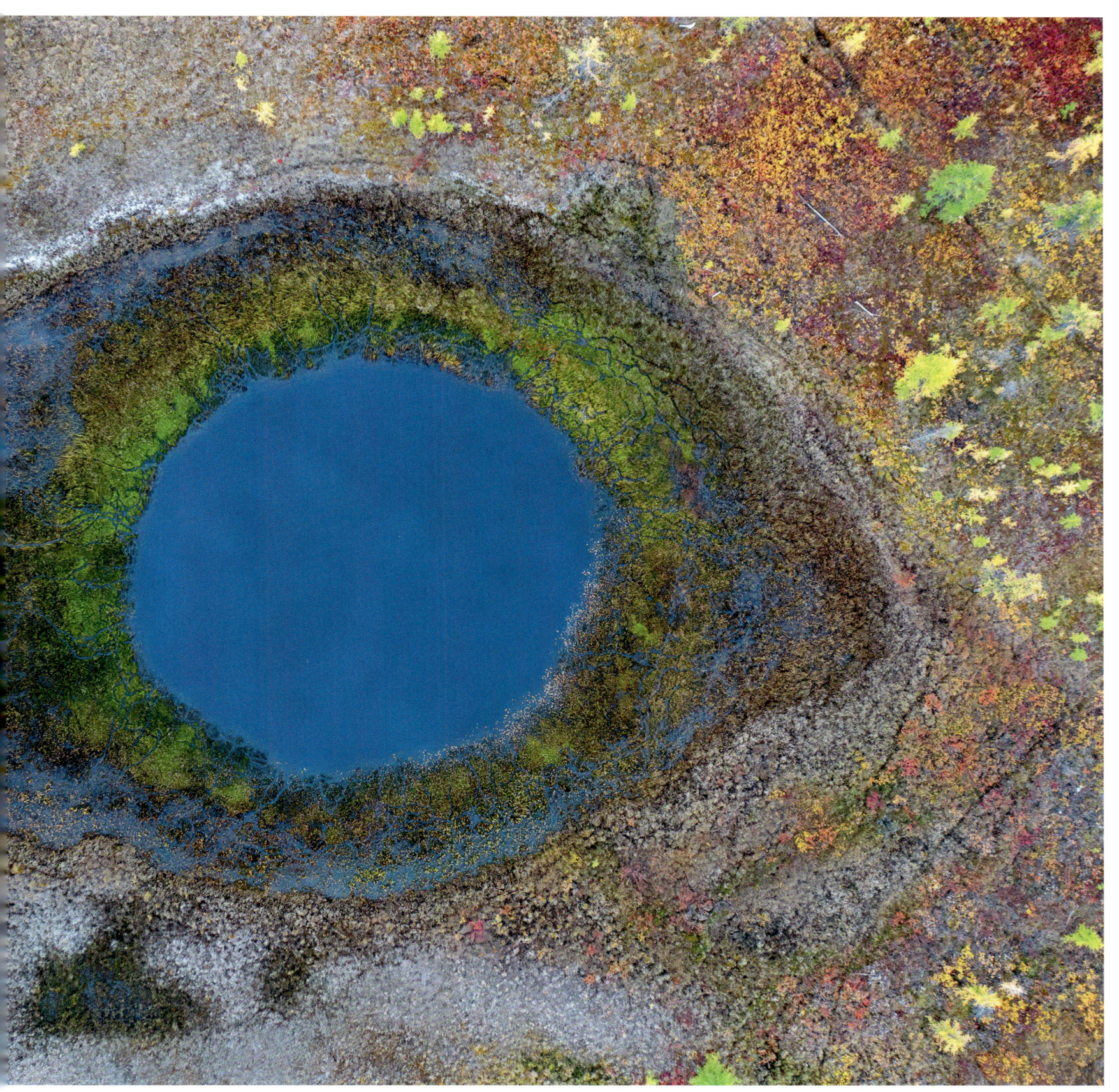

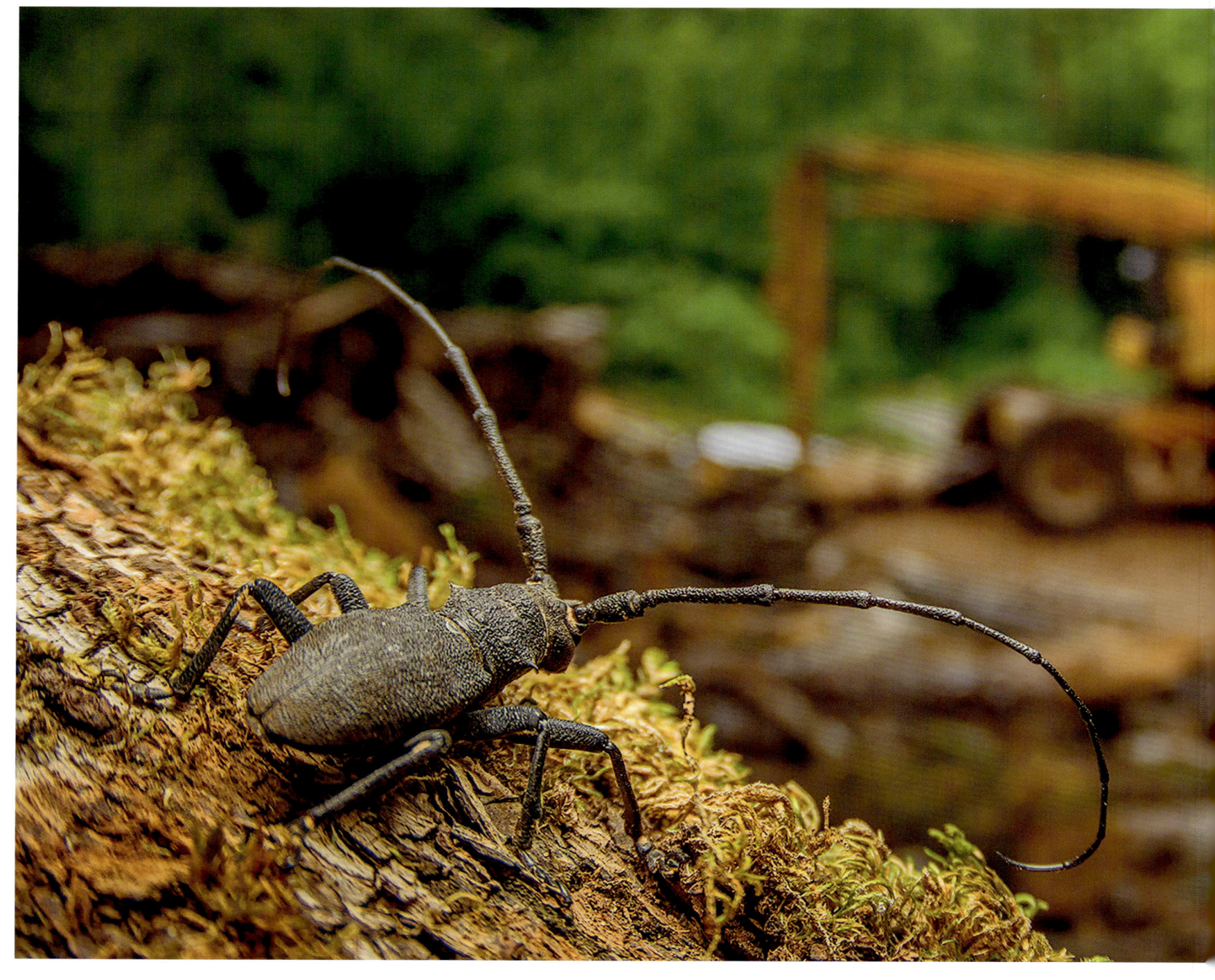

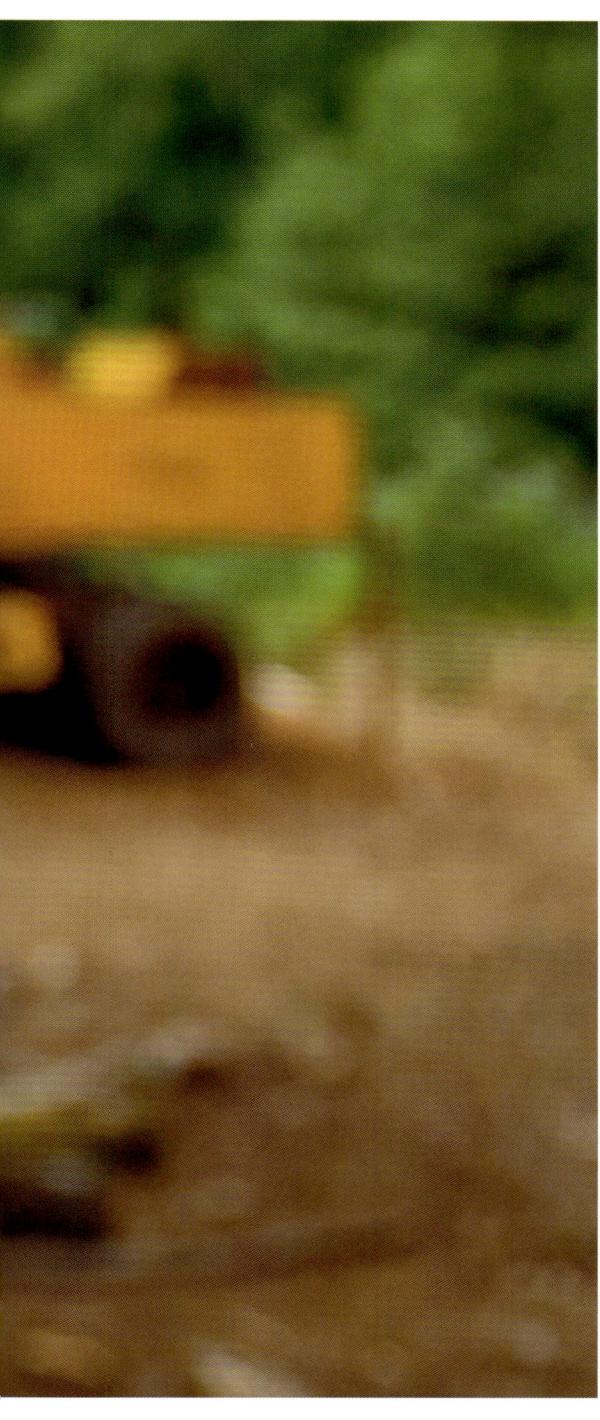

The Young Wildlife Photographer of the Year 2025 Award

This year's grand title is awarded to Andrea Dominizi of Italy. He is also the winner of the category for young photographers aged 15–17 years. Andrea's photograph has been judged to be the most memorable of all the entries by photographers aged 17 or under.

Andrea Dominizi

ITALY

Andrea took up wildlife photography four years ago. He specializes in macro photography, inspired by the many small arthropods he sees in the countryside near his home in central Italy. Andrea aims to tell creative stories with a conservation focus.

After the destruction

As if standing guard over its domain, a mature longhorn beetle resembles a forest sentinel observing a dangerous intruder into its woodland home. Andrea chanced upon it while walking in the Lepini Mountains of central Italy. This area of the mountains had been logged for its old beech trees; although the machinery in the background suggests ongoing activity, operations had ceased. Longhorn beetles inhabit old-growth forests across much of southern Europe, and seek out deadwood in the form of fallen tree trunks and branches, stumps and rotting bark, to lay their eggs. After hatching, longhorn larvae take several years to develop and will remain within the same piece of wood to feed and mature. The loss of ancient woodlands is a potential death knell to the beetles, as well as to other insect species. While Andrea and his friends were free to explore this patch of cleared forest and beyond, the beetles rarely move more than 500 metres (1,640 feet) from the deadwood home where they first emerged as larvae. As with other woodland species, logging and forest fragmentation poses a major threat to the beetle's lifecycle. Choosing wood and timber products that are certified as sustainably harvested is one way the public can help prevent the destruction of wildlife-rich old growth forests.

Nikon D7100 + Tokina 10–17mm f3.5–4.5 fisheye lens at 17mm; 1/80 at f8; ISO 400; Godox TT350 off-camera flash and diffuser.

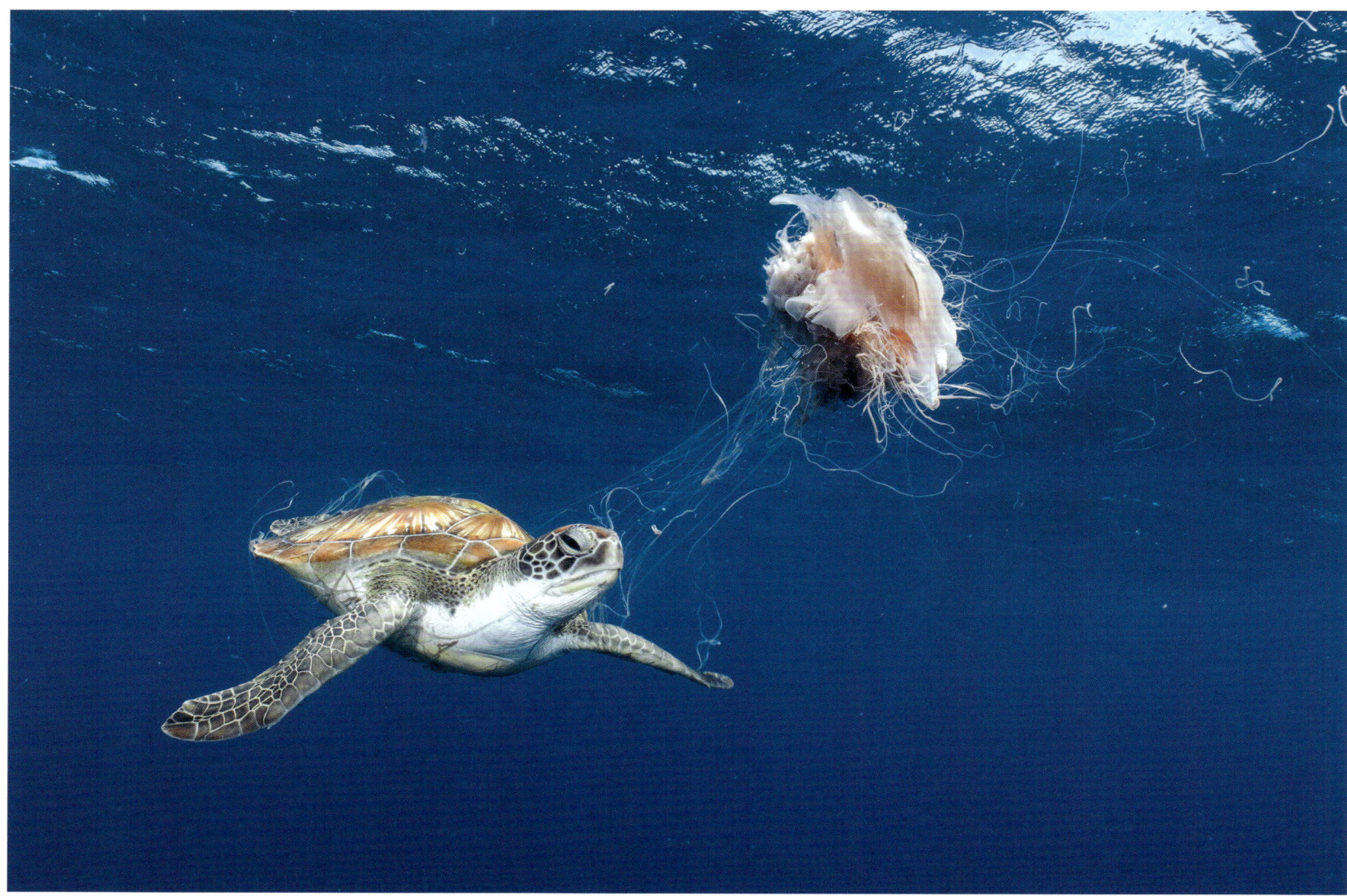

RUNNER-UP

Jellied meal

Tinnapat Netcharussaeng

THAILAND

While human swimmers should be wary of the long, stinging tentacles of this lion's mane jellyfish, they are just another food source for a green sea turtle. Tinnapat watched as the endangered reptile bit chunks out of its invertebrate prey while he was scuba diving off Koh Losin, a rocky islet in the Gulf of Thailand. Among marine turtles, adult green sea turtles are unusual in subsisting almost entirely on seagrass, but juveniles are known to eat some invertebrates, including jellyfish and sponges. Tinnapat was rewarded with several sharp stings as he moved in to take the picture, but says they were 'a small price for achieving a photograph with the vision I wanted.'

Sony α1 + 28–60mm f4–5.6 lens; 1/125 at f22; ISO 640; Seacam 160D flash; Nauticam NA-α1 housing; Nauticam WACP-1 wide-angle conversion port.

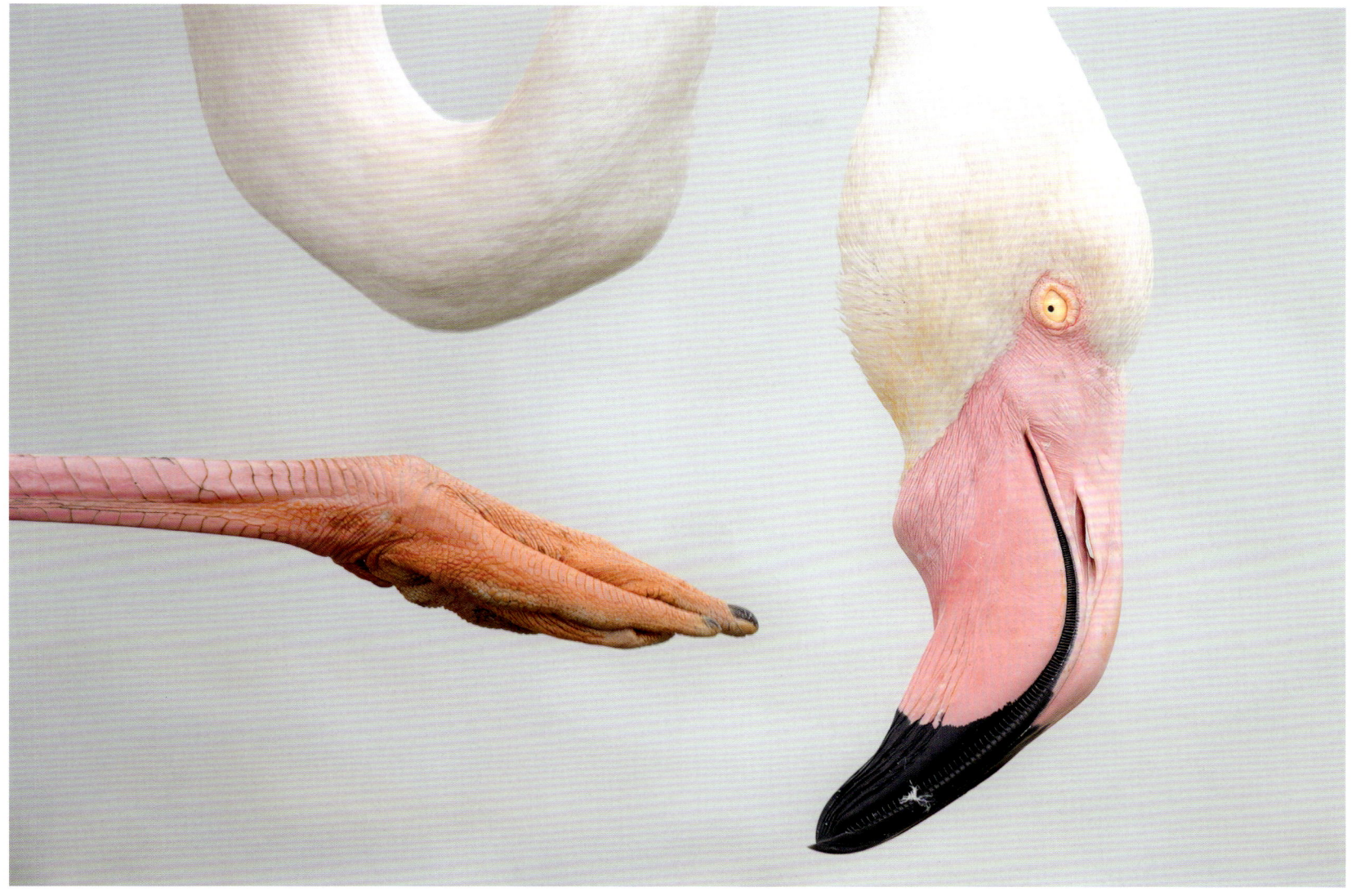

Pink pose

Leana Kuster

SWITZERLAND

A greater flamingo is caught in the mundane act of scratching its head with one of its unmistakably long legs. Leana had been watching the flamingos in the Camargue, the iconic wetlands of southern France, while on a family holiday. Although it was raining at the time, she sat for hours on the wet ground, fascinated by their foraging behaviour as they moved gracefully through the saline shallows, filter feeding for molluscs and crustaceans. Flamingos use their tongues to force water through their specially adapted bills, lined with many rows of fine comb-like plates, to trap a species of brine shrimp called *Artemia salina*, which gives the birds their famous pink hue. The Camargue is France's largest wetland and the only region in the country where flamingos nest. While many migrate to North Africa, Spain and Turkey for the winter, some will stay here all year round.

Nikon D810 + Tamron 150–600mm f5.6 lens; 1/500 at f6.3; ISO 250.

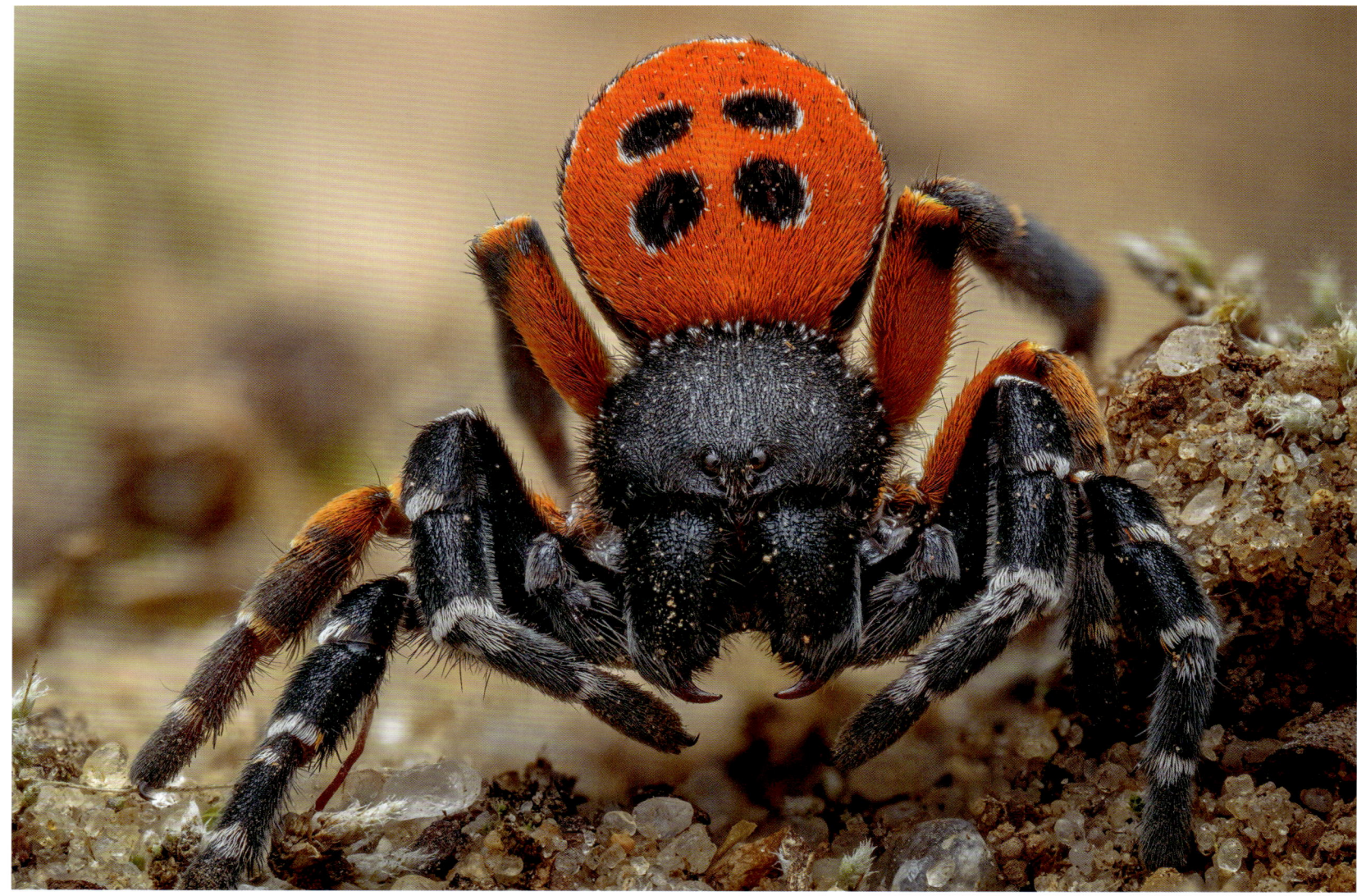

Red alert

Alexis Tinker-Tsavalas

GERMANY

With its distinctive red abdomen and four black spots, it's easy to see why this arachnid acquired the common name of the ladybird spider. Males develop the vivid red abdomen with black spots once they are mature and ready to reproduce. The spiders are found on heathlands in northern and central Europe, and possibly into central Asia. Across Europe, the spider's heathland habitat is at risk through conversion to agriculture, housing and forestry. Alexis took this photo at Döberitzer Heath, a former military training area near Berlin, protected as a nature reserve since 2004. He used a technique called focus stacking (where multiple images are captured at different focus planes) to achieve greater depth of field, and thereby maximize the impact of the spider's brilliant red abdomen.

Fujifilm X-H2 + Laowa 65mm f2.8 2x ultra macro lens; 1/250 at f5.6; ISO 320; Godox V860iii flash; Cygnustech diffuser; focus stack of 102 images.

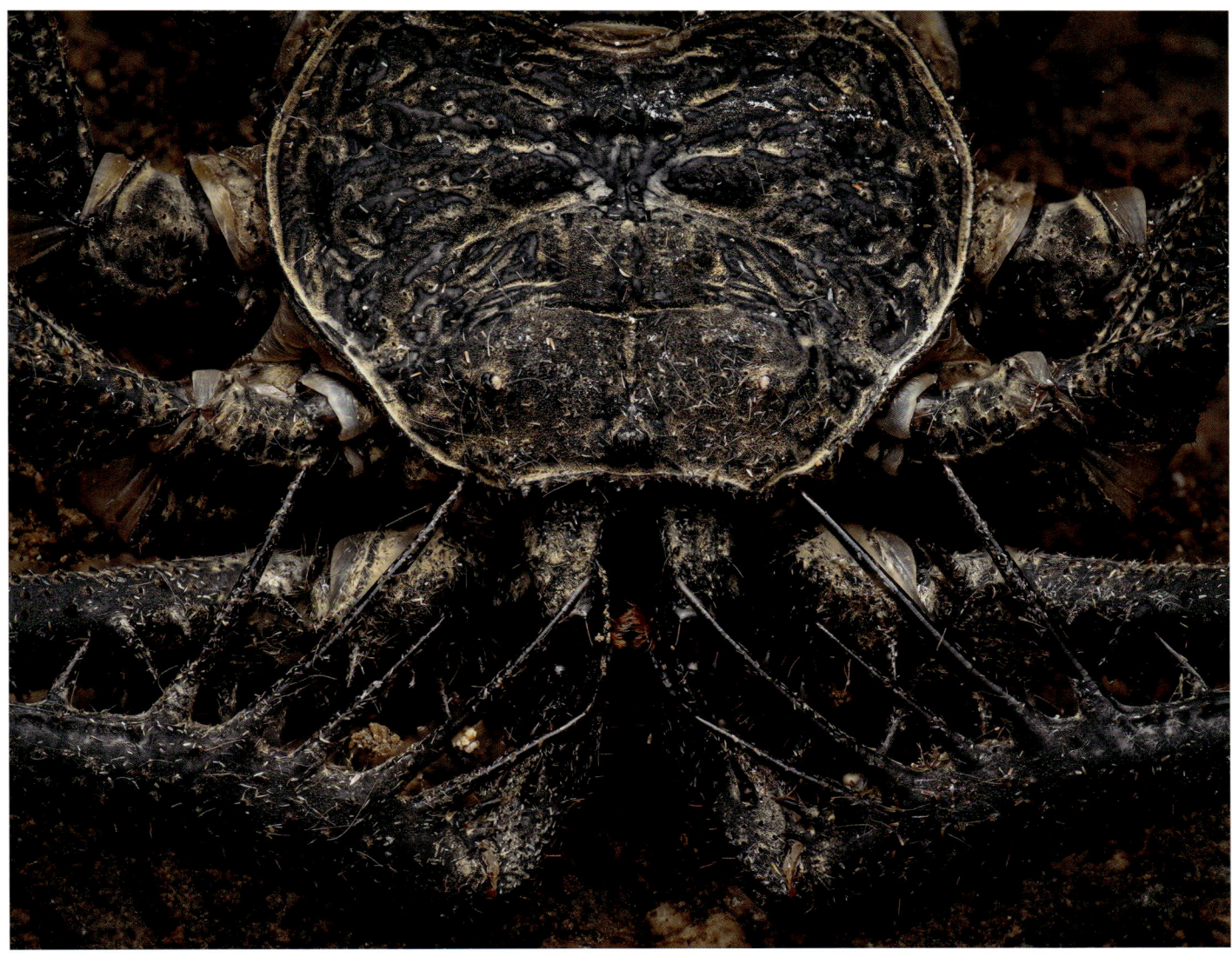

Cave stalker

Beckett Robertson

CANADA

Some creatures might be scary to look at, but looks can also deceive. This is an amblypygid, a nocturnal arachnid belonging to a group of animals also known as whip spiders, because the front pair of legs have evolved into long, whip-like limbs used as sensors. Beckett found this species, *Phrynus longipes*, in the Cueva del Boulevard Turístico del Atlántico, Dominican Republic. He estimated its leg span at 46 centimetres (18 inches). Whip spiders possess thorn-like spines on their pedipalps to grasp and consume prey. They seek caves, crevices and other dark hiding places in the Caribbean rainforests by day, before emerging at dusk to ambush prey. Unlike most spiders, *Phrynus longipes* can't produce silk or spin a web; nor does it possess any venom glands. So, despite the fearsome appearance, it is harmless to humans.

OM System OM-1 + 60mm f2.8 macro lens; 1/400 at f10; ISO 250; Godox TT350 O flash + Cygnustech macro diffuser.

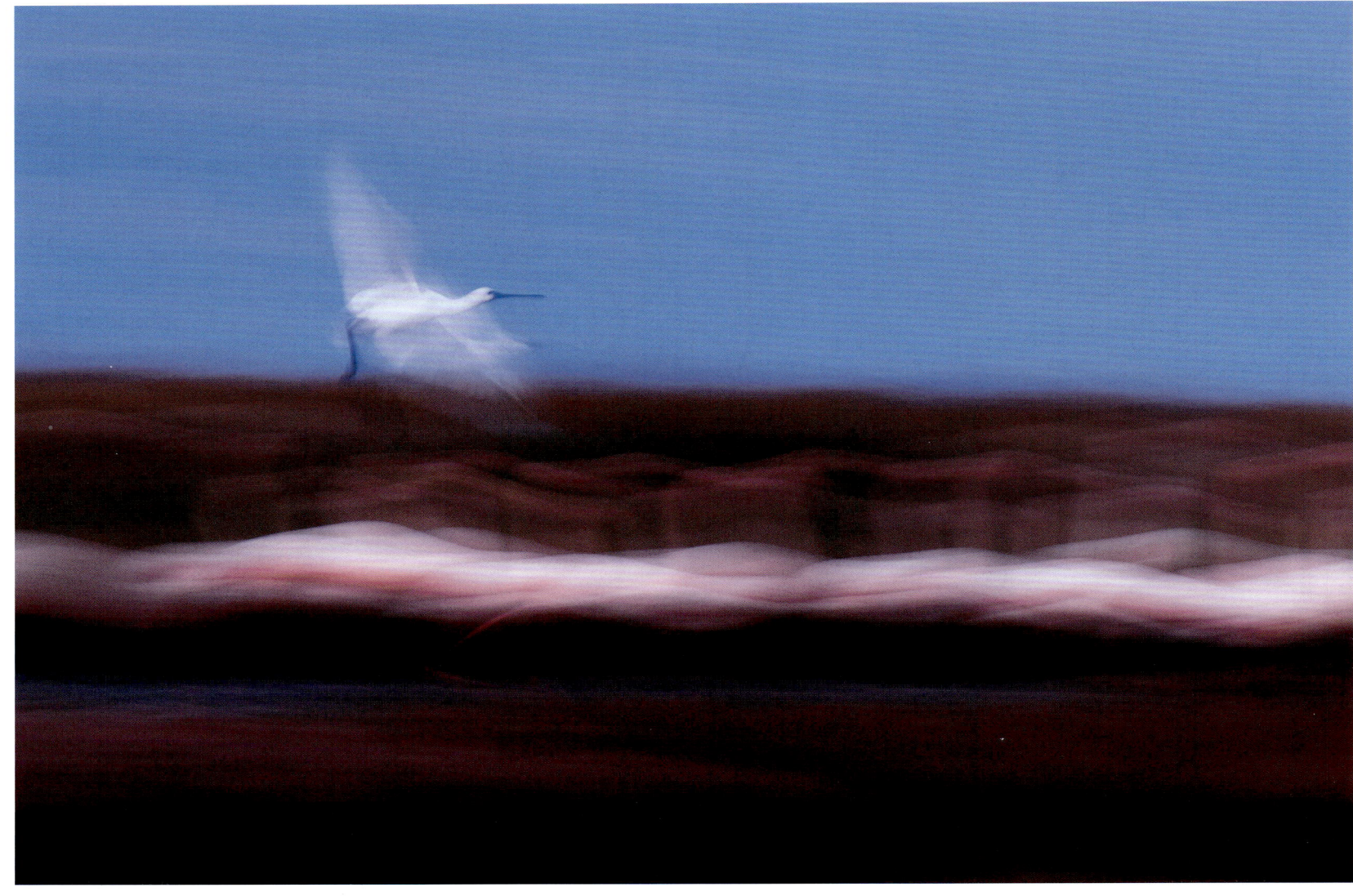

White over pink

Tomasz Michalski

POLAND

Moving his camera deliberately, Tomasz captured the moment he saw a Eurasian spoonbill fly over a flock of greater flamingos, standing in a salt marsh on the Greek island of Lesvos. He had spent several days photographing the flamingos filter-feeding on algae and tiny aquatic invertebrates near the town of Kalloni, and decided to experiment with a technique known as intentional camera movement. This involves moving the camera slightly while pressing the shutter at a slow speed to create a blurred, almost impressionistic effect. Though spoonbills are not rare on Lesvos, this one was the first Tomasz had seen on his trip. Both spoonbills and greater flamingos have a widespread Eurasian and (to a lesser extent for spoonbills) African distribution, with the European populations of both species currently increasing.

Nikon Z8 + Tamron 150–600mm f5–6.3 lens; 1/4 at f/20; ISO 100.

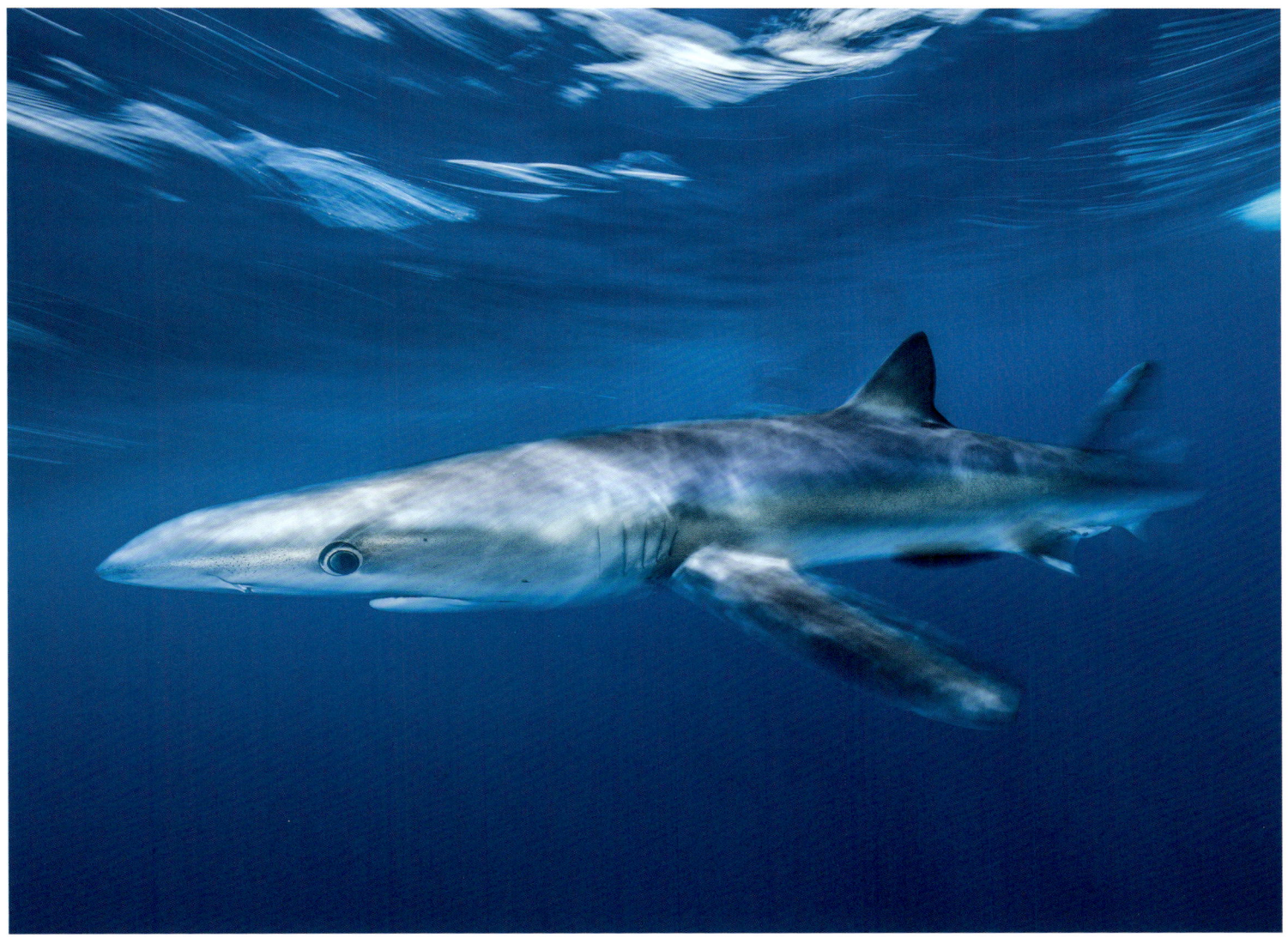

Blue streak

Tinnapat Netcharussaeng

THAILAND

There can be no mistaking the aptly named blue shark seen here in Tinnapat's photo, taken off the southern tip of Baja California, Mexico. The shark's striking blue back and white underside are an example of countershading, a type of camouflage whereby their back matches the blue of the ocean when viewed from above, and the white underbelly the light from the surface when seen from below. Blue sharks should not be feared; although often seen around divers, unprovoked bites are rare. They are the most migratory of sharks, covering about 9,000 kilometres (5,600 miles) annually, but heavily fished – an estimated 20 million individuals are caught globally each year, often as bycatch. Fortunately, blue sharks are prodigious breeders, with females giving birth to an average of 35 pups in each litter.

Sony α1 + 12–24mm f2.8 lens; 1/5 at f22; ISO 50; Seacam 160D strobe; Nauticam NA-α1 housing; Seacam Superdome port.

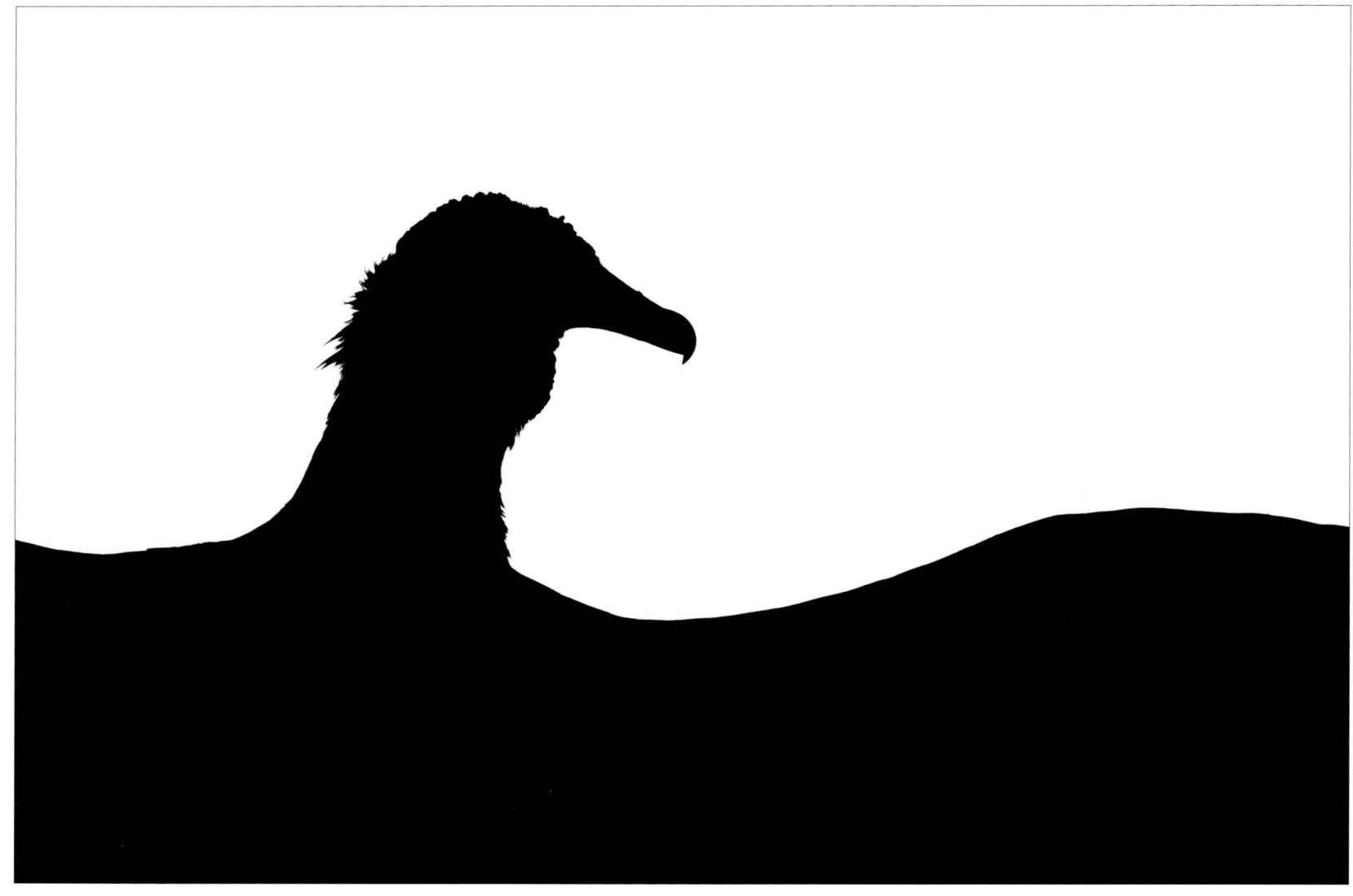

The silhouette

Tomasz Michalski

POLAND

Considering they are the most numerous vulture in the western hemisphere, Tomasz experienced many encounters with black vultures during a visit to Nicaragua. However, he hadn't taken any pictures that pleased him – until he saw this individual fanning out its wings to dry after a rain shower. This prompted Tomasz to attempt a silhouette effect, rendering the vulture's profile plain black (as befits its name) against a white sky. Public opinion about vultures is as black and white as this image: as scavengers, the birds gather to feed on carrion, but farmers in North and South America say they kill calves and lambs. Scientific evidence says the extent of predation is exaggerated. Instead, they should be valued for their ecological role when cleaning carcasses, thereby reducing the spread of pathogens and disease.

OM System OM-1 Mark II + Panasonic Leica DG Vario-Elmar 100-400mm f4.0-6.3 lens; 1/320 at f22; ISO 125.

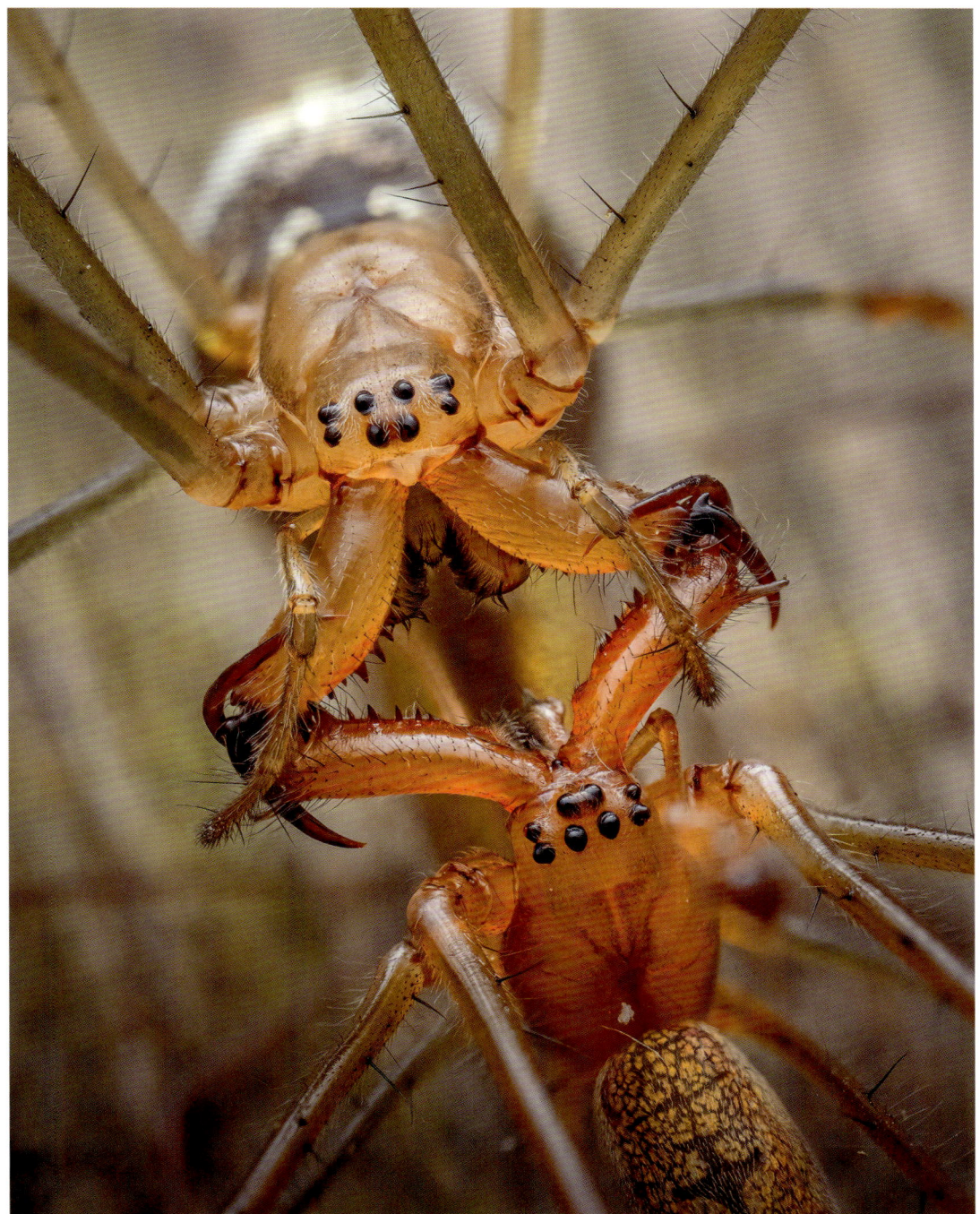

Long jaws locked

Alexis Tinker-Tsavalas

GERMANY

This pair of long-jawed orb weaver spiders appear to be locked in a battle that neither can win. In fact, they are a mating male and female, and their jaws, known as chelicerae, are joined together while the smaller male (below) transfers sperm to the female from one of its pedipalps. Known also as stretch spiders, their horizontal webs are usually spun just above the surface water of a pond, stream or marsh to catch aquatic insects that emerge in their winged adult forms. Alexis spotted this scene in a Berlin wetland. From a fixed position, he made a focus stack of 27 images, a technique whereby multiple exposures are taken at different focal planes then combined into one image using specialist software to maximize the subject's depth of focus.

Fujifilm X-H2 + Laowa 65mm f2.8 2x ultra macro lens; 1/200 at f5.6; ISO 200; Godox V860III flash; Cygnustech diffuser; focus stack of 27 images.

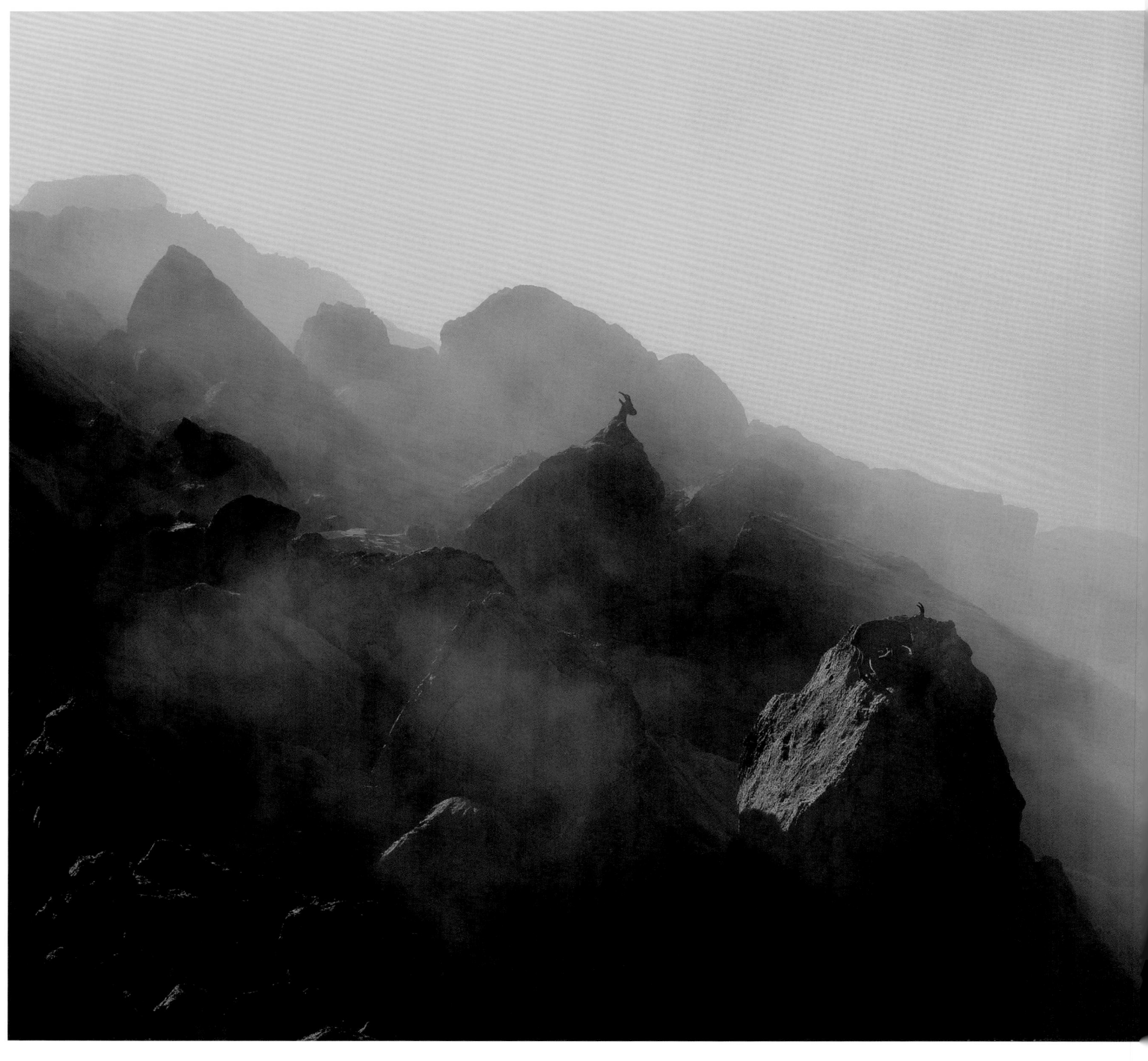

Young Wildlife Photographers: 11–14 years

Alpine dawn

Lubin Godin

FRANCE

Two female Alpine ibex, the nearer with a kid, rest atop the jagged limestone crags of Col de la Colombière, in the French Alps. Endemic to Europe, the species was hunted close to extinction in the early 1800s. Protection and reintroduction programmes now see it back across the Alps, albeit with very low genetic diversity and high inbreeding, which may reduce its ability to survive the fast-changing climate. As alpine temperatures rise, scientists predict ibex will be forced to forage in limited areas closer to mountain peaks, thereby restricting the range of suitable habitat. Females give birth from early June, usually to one kid, capable of following its mother across the rugged terrain at just a day old. Though hunting Alpine ibex is illegal in France, controversial culling is being carried out to control brucellosis, a bacterial disease that also affects domestic livestock and humans. Lubin noticed the ibex resting above a sea of clouds as he made an early morning ascent in August. Glancing back later, he saw the mist rising as the sun was breaking over the crags and quickly retraced his steps to capture this ethereal moment before the fog thickened and the light faded.

Canon EOS R7 + 100–400mm f4.5–5.6 lens at 140mm + 1.4x teleconverter; 1/640 at f8; ISO 100.

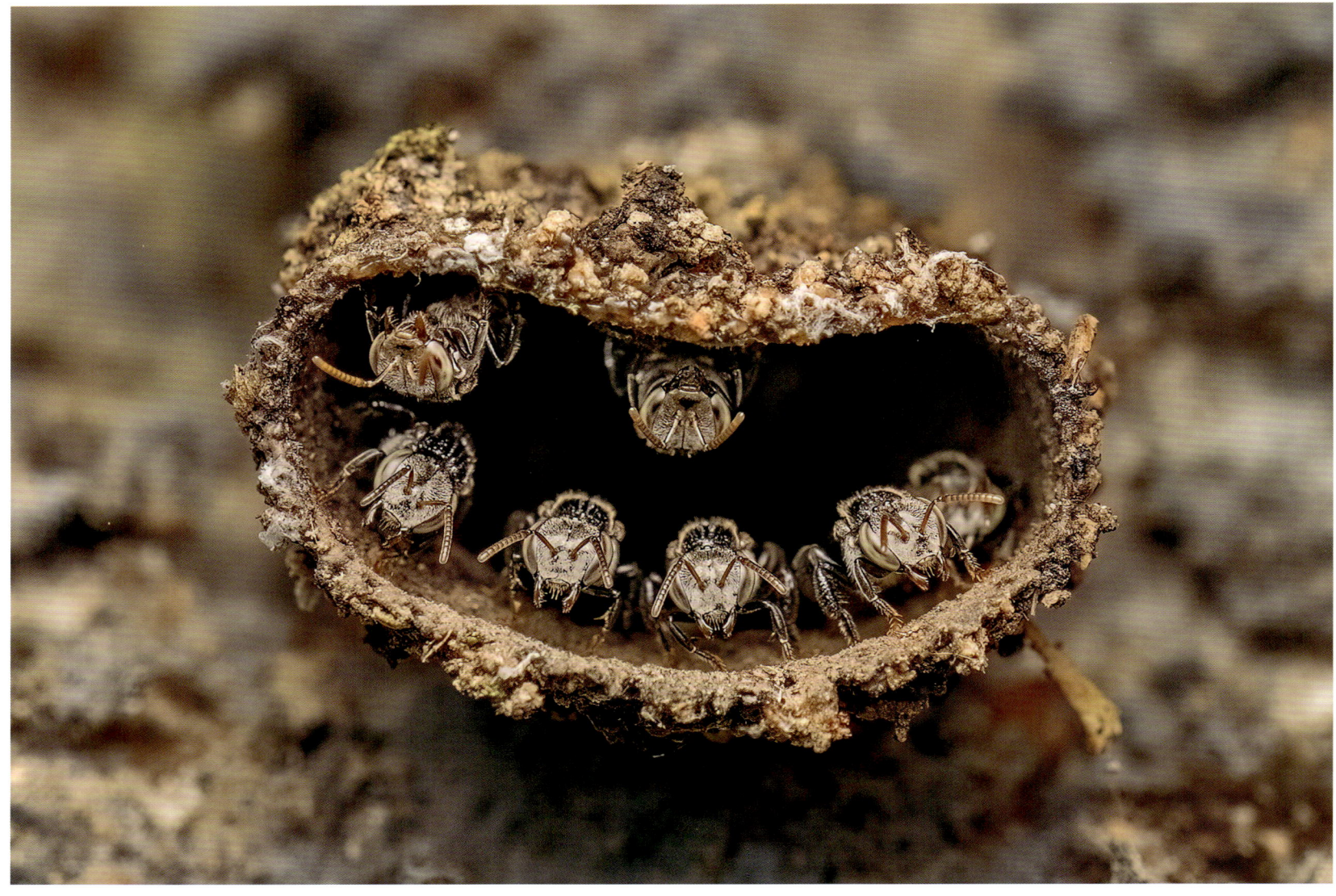

RUNNER-UP

On guard

Rithved Girishkumar

INDIA/UNITED ARAB EMIRATES

A band of worker stingless bees stand guard at the tube-like entrance to their nest, in Kerala, southwest India. These sentries, a few millimetres long, lack effective stings but can bite an intruder or invade its nose and ears. Their nest (built with wax, resin and mud) was hidden within an old wall, but Rithved spotted the comings and goings of a few foragers. Stingless bees are important and prized pollinators – although the smallest of the honey-producing bees, their honey fetches a higher price because of its medicinal values. Careful not to disturb the bees, Rithved crouched down, braving ants and thorny shrubs, to capture them face on.

Nikon D850 + Sigma 105mm f2.8 macro lens; 1/400 at f11 (-0.3 e/v); ISO 160; Rollei flash 58F; Radiant diffuser.

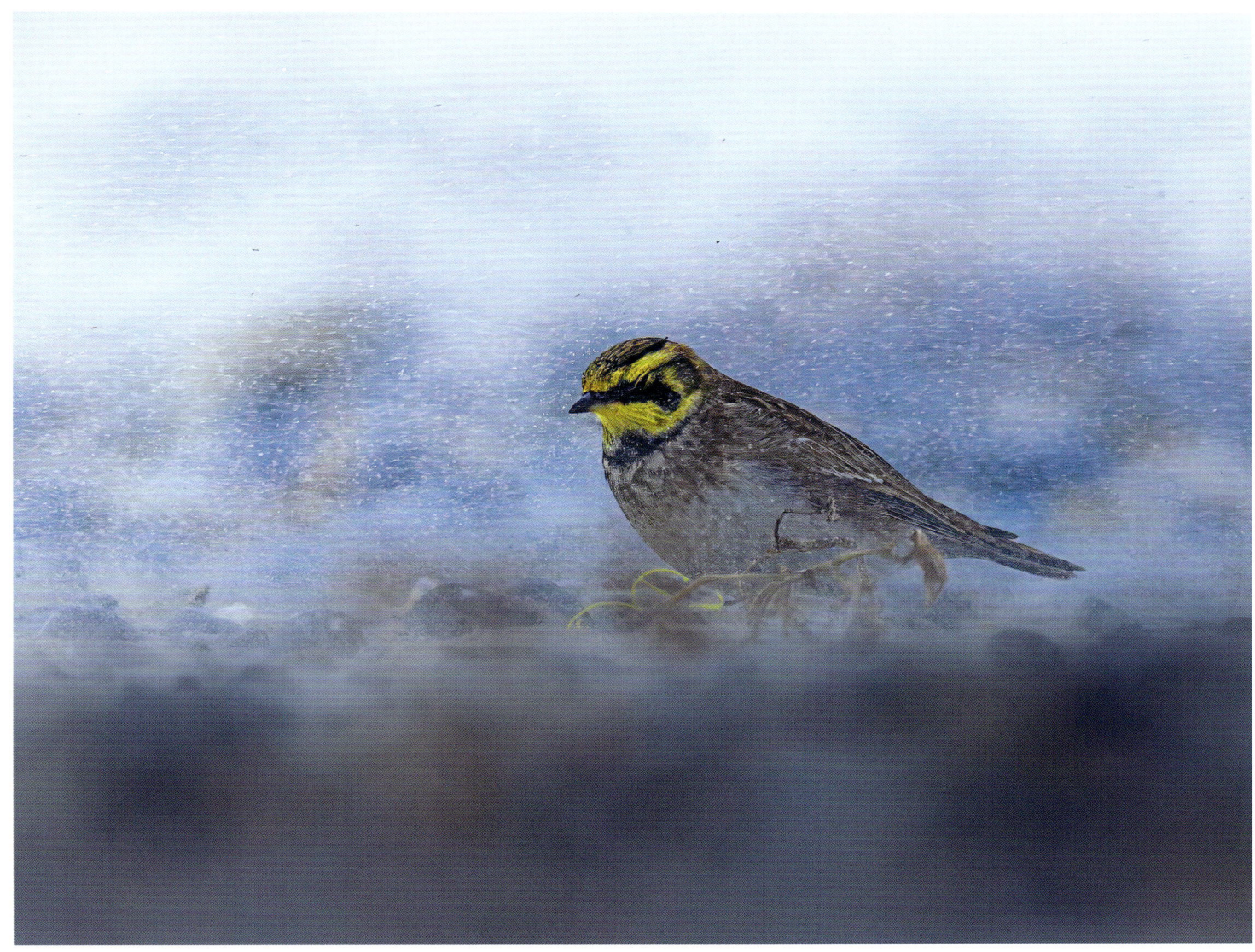

Sand-swept lark

Néo Koslowski

GERMANY

As the wind whipped up on the small, North Sea island of Düne, in the German archipelago of Heligoland, many creatures sought shelter. But Néo pressed himself into the sand, his eyes on a defiant male horned lark that had been gradually approaching him as it searched for food. This songster – the only lark to have colonized tundra and alpine habitats – is widespread and abundant but has declined steeply in North America over the past 50 years, largely due to agricultural changes. In Eurasia, it breeds in Scandinavia and Arctic Russia, migrating south in autumn, with small numbers visiting North Sea coasts. The lark paused, head to wind, closing its eyes against the swirling sand. Néo deftly captured the scene, then spent an hour or so removing sand from his kit and ears.

Canon EOS R5 + 100–500mm f4.5–7.1 lens at 500mm; 1/1250 at f7.1 (+1 e/v); ISO 1000.

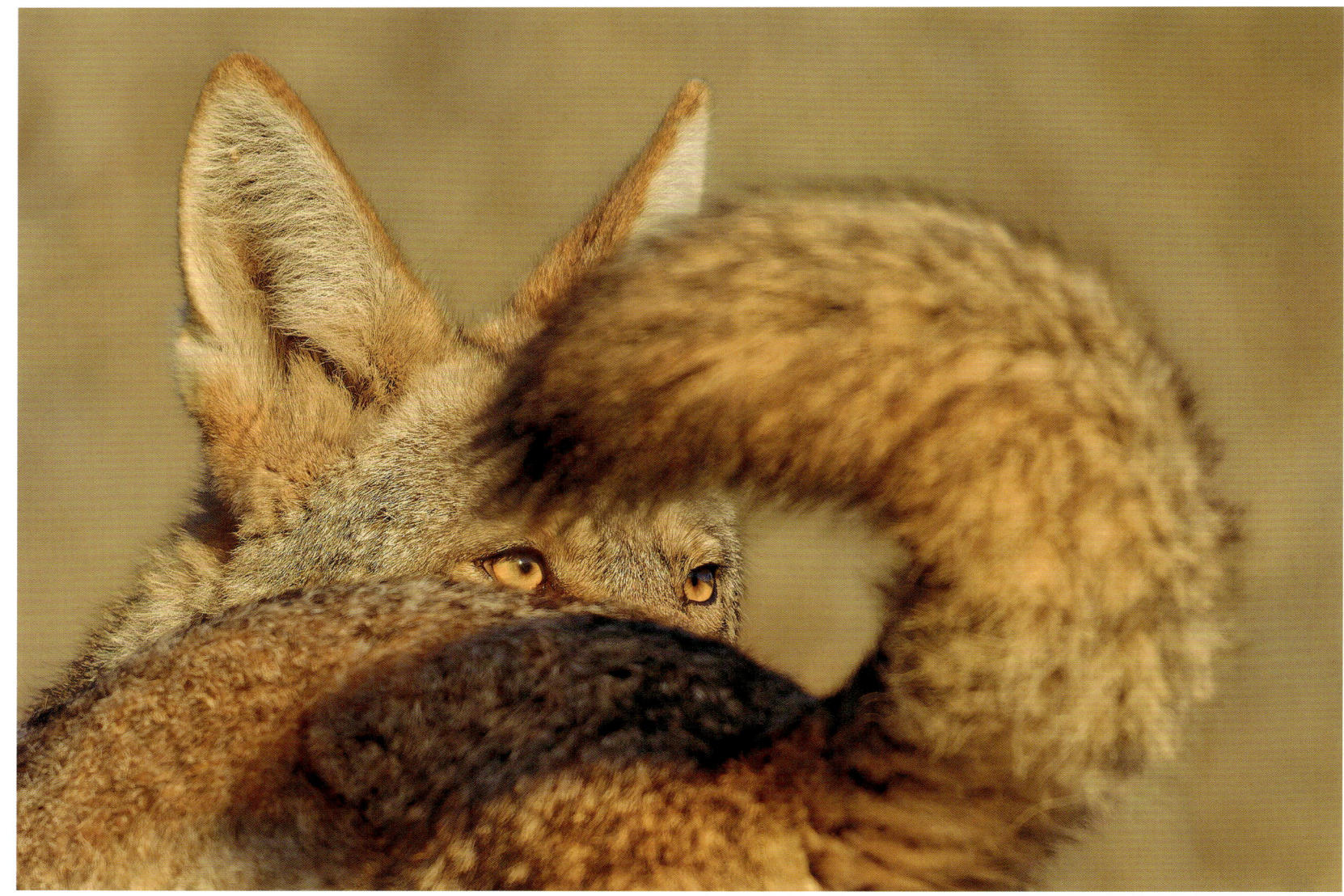

A tale of two coyotes

Parham Pourahmad

USA

A female coyote playfully wags her black-tipped tail as she trots past a male, possibly her brother, framing his amber eyes in the morning light of Bernal Heights Park, San Francisco, USA. Abundant across North America and into Central America, this largely crepuscular species is so versatile that it can utilize almost all habitats, including urban areas, and hunt a wide variety of prey. In recent decades, coyotes have repopulated San Francisco, coming into conflict with humans when scavenging food waste, although their diet includes rodents and other small mammals. Courtship and mating takes place from late winter to early spring, producing an average of six pups per litter. Parham followed these two coyotes across the rocky hillside and quickly framed his shot before the male turned to nuzzle the female.

Nikon Z8 + 180–600mm f5.6–6.3 lens at 600mm; 1/1250 at f6.3; ISO 800.

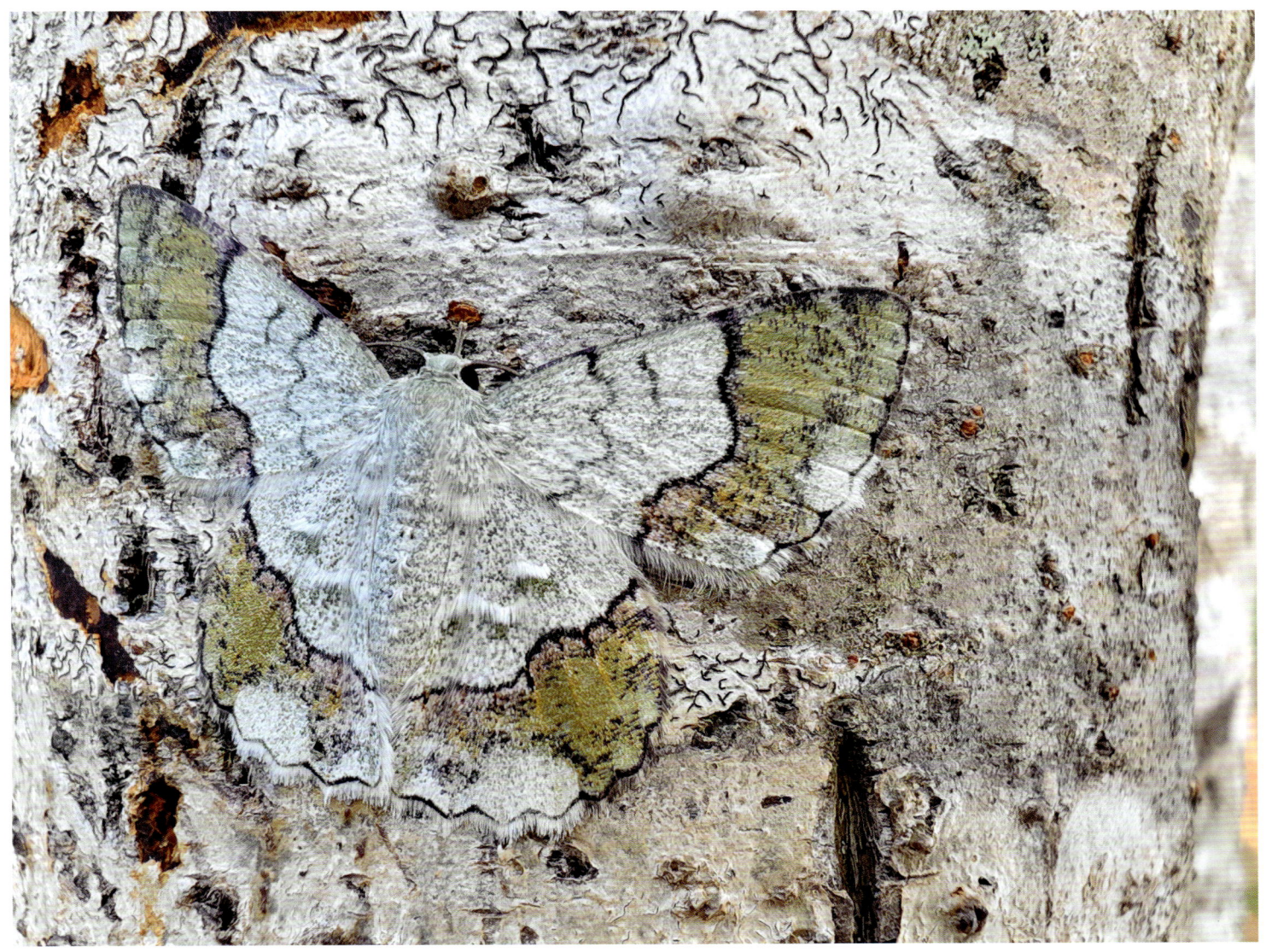

Hiding in plain sight

Zhixuan Sun

CHINA

Intrigued by a pattern on the silvery bark of a tree in Xishuangbanna Tropical Botanical Garden, Yunnan, China, Zhixuan went for a closer look. His curiosity led him to a bordered duster moth resting on the trunk, a species well camouflaged from above but with bold bands of black, white and yellow on its underwings. It belongs to the large Geometridae family, named after the characteristic looping locomotion of their caterpillars (also known as inchworms), as if they are measuring the ground beneath them. Adult geometrids can resemble butterflies, their broad wings held flat when resting, but unlike butterflies, their antennae are never clubbed. Afraid the moth would fly away, Zhixuan grabbed his smartphone and slowly moved closer, shooting in macro mode to get the best results.

Vivo X100 Ultra + 23mm built-in lens; 1/265 at f2.2 (+1.5 e/v); ISO 71.

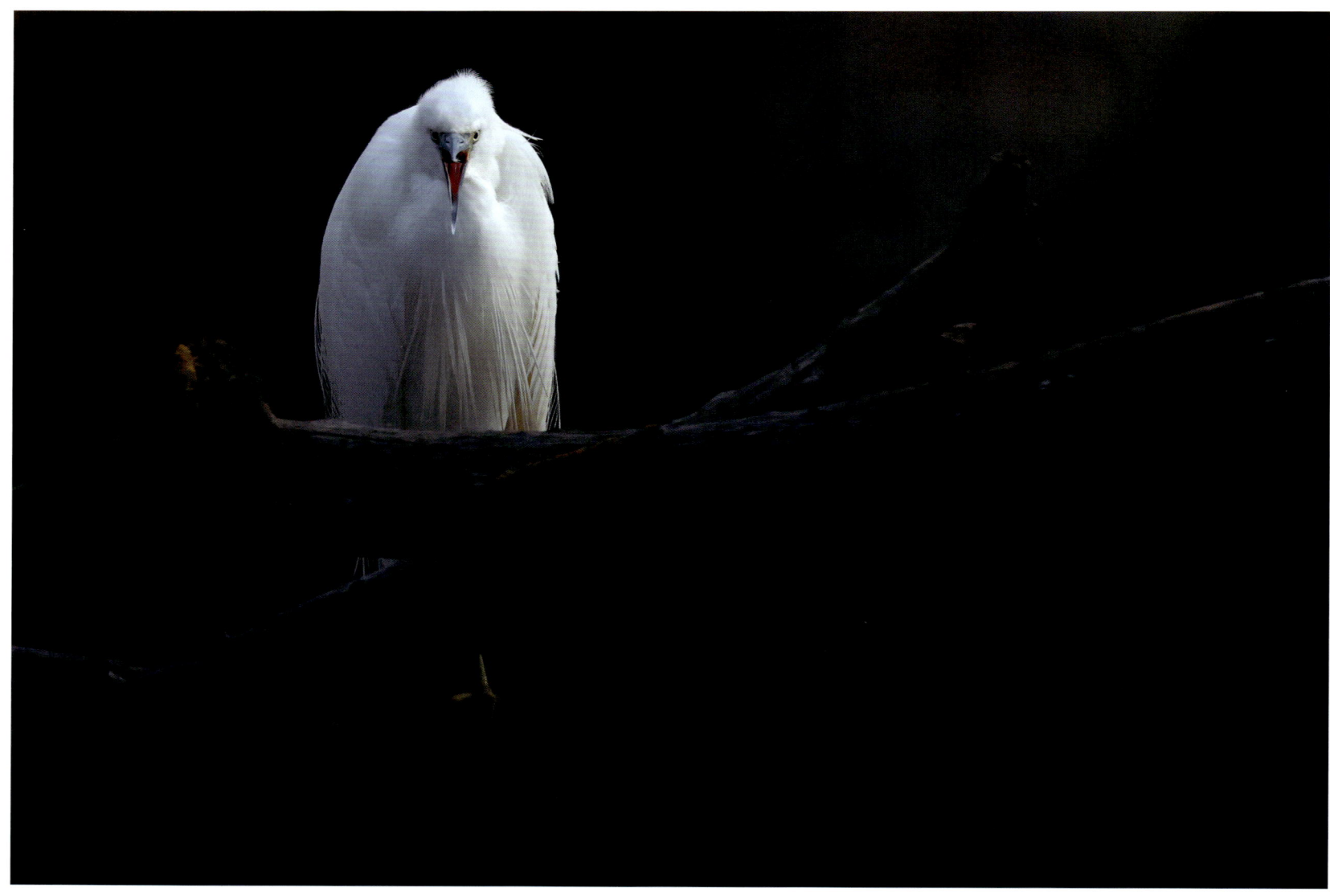

Spirit of the marsh

Lubin Godin

FRANCE

In the gloom of a grey February morning on the Marais du Vigueirat, a nature reserve in the Camargue, France, the brilliant white of a little egret caught Lubin's eye. Its black legs and yellow feet were almost lost in shadow as it rested on a branch. For centuries, snowy, great and little egrets were exploited for their plumes for the fashion trade, wiping them out from much of their range. This adaptable, small heron species has since recovered and is widespread across much of Eurasia, Africa and Australia. Today, little egrets are threatened by loss and degradation of their wetland habitat to agriculture, and susceptible to future outbreaks of avian flu. Lubin stood on tiptoes, shivering in the icy wind, when the bird opened its dagger-like bill. 'It gives the egret a rather unfriendly look,' he says, 'but it was just yawning.'

Canon EOS R7 + 100–400mm f4.5–5.6mm lens at 400mm + 1.4x teleconverter; 1/1250 at f8; ISO 800.

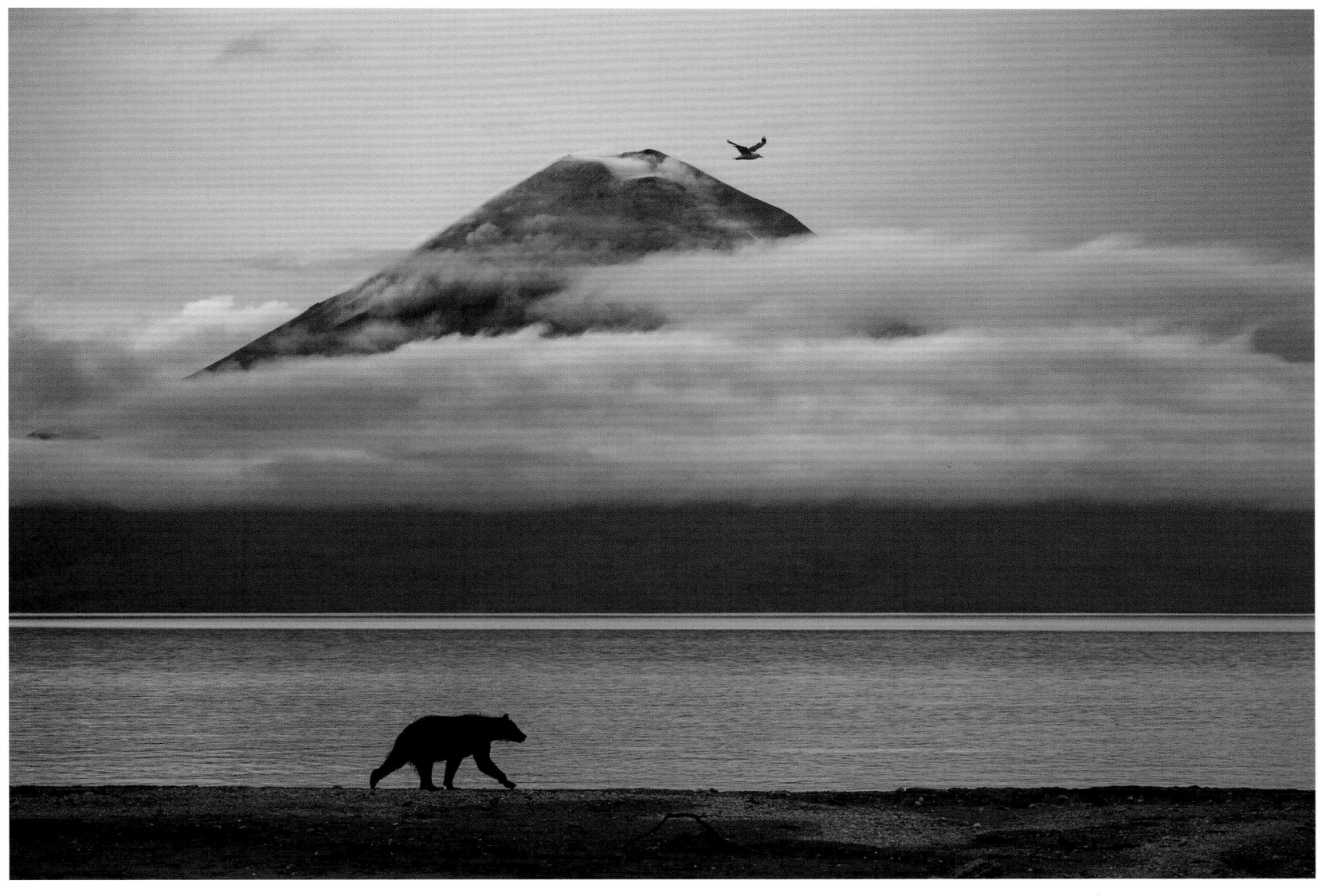

Essence of Kamchatka

Kesshav Vikram

INDIA

Kesshav waited days for the elements he had in mind to come together: a brown bear strolling along the shore of Kurile Lake on the Kamchatka peninsula, in Russia's far east, coinciding with the emergence of the Iliinsky volcano from the clouds. Generally solitary, the bear was going to feast with others on the glut of sockeye salmon, migrating up river from the Pacific to their natal lake to spawn. This volcanic caldera lake is the largest sockeye salmon spawning ground in Eurasia. The bears dine well on the high-calorie fish, fattening to 500 kilograms (1,100 pounds) or more, before environmental cues prompt their six-month hibernation. The surprise flypast of a slaty-backed gull, aligned with the summit of the volcano that last erupted in 1901, added the final touch to capture the character of this remote wilderness.

Nikon Z8 + 100–400mm f4.5–5.6 lens at 100mm; 1/4000 at f4.5 (+0.3 e/v); ISO 1000; beanbag.

Young Wildlife Photographers:
10 years and under

The weaver's lair

Jamie Smart

UK

On a cold September morning in mid-Wales, a gorse orbweaver sits tight inside its silken retreat. Roaming her garden, camera in hand, Jamie spotted the dew-laden threads first, spun on a dock plant, before realizing their maker was lying in ambush. As with others in the Araneidae family, this spider spins an orb web – the classic bicycle-wheel shape, constructed from a scaffold of radial threads, overlaid with a spiral of silk, which is coated in a sticky substance to hold ensnared insects in place. A lattice of silk threads spans the hub, from which a strong signal thread extends to the spider's nearby hiding place. This transmits vibrations from struggling prey, triggering the lurking spider to rush out and grab its meal. The species is widespread in England and Wales and across most of western Europe, where it is usually found on gorse bushes, heather and other low vegetation. This specimen was deep in its web and a little restless, but with the patience and steadiness needed to focus manually and to keep her subject well lit and symmetrical, Jamie captured this low-lying arachnid in a single shot.

Nikon Z9 + 105mm f2.8 lens; 1/200 at f10; ISO 80; Nikon SB-910 Speedlight flash; Cygnustech diffuser.

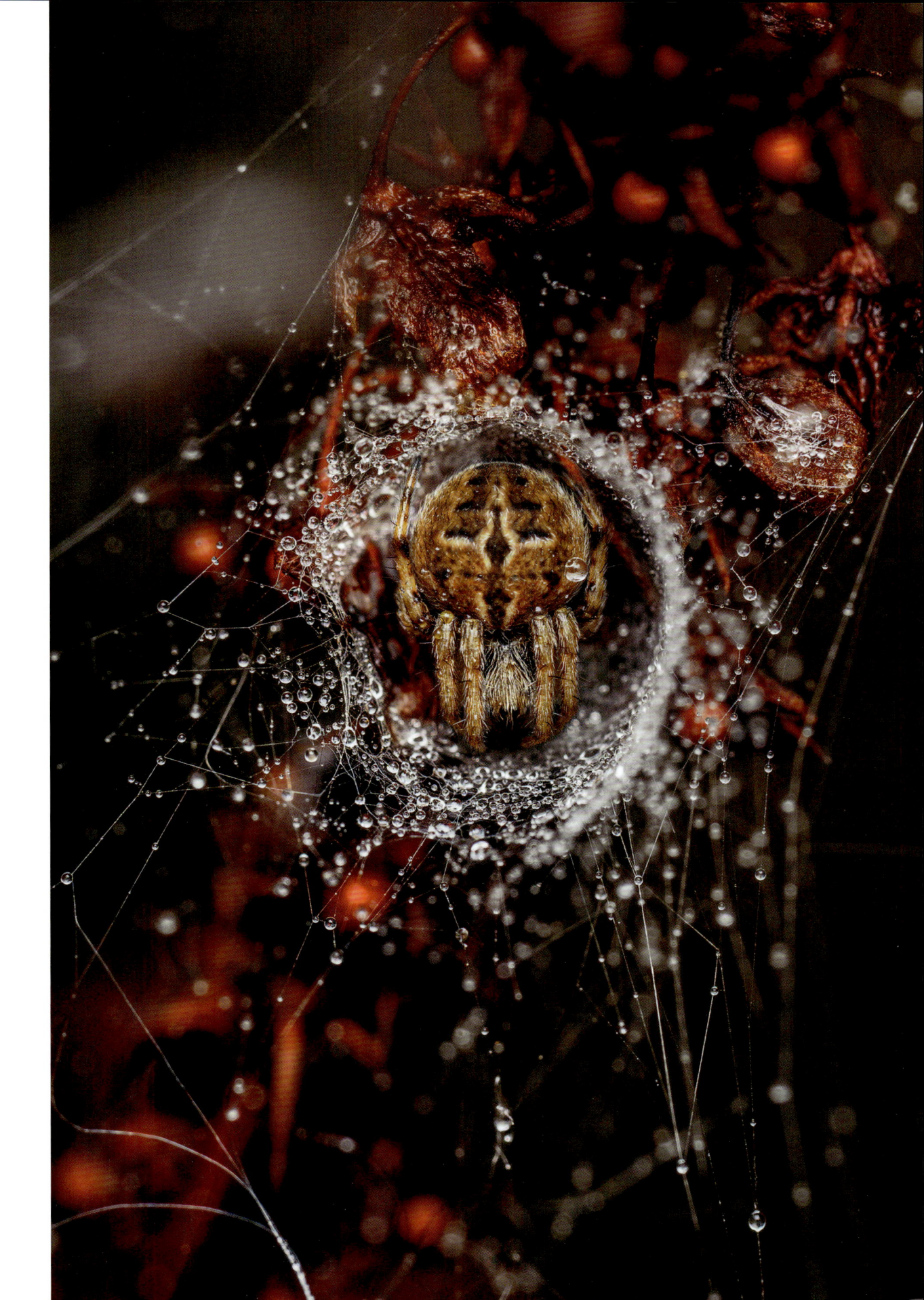

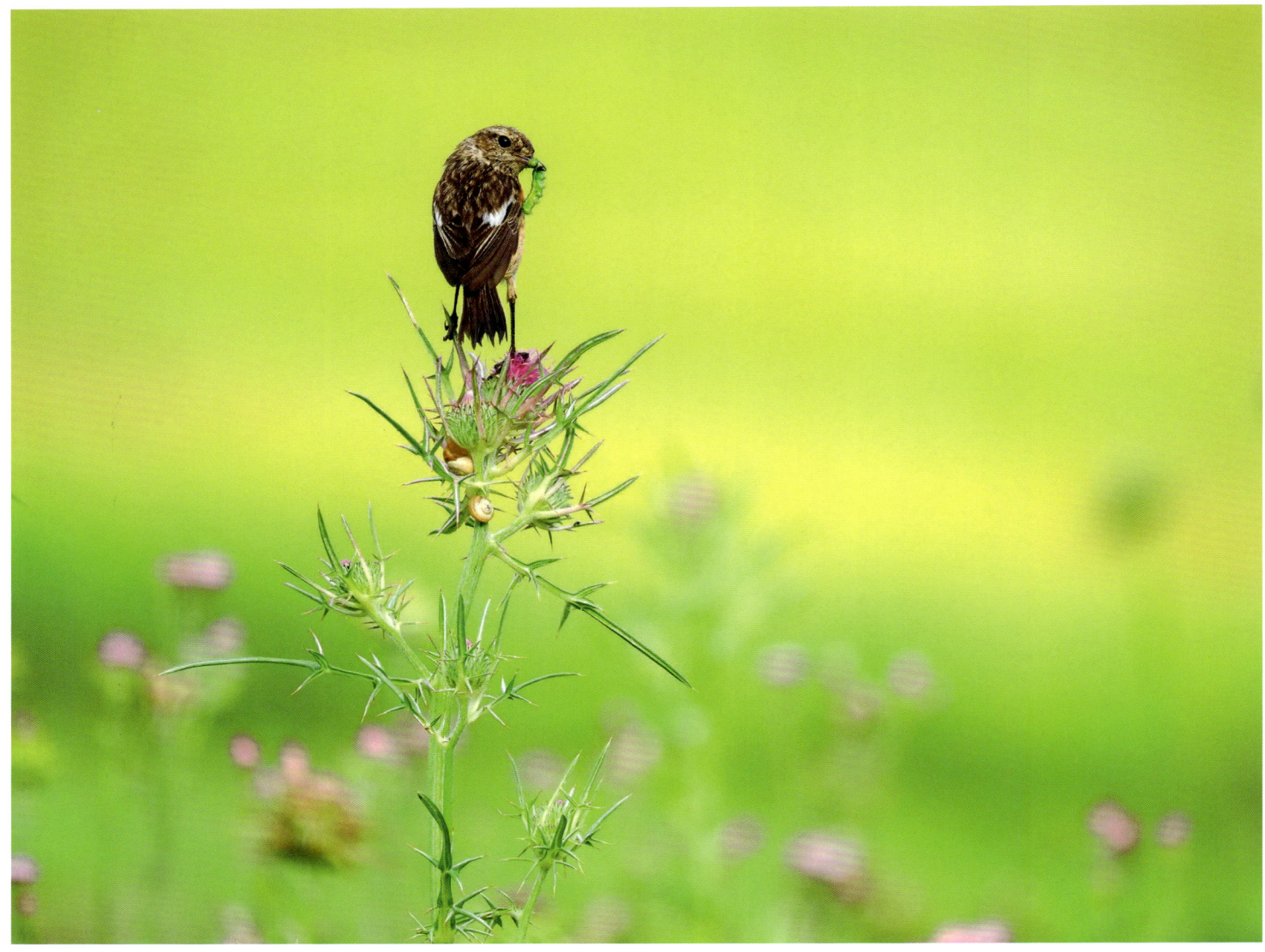

Meal stop

Alberto Román Gómez

SPAIN

With his camera poised through an open car window on a spring afternoon, Alberto observed this female European stonechat, hunting invertebrates to feed her young in Sierra de Grazalema Natural Park, southern Spain. She repeatedly dropped down to the ground to find prey, before flying back up to a perch – and Alberto spotted that this budding purple milk thistle was a favourite landing spot. Framing his shot around this plant, he waited for the moment the small bird returned with a caterpillar, giving a backward glance to check for predators, before delivering the meal to her offspring, hidden in a softly lined nest in the long grass.

OM System OM-1 + 100–400mm f5–6.3 lens at 400mm; 1/320 at f6.3 (+1 e/v); ISO 800; bean bag.

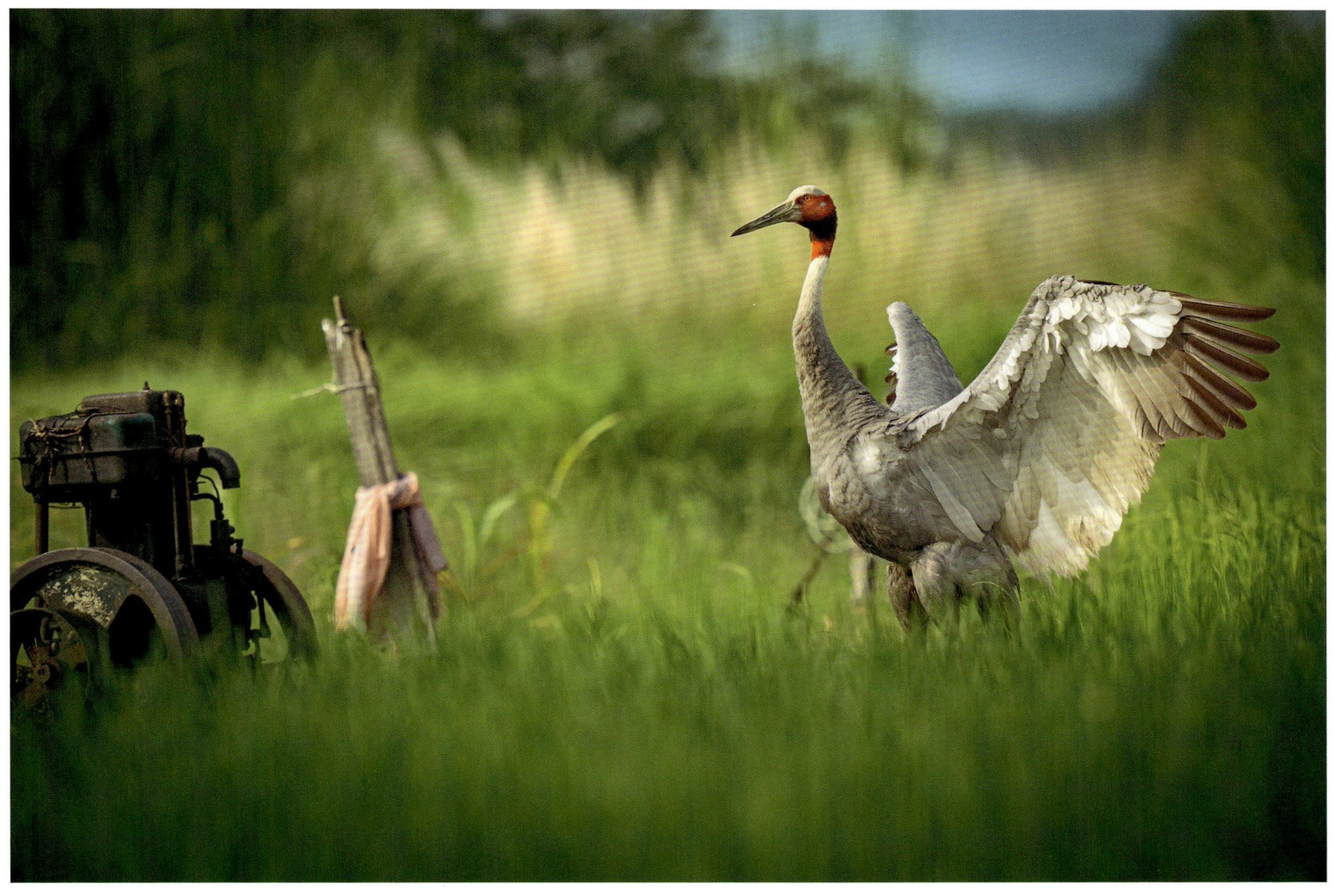

Height advantage

Shreyovi Mehta

INDIA

A sarus crane – at more than 1.5 metres (5 feet), the world's tallest flying bird – stumbles across a water pump, while foraging in Dhanauri Wetlands, Uttar Pradesh, northern India. Despite being the most populous state in India, Uttar Pradesh is the stronghold of this vulnerable species. Sarus cranes are known for their adaptability to human settlements, on open and irrigated fields, and are well tolerated by local people. However, they are threatened by the loss of wetland habitats, ingestion of pesticides, and hunting. Shreyovi's patience was rewarded when this lone individual appeared while feeding on aquatic plants, grains and small vertebrates in its path. Using a long lens and teleconverter to keep her distance, she quickly captured its reaction, highlighting the crane's elegance alongside the squat and static metal pump.

Sony α1 + 400mm f2.8 lens + 2x teleconverter; 1/800 at f8; ISO 500.

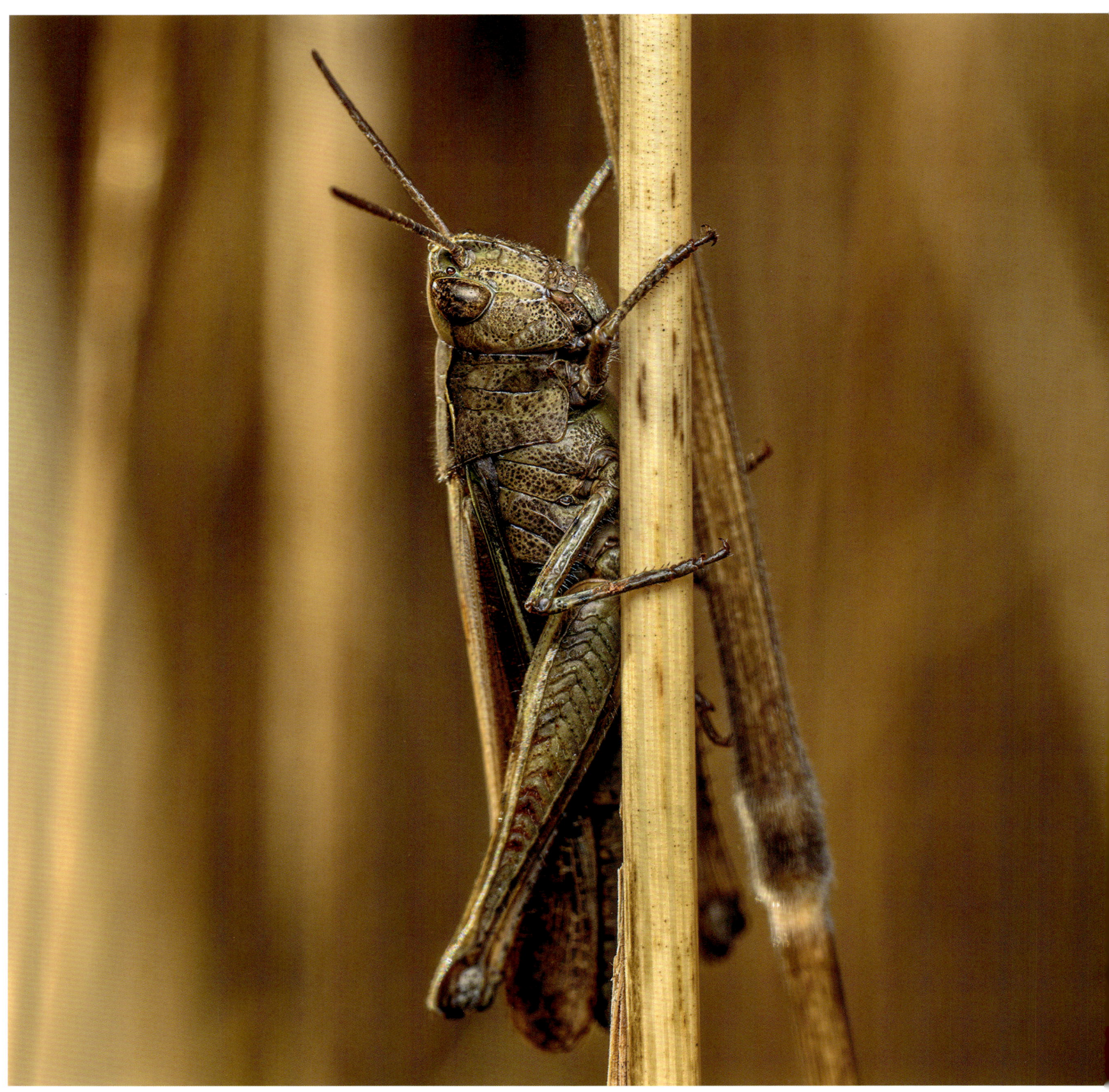

Morning hopper

Jamie Smart

UK

Jamie was up and out before breakfast, hunting for what she calls 'mini beasts' in her garden in mid-Wales, as the sun started to break through the autumn mist. 'The light was just perfect,' she enthuses. Despite the mottled brown colours of this common field grasshopper – highly effective camouflage against some predators – her sharp eyes soon picked it out, low in the long grass, slowly warming up after a chilly night. Acting quickly in the rapidly changing light, Jamie gently drew back a few stems to get a clear view of her subject without disturbing it. Like most grasshoppers, this small, widespread species has short antennae and powerful hind legs. They are ideal for jumping and, when rubbed against its wings, for producing its characteristic, intermittent chirps, which are detected by sensory organs on the abdomens of other grasshoppers. Jamie chose to shoot into the sun to highlight the grasshopper's back, and added flash with a diffuser to bring out its details in the shadows, while illuminating a backdrop of soft lines of grass that hint at the grasshopper's hiding place.

Nikon Z9 + 105mm f2.8 lens; 1/200 at f13; ISO 64; Nikon SB-910 Speedlight flash; Cygnustech diffuser.

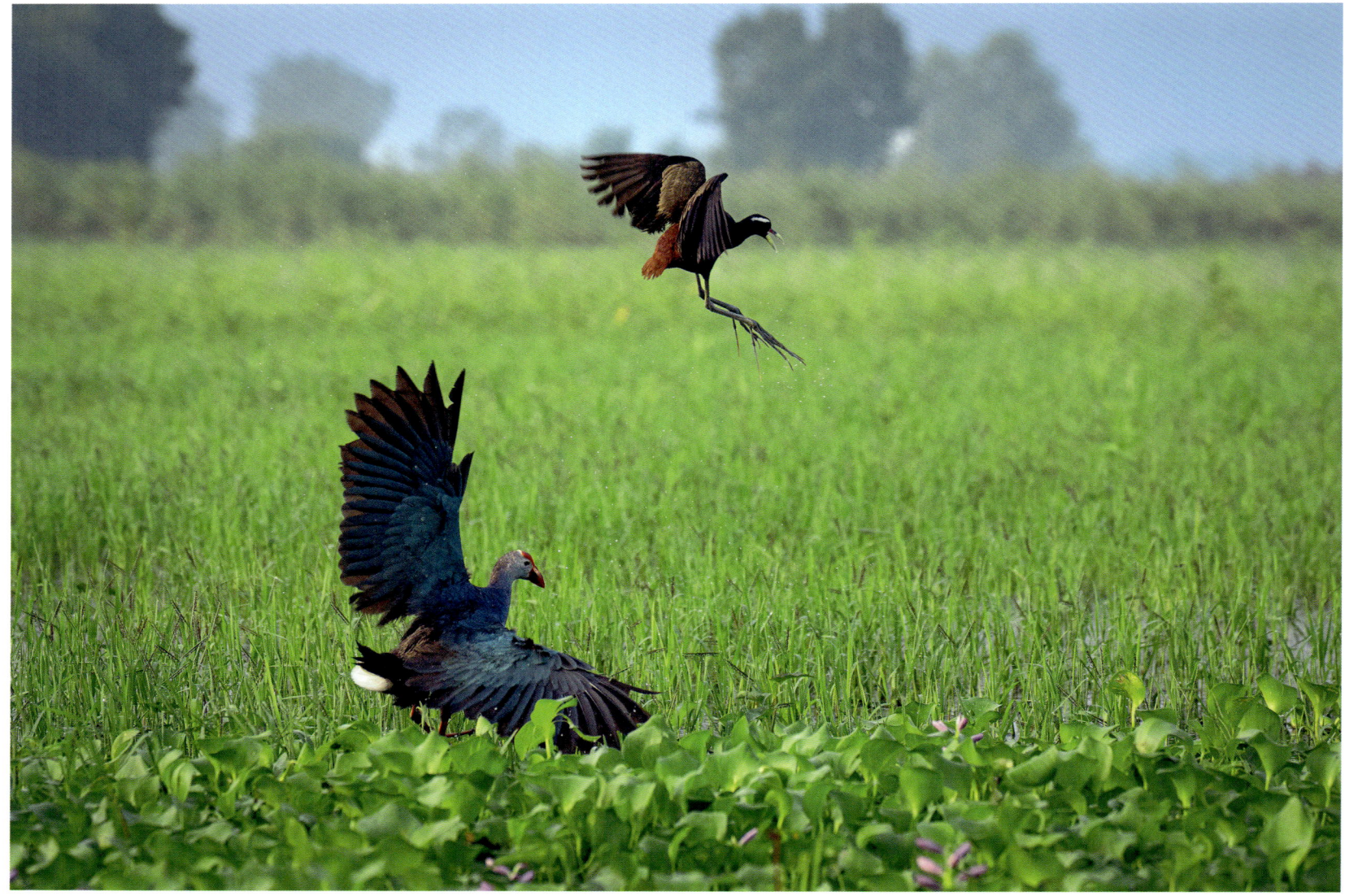

Wetland spat

Shreyovi Mehta

INDIA

When Shreyovi spotted a bronze-winged jacana (right) approaching the purple swamphen, she zoomed out her lens, anticipating some interaction. These two inhabitants of the Dhanauri Wetlands, Uttar Pradesh, northern India, have similar tastes in food: mainly plant matter but also invertebrates, such as snails and insects. Unwilling to share with the gangly, white-browed intruder, the swamphen threw a determined flap in its direction. Shreyovi was hidden behind a bush next to a trail with her camera mounted on a tripod. Using a fast shutter speed, she captured the swamphen's wings at full stretch and the jacana's instant departure, softly framed by the lush vegetation. The broad-leaved plants in the foreground are water hyacinth, an invasive species introduced to India in the late nineteenth-century.

Sony α1 + 100–400mm f4.5–5.6 at 185mm; 1/1250 at f7.1; ISO 2500; Benro tripod + Sachtler fluid head.

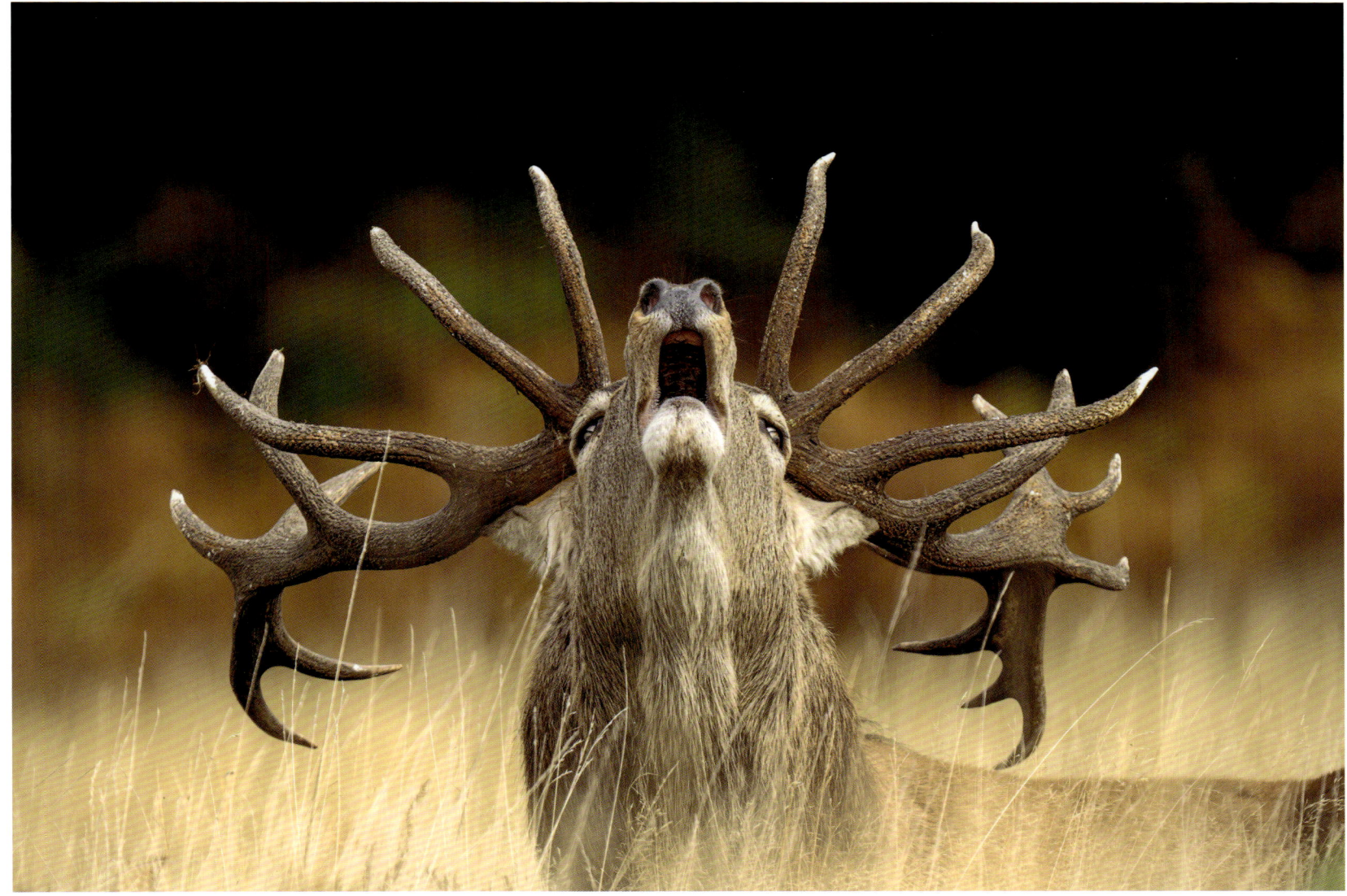

Rutting call

Jamie Smart

UK

Lying in the long, straw-coloured grass in Bradgate Park, Leicestershire, England, a red deer stag emits a mighty bellow during the autumn rut. This mature male could hear the distant roars of rivals and responded repeatedly to assert his claim over seven females grazing nearby. The stag's antlers have regrown since their annual shedding in early spring, initially covered in a velvet-like soft skin, now rubbed off to expose the bone beneath. For the first few years, each new set of antlers is larger, with more complex points, called tines, crowning the heads of mature males. To frame the symmetry atop the stag's moving head at just the right moment, Jamie moved up and down the track at a safe distance, stretching herself up tall to avoid any long grass in the foreground from spoiling her shot.

Nikon Z9 + 800mm f6.3 lens; 1/800 at f6.3; ISO 450.

Index of Photographers

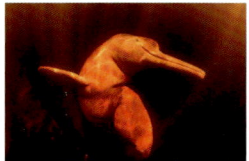

52
Hussain Aga Khan
SWITZERLAND
@focusedonnature

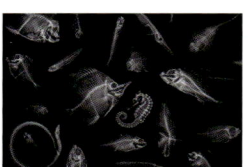

78
Sirachai Arunrugstichai
THAILAND
shinsphoto.com
@shinalodon

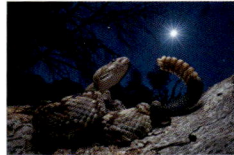

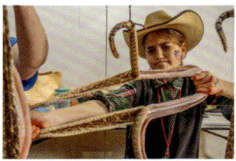

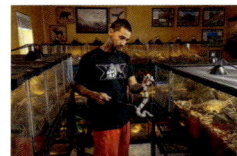

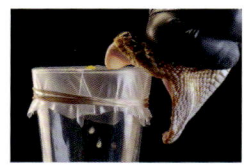

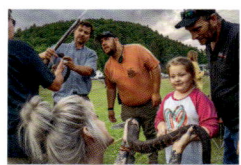

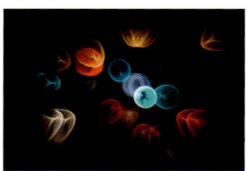

110–115
Javier Aznar González de Rueda
SPAIN
javieraznarphotography.com
@javier_aznar_photography
facebook.com/
javieraznarphotography

64
Simone Baumeister
GERMANY
naturfoto-baumeister.com
@simone_baumeister

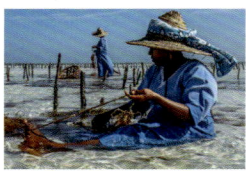

76
Anna Boyiazis
USA
annaboyiazis.com
@annaboyiazis
Agent: Sid and Michelle Monroe,
monroegallery.com,
info@monroegallery.com

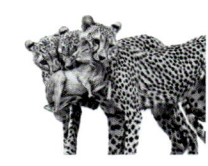

17
Marina Cano
SPAIN
marinacano.com
@marinacano
facebook.com/MarinaCano
Wildlifephotographer

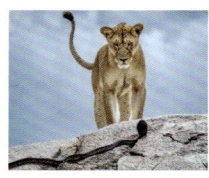

9, 16
Gabriella Comi
ITALY
@la_zia_gabri

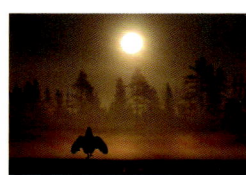

26
Marc Costermans
BELGIUM
marc.costermans.be
facebook.com/
MarcCostermansPhoto

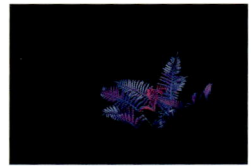

100
Juan Cuetos
SPAIN
@juancuetos73

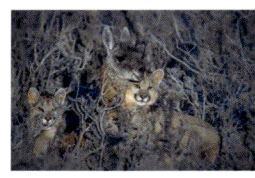

18
Hua Dai
CHINA
Agent: Ke Han,
megrezclub@gmail.com

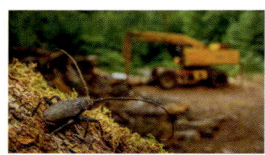

130
Andrea Dominizi
ITALY
@a.andrea.do

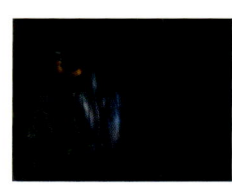

56
Philipp Egger
ITALY
philipp-egger.com
@philipp_egger_photography
facebook.com/BananeFisch

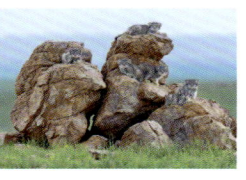

60, 62
Amit Eshel
ISRAEL
amiteshel.com
@siberianart
facebook.com/eshelamit

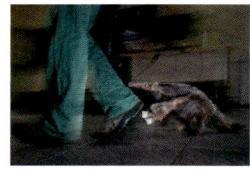

104
Fernando Faciole
BRAZIL
fernandofaciole.com
@Fernando.faciole

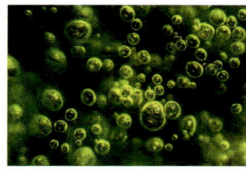

90
Sebastian Frölich
GERMANY
froelich-natur-fotografie.com
@sebastianfroelich
facebook.com/galeriedermomente

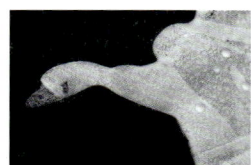

66
Fortunato Gatto
ITALY
fortunatophotography.com
@fortunato.gatto
facebook.comFortunatoPhoto

88
Stefan Gerrits
FINLAND
stefangerrits.com
@stefangerrits_photography
facebook.com/
StefanGerritsPhotography

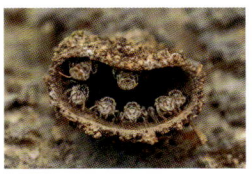

142
Rithved Girishkumar
INDIA/UNITED ARAB EMIRATES
@rithvedgirish

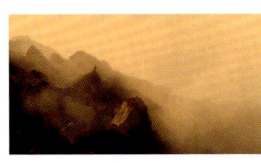

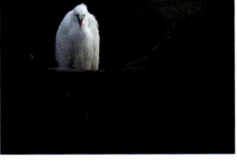

140, 146
Lubin Godin
FRANCE
@nidonibul
facebook.com/Nidonibul

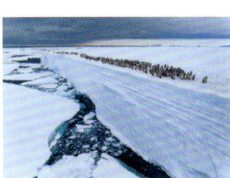

82
Bertie Gregory
UK
bertiegregory.com
@bertiegregory

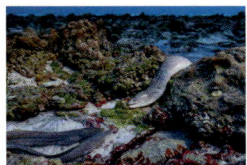

80
Shane Gross
CANADA
shanegross.com
@shanegrossphoto
facebook.com/
shanegrossphotography

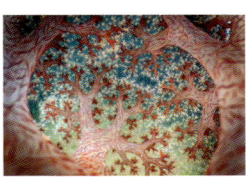

7, 68
Ross Gudgeon
AUSTRALIA
bluefishphoto.com.au
@ross_gudgeon
facebook.com/ross.gudgeon.7

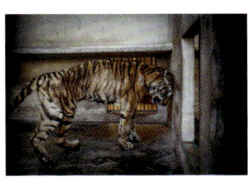

107
Amy Jones
UK
amyrjones.com
@amyjonesphoto

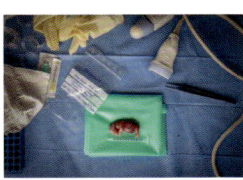

102
Jon A. Juárez
SPAIN
@jonjuarez.photo

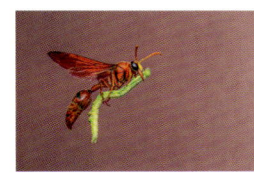

2, 34
Bidyut Kalita
INDIA
@bidyutkalita_
facebook.com/bidyut.
kalita.3720

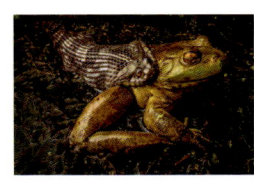

30
Nick Kanakis
USA
nickkanakis.com
@nick_kanakis

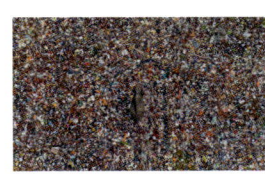

108
Lakshitha Karunarathna
SRI LANKA
lakshithak.com
@lakshithak
facebook.com/lakshitha.
karunarathna.8

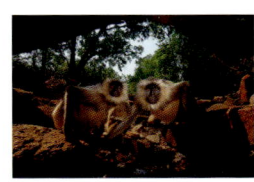

58
Nayan Khanolkar
INDIA
@NayanKhanolkar
facebook.com/NayanKhanolkar

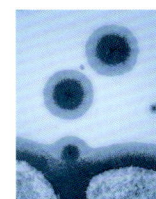

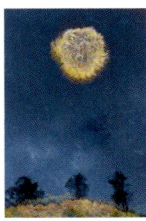

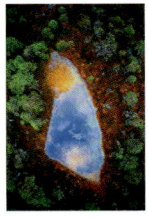

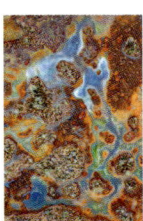

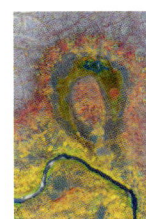

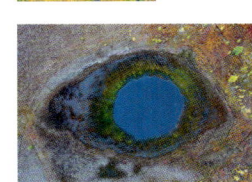

122–129
Alexey Kharitonov
ISRAEL/RUSSIA
alexey-kharitonov.pixels.com
facebook.com/akharitonoff

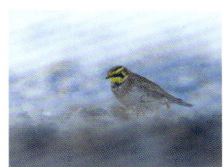

143
Néo Koslowski
GERMANY
@neowitsch_photo

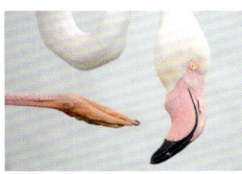

133
Leana Kuster
SWITZERLAND
leanakuster.wixsite.com/my-site-1
@leana.kuster_photography

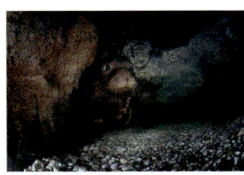

54
Greg Lecoeur
FRANCE
greglecoeur.com
@greg.lecoeur
facebook.com/greglecoeurUW
Photography

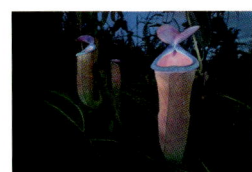

98
Chien Lee
MALAYSIA
chienclee.com
@chienleephotography
facebook.com/
chienleephotography

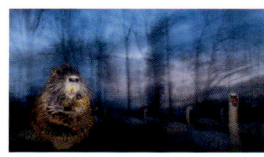

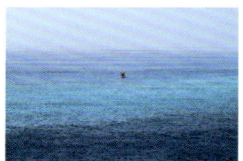

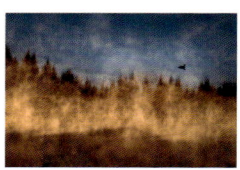

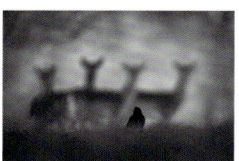

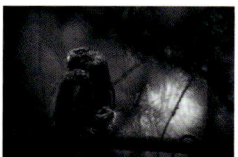

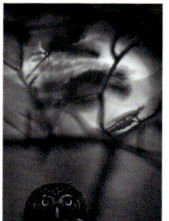

**116–121
Luca Lorenz**
GERMANY
lucalorenz.de
@luca_lorenz_wildlife

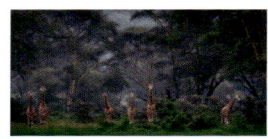

**84, 87
Roberto Marchegiani**
ITALY
joyoflight.it
@joyoflight_
facebook.com/roberto.
marchegiani.520

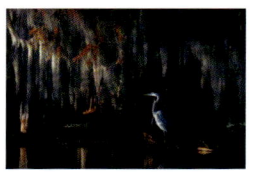

**28
Quentin Martinez**
FRANCE
quentinmartinez.fr
@quentin_martinez_wildlife
facebook.com/
quentinmartinezphotographer

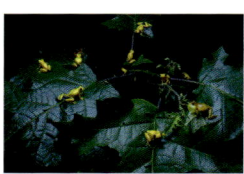

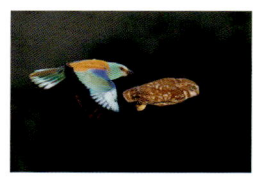

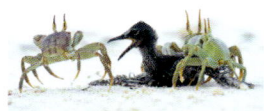

**24, 38
Bence Máté**
HUNGARY
bencemate.com
@bence_mate_photography
Agent: Andrea Reichenberger,
office@matebence.hu

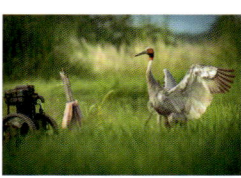

**151, 154
Shreyovi Mehta**
INDIA
@shreyovi_mehta

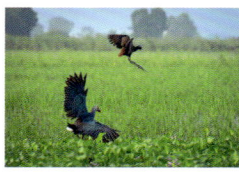

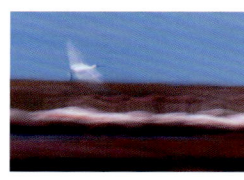

**136, 138
Tomasz Michalski**
POLAND
@tomekmichalski.fot

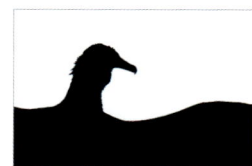

**59
Santiago José Monroy García**
COLOMBIA
@santiagomonroywildphoto

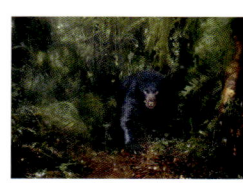

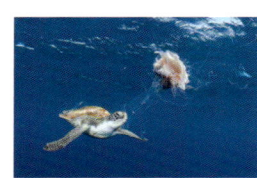

**132, 137
Tinnapat Netcharussaeng**
THAILAND
@punpun_tp_nc

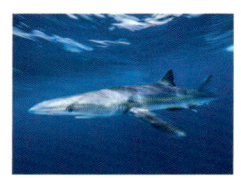

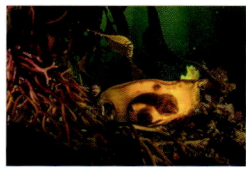

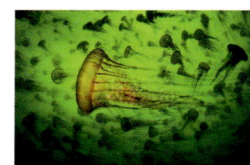

**48, 50
Ralph Pace**
USA
ralphpace.com
@ralphpace
Agent: Minden Pictures,
www.mindenpictures.com,
info@mindenpictures.com

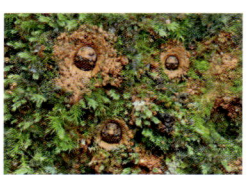

**35, 44
Jithesh Pai**
INDIA
@Jithesh_pai
facebook.com/mjithesh.pai

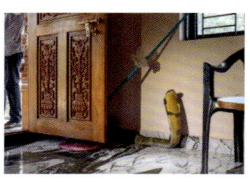

**101
Imre Potyó**
HUNGARY
@imrepotyo
facebook.com/imre.potyo/
photos_by

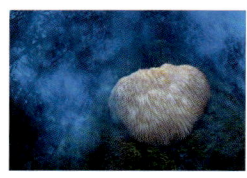

**144
Parham Pourahmad**
USA
@wildphotop

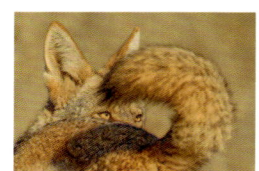

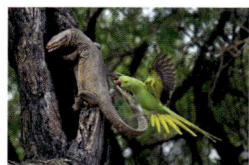

**25
Hira Punjabi**
INDIA
@hirapunjabi3
facebook.com/hirapunjabi

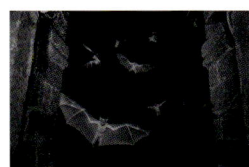

46
Sitaram Raul
INDIA
sitaramraul.com
@shawshaank_
facebook.com/raul.shashank

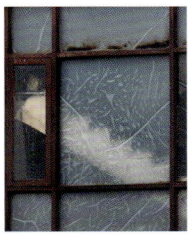

45
Chaitanya Rawat
INDIA
chaitanyarawat.com
@chaitanyarawatphotography

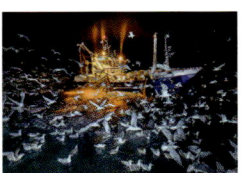

74
Audun Rikardsen
NORWAY
audunrikardsen.com
facebook.com/
audunrikardsenphotography

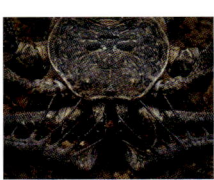

135
Beckett Robertson
CANADA
beckettsmacro.com
@beckettsmacro

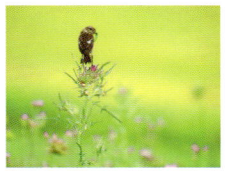

150
Alberto Román Gómez
SPAIN
@albertoromangomez

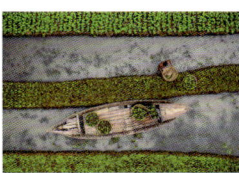

92
Azim Khan Ronnie
BANGLADESH/FRANCE
azimronnie.com
@azimronnie
facebook.com/azimronnie

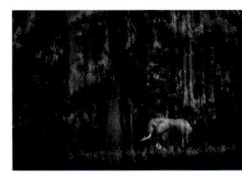

70
Rahul Sachdev
INDIA
rahulsachdev.net
@rahulsachdevphotography
facebook.com/
rahul.sachdev.756412

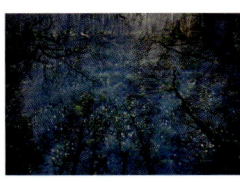

69
Thomas Schwarze
GERMANY
ts-home.de
@tioem

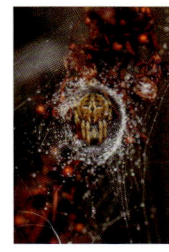

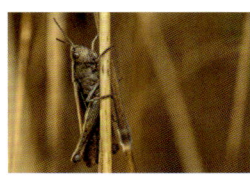

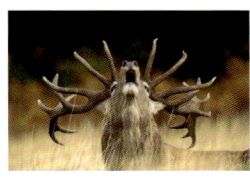

148, 152, 155
Jamie Smart
UK
eagleeyedgirl.co.uk
@eagle_eyed_grl
facebook.com/eagle_eyed_girl

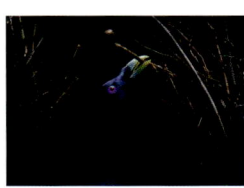

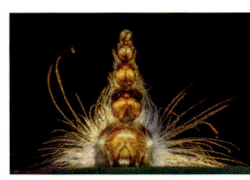

22, 32
Georgina Steytler
AUSTRALIA
georginasteytler.com.au
@georgina_steytler
facebook.com/georginasteytler

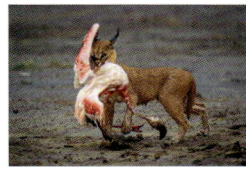

12
Dennis Stogsdill
USA
dennisstogsdill.com
@dstogs_photography

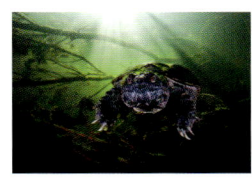

53
Jake Stout
USA
jakestout.photoshelter.com
@JakeStoutphoto

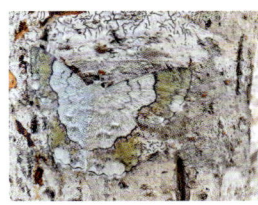

145
Zhixuan Sun
CHINA

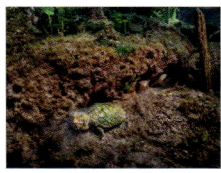

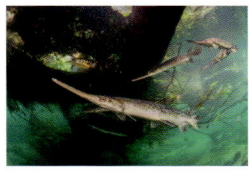

31, 94
Isaac Szabo
USA
isaacszabo.com
@isaacszabo
facebook.com/
isaacszabophotography

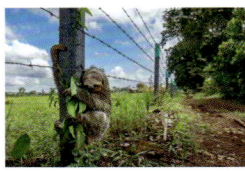

4, 42
Emmanuel Tardy
FRANCE
@instagram.com/emmanuel.
tardy

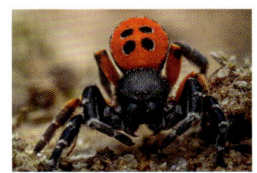

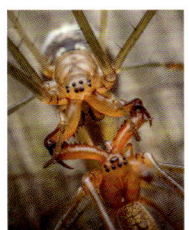

134, 139
Alexis Tinker-Tsavalas
GERMANY
@naturefold

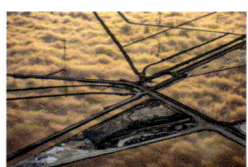

96
Jassen Todorov
USA
jassentodorov.com
@jassensf
facebook.com/jassensf

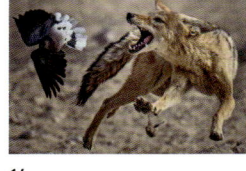

14
Willie van Schalkwyk
SOUTH AFRICA
500px.com/willievs
@vanschalkwykwillie

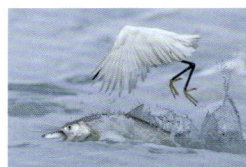

20
Qingrong Yang
CHINA
Agent: Ke Han,
megrezclub@gmail.com

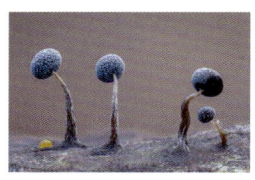

72
Kutub Uddin
BANGLADESH/UK
@kutub_uddin_macro_man
facebook.com/kutub.uddin.777

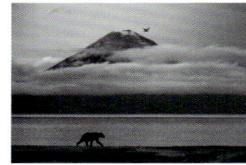

147
Kesshav Vikram
INDIA
kesshavvikram.com
@kesshavvikram

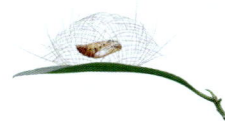

36
Minghui Yuan
CHINA
artron.net

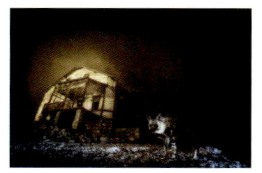

10, 40
Wim van den Heever
SOUTH AFRICA
tuskphoto.com
@wim_van_den_heever
facebook.com/Wimvanden
HeeverWildlifePhotographer

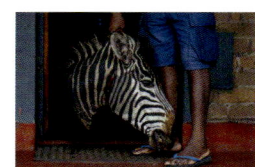

106
Marcus Westberg
SWEDEN/PORTUGAL
@marcuswestbergphotography
facebook.com/
marcuswestbergphotography

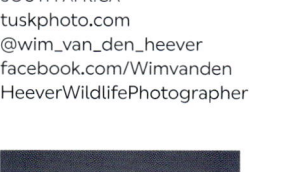

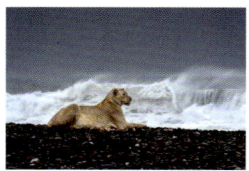

86
Griet Van Malderen
BELGIUM
@grietvanm
facebook.com/grietvanm